Jurisprudence

Themes and Concepts

SECOND EDITION

Jurisprudence: Themes and Concepts offers an original introduction to, and critical analysis of, the central themes studied in jurisprudence courses. The book is presented in three parts each of which contains general themes, advanced topics, tutorial questions and guidance on further reading:

- Law and Politics, locating the place of law within the study of institutions of government
- Legal Reasoning, examining the contested nature of the application of law
- Law and Modernity, exploring the social forces that shape legal development.

This second edition includes enhanced discussion of the rise of legal positivism within the context of the rise of the modern state, the changing role of natural and human rights discourse, concepts of justice in and beyond the nation state, the impact of emergency doctrines in contemporary legal regulation, and challenges to the rule of law in light of shifting and competing demands for new types of social solidarity.

Accessible, interdisciplinary, and socially informed this book has been revised to take into account the latest developments in jurisprudential scholarship.

Scott Veitch is Professor of Jurisprudence at the University of Hong Kong.

Emilios Christodoulidis is Professor in Legal Theory at the University of Glasgow.

Lindsay Farmer is Professor of Law at the University of Glasgow.

Jurisprudence

Themes and Concepts

SECOND EDITION

Scott Veitch, Emilios Christodoulidis
and Lindsay Farmer

Routledge
Taylor & Francis Group

LONDON AND NEW YORK

Second edition published 2012
by Routledge
2 Park Square, Milton Park, Abingdon, Oxon, OX14 4RN

Simultaneously published in the USA and Canada
by Routledge
711 Third Avenue, New York, NY 10017

Routledge is an imprint of the Taylor & Francis Group, an informa business

© 2012 Scott Veitch, Emilios Christodoulidis and Lindsay Farmer

Previous editions published by Routledge-Cavendish
First edition   2007

British Library Cataloguing in Publication Data
A catalogue record for this book is available from the British Library.

Library of Congress Cataloging in Publication Data
A catalog record for this book has been requested.

ISBN: 978-0-415-67972-5 (hbk)
ISBN: 978-0-415-67982-4 (pbk)
ISBN: 978-0-203-11895-5 (ebk)

Typeset in Times New Roman
by RefineCatch Limited, Bungay, Suffolk

MIX
Paper from
responsible sources
FSC
www.fsc.org   FSC® C004839

Printed and bound in Great Britain by
TJ International Ltd, Padstow, Cornwall

For Neil MacCormick (1941–2009), teacher and friend

Contents

Acknowledgements and attributions   xi
Notes on contributors   xiii
Abbreviations   xiv
Introduction   1

PART I: LAW AND POLITICS   7

1   General themes   9
      1.1 Introduction to the relationship between law and politics   10
           On power – political power and legal power   10
           Elements of the constitutional state   11
           Jurisdiction, state and legal system   13
      1.2 Sovereignty   15
           Sovereignty: a contested concept   15
           Attributing sovereignty – to whom or what?   16
           Post-sovereignty?   18
      1.3 The rule of law and the 'inner morality of law'   20
           The rule of law – meaning and value   20
           Challenges to the rule of law   20
           An inner morality of law   22
      1.4 Rights   26
           Civil, political and social rights   28
           Politicising law – legalising politics   29
           The indivisibility of rights?   30
           Rights in international and global context   31
      1.5 Identifying valid law   33
           Hart's concept of law   35
           Kelsen's pure theory of law   38
           Legality and validity   40
           Injustice and invalidity   44

2   Advanced topics   50
      2.1 Justice   51
           Introduction   51
           Utilitarianism versus libertarianism   52
           Liberalism: Rawls's justice as fairness   56
           Socialism   59

2.2 Constitutionalism and citizenship 65
The paradox of constitutionalism 65
Representation and foundation 67
Constitutional 'moments' 68
Citizenship: liberal and republican 70
2.3 Law, politics and globalisation 74
Globalisation and the reconfigured State 74
Sovereignty after globalisation 75
Constitutionalism beyond the State 78
2.4 Law and the state of emergency 81
Emergency, derogation and the 'war' on terror 81
Carl Schmitt: Sovereignty and the exception 84
2.5 The rule of law in political transitions 88
Dilemmas of the rule of law 88
Difficulties in establishing accountability and responsibility 89
Forms of justice 90

Tutorials 96

PART II: LEGAL REASONING 111

1 General themes 113
1.1 Introduction to legal reasoning 114
1.2 Legal formalism 117
What is formalism? 117
The 'pure theory of law' and the notion of
self-containment 118
Formalism and deduction 120
The promise of formalism 122
1.3 American Legal Realism 123
'The Path of the Law': law as prophecy 125
Rule-scepticism 126
Fact-scepticism 128
The faith in science 129
1.4 Rules, 'open texture' and the limits of discretion 131
HLA Hart and the 'open texture' of legal language 131
Neil MacCormick: the defence of an 'extended formalism' 133
1.5 Law as a practice of interpretation 137
Dworkin on 'hard' cases 137
The 'right answer': law as integrity 140
1.6 Critical Legal Studies 142

2 Advanced topics 148
2.1 Justice, natural law and the limits of rule-following 149
Moral reason and hard cases 149
John Finnis and the morality of the law 150

2.2 Equality, difference and domination: feminist critiques of
adjudication 154
Initial challenges 154
Critiquing the *form* of legal reasoning 155
Comparing approaches 157
2.3 Trials, facts and narratives 159
The legacy of fact-scepticism 159
Trials and perceptions of fact: language and narrative
in the courtroom 162
Trials, regulation and justice 165
2.4 Judging in an unjust society 168
2.5 Law and deconstruction 174

Tutorials 187

PART III: LAW AND MODERNITY 201

1 General themes 203
1.1 The advent of modernity 204
1.2 Law and social solidarity 210
1.3 Law, power and exploitation 215
The function of law 218
Ideology 219
Marxists and the law 222
1.4 Formal legal rationality and legal modernity 224
Forms of legal rationality 224
Forms of political authority 226
The development of legal modernity 228
1.5 Transformations of modern law 233
The materialisation of modern law 233
Law in the welfare state 235
The welfare state and globalisation 239
'Unthinking' modern law 241

2 Advanced topics 247
2.1 Legal pluralism 248
Classical and contemporary legal pluralism 248
Strong and weak legal pluralism, and the position of
the State 250
Empirical, conceptual and political approaches to
legal pluralism 251
Future directions in legal pluralism 253
2.2 Juridification 255
Introductory remarks 255
Habermas on juridification 257
Juridification and the 'regulatory trilemma' 258

Juridification as depoliticisation ... 260
A fifth epoch? ... 262
2.3 Displacing the juridical: Foucault on power and discipline ... 264
Introductory remarks ... 264
Discipline and biopower ... 265
Governmentality ... 268
A theory of legal modernity? ... 269
2.4 Law in the risk society ... 271
Introduction ... 271
Features of the 'risk society' ... 272
Law in the risk society ... 274
Individualisation ... 276
2.5 Law and autopoiesis ... 278
The concept of autopoiesis ... 278
An inventory of concepts ... 279
The coding of social systems ... 281
Society, sub-systems and the law ... 283
How does 'the law think'? ... 284

Tutorials ... 290

Index ... 299

Acknowledgements and attributions

When we wrote the first edition of the book, we little thought that we would ever be writing a second. That we have been asked to is hopefully an indication that at least some students and teachers have enjoyed using the book and agree with its general approach to the subject. That said, we also received some constructive feedback on the first edition and we have been able to draw on this in putting the second edition together.

The main shape of the book remains the same. It is divided into three broad themes, which are themselves divided between the general and the advanced topics. We received some comments that in seeking to break with a certain approach to the teaching of jurisprudence, we had perhaps gone too far in not providing sufficient of an introduction to certain key theorists, such as HLA Hart, Hans Kelsen or Emile Durkheim, or that we had dealt with other topics of central importance, such as validity or justice, too quickly. We have accordingly sought to address these concerns. The content of the general sections has been rearranged, some sections rewritten to provide more systematic coverage, where necessary, and some issues which were perhaps a bit too complex have been moved into the advanced sections. There have also been changes made to the content of the advanced sections, with some new topics added, notably on law and deconstruction (in Part II) and on law and autopoiesis (in Part III).

As before we have benefited greatly from the generosity of friends, colleagues and students and we are pleased to acknowledge these debts. Some have contributed whole sections; others have assisted by updating or amending sections that were contributed to the first edition; and in some cases we have taken text from the first edition and reworked and updated this ourselves on the basis of feedback from students and colleagues. The more substantial contributions of certain colleagues are recognised in the attributions below.

In one instance the need to make updates ourselves has been forced upon us by circumstances. Neil MacCormick, who contributed enormously to the first edition by providing sections on sovereignty and the rule of law, died in April 2009. We have accordingly updated and lightly amended these sections as seemed necessary. More generally, though, Neil demonstrated through his life and work how jurisprudence could be seen as part of the project of government broadly conceived and he was always alert to the need to engage widely with political and social issues. It is in recognition of this spirit that we dedicate this second edition to him.

SV/EC/LF
November 2011
Glasgow and Hong Kong

In Part I, the introduction, the sections on sovereignty and the rule of law were originally written by Neil MacCormick. The section on the inner morality of law was originally written by Zenon Bankowski. The sections on 'rights' and on 'law, politics and globalisation' were written by Gavin Anderson.

In Part II, the section on law and deconstruction was written by Johan van der Walt.

In Part III, part of the sections on the transformations of modern law and the whole of 'legal pluralism' were written by Gavin Anderson.

Notes on contributors

Gavin Anderson is Senior Lecturer in Law at the University of Glasgow.

Zenon Bankowski is Professor of Legal Theory at the University of Edinburgh.

Emilios Christodoulidis is Professor of Legal Theory at the University of Glasgow.

Lindsay Farmer is Professor of Law at the University of Glasgow.

Neil MacCormick was formerly Regius Professor of Public Law and the Law of Nature and Nations at the University of Edinburgh.

Scott Veitch is Professor of Jurisprudence at the University of Hong Kong.

Johan van der Walt is Professor of Legal Theory at the University of Luxembourg.

Abbreviations

ADR	alternative dispute resolution
CJ	Chief Justice
CLS	Critical legal studies
EC	European Community
ECHR	European Convention on Human Rights
ECJ	European Court of Justice
EEC	European Economic Community
EU	European Union
GDP	gross domestic product
ICC	International Criminal Court
ILO	International Labour Organisation
IMF	International Monetary Fund
MEP	Member of European Parliament
MP	Member of Parliament
NGO	non-governmental organisation
PFIs	private finance initiatives
PPP	public private partnerships
PVS	persistent vegetative state
TRC	Truth and Reconciliation Commission (S Africa)
UDHR	Universal Declaration of Human Rights
UK	United Kingdom
UN	United Nations
UNIDROIT	International Institute for the Unification of Private Law (Fr)
US	United States
WTO	World Trade Organization

Introduction

In a series of lectures delivered at the University of Glasgow beginning in 1762, Adam Smith, the Professor of Moral Philosophy, delineated the province of jurisprudence. He defined it in general terms as 'the theory of the rules by which civil governments ought to be directed', otherwise, 'the theory of the general principles of law and government' (Smith 1978/1762, pp 5 and 398). This he saw as comprising four main objects: the maintenance of justice, the provision of police, the raising of revenue and the establishment of arms. What immediately strikes the modern reader of this definition is its breadth. He includes subjects such as taxation or police and security that obviously concern relations between state and citizen, but which are all too often viewed as purely technical areas of government. Just as importantly a theory of law and government for Smith requires that we attend not merely to matters of the definition or application of law, but also of how these relate to politics and the practice of governing. His approach to these questions is striking, for he approaches the topic with a method that is (in contemporary terms) both historical and sociological: that is to say that he is concerned with both the question of understanding the historical development of forms of law and government, and that of how it relates to stages of social and economic development of the society to be governed

The contemporary study of jurisprudence rarely aspires to a comparable breadth in either subject matter or method. Anglo-American jurisprudence, indeed, has for a long time been more interested in law than government, has focused more on abstract rules than institutions, and has paid only patchy attention to the historical or sociological context within which law and legal and political institutions develop. While we do not have the space here to address the question of why it has come about that the scope of province of jurisprudence has narrowed so dramatically, we would argue that the contemporary approach is too narrow and too technical. It not only risks losing the interest of students, but more importantly risks undermining the relevance of the subject itself. The aim of this book, then, is to restore some of the breadth of subject matter and method that animated the studies of our illustrious predecessor here at the University of Glasgow.

Our starting point in this enterprise is that jurisprudence is the study of law and legal institutions in their historical, philosophical and political contexts. The study of law in this sense cannot be abstracted from the questions of the nature and theory of government; indeed, the two must necessarily be considered in their relation to each other. This book offers a range of competing interpretations of how the role of law is best understood, considering among other things the relation between law and politics, law and the economy, law and moral values, the role of judges in a democracy, and the virtues of the rule of law and threats to its realisation in practice. The book provides students with an introduction to, and overview of, the historical and philosophical development of understandings of a range of profoundly important social concerns, with the aim of enabling them to analyse and reflect on the role of law and legal practice more broadly.

These are complex issues that invite complex answers. We have attempted to navigate through the complexity by organising the material around three broad thematic axes: law and politics, legal reasoning, and law and modernity. The first seeks to locate the place of law within the study of institutions of government; the second examines the application of law in particular cases, with specific reference to the relation with other disciplines or rationalities; and the third attempts to place the study of law within the specific historical context of the development of modernity. We shall have more to say about each of these themes shortly, but before doing so, we want to say a little more about our 'thematic' approach to this subject.

All too often, in our experience, jurisprudence is taught in one of two ways. Either it is presented as a series of imaginary debates between positions or approaches that seem to have little in common (natural law v positivism, conceptualism v realism, and so on), or it is taught as a stately progression from one great thinker to another (Bentham to Austin to Hart to Dworkin, and so on). The problem with the first approach is that it presents the debates in a rather abstract way, wrenching them out of any sort of context in which the debate might be considered meaningful. It is difficult, especially for a student encountering jurisprudence for the first time, to care much about the relative merits of natural law and positivism in the abstract, and so the exercise becomes one of the rote-learning of the 'strengths' and 'weaknesses' of the different positions. However, we consider that these kinds of debates can become much more meaningful when considered in the context of what they can say about different theories of sovereignty, of the relation between legal power and political power, or the day-to-day realities of the judicial interpretation and application of legal rules. Likewise, presenting ideas through the theories of thinkers who advanced them, can make the study of jurisprudence seem a hermetically sealed world, developing with reference only to its own history and where jurists engage only with other jurists. Against this we would argue that it is important to understand something of the historical context in which particular theories were developed, or of the problems of state and law that the theorists were addressing. Jurisprudence, in other words, should neither be understood nor taught as a purely abstract or philosophical subject. The most important jurists and the major jurisprudential theories have much to say about the pressing legal and political issues of their, and our own, time.

The way in which we have sought to address these shortcomings in this book is to address theoretical debates and issues through the three broad themes and a series of 'sub-themes' and concepts. The themes lay out certain broad contexts within which questions of law and government should be considered; and sub-themes develop issues and debates, showing how particular debates, far from being abstract or distant from the 'real world', are often addressing matters of central political or legal concern. Our aim in doing this is to try and make the subject of jurisprudence easier to understand by relating it to the kind of subjects that are already being studied in the curriculum of the LLB. Thus, for example, we take concepts such as sovereignty or citizenship which already have an established place within the law curriculum, but address them in a way that seeks to broaden and deepen the issues around them, so that the student can see that they are not just matters of technical, positive law, but are also related to contemporary social and political issues.

This has three other consequences that we should note. We have, so far as possible, eschewed an approach that looks at the 'complete' theory of a particular philosopher, or indeed (within limits) an approach that looks at discrete thinkers at all. Instead, our thematic approach means that we focus primarily on issues, and thus what particular thinkers had to say about these issues, rather than addressing a corpus of thought. This means that the work of certain theorists, such as HLA Hart or Max Weber appear at different places in the book, where we address different aspects of their overall work in order to illuminate the topic under discussion. What is lost in the failure to cover the 'complete' theory is hopefully made up for by the fact that we are able to present a range of positions in relation to the issues. This also has consequences for the way that certain concepts are addressed, as the thematic approach means that certain issues will appear more than once, in different sections of the book, and will be addressed differently in the light of the context established by the overall theme. Thus, for example, the issue of globalisation is discussed in relation to theories of sovereignty and the rule of law in Part I, but is then discussed again from the different perspective of theories of legal modernity and globalisation in Part III. This should underline the point that there is not necessarily a single correct approach to an issue, but that the approach or understanding might depend on the context or perspective from which it is addressed. The third consequence relates to the range of issues covered. The book misses out certain issues that might normally be covered in a jurisprudence course – such as theories of punishment or responsibility – while also including others that are not, perhaps, part of the conventional course. This is not because we do not think that these things are important – far from it. However, in seeking to present a relatively short introduction to the subject we have preferred to focus on the issues that we take to be related to our three central themes – and which are also related to our own research and writing in the area. We are not so much setting out to define the scope of the subject as to set out a method and themes that will whet the appetite of the student and hopefully lead them on to a fuller study of the subject.

In doing so we are thus moving away from what has become in recent decades an unfortunate tendency to channel jurisprudence through the distorting lens of analytical jurisprudence. This tendency has resulted both in an increasingly narrow specialisation which separates the study of jurisprudence from other disciplines, and its marginalisation from other parts of the law curriculum. By seeking to challenge these unhappy exclusions we hope to engage students' curiosity about the role and worth of law, its promises and its drawbacks, its history and the challenges it faces now and in the future.

The themes

As we have suggested above, each of the themes is intended to set out a broad framework or context within which we can address more specific issues about the role and function of law. Each broad theme thus sets out a general problematic – the relation between law and politics; the nature of legal reasoning or argumentation; law and modernity – and discusses a range of theoretical issues and perspectives. There is a certain logic to this approach for it is our starting point (with Smith) that a central aim of jurisprudence must be a theory of the general principles of law and government. Thus we begin by looking at the relationship between law and politics.

The articulation of law and politics is one of legal and political theory's most perplexing questions. On the one hand, law is an expression of political sovereignty, the product of political processes of will-formation and entrusted to the political apparatus of the state for its administration and enforcement. And yet at the same time it claims autonomy from politics, an objective meaning of its own, an expression of principle, even justice, somehow above and beyond the 'messy' world of politics. Moreover, in recent decades, legal organisation and society generally have seen massive shifts in the political landscape through the emergence of regional institutions such as the European Union, as well as the pressures that are associated with processes of globalisation. How law is involved in, and responds to, these developments requires scrutiny if we are to understand more fully the nature of the contemporary relationship between law and politics.

Under the second category we collect theories and issues that surround legal reasoning. The questions here are often more technical, but arguably no less political or controversial. The question is whether law invites and deploys a mode of reasoning that is peculiarly its own, characteristically involving the application of rules to cases, or whether and to what extent ethical and political concerns, perspectives and imperatives impact on legal reasoning. Again, the stakes are high, particularly given that there is a common expectation that legal rules, once instituted, are to be largely insulated from disagreements that we might call political or ethical, which might be thought to be more properly debated in the political rather than the legal domain. But if that is the case, is a politics of legal reasoning feasible, and if yes, is it also desirable?

Finally, in the category of 'law and modernity' we take a step back into the sphere commonly referred to as the sociology of law, to ask more general questions about the role that law plays in society, its function in maintaining social structures and its role in realising the project of modernity. Here we attempt to place some of the issues that have been addressed in the first two sections of the book in a social and historical context. How, for example, has the relationship between law and politics, or the modern state, developed? How is this conception of the state related to the social and economic structures of society, and how might it change in the context of developments such as globalisation? The aim here is to question whether the projects and ends of modern law continue to be adequate in contemporary social conditions.

How to use this book

This book is introductory. We expect it to work as a point of departure rather than an end point in itself, particularly since not all that can wisely be covered in such a course of study is covered here. Rather our aim is to engage students new to the subject by providing some initial coverage of themes and concepts we think important, and by provoking them into pursuing further reflections and research on topics raised here, among others. We have, for that reason, not attempted to be comprehensive in our coverage, but to focus on issues and debates, and to connect these to more general themes.

Each part is divided into general themes and advanced topics. It is intended that the general themes provide an overview of central aspects of the subject under consideration. The advanced topics focus on more specific sets of problems, which develop in some detail aspects of the main themes. They are also pitched at a more advanced level and presuppose that the 'general themes' have already been covered.

Throughout all three parts we have provided readings that we see as indispensable to the comprehension of the text: these follow each section of the 'general themes' and come at the end of each 'advanced' topic, along with further reading, which is provided mainly for purposes of further research on the topic. Each part also contains a series of tutorials that might be used as the basis for discussion of issues covered in that part of the book. There are three types of tutorial, each of which is designed to encourage different types of skill in the student. The first type are problem-solving, a form which is familiar to most law students, though perhaps less common in the teaching of jurisprudence. These describe a scenario, often based on actual cases, and ask the student to think through certain issues as they are dramatised in the factual situation. The second type are aimed at developing skills in the critical reading of texts. We have either provided extracts from a text, such as a judgment, or have directed the student to a journal article or section from a book, and provided a series of questions that should assist the student in reading and analysing the text. The third type are more open-ended 'essay'-style questions, in response to suggested readings either from this book or other texts. These can provide the basis for classroom discussion, or alternatively students might be asked to prepare presentations on the basis of the questions.

Finally we should note that there are two levels of tutorials. The first type are introductory in scope and are related only to issues covered in the general section of each part; the second type are identified as advanced level tutorials and are better suited to those courses which are exploring issues in greater depth and complexity. These might relate to the advanced topics, or offer a more advanced engagement with issues covered in the general topics.

The book can thus be used in a number of different ways. It is intended primarily as a textbook for a basic course on jurisprudence, which could focus on the three themes, allowing the teacher either to address the tutorials and advanced topics included in the book or to introduce their own according to their own interests. The purpose of the book is thus to provide the students with a basic introduction to some central issues in jurisprudence and to encourage them to tackle some of the primary texts in the area. Alternatively, the book may be used in a more advanced course, focusing primarily on the advanced topics, where we have given both an overview of the issues and sufficient guidance that they can go on and read some of the primary texts.

That said, there is of course no correct way to use the book; our main hope is that students find it lively and interesting and that it stimulates them to read more widely in the subject.

Reference

Smith, A, 1978/1762, *Lectures on Jurisprudence*, RL Meek, DD Raphael and PG Stein (eds), Oxford: Oxford University Press.

Part I

Law and politics

| 1 | General themes | 9 |
| 2 | Advanced topics | 50 |

Chapter 1

General themes

Chapter Contents

1.1	Introduction to the relationship between law and politics	10
1.2	Sovereignty	15
1.3	The rule of law and the 'inner morality of law'	20
1.4	Rights	26
1.5	Identifying valid law	33

1.1 Introduction to the relationship between law and politics

On power – political power and legal power

Law and politics both concern power – power relations and the exercise of power. They interact in many important ways. Yet, they are distinct. They differ because they involve different kinds of power. All power is relational, so the task is first to identify the element common to all kinds of power relation, and next to identify the elements.

Common is the idea of a relationship such that one person, group or corporate entity is able to affect some other persons, groups or entities in their reasons for acting and indeed in how they act. To have interpersonal power is to be able to get somebody to act in ways s/he would not otherwise choose to do. This is done by manipulating in some way the reasons in response to which other people govern their actions. If I care for my bodily safety, and you credibly threaten me with physical violence unless I act in a certain way, you give me reason to act in that way, though it is perhaps an action I would not otherwise consider performing. That is a case of coercive *physical* power. If you have control of economic resources to which I need to have access, and you grant me access to them only on condition of my acting in a certain way, you exercise *economic* power. Your decisions materially affect my reasons for acting and thus my possible decisions and courses of action. In as many ways as one person can, by virtue of general features of their position, affect the reasons others have for acting, and can thus affect the way they act, so many are the kinds or forms of power. Yet all those we have considered so far concern one's ability in fact to change reasons for acting because of physical or economic or other relations actually existing between people.

A different case is where some 'ought propositions' or 'norms', apply to a person, and these include norms according to which one person or set of persons ought to act in accordance with decisions of another person. The latter can then, by announcing appropriate decisions, give the former new reasons for acting, namely, reasons to act in accordance with the announced decision. Such is a case of power that is *normative* in character. Where some person has a standing or position that enables him or her under a certain normative conception to govern others' reasons for acting over a determined range of issues, that person has normative power, or *authority*, over those others in respect of those issues. The biblical commandment to 'honour thy father and mother' can be interpreted as implying that children ought to be governed by the commands, requests and guidance given to them by their parents. So understood, it implies a normative power of parents over children, as a matter of God's law, or of the moral law, or whatever one takes to be the character of the commandments. A constitution that grants competence to a legislature to make laws concerning the peace, order and good government of a country, similarly confers normative power on the legislature over everyone who is subject to that constitution.

In some settings, interest in power relations focuses primarily on the question of how far and by what means one person or group can in fact bring about certain courses of conduct by others, by virtue of some standing feature of the persons involved and the relations between them. *Political* power is an idea best explicated along those lines. Political power consists in being able in fact to exercise effective governance within a defined territory, through manipulating the reasons other people have for acting, and thus affecting their action so as to bring about desired rather than undesired behaviour within the subject group.

In other perspectives, the question is not so much who can *in fact* do certain things, but who has the *right* to do so. The latter question amounts to asking whose rules or commands ought to be obeyed if issued on certain subjects and following prescribed procedures. Such a person has a position defined by some normative order empowering them in this normative, rather than factual, sense to lay down what others must receive as, for them, valid or binding norms or reasons for action. Here, what is in issue is authority; power in its normative form. *Legal* power, that is, legal authority is normative in character, for laws are essentially normative in character.

Of course, any separation between legal and political power is purely conceptual. If no one pays any attention to the acts and decisions of a person claiming to exercise ultimate legal authority on some matter, the claim becomes an empty one. There can be no real legal authority without some political power. Conversely, the prospects of exercising political power over any extensive territory are highly dependent on some sense of legitimacy, and legitimacy is largely, though not exclusively, a matter of holding a legal–constitutional position of authority. So there is rarely real political power without some legal authority. This is mutual interdependence, not conceptual identity.

Elements of the constitutional state

In contemporary constitutional states, political activity concerns competition for and, for successful competitors, exercise of, elective office, which in turn involves the exercise of power. Election may be either to membership of a legislature or to executive office. In parliamentary systems such as that of Germany, the United Kingdom (UK), Italy or Ireland, executive office is achieved through the securing of a majority in the legislature and is held by the leaders of the largest party. In presidential systems, such as in France or the United States (US), election to the highest executive office is by direct election, and the legislature with its elected members is more clearly separated from the executive than in parliamentary systems. In parliamentary systems, the headship of state is a mainly ceremonial office, whether held by an elected president or by a hereditary monarch. Kings or queens and presidents may, however, have considerable influence by virtue of their public standing, and sometimes have particular duties in respect of safeguarding the constitution itself.

The legislature and the executive are two of the great branches of government in constitutional states. The third is the judiciary. Maintaining some form of separation between these three branches has long been understood to be a necessity for the sake of free (rather than tyrannical) government. The tasks of the three branches are those of:

- making law and keeping the executive under scrutiny – the legislature;
- executive government concerned with the pursuit of public policy in implementation of the law or otherwise within a legal framework – the executive;
- adjudication aimed at upholding the law, both in disputes between private persons and in matters involving private persons and public authorities – the judiciary.

Some, not necessarily perfect or complete, separation of these powers among different persons and institutions is a defining feature of the constitutional state. Democratic forms of election to public office as a member of the legislature or as the chief or a member of the executive government, though not (with a few exceptions) to judicial office, have also come to be a feature of these states. Fully democratic electoral systems, based on 'one person one vote', emerged later than the separation of powers, and would be all but impossible to achieve or sustain in other circumstances.

All states, whether or not conforming to this constitutional pattern, have five essential characteristics: (a) they have a *territory*, over which they claim to exercise effective control by the use, if necessary, of coercive force against external and internal threats; (b) they claim that this territorial control is *legitimate*, in that their governing authorities exercise it as of right on some moral-cum-political ground; (c) they claim universal *jurisdiction* within the territory, involving authority to make laws and to try all allegations of crime and legal disputes arising within it; (d) they claim *independence*, on the ground that the people of the state are entitled to a form of government free from external interference by other states; (e) *recognition* of these claims to territoriality, legitimacy and independence is accorded by other states. In international law, indeed, a state is defined as a territory with a *recognised and effective government*, and each state is entitled to respect under the principle of mutual non-interference.

Government concerns the maintenance of order and the pursuit of some conception of a common good or of the public interest of the state and its citizens. Where the separation of powers is maintained in any of its possible versions, the activities of the executive branch of government and of law-enforcement agencies such as the police are carried out under general rules that are the responsibility of the legislature. The legislature can also hold the executive to account politically. So far as concerns the legality of all exercises of governmental power, the judiciary has a final say upon what are the limits of the law laid down by the legislature or contained in a constitution itself. In short, there are rules that permit official use of force in reasonably defined circumstances, and these rules also prohibit non-official uses of force save in exceptional cases of self-defence. By this means, the state acquires a monopoly of the legitimate use of coercive force in its territory – not that such a legal monopoly is ever fully effective in real life. States can thus be identified primarily in territorial and political terms, but the idea of legitimacy and of mutual recognition has a basis in international law as this emerged in the period subsequent to the Peace of Westphalia of 1648, and came to be expressed by theorists of international law starting with De Vattel in 1758 (see Vattel 1883). (In a slightly anachronistic way, it has become common to describe states in the form they had acquired by the twentieth century as 'Westphalian' states.)

The 'rule of law' is the ideal according to which all political and governmental power is in fact exercised under rules of law. Yet obviously effective government cannot just be a matter of 'rule-following' – it calls for statesmanship and political commitment, and its ends are expressed in political programmes, not legal codes. A constitution, whether a formally adopted constitutional text, or a mixed body of law and custom such as makes up UK constitutional law, has to designate the functions of various office holders and the method of their election or appointment to office.

It must leave considerable scope to the discretion and judgement of those exercising the various offices of state. Yet at the same time it must enable them to exercise effective checks and balances to prevent the holder of any one of the powers of state from coming, in fact, to enjoy unlimited power rather than the defined, but extensive, power the constitution confers. This means that the legislature, in further empowering the executive or in regulating its powers, must never grant unlimited discretion, and the courts must exercise scrutiny of governmental conduct to ensure that limits are respected. When that is so, it is possible for the conduct of the affairs of state to be genuinely carried on under law.

In this context, citizens – and indeed everyone within the jurisdiction – can have confidence that their activities will be judged in accordance only with established rules and principles of law. Thus their personal liberty and liberty to conduct business affairs is subject to restraint only by virtue of legal powers clearly vested in persons acting with the authority of the state under the constitution or under legislation as interpreted by the judges in courts of law. Civil liberty in a free society depends on respect for the rule of law. Citizenship is above all concerned with the right to participate in the political processes of a state, at least by the exercise of the vote, and by the opportunity to participate in political and non-political organisations within the 'civil society' which the state sustains.

Jurisdiction, state and legal system

All this presupposes that law can be considered as a kind of normative order – that is, it is concerned with providing or maintaining a basis for order in human conduct and affairs, through reference to standards of conduct that lay down how people ought to or must behave. Law is (in several senses) *institutional*, for it is made or reformed by legislatures, implemented by executive agencies and law-enforcement officials, subjected to adjudication by courts, and practised by separate bodies of professionals such as solicitors and advocates. When a court finally reaches judgment, that judgment is coercively enforceable by relevant processes using specialised agencies, depending on whether criminal penalties or civil remedies are in issue.

The law of modern states is thus also *coercive* in character, with the executive and enforcement agencies of the state exercising physical force (and claiming a monopoly on the legitimate exercise of such force) to ensure implementation of judgments by the courts, based on laws laid down by legislatures or developed through judicial precedent. State law is thus normative (concerning what ought to be or must be done or omitted) and institutional, as well as coercive: implemented by *physical* force used along with a claim that this is a monopoly of *legitimate* force.

The *system* element depends on the way in which the activities and practices of the institutions and agencies hang together in a relatively coherent way. This depends on the institutions acknowledging a common body of constitutional or sub-constitutional rules and principles that empower each of them to act as they do and that seek to co-ordinate their activity, as well as regulating and empowering conduct of citizens. Where the 'separation of powers' exists the 'rule of law' is possible, in that each of the institutions keeps or is kept to carrying out functions only in accordance with established law, taking action against citizens only when empowered by law and only in case of violation of the law by citizens. In this context a vital role falls to the courts as the final interpreters of the rules that confer legal power and authority on all the institutions, including the courts themselves.

All the relevant rules and principles of conduct can be seen as systematically interrelated because the courts, especially the highest courts, accept it as obligatory to implement only rules that satisfy common criteria concerning their origin or content. They do so in accordance with a shared interpretation of the relevant criteria. This view of 'system' is thus dependent on a court-centred view of law (other views are possible, for example, those focusing on legislatures, or the democratic underpinnings of a legislature's position). But the court-centred view is appropriate to those who study legal systems as such. This branch of study is essentially court-oriented, though legal systems are also dependent on the legislature for its output of enacted rules. Otherwise, activity within the legislature, and the interaction of legislature and executive, belong more to the political system than to the legal, though they do have to work within the given legal–constitutional framework.

Since states are territorial in character, their legal systems also have a geographical or territorial extent (what Hans Kelsen called a 'spatial sphere' of validity). This can be quite complex and layered, as one can illustrate by reference, for example, to the UK. There are three internal jurisdictions, namely England and Wales, Scotland and Northern Ireland. The legal system applicable in each internal jurisdiction (English law, Scots law, or Northern Irish law) comprises all those rules that the relevant courts are obligated to apply in trials and lawsuits arising within their jurisdiction. Some of these rules are peculiar to one region alone, deriving from institutional writings, from precedents of regional courts, or laws passed by the regional legislature. Others derive from legislation of the central legislature – the UK Parliament – expressed as having specific regional application. There are also rules laid down by that Parliament, which establish common rules applicable generally throughout the whole UK, or derived from precedents of courts exercising a similarly comprehensive jurisdiction.

As a Member State of the European Union (EU), which is a form of supranational legal order, the UK is bound to observe the treaties establishing the European Community (EC) and EU and any regulations or directives validly made under these treaties. Hence, the rules that UK courts must recognise as binding include those laid down in the treaties or in the exercise of legislative powers that they confer. Such rules are, in principle, EU-wide in their application, so laws binding in the UK are also binding in the same terms on all other Member States (though EU directives normally have to be incorporated into national law by specific legislative acts, and these may tailor general provisions to local conditions).

Most European states have also agreed to be bound by the rules laid down in the Council of Europe's European Convention for the Protection of Human Rights and Fundamental Freedoms, which is a binding treaty under international law. It applies even more widely throughout Europe than just in the EC/EU. This is not 'supranational law' in the same sense as the law of the EU and Community. Since the Convention is an international treaty, its rules about fundamental rights do not have automatic direct applicability in states that are parties to it. This comes about only to the extent that a country's national constitutional law (as in the Netherlands) makes them so applicable, or to the extent that this is achieved by specific national legislation (as in the UK's **Human Rights Act 1998**, together with the **Scotland Act 1998**). In the contemporary world, states (especially in Europe) tend to have a complex and layered form of legal geography. The illustration of this given here in respect of the UK and its several internal jurisdictions, applies to all other Member States of the EU in respect of the nesting of the national legal system within Community law and Convention law on human rights. In all the larger states with forms of federation or internal autonomies or schemes of devolution there is an internal geographical complexity analogous to that of the UK. Everywhere, a specific set of courts with a hierarchical structure of appeals lies at the heart of the legal system or sub-system, which is both the framework of their work and yet also its output.

Reading

For an expanded analysis of types of power, see MacCormick (1999) ch 8. On the idea of law 'making politics safe' see MacCormick (1989) and (2007) chs 10 and 11.

On law as institutional normative order see MacCormick (1999) ch 1 and (2007) chs 1–3. For a concise statement of Kelsen's thought on these matters see Kelsen (1992) chs V and VIII; and see 1.5 below.

For a fuller treatment of constitutionalism and citizenship see Part I 2.2.

1.2 Sovereignty

Sovereignty: a contested concept

Sovereignty, like so many terms that straddle the boundary between law and politics, is a concept denoting a cluster of related ideas rather than one single clearly defined one. Moreover, in nearly all its clustered elements, it is a contested concept, in the sense that different theoretical approaches dispute over its correct explanation or definition, usually also disagreeing about its practical relevance. Sometimes it is used mainly in a *political* sense, to denote a kind of untrammelled power of rulers over those they rule. Sometimes it is conceived of in *legal* terms, as a kind of supreme normative power or highest possible legal authority. It is not even agreed what kind of entity it primarily applies to. Some treat it as an attribute of a person, or entity or agency within a state, such as an emperor, a king, a dictator or a parliament. Some treat it as an attribute primarily of the state itself – a 'sovereign state' being one that is fully self-governing and independent of external control. Some treat it as mainly belonging to the people of a territory, on the ground that they are ultimate and self-governing masters of the institutions of the state established there. 'We the people' adopt a constitution and establish a state with constituted organs of government, limited by the terms of our grant of power to them. Thereafter, 'we' can exercise our sovereignty only through the constitutionally established organs of government, with their powers divided and limited according to the constitution whereby 'we' established them. Alternatively, but only in accordance with constitutionally prescribed procedures, we can exercise the constitutional power of constitutional amendment. In the moment of its exercise, absolute popular sovereignty transforms itself into limited constitutional sovereignty.

Attributing sovereignty – to whom or what?

However that may be, there could be other possible points of attribution of sovereignty apart from 'the people'. One starting point that seems useful towards figuring out some features of the clusters of related-but-contested concepts is the English common lawyers' view of the sovereignty of the UK Parliament. This affords one striking instance of the ascription of sovereignty to an entity within a state. Strictly, this is sovereignty of a composite body, namely, 'the Queen in Parliament', which is the monarch acting in procedurally fixed ways along with the two Houses of Parliament – the Lords and the Commons. With the growth and eventual triumph of democracy as the underlying ideology of governance, however, the House of Commons has become the predominant element in this composite sovereign. At the same time, the electoral power of political parties in a system of representative democracy gives party whips and party leaders in normal circumstances a tight grip on the voting behaviour of individual Members of Parliament (MPs). Hence, when a party has a comfortable majority in the House of Commons, its leader, as Prime Minister, can, with the support of a Cabinet, each of whose members is appointed and can be dismissed by that same Prime Minister, acquire a personally predominant position: a highly concentrated form of power at the disposal, temporarily at least, of a single political leader. Hence parliamentary sovereignty meant the legally unlimited power of Parliament to enact any law it chooses, except one that would have the effect of binding later parliaments; but what the law ascribed to Parliament was politically exercisable in a much more autocratic way.

The jurisprudential reflection of all this is found in the legal positivism of Jeremy Bentham and John Austin, which exercised so powerful a hold on the British juristic imagination during much of the nineteenth and twentieth centuries. They were building to a great extent on ideas originally advanced by Thomas Hobbes (1996) in the context of a very minimalist view about natural law – law in a state of nature. In such a state, he contended, people would effectively face a war of all against all with no binding rules among them, and the only way out would be to agree on having a sovereign with absolute power to make and enforce rules establishing and protecting rights and property. While Bentham and Austin rejected the fiction of the state of nature and the social contract as a way out of it, they nonetheless argued for the thesis that law always depends on some sovereign person or assembly of persons whom others in a certain territory do in fact habitually obey, for whatever reason. Laws then are whatever the sovereign issues by way of general commands.

As democratic ideas have extended their scope and become the dominant ideology of governmental legitimacy throughout the whole world in our times, so has the idea of the sovereignty of the people extended its sway. Sovereignty was claimed by (and for) the people who adopted the constitution that determined the way they were to be governed, indeed were to exercise their self-government. Always, of course, there was a vanguard of 'founding fathers', but the constitutions they drafted required, by their own terms, ratification by the people through what were considered appropriate forms of popular legitimation. A widely prevailing model of constitutional legitimacy is one whereby representative authors prepare constitutional drafts that are to take effect when, and only when, approved by the people they represent, through a referendum under conditions of universal adult suffrage. This model is already actualised fairly generally in most mainland European countries of the EU, and indeed in Ireland as well. In such a context, the attribution of sovereignty cannot credibly be to any single organ of government within the state, and the concept of the people themselves as the sovereign, for all the paradoxical quality in this idea, may again come into its own.

An alternative, which may escape the paradox, is to attribute sovereignty to 'the state' itself. The existence of a sovereign in the Austinian sense of the term, where sovereignty is attributed to a person or institution, implies effective governance of some territory and of the people living in it. Where sovereigns of this kind exist, they are holders of a power that is logically independent of any higher power of the same kind. There can, of course, be different sovereigns in different territories. Logically, they must be mutually independent, for if one ruler were in effect the overlord of another, that other would cease to have sovereignty. Mutual independence is a necessary attribute of sovereigns, as is territorial separation.

However, where constitutional government has developed in ways expressive of some conception of popular sovereignty, it is most likely that the constitution does not allow for or constitute any sovereign official or institution – indeed, a constitution such as that of France expressly prohibits this. In polities of this kind, the constitutional framework typically establishes some version of the classical 'separation of powers' discussed above. At a minimum, executive, legislative and judicial powers are assigned to distinct agencies, with some form of checks and balances among the agencies. In large polities, federal or quasi-federal forms of government may further complicate the constitutional picture, insofar as there are separate states, each with its own internal separation of powers, and a division of competences between the authorities of each state and those of the federal government. In such contexts, there is no single person or institution that exercises an unfettered supreme power; that is, there is no 'sovereign' in the Austinian sense.

But a country under such a constitution – whether it be a unitary state or a federal state – may enjoy as complete legal and political independence from power exercisable by other like entities as a state ruled by a sovereign monarch or dictator or a sovereign parliament. The state or federation may, in that sense, enjoy sovereignty. It is often, indeed usually, the case that the constitution of the state or federation was established by some method of popular approval, expressed through a referendum, a constitutional convention or the like. It is also normal that the constitution provides for its own amendment by similar processes. Where all this is so, popular sovereignty connects in an obvious way with state sovereignty. The state is sovereign in its external relations with other states. Internally, the power to determine or alter the legal frameworks in which government is carried on belongs to the people acting in constitutionally stipulated ways. Democratic forms of government also involve the will of the people, usually expressed through political parties, to determine or at least strongly influence the course of legislation and the policies pursued by the executive.

The idea of the state as itself the repository of sovereignty is implicated in the idea, introduced earlier, of the 'Westphalian state'. Each such state is conceived as independent of every other and the rule of mutual non-intervention applies equally to all. This naturally entails the absence of any superior authority above the state level, though it does not preclude voluntary associations of states agreeing on common treaties or conventions that establish criteria of right conduct among them – like the

Hague Convention on prisoners of war, or the Vienna Convention on Diplomatic Immunity, or even the United Nations Covenant on Civil and Political Rights or on Economic and Social Rights. From the viewpoint of sovereignty theory, however, the truly legal character of such solemn international undertakings can be problematic. Austinian theories that make the existence of genuine law conditional on the existence of a common sovereign with political power to enforce sanctions in case of breaches imply that 'international law' is not true law, but some kind of solemnly announced 'positive morality' among states.

Post-sovereignty?

The very fact that Austinian sovereignty theory leads to such an insipid characterisation of solemn undertakings among states may itself weaken the case for favouring sovereignty in that sense. But one of the things that may then also be weakened is the doctrine of 'parliamentary sovereignty', so fundamental to the British constitutional tradition, especially according to those who interpret it from the standpoint of English law. This is a sense of sovereignty that might plausibly have become redundant under the developments of the last three decades of the twentieth century. For a start, most modern polities, and all democratic law-states, simply do not fit the Austinian picture, even when this is re-expressed in terms of common-law principles. Among European states, including the UK, the development of the EU has had decisive significance, along with other developments such as the (European) Convention for the Protection of Human Rights and Fundamental Freedoms, especially as this has come to be implemented by the European Court of Human Rights.

Of course, it may be argued that the positivistic conception was based all along on a conceptual mistake, and that sovereignty was never anything like the positivists' imaginings of it. Sovereignty was always something quite different, for example, 'an expression of a political relationship [that is, a political rather than an economic or a narrowly legal relationship, or one based on pure brute force or on property interests] between the people and the state' (Loughlin 2003, pp 82–3). Thus sovereignty has both political and legal implications, depending on whether one focuses on power in fact or on normative power, as discussed earlier. It remains doubtful how far either sense has full application in an EU that is increasingly pluralistic in its legal structures.

Since its inception in 1958, the European Economic Community (EEC), along with related Communities, and subsequently the 'European Union' (since the Treaty of Maastricht of 1992) has undergone a process of 'constitutionalisation'. The foundational Treaties, especially the Treaties of Paris (1950) and Rome (1957), came to be interpreted as a kind of 'constitutional charter' for the Communities and then the Union. This was tied up with decisions by the European Court of Justice (ECJ) that the Treaties and Regulations or Directives made under them enjoyed both supremacy over the laws of the Member States, to the extent of any conflict between them, and direct effect on and in favour of citizens of the states, not only the states themselves. This involved characterising EC law as being a new kind of law 'sui generis' (of its own kind, neither national law nor international law, but something quite novel). One implication of this for the UK became clear in 1991 with the case of *Factortame v Minister of Transport*, which held as a matter of law that the UK must 'disapply' as against EU citizens involved in fisheries the material provisions of the **Merchant Shipping Act** enacted by the Queen in Parliament in 1988.

In this light, one can no longer adhere to the traditional doctrine of parliamentary sovereignty. It must be radically reinterpreted or even abandoned. Yet this is not because a new European Sovereign has come into existence. The EU is a 'sui generic' legal order, but certainly not one characterised by sovereignty in the Austinian sense.

What about other senses? It is instructive to reflect on constitutional developments in the period 2001–2005. The European Council at Laeken in December 2001 called into being the Convention on the Future of Europe under the Presidency of Valéry Giscard D'Estaing. Over a period of 18 months, this Convention produced a 'Draft Treaty establishing a Constitution for Europe'. In October 2004, the representatives of the Member States at an Intergovernmental Conference signed a revised version of this draft, and made it open to ratification by each state according to its own constitutional processes within the two following years. It is controversial how far a 'constitution', thus adopted state-by-state, with resort to a referendum in some countries but not others, would satisfy purist theories of popular sovereignty.

In any event, substantial negative referendum votes in France and the Netherlands in May/June 2005 derailed the project of adopting this constitution, probably permanently. But even if the Constitution had been – or were to be – ratified in every Member State, and even if every state eventually held an affirmative referendum, there would remain a problem about the location of sovereignty. Would it be vested in the total population of the Union, or in the peoples of the states, or in some way shared? Or would it have been, indeed is it, a collective possession of the states, which remain in the last resort collectively masters of the Treaties? Can sovereignty be divided or shared, and can it exist in the absence of a single European people or nation self-constituted by the very act of adopting a constitution? These are questions it would be difficult to answer with confidence. What they suggest is, strongly, that sovereignty is currently a concept in transition in Europe, and that our understanding of law should be used to cast light on difficult questions about sovereignty. Explanations of law in terms of sovereignty would amount to explaining a difficult idea in terms of a complex, contested and obscure one.

Reading

For Austin's account of sovereignty see Austin (1954). On the 'Benthamite Constitution' see MacCormick (1999) ch 5.

Hart's critique of the command theory of sovereignty and his own analysis on the basis of primary and secondary rules is in Hart (1961) especially chs IV–VI. Cf MacCormick (1999) ch 4 and ch 6, and MacCormick (2008).

For an expanded account of 'post-sovereignty' see, generally, MacCormick (1999) and especially ch 8. For a useful overview see Walker 'Late Sovereignty in the European Union' in Walker (2003) and Walker (2010).

For a defence of modern sovereignty see Loughlin, 'Ten Tenets of Sovereignty' in Walker (2003), and Loughlin (2000) chs 9 and 10 on changing conceptions of sovereignty.

These issues are addressed in more detail in Part I 2.3, 'Law, Politics and Globalisation'.

1.3 The rule of law and the 'inner morality of law'

The rule of law – meaning and value

We have made reference to the 'rule of law' earlier, but we should now consider it in greater depth. Only where officials faithfully observe the constraints laid down in laws and constitutions does the rule of law obtain. It is commonplace that societies that live under the rule of law enjoy great benefits by comparison with those that do not. The rule of law is a possible condition to be achieved under human governments. Among the values that it can secure, none is more important than legal certainty, except perhaps its stablemate – security of legal expectations and safety of the citizen from arbitrary interference by governments and their agents.

Where the rule of law is observed, people can have reasonable certainty, in advance, concerning the rules and standards by which their conduct will be judged, and the requirements they must satisfy to give legal validity to their transactions. They can then have reasonable security in their expectations of the conduct of others, and in particular of those holding official positions under law. They can challenge governmental actions that affect their interests by demanding a clear legal warrant for official action, or nullification of unwarrantable acts through review by an independent judiciary. This is possible, it is often said, provided there is a legal system composed principally of quite clearly enunciated rules that normally operate only in a prospective manner, that are expressed in terms of general categories, not particular, indexical, commands to individuals or small groups singled out for special attention. The rules should set realistically achievable requirements for conduct, and should form overall some coherent pattern, not a chaos of arbitrarily conflicting demands.

This is attractive in itself, yet it must not blind us to the extent to which in a free society law necessarily also has an argumentative quality. Any legal text may be open to several interpretations in the light of contested principles and values that are taken to underlie this or that rule of law or branch of law. People are entitled to argue for one favoured interpretation against another, and in disputes between citizen and citizen, or citizen and state, each side may seek interpretations favourable to their own view of the matter (and hoped-for outcome). It is indeed right to look at every side of every important question, and not come down at once on the side of prejudice or apparent certainty.

Challenges to the rule of law

This can, however, lead to a degree of scepticism concerning the possibility of a genuine 'rule of law' that does uphold tolerable certainty in human affairs. If everything is arguable (or even if rather many points are arguable) and open to a decision either way, the decision is a matter for the discretion of judges. How the judges decide, on whatever grounds they favour, determines legal outcomes both for individuals and, through the system of judicial precedent, for society at large. The 'rule of laws, not men' becomes no better than a rule by one set of men (the judiciary) rather than another (the legislature). Moreover, the prized 'separation of powers' is revealed as something of a sham, and with it the distinction laboriously drawn earlier between law and politics.

There are two possible manifestations of this scepticism. One is a scholarly one, concerning the false consciousness implicit in (and generated by) theorising about the rule of law and the separation of powers. People may be taught to believe in the virtue of legal certainty and its possible achievement under the rule of law or in a *Rechtsstaat*, a 'law-state'; but the belief is an illusion. They may be comforted by the thought that it is actually achieved in their own state, but the thought is false. It is not true that even when substantive results in lawsuits go against one's own individual interest or class interest, at least formal justice is achieved, or that we all live under the same rules, and they are fairly enforced. Enforcement is capricious and biased, and cannot be otherwise. Legal uncertainty is pervasive and legal decision-making is done in response to ideology under cover of rule-of-law talk.

The other response is political, expressed, for example, in conflict between the executive and the judiciary. In the UK in 2004–2005, Prime Minister Blair's government was greatly concerned with terrorist threats coming from militant Islamists allied to the Al-Qaida network. Indeed, since the '9/11' attack on New York's World Trade Center Towers, the British and all Western governments had active concerns about this, and the terrorist bombings in Madrid in May 2004 and in London in July 2005, showed how serious were the grounds for concern. At the same time, however, the courts have had to adjudicate on the lawfulness of certain countermeasures involving, for example, detention without trial of terrorist suspects or the contestable character of evidence obtained, or allegedly obtained, through torture. Litigation on this has raised issues both about long-standing principles of the common law and about human rights, in the context of the UK's **Human Rights Act 1998**, which imported into domestic law a very substantial part of the European Convention on Human Rights. The judiciary have reached decisions against the government in some very salient cases, and ministers have responded that the judges are crossing the boundary of judicial deference to law and have invaded the role of the executive. The judges have responded that they are only giving effect to the clear meaning of the law. Can this be true? Are the judges or the politicians more in the right in this matter? Do they really have different grounds and methods of deciding or are the 'legal' decisions just political ones through and through?

To respond fully to these points would call for a fairly thorough-going account of legal reasoning and of the extent to which, and grounds on which, one can ascribe objective rightness or wrongness to decisions about contested matters of law. (These issues are explored more fully in Part II.) It is sufficient here to note that 'rule-of-law' theory may tend to exaggerate the possibility of legal determinacy and certainty, and the possibility to settle everything in advance by well-drafted and clearly conceptualised rules of statute law (far less, case law) meshing coherently across a whole legal system. (Indeed, as commentators like F A Hayek point out, excessively detailed regulatory interventions actually undermine the kinds of freedom the rule of law ought to serve, which is achieved best under broad principles of common law – evolved law rather than designed law.) Nevertheless, law is less radically indeterminate than critical theorists suggest, and the canons of good legal reasoning, fortified by a sense of reasonableness can in fact settle quite clear bases for discriminating between sound and unsound, or better and worse, legal arguments in disputed cases. Certainly judges from time to time make mistakes – but the very fact that they can be seen as mistakes indicates there really is a possibility that on other occasions they make no mistake, that is, reach an objectively correct decision.

The kinds of liberty supposedly upheld by respecting the rule of law are thus genuinely, albeit never perfectly, achievable, and are of real value. But such 'liberal liberty' may itself be insufficient. Anatole France famously remarked that the law in its majestic equality forbids the rich and the poor alike to sleep under the bridges of Paris. Equality before the law and liberty under the rule of law are compatible with very great economic and social inequalities and indeed injustices. Where law produces what seem substantively unsatisfactory outcomes for people, why should they accept that there is any value at all in the 'majestic equality' of the impartial administration of rules that affect very differently the interests of different individuals and different classes?

The possibilities implicit in democratic institutions may afford one answer to this. One reason to put up with bad laws and indeed to demand that they be fairly and regularly administered is because they can be changed, and the same logic will then demand fair and regular administration of reformed laws. Those who want laws changed only have to mobilise politically and secure a majority in the legislature to enact suitable reforms. These, if fairly administered, will generate different outcomes for the interest groups affected. Whether this is a reasonable hope or yet another illusion in the conditions of post-industrial global capitalism is another question, and for present purposes must be left as an open question.

An inner morality of law

In our society, democratic liberty is best expressed by the rule of law or government under law. What does this mean? According to Neil MacCormick, 'It is that stance in legal politics according to which matters of legal regulation or controversy ought to, so far as possible, be conducted in accordance with predetermined rules of considerable generality and clarity in which legal relations comprise rights, duties, powers and immunities reasonably clearly defined by reference to such rules and in which acts of government however desirable teleologically must be subordinated to respect for such rules and rights' (1989, p 184).

There appear to be two general sorts of reasons that seem to show why the law might be desirable. First, 'justice reasons'. The legal regulation of social relations is to take place through general rules applied in an impartial fashion to all persons alike and known in advance. The rules are to be applied by impartial specialists in law according to the internal logic and validity of the system and excluding any personal or non-legal considerations. Hence generality and reference to formal sources guarantee certain fundamental notions of fairness. The rule of law means (1) equality of legal subjects before the law in that individual cases are dealt with in terms of their facts alone and no one may be exempt; (2) government accountability and hence control of arbitrary action (including the actions of judges) – the doctrine of separation of powers means that judges should merely apply rules, not create them; (3) since legal systems involve coercion and stigmatisation, the rule of law attempts to make coercion 'the friend of freedom' by regulating its use. Is it not a good thing if private persons (pursuers or plaintiffs) and public officials (procurators fiscal, police) can call upon courts to do such coercing/stigmatising only by offering to prove – and to prove that there is some legal warrant for this – some 'major premise' which is a legal rule and that some relevant facts or 'minor premises' hold good? We can consider all these as aspects of the phrase 'government of law not men'.

Secondly, there are what may be called 'instrumental reasons'. The rule of law offers an efficient technique of social management in governing a pluralist market society where no underlying consensus of values can be presumed and there are conflicts of interests. The uniformity and predictability of law facilitates personal and commercial planning, entrepreneurial initiative in the market and in private spheres of action. Clear and technically authorised general rules are the perfect instrument for pursuing social and individual goals, whatever they may be. Weber thought of the rule of law in the shape of general formal and abstract rules as being instrumental in the rise of capitalism, and Marxist writers, who also saw it as inextricably connected with capitalist society, criticised it in its role in legitimating an unjust social order (see, further, Part III).

In one of the most interesting and influential jurisprudential accounts of these problems, Lon Fuller elevates the core features of the rule of law to nothing less than what he calls the 'inner morality of law'. Legality, for Fuller, is the 'enterprise of subjecting human conduct to the governance of rules' (Fuller 1969, p 106). As such, its tendency is to minimise irrationality in human affairs. Its purpose is to prevent our being governed by arbitrary will. What this means is that law is an essential element in the governance of civil power through the rational principles of civic order. It is there in order to prevent our domination by the arbitrary will of officials and others who claim to know what is best for us – there being no curb on their power. It is there to open up, and to preserve, free communication between people. For Fuller, the proper way of 'putting ourselves under the governance of rules' is through legality, that complex ideal embracing standards for assessing and criticising decisions that purport to be legal. Where this ideal exists, according to Fuller, official action is enmeshed in and restrained by the web of rules, and no power is immune from criticism or completely free to follow its own bent, however well intentioned. Law is to be seen as intrinsically involving a procedural 'inner morality'. This inner morality offers some fundamental constraints simply through law's formal features.

What are the features of this inner morality? What are the characteristics of legality? Fuller sets out the eight necessary features. These eight features must, in some degree, all be present in a legal system as a whole. Legality is an art and we must balance them against each other so that we get the best mix. But the condition of something being called a legal system is that this mix is present.

1   There must be rules: This is interpreted as the demand for generality. There must be rules of some kind and their essential feature is that they must be general in scope.

2   Promulgation: The demand that the law be made public, not kept secret. Citizens are not likely to know the content of all the laws, but they must be able to find out.

3   No retroactivity: Rules must be prospective. That is, in order to govern human behaviour they must be set out in advance in order that citizens are able to decide whether to conform to them or not. The basic human right of no punishment without a law expresses this principle.

4   Clarity: Rules must so far as possible be clear in order that they may be understood and followed. While some interpretative leeway is inevitable, and some flexibility of standards desirable, rules that are deliberately unclear contradict the possibility of ordering human conduct according to them.

5   No contradiction in laws: Rules that demand competing actions give no clear guidance as to what behaviour is expected by the law.

6   Laws must not require the impossible: Laws that demand behaviour over which citizens have no possible control cannot allow the fulfilment of subjecting their conduct to rules.

7   Constancy: Laws must not keep changing rapidly if they are to produce stable expectations of what the law requires of its citizens, though of course this does not mean that they cannot change in order to meet the needs of a changing society.

8   Congruence between official action and declared rules: What officials do must be in accordance with the laws set out in advance, otherwise what the rules required and their application would differ in such a way as to leave citizens subject to the arbitrary powers of those in authority.

In defining the conditions under which the ideal of the rule of law can be realised, Fuller borrows from the German sociologist Simmel the idea that 'there is a kind of reciprocity between government and the citizen with the respect to the observance of rules. Government says to the citizen in effect, "These are the rules we expect you to follow. If you follow them, you have our assurance that they are the rules that will be applied to your conduct." When this bond of reciprocity is finally and completely ruptured by government, nothing is left on which to ground the citizen's duty to observe the rules' (Fuller 1969, pp 39–40).

While the ideal of reciprocity requires a firm commitment to the fulfilment of all eight principles of legality, this does not mean – with the exception of publicity – that they can all equally be fully realised on all occasions. For example, clarity is always an aspiration rather than something that can easily be achieved in the writing of all laws; laws do require change over time; principles of strict liability do in some sense demand the impossible where they hold actors liable for consequences that they may have done everything in their power to prevent; and sometimes in the case of common-law judgments, which change or 'develop' the law, the principle of non-retroactivity may appear to be compromised (see, for example, the 'marital rape' cases, *Stallard v HMA* in Scotland or *R v R* in England).

For Fuller the instantiation of each principle is required in a legal order in order that law's fundamental purpose, namely the subjection of human conduct to the governance · of rules, be fulfilled. These principles constitute an 'inner morality of law', that is, they are intrinsic to what it means to have law at all. They are the necessary and sufficient condition for the possibility of bringing about the framework of 'reciprocity', which is law's achievement, in that law is distinct from merely instituted power and acquires a 'moral' dimension. Let us have a closer look at why.

One prominent objection to this has been that it is a purely formal account of the rule of law that has no necessary moral dimension as such. After all, couldn't even a fascist, or racist, or other totalitarian government meet these ideals without sacrificing its programme? For HLA Hart this 'inner morality' is perfectly compatible with the pursuit of immoral ends and he gives the example of the 'morality of poisoning'. Fuller's principles ensure the effectiveness or efficiency of a particular practice – even one such as 'poisoning' – regardless of moral judgements about that activity. Fuller correctly replies that before you make that argument about law you have to know the point of law. If you see law as a social technique for the ordering of society then the objection may have some bite. For then, law is seen as nothing more than a neutral technique for managing a society, and with the separation of means and ends, perhaps the question of effectiveness becomes something distinct from moral value. But if, like Fuller, you see law as something more than a neutral technique, with a moral purpose of its own – that of bringing about reciprocity – then the means of achieving it (clarity, prospectivity, etc) acquire a moral dimension of their own, as making possible that reciprocity. Following Aristotle, the conditions of excellence of a practice are internally derived. Fuller argues then that law is not just a technique and that it has a moral purpose of its own, and this is encapsulated in the 'enterprise of subjecting oneself to rules' and eliminating the arbitrary from everyday life.

Is Fuller right to argue that law has a moral purpose? Isn't it merely a *means* of getting at goals, even if these goals are sometimes morally worthy, like justice? A robust defence of the morality of law has come more recently from John Finnis who moves away from the idea that law is, in *any* sense, a 'necessary' evil. One thing, he claims, which any healthy community requires, is some common authority. Unless we all in common accede to the authority of some common code of conduct we cannot live together in community at all. And the implementation of any common code of conduct requires the institutionalisation of some agency or agencies, which adjudicate upon breaches of the common code. The more complex a political society becomes, the more rich and varied are the opportunities it presents for diverse manifestations of the good. But the more that is so, the more we face problems of co-ordination with each other. Hence the more sophisticated are the common public agencies we need for adjudication, administration, enforcement and amendment or enrichment of our common and authoritative code of social conduct. The achievement of co-ordination, which is the achievement of law, becomes in this way of thinking a means of human flourishing – the achievement of moral good. Law is both part of the procedure for arriving at things and part of the good itself. It is a substantive thing, which becomes a moral good itself.

It is this then that lends further credence to Fuller's view that law requires reciprocity and connection. It is more than a neutral means of organising a society; rather, it is something that is a moral enterprise in itself. That way of living is *in itself* morally good for us. It is in this way that the rule of law becomes something more than a one-way street of norms standing above, to be a shared interaction that both protects and enriches us. And it is thus part of a democratic arrangement even though it appears to stand above us – insulated from us.

Hence legality can be seen in the manner of a flexible grammar: something that partly determines our language and thus helps us to write, but also something that, because of its flexible interaction, is embedded in it and thus is part of the enrichment and good of our lives and not just a means to an end.

Reading

On the tension between certainty and the 'argumentative' character of law, see MacCormick (2005) ch 2, and ch 13 on the meaning of objectivity.

For Hayek's influential defence of the rule of law and the challenges it faces in practice, see Hayek (1944) ch 6. See also Raz's essay 'The Rule of Law and its Virtue' in Raz (1979).

Craig (1997) offers a survey in the context of public law, and see also Dyzenhaus (2000b).

For a helpful overview of a range of critiques of the rule of law, see Sypnowich (2000) 178–91.

For a brief, influential and controversial account from a Marxist perspective, on the rule of law as 'an unqualified human good' see Thompson (1977) 265–9.

For a full account of MacCormick's treatment of legalism and its ethical value, see MacCormick (1989). Shklar (1986) offers a critical assessment of legalism and its role in landmark political trials.

Fuller's analysis is found in Fuller (1969), especially ch 2 ('The Morality that Makes Law Possible').

Hart's criticisms can be found in the debate with Fuller in *Harvard Law Review* 71 (1958) 595 and 630 respectively. See also Fuller's 'A Reply to Critics' in Fuller (1969).

Waldron (2008a) and (2008b) are very helpful assessments of these authors' debate, as well as providing interventions on the subject in their own right.

For Finnis's restatement of natural law see Finnis (1980), and for a valuable engagement in response, MacCormick (1992). See also Part II 2.1.

1.4 Rights

Rights represent a particular way of talking about law and politics. Historically, rights were associated with revolution: for example, the 1789 French Declaration of the Rights of Man, in defiance of the old aristocratic order, asserted that 'men are born and remain free and equal in rights'. Today, many people regard society as being in 'the age of rights', which reflects the extent to which rights have come not only to predominate in legal and political argument, but to provide the basic standards to which those exercising power must conform. But opinion divides now, particularly in the context of contemporary globalisation, over whether rights can and do still retain their radical character, as a weapon for the powerless in the struggle against oppression.

Rights are a special type of political claim, grounded in a distinctive form of argument. A distinction is often drawn between rights-based and utilitarian arguments in political and legal theory. The former employs what is called a deontological form of reasoning, that is that we should follow a certain course of action because it is the morally correct thing to do; the latter employs consequentialist reasoning, that is that our actions should be guided by results, in particular what will produce the greatest happiness for the greatest number.

We can trace the origins of rights claims to the development of natural law doctrines in the seventeenth century, and in particular, the writings of John Locke. Locke suggested that humans originally lived in a state of nature in which they were free and equal, and possessed certain natural rights, particularly the right to property. The purpose of agreeing to organised rule through government was that these natural freedoms could be better protected by the state – accordingly, with the formation of political society natural rights do not disappear, but are now guaranteed by positive law through a process of instituting government by consent. At the time, this was a revolutionary way of thinking, marking a sharp break with classical political thought. Previously, individuals had been regarded as subjects under a duty of obedience to their rulers. They were now to be considered as the holders of inalienable rights, that is these rights cannot be given or taken away. On this account, natural rights enjoy priority – both in chronological terms, and against laws that might interfere with them. They also have finality in the sense that they provide closure to political disputes – to adopt contemporary language, they are trumps which prevail over political claims framed in consequentialist terms.

This framework gives rise to the important distinction between the right and the good in liberal political philosophy. In advancing their conception of the good society, it is open to governments to pursue a variety of goals, and choose, for example, between laissez-faire and interventionist forms of economic management. However, the idea of the right states that there are certain limits, in the name of individual freedom, to what governments can do, no matter what conception of the good is being implemented. These limits may concern both the substantive content of rights – Locke, for example, argued that 'the great and chief end . . . [of] government is the preservation of their property' (Locke 1988, pp 350–1) – as well as the form of their protection, namely through processes established according to the rule of law.

We can get a sense of the main issues involved in delineating the scope of rights claims by considering Martin Loughlin's argument that the rights movement should be understood as 'an evolutionary process' marked by four trends:

> 'generalization' (as greater numbers of political claims are expressed in the language of rights), *institutionalization* (as such claims increasingly acquire recognition in positive law), *collectivization* (as claims extend beyond the abstract individual to embrace social groups), and *internationalization* (as rights discourse enters the domain of international relations).
>
> (Loughlin 2000, p 208, emphasis in original)

Loughlin further suggests that each trend promotes an increasing '*politicization*' of rights, which has had a major impact on our understanding of law.

Civil, political and social rights

The last fifty or so years have witnessed a significant colonisation of political argument by rights discourse, whether by oppressed minorities (and majorities) seeking the right to equal treatment, campaigners seeking to vindicate either the rights of women to choose an abortion or the rights of foetuses to life, or the starving and poor seeking the right to basic subsistence and shelter. From the vantage point of history, this latter-day ascendancy of rights was by no means guaranteed. Natural rights had been subject to sustained critique, which downgraded their standing in political thought. Bentham famously denounced natural rights as 'nonsense upon stilts', while Marx saw rights as tools of bourgeois legitimation, each contrasting the rhetoric of rights with the material lack of freedom on the part of many. However, there was a revival in natural rights thinking in response to the atrocities of the Second World War. Leading Nazis were tried at Nuremberg for crimes against peace and humanity, and in 1948, the United Nations (UN) set out in the Universal Declaration of Human Rights (UDHR) a list of basic human rights that should never again be violated on such a massive scale.

According to TH Marshall, the modern growth of rights is related to the demands of three different, but related, elements of citizenship: civil, political and social. Civil rights provide the basic requirements of individual freedom, such as freedom of expression and religion, and personal liberty. The formative period for civil rights was the eighteenth century, when, reflecting their radical roots, they were deployed in the fight against authoritarian rule. Civil rights thus understood are closest to the freedoms Locke envisaged in the state of nature, particularly if we include the right to private property. In the nineteenth century however, these rights, while necessary, were seen by some as insufficient in ensuring equal citizenship, and attention turned to the realisation of political rights, enabling individuals to participate in decisions where political power is exercised. For groups such as the Chartists and Suffragettes, restricting the right to vote on the basis of property or gender rendered it defective, and so the main objective of the movement for political rights was the universal franchise, finally achieved in the UK in 1948. In the twentieth century, it has been argued that full citizenship also required the protection of social rights. Campaigners contrasted the formal equality granted by civil and political rights with the substantive inequality which these rights seemed unable to remedy, and contended that to enjoy freedom in material terms, it was necessary to guarantee rights such as education, adequate housing and minimum levels of subsistence.

Marshall's analysis underscores the breadth of claims now made in the name of rights. However, highlighting the diversity of rights also reveals that they are potentially in conflict. Whichever type of rights has priority will affect the scope for governmental action by drawing the line between the right and the good in a different place. For example, a strong conception of civil rights could restrict interference with private property, whereas an emphasis on social rights may require the redrawing of existing patterns of wealth and ownership, which may require the state to take private property or at least restrict enjoyment of it. Accordingly, one of the consequences of expanding rights discourse has been fierce political debate over the requirements of freedom: is this better satisfied in negative terms, that is freedom from external constraints, or in positive terms, that is freedom to exercise one's autonomy.

Politicising law – legalising politics

For much of their existence, rights were part of political struggle and debate directed towards criticising and changing the existing ruling order. Even where enshrined in constitutional texts, they were largely dormant as legal instruments; for example, although the US Bill of Rights dates from 1791, it was only in the twentieth century that the courts began to play a more active role in upholding constitutional rights. However, the recent history of rights has seen a general move towards greater legal protection. This is manifested in two developments: first, the adoption of international and regional treaties following the Second World War such as the European Convention on Human Rights (ECHR), and second, the spread of liberal democratic ideas and practices after the fall of the Berlin Wall in 1989, for example, the adoption of constitutional charters of rights throughout Central and Eastern Europe.

That the institutionalisation of rights has primarily taken legal form rests on certain ideas about the separation of powers, which justify treating courts as the guardians of fundamental rights. In part, this is an argument about judges' institutional status, that as they are not elected to serve the wishes of the majority, they are less prone to popular pressures which might seek to restrict the rights of minorities. It is also in part an argument from democracy, that rights provide the infrastructure of the political process, and so there needs to be some external check on elected politicians to ensure rights are not abused.

This emphasis on legal institutional forms tends to promote a particular conception of rights. Stronger international machinery exists for the protection of civil and political rights, and these are more readily enforced under national constitutions than social rights, which are often instead seen in more aspirational terms. This is linked to a number of perceptions about the nature of rights and adjudication. First, that we can draw a distinction between negative rights, which prevent the state from doing something, and positive rights, which may require the state to act. Second, that the good constitution promotes freedom by entrenching negative rights to prevent state encroachment on individuals' private spheres. Third, that this is best achieved through the judicial enforcement of civil and political rights. According to Ronald Dworkin (1985), the foundational constitutional principle is that everyone be treated with equal concern and respect, and so it is the duty of the courts in upholding the rule of law to ensure minimal non-interference with individual autonomy. Moreover, cases involving negative rights are suited to courts as they determine the rights and duties of two parties, to which Dworkin argues there is always a legally right answer. Positive rights, on the other hand, raise questions involving the allocation of resources that affect the whole population, to which there can only be politically preferable answers.

These arguments are not uncontroversial. Whether a claim should be framed as a positive or negative right is often open to discussion. For example, does freedom of expression simply require the state to refrain from censorship, or does it impose a duty on the state, say, to provide access to the media? Also, while the priority of negative rights is asserted, it is generally accepted that only some rights are absolute (for example, the right not to be tortured), and most texts permit rights to be limited, either in general terms, such as when necessary in a democratic society, or on specific grounds, such as the interests of national security or the protection of health and morals. Resolving these questions involves courts in difficult line-drawing exercises, and there are often sharp differences of judicial opinion within and between cases over what the right answer is. For some critics, the political nature of rights claims does not disappear when they are discussed in a court of law, and in deciding these cases judges inevitably draw on contentious political assumptions over which there can be reasonable disagreement. The extent to which such questions are now the mainstay of legal discourse leads Loughlin to conclude that greater institutional protection of rights inevitably leads to the politicisation of law.

The other side of this story is the legalisation of politics as more disputes over matters of public policy are resolved in the courts. One consequence of advancing rights claims in legal guise is to change the form of argument; for example, rather than debating whether aircraft should be able to land during antisocial hours on grounds of health and safety, this now becomes an aspect of the right to privacy. If those affected by the aircraft passing over their homes can convince the courts that this disproportionately affects their right to privacy and family life then the aircraft will not be able to take off and land, no matter how strong the interest of society in allowing this to happen. Following the lead of the US, there has, comparatively speaking, been an upsurge in rights litigation, which some see as beneficial in correcting basic flaws in the democratic process, particularly in protecting minorities. For others, though, the filtering of political claims through the courts leads to a thinning out of democracy, as it reduces the range of political argument by privileging an individualistic outlook, while limiting the participants to those who can afford the cost of legal action.

The indivisibility of rights?

The historical priority accorded to civil and political rights has recently been challenged, and instead there have been calls for a different, more collective, approach. Some writers speak in terms of generations of rights: first-generation civil and political rights focus on the abstract individual; second-generation social and economic rights are enjoyed by particular groups (for example, the right to health care addresses the needs of the sick); and third-generation solidarity rights are claims that affect humankind as a whole, such as the right to a clean environment. There has been a gradual move towards giving these rights greater international and constitutional recognition, although often with weaker enforcement machinery. We should be careful though not to equate the institutionalisation of rights solely with their enumeration in formal texts – for example, with the establishment of the welfare state, it could be said that social rights in practice predominated in post-war Britain, even if they were not called rights.

The argument that second- and third-generation rights should have equal status to first-generation rights seeks to minimise the supposed differences between them. For example, against the claim that social rights distinctively require expenditure and state intervention, it is said that civil and political rights also have financial implications and entail positive action, such as the maintenance of a system of courts. On the other hand, it is said that giving full constitutional protection to social rights would embroil courts in political controversy. But, as we have seen, the charge of politicisation of law also arises with respect to civil and political rights. However, while both sets of rights involve decisions over potentially irresolvable conflicts of values, social rights are seen as being more overtly concerned with questions of distributive justice. Thus to the extent that social rights can be perceived as more political than legal, this often works to enhance the higher institutional standing of civil and political rights.

The case for the second and third generations is based on ideas of the indivisibility of rights. In particular, it is argued that a basic standard of living is a prerequisite to being able to enjoy civil and political rights: for example, the right to a fair trial or freedom of speech may be quite useless to someone dying of starvation. Moreover, some see prioritising the first generation as promoting a partial vision of rights that seeks to universalise Western values. It is suggested that regarding rights as claims by individuals made against the state fosters an atomistic view of society, and obscures the systematic widespread abuse of rights often visited on groups, for example, the millions of humans who are denied the basic right to food. Arguments in favour of collective rights seek to recover neglected, including non-Western traditions of rights, which reflect more organic notions of society. This approach again changes the focus of rights discourse. Upendra Baxi argues that in the dominant tradition, the privileged bearer of rights was the white European male. Accordingly, Western notions of rights made human suffering invisible, particularly in the context of colonisation, as they did not treat non-Europeans as fully human and so their rights were imperilled by genocidal practices. In contrast, regarding all peoples as bearers of rights brings to the fore violations of their ultimate collective right to self-determination, and so has as its principal focus taken suffering seriously.

Rights in international and global context

Reference to the right to self-determination highlights the role human rights have played in international politics. While self-determination itself first came to prominence at the 1919 Versailles Conference, the main impetus for the internationalisation of rights was the UN's adoption of the UDHR in 1948. There is now a raft of international treaties dealing with a range of subjects such as the abolition of torture or combating discrimination. These developments have two important consequences. First, rights are now genuinely human rights, possessed by everyone by reason of their humanity and without distinctions based on geographical origin. Second, and related, as these human rights are universal, they potentially challenge the principle of state sovereignty and can justify humanitarian intervention by the international community, for example, to prevent the genocide of one ethnic group by another within the same state.

While internationalisation can in many ways be seen as providing a step change in the career of human rights, this is not without its dangers. Rights can become pawns in the power play of international diplomacy. During the Cold War, rights became an ideological tool, as the West argued that lack of respect for civil and political rights undermined the legitimacy of state communist regimes, while the

East countered that capitalist societies failed to protect social and economic rights. Throughout this period, each side was prepared to overlook gaps between their own rhetoric and practice in client states, enabling dictatorial regimes to escape scrutiny for rights violations. The fall of the Berlin Wall dramatically changed this context, and ushered in a new consensus on human rights. Today, some international lawyers suggest the right to democratic governance has become the norm, supported by the record number of countries now living under some form of parliamentary rule. Combined with the spread of charters of rights and judicial review, some commentators speak of the globalisation of human rights.

However, while some see this as a cause for celebration, others suggest that the key challenge for human rights concerns how these developments relate to broader patterns of globalisation. In particular, can rights operate as a check on new forms of power associated with the global economy, such as that wielded by multinational corporations, which may now present the strongest threat to individual autonomy? And should they be expected to? Some commentators suggest such an outcome is not envisaged, and that the institutional form of rights that are being globalised reflects a pared-down vision of democracy satisfied by fair procedures at elections. Others argue that the spread of rights and global capitalism reflect the same values, as each seeks to carve out an area of private activity free from state interference.

Baxi captures these concerns by juxtaposing two ways of thinking about human rights – one is the universal paradigm, grounded in the 1948 Declaration; the other is of what he calls the 'trade-related market-friendly paradigm' of human rights. The latter reflects the extent to which corporations have been able to advance their interests through rights – for example, by arguing that restrictions on tobacco advertising limit their freedom of expression – and also how rights claims are being reframed in the language of the market – for example, the right to shelter is translated into profit opportunities for construction companies. He suggests that these paradigms reflect an ongoing clash between the politics *of*, and the politics *for*, human rights. The politics *of* human rights uses rights as a means to promote established patterns of power, as happened during the height of the Cold War. By contrast, the politics *for* human rights views rights as a way of disturbing oppressive power relations, as when colonised peoples asserted self-determination against imperial rule. Baxi argues that the relative ascendancy of the 'trade-related market-friendly paradigm' shows the extent to which the politics *of* human rights has been appropriated for global capital. He warns that the future of human rights depends on developing a more thorough-going politics *for* human rights at the global level, which has as its object 'that order of progress which makes the state more ethical, governance progressively just, and power increasingly accountable'.

Reading

For the development of natural rights theories, and a discussion of some of its principal critiques, see Waldron (1987) chs 1 and 6. The best short introduction from a historical perspective remains d'Entreves (1951).

John Locke's account of the state of nature and its relation to natural rights is in Locke (1988) chs II, VIII and XI.

One of the most famous, and influential, defences of natural rights is Paine's *Rights of Man*, Paine (1961).

TH Marshall's analysis of the development of rights is in Marshall (1992), pp 8–17 and 27–43.

The distinction between negative and positive liberty is explored in Berlin (1969) pp 121–34. For the difference between negative and positive rights, see Laws (1996) pp 627–35.

Loughlin's analysis of the 'age of rights' is in Loughlin (2000) ch 13. On the inevitably political nature of rights resolutions see Griffith (1979) pp 7–18. Dworkin's account of the proper scope of the judicial role in rights adjudication is elaborated in Dworkin (1985) chs 1 and 8.

For a statement on the indivisibility of human rights, see the 'Bangkok Declaration' (1993). Craven (1995) pp 6–16 provides an overview of the conceptual issues relating to social and economic rights.

For a discussion of the 'sociality' of human rights, see Stammers (2008) ch 2.

Pogge (2002), 'General Introduction' and ch 1, offers an influential account of the foundational nature of basic subsistence rights.

Henkin (1999) discusses human rights and contemporary international politics.

For a critique of the tendency to regard human rights as exclusively Western, see Baxi (2008) pp 33–50 and Santos (2007), and on their entwinement with capitalism (Baxi, 2008), pp 252–64.

1.5 Identifying valid law

One way of interpreting the relationship between law and politics raises a more general concern about the relationship between law and other kinds of values. We have seen that we can distinguish political, economic and legal power (section 1.1 above), but does this mean that law can be understood without including any necessary reference to those values that it may seem desirable for law to embody: values such as justice, fairness, equality and non-discrimination? Is it possible, in other words, and is it desirable, to identity valid law *without* reference to other kinds of normative or evaluative standards?

The tradition of *legal positivism* gives an affirmative answer to these questions. Legal positivism emerges as a distinct approach to legal analysis in the work of Jeremy Bentham and John Austin, English jurists writing in the late eighteenth and early nineteenth centuries, and it received great impetus in the work of two twentieth-century legal philosophers, Hans Kelsen and HLA Hart. These authors differ in their approaches, yet they all see as important the need to identify valid law without collapsing this into questions of political or moral values. They argue that what the law is, and what it ought to be, are different questions and require different kinds of answer. As Austin famously put it, 'The existence of law is one thing, its merit and demerit another. Whether it be or be not is one enquiry; whether it be or be not conformable to an assumed standard, is a different enquiry' (Austin 1954/1832, p 157).

The possibility of 'value-free' analysis was influential across diverse areas of intellectual enquiry throughout the nineteenth century in the emerging social sciences. It had philosophical roots in David Hume's observations that, first, there is a crucial difference between factual statements (that such and such *is* the case) and evaluative statements (that such and such *ought* to be the case), and secondly, that the latter cannot be logically derived from the former. For Hume, descriptive (factual) accuracy should not be conflated with (evaluative) desirability: 'The anatomist', he wrote, 'ought never to emulate the painter' (Hume 1978/1739, p 620). Taking the lead from Hume's insight, legal positivists sought to clarify our understanding of law – a description of what the law *is* – by freeing it from value judgements about what it ought to be.

Yet if this 'analytical jurisprudence' sought clarity, it did not disavow the very real importance to society of pursuing moral and political values, such as justice and equality and so on. In fact, the major legal positivist authors wrote a great deal about what such values were and how they may be best pursued, including through legal means. But this kind of enquiry, they maintained, was separate from the problem of identifying valid law. Moreover (and it sounds rather odd at first hearing), for legal positivists there were good *evaluative* reasons for pursuing a non-evaluative theory of law. If we could describe accurately which laws were in force in any given juris-diction then we could make a clear and coherent assessment of them as a matter of independent critical evaluation. A legal system whose legislation was, for example, racially discriminatory would still contain valid laws (assuming they were proce-durally enacted properly) even though many citizens and observers would consider them politically and morally abhorrent. To mix the undesirability of these laws from a political or moral point of view with the question of whether they were legally valid fused two different things: what the law is (here and now) and what it ought to be if it were more just and equal. And it was important to make this point not just for analytical reasons but because legal reform itself depended upon being able to give an accurate description of what the law is and how it is changed, in order to be able in turn to make it better. The anatomist, Hume concluded, is not expected to be creative like the painter is, yet he 'is admirably fitted to give advice to a painter . . . We must have an exact knowledge of the parts, their situation and connexion, before we can design with any elegance or correctness' (ibid, p 621). Hence conflating legal validity with moral or political judgement simply muddied the waters of analysis and potential reform.

It is important to realise that as an analytical project legal positivism is not appropriately comparable with what is commonly called the 'natural law' tradition. The goals of the two are quite different and hence it is not comparing like with like to set them in opposition to each other (Finnis 2007). The former is far narrower and technical in scope, while the latter is much wider in ambition and resources, and in which the question of legal validity is only a very small component of a far richer exploration of human values over times and contexts. However, although its descriptive successes and the merits of its method of 'value-free' analysis have been widely criticised, legal positivism's analytical approach has been, and to an extent remains, influential. In the following sections we therefore set out some of the key ideas of Hart and Kelsen and consider some differences between the two. The lens through which we look at their theories here is specifically as part of a thematic concern with the role of political and moral values in the law. (We return to different aspects of their work later.) We conclude the section by highlighting some prominent criticisms of the work of the legal positivists in that regard.

Hart's concept of law

Sympathetic to Bentham and Austin's legal positivism, Hart nonetheless identified a number of problems in their analyses. For Austin, law 'properly so called', is the command of a sovereign backed by the threat of a sanction. He defined the sovereign as 'a determinate human superior, not in the habit of obedience to a like superior, [which] receive[s] habitual obedience from the bulk of a given society' (Austin 1954/1832, p 166). This 'command theory' of law, as Hart saw it, may well resemble common perceptions of the criminal law, but it was inadequate as a full description of law. One of the main reasons why is that there are different *kinds* of laws many of which do not operate as commands at all, but rather involve the conferring of powers. These powers may be found in the domain of public law, such as with jurisdictional powers – laws, for example, establishing or varying the jurisdiction of courts or tribunals – as well as in the myriad private law powers to make contracts or wills or establish corporations. In all such cases, and they are very many, it is not accurate, said Hart, to describe the relevant laws as commands. Nor is it appropriate to see their use as involving the threat of sanctions. For Hart, an alternative understanding was required if the legal positivist tradition was to remain persuasive.

This new understanding involved shifting attention from commands to *rules*. For Hart, a legal system was best understood as the 'union of primary and secondary rules' (see Hart 1961, ch V). Primary rules imposed obligations. Tax law, for example, or the law of negligence imposed on citizens legal obligations: duties to do, or refrain from doing, certain actions. These laws came in the form of rules, not commands. Importantly, there is something about the quality of rules that makes them different from commands: a robber in the street, argued Hart, may demand that you hand over your money. You may feel obliged to do so. But it would be wrong to say that you had 'an obligation' to do so. What a 'tax demand' did, by contrast, was precisely to impose obligations to pay money, and these obligations had their source in legal rules established by legislation. You may or may not feel obliged to pay your taxes. But that was different from saying you had an established legal obligation to do so. Primary legal rules of this sort were therefore duty imposing rules: rules that established binding legal obligations.

But as we have already noted, not all legal rules are of this kind. There were also, Hart argued, secondary rules. They were, 'on a different level from the primary rules, for they are all *about* such rules' (Hart 1961, p 92, original emphasis). The importance of these rules lay in their relation to primary rules in such a way that established a legal *system*. According to Hart, here are three types of secondary rules. First, there were those power, conferring rules that established who, or which institutions, had the legal authority to decide legal disputes and impose penalties for breach of obligations. They also established the procedures that were to be followed to make such judgments. These Hart called rules of *adjudication*. They allowed for a certain efficiency in, for example, the processing of legal disputes by identifying authoritative bodies and procedures to determine legal outcomes.

Secondly, there were those power-conferring rules that established who, or which institutions, and according to what procedures, were legally authorised to make changes to legal rules. These were secondary rules of *change*. In the most obvious sense, such rules established the conditions according to which new primary rules could be introduced or older rules amended. This includes the power to make legislative-type change. This will likely be available at a variety of possible levels such as the powers that are normally conferred on local government to vary legal standards with respect to areas within their jurisdictional competence. But rules of change are not limited to this form for there are also rules of change which confer powers in private law that allow individuals to change their legal position or status in certain defined ways. For example, the power to change your legal status by way of marriage; or to establish a corporation, and so on. These may in turn create new (to you) primary legal obligations, but they require powers being conferred, as Hart said, at a different level from such primary rules.

The third type of secondary rule is the rule of *recognition*. At its most simple, it is 'a rule for conclusive identification of the primary rules of obligation' (Hart 1961, p 92). In complex legal systems there may be, says Hart, a number of such rules and they may take different forms. But what they have in common is that characteristic of establishing definite criteria to *identify* valid law. It is the rule of recognition, or in a complex setting, an 'ultimate rule of recognition' that does this. The content of such an ultimate rule will vary from jurisdiction to jurisdiction: in the United Kingdom, for example, Hart noted that the ultimate rule of recognition was 'Whatever the Queen in Parliament enacts is law.' In addition to providing criteria for recognising valid law, this rule also introduces the key idea that all the rules together, primary and secondary, form a legal *system*: 'the rules are now not just a discrete unconnected set but are, in a simple way, unified' (Hart 1961, p 93).

It is in this sense that a legal system is best understood as 'the union of primary and secondary rules'. But it is of course also necessary that the rules of the legal system, and especially the rules of obligation, are generally effective; most of the people most of the time must act in accordance with legal rules and be liable to sanction where they do not. This is a necessary *condition* for the existence of a legal system. But this fact of efficacy is not the reason for the validity of its rules. *That* requires that the rule of recognition, which provides the criteria of validity for all the other rules, be accepted as a common standard at least by the *officials* of the system. Rules, said Hart, had two aspects: an 'external' aspect, where rules were essentially predictions of how people would behave (for example, when the traffic light is at red we can predict that drivers will stop); and an 'internal' aspect where, seen from the *participants'* point of view, rules provided *reasons* for people to act in certain ways (the red traffic light is the internalised reason *why* drivers stop). In complex societies, said Hart, most of the people need not accept legal rules from the internal point of view. Instead, 'The rule of recognition, if it is to exist at all, exists only as a shared social rule *accepted as a binding common standard of behaviour* by those whose official power as a "legal power" is dependent ultimately upon that very rule' (MacCormick 2008, p 34, original emphasis). The ultimate rule of recognition in a legal system is not itself a legal rule, but a conventional rule: 'It "exists" . . . by the custom and usage of those bound by it' (ibid, p 137). And so it is, concludes Hart, that the ultimate rule of recognition 'can neither be valid nor invalid but is simply accepted as appropriate for use in this way' (Hart 1961, pp 105–6).

Part of the significance of Hart's legal positivist approach lies in its description of legal validity as having no *necessary* connection to political or moral values. One legal system may, for example, impose the death penalty, another not; one may allow discrimination on the grounds of race or gender, another declare these as illegal. In all, or any, such cases, the question of legal validity does not depend on its correlation to particular political or moral values. It is, rather, answerable by reference to the system's ultimate rule of recognition which is itself ultimately a matter of officials' practice.

Hart does note that all societies will normally have certain basic rules and values enshrined in their law: rules against violence, theft, fraud and so on (what he describes as a 'minimum content of natural law'). And he will also argue for a set of moral and political values that he espouses as desirable in a decent society and which the content of its laws would ideally reflect. But such desirability, and the contingency of laws enshrining certain values, should still not be confused with a description of what constitutes validity in a legal system. Here a certain 'anatomist's' realism must prevail. Even politically and morally atrocious governments can make and enforce valid laws that cause great harm to a great many of those subjected to them. Even there, argues, Hart, 'The society in which this was so might be deplorably sheeplike; the sheep might end in the slaughter-house. But there is little reason for thinking that it could not exist or for denying it the title of a legal system' (Hart 1961, p 114).

We will return later in this section to collect certain criticisms of such an approach. But for now we can note one insight made by MacCormick in the course of his sympathetic treatment of Hart's work. MacCormick observed that 'Perhaps everywhere there is a line to be drawn between "law" and "politics", but one of the more obvious facts of cross-cultural comparison is that it gets drawn differently in different places' (MacCormick 2008, p 8). For all that Hart's concept of law was intended as generally applicable, it inevitably bears the hallmark of its time: 'it is clearly recognisable as the work of an English lawyer of the twentieth century' (ibid). In that time, and indeed for some time before, matters of political and social justice belonged entirely in the realm of the 'political nation'. It was here, according to MacCormick, that questions of entitlement and rights were argued over and settled, and the outcomes of these conclusions, where appropriate, enacted into law. In such a system, legal officials were expected to apply the law declared by the political system, and for this they needed clear criteria – rules of recognition – for what counted as legally valid and binding rules and what did not. The political morality of these rules was not something officials, and in particular judges, were required to engage with.

Even without comparing different types of legal and constitutional traditions and practices, it is clear, says MacCormick, that the British understanding Hart imbibed and described as to where the line between law and politics is drawn has itself changed markedly in recent decades. Two factors stand out. One involves the large-scale impact of supra-state entities (in particular the law and policies of the

European Union) and the simultaneous effects of internal devolutionary adjustments (a Scottish Parliament, and Assemblies in Wales and Northern Ireland). The other is the incorporation of the European Convention on Human Rights into domestic law which has, among other things, resulted in an increasingly direct role of the judiciary in what were formerly taken to be within the exclusive domain of the political nation. These, combined with the fragmentations and recombinations of sovereignty, the pluralisation of legal orders, and the existence of competing and overlapping juris-dictions have together made the legal landscape quite different from when Hart's work was developed. On the one hand, such developments make far more complex the problems of identifying valid legal rules according to an ultimate rule of recog-nition that would provide unity for a single UK legal system. But more importantly they have challenged the very notion of the autonomy of law where (as we saw above) the politicisation of law and the legalisation of politics mark a clear shift in where it is appropriate to draw the line between law and politics. Together these make much more problematic the descriptive endeavours of a legal positivist approach that would seek to maintain a conceptual separation between law and political and moral values.

Kelsen's pure theory of law

The question of the autonomy of legal validity from political and moral values is addressed in a second version of legal positivism, that developed by Austrian jurist Hans Kelsen. Following again Hume's insight on the underivability of normative ('ought') statements from factual ones, Kelsen argued that the validity of norms could only be derived from other norms, not from factual statements about the way the world is or human beings are. With respect to law, therefore, Kelsen noted that 'It is a peculiarity of law to regulate its own creation' (Kelsen 1957, p 365). Yet his approach differed from Hart's in important ways as we will now see.

According to Kelsen, there is a science of legal norms. 'Its exclusive purpose is to know and to describe its object' (Kelsen 1967, p 1). Its object is positive law. The proper method for analysing legal norms must be objective; it cannot, he argues, refer to other, subjective, criteria: whether the law is good, fair, or just, for example. Legal science thus offers a 'pure theory of law', purified from these other, subjective, 'alien elements'. It is in this sense that jurisprudence is 'value free'.

Kelsen distinguishes between the subjective and objective meaning of acts. For example, you might write down a wish-list of who you want to benefit from the things belonging to you when you die, and sign your name at the end. The existence of this piece of paper and what it means to you can be distinguished from its objective legal meaning. If your legal system recognises such an act as sufficient to create a will, there now exists a legally valid document, the content of which creates certain legal rights and obligations that can be legally enforced, if need be by a court of law, on your death. Contrarily, you may do exactly the same act – producing a piece of paper with your wish-list and signature – but if the law of your country requires your signature to be witnessed, then that piece of paper fails to create a legally valid document: its objective meaning (in this instance that the signed document creates no enforceable legal rights and obligations) is quite different, despite your subjective act being the same. The law, for Kelsen, therefore provides a 'scheme of interpreta-tion' which confers objective legal meaning on actions: 'The judgment that an act of human behaviour, performed in time and space, is "legal" (or "illegal") is the [...] of a specific, namely normative, interpretation' (Kelsen 1967, p 4). It is that norm [...] tive schema specific to law – the norms of positive law – that is the object of legal science, and, says Kelsen, we can and should analyse it without reference to questions of moral or political worth.

Legal norms confer objective meaning on human actions. But what makes these legal norms valid? That is, what makes them binding in such a way that 'an individual ought to behave in the manner determined by the norm'? (Kelsen 1967, p 193). Consider an example we used earlier: there is a letter from the tax office notifying you that you are liable to pay the amount of tax calculated by them. What makes this tax demand legally valid? For Kelsen, like Hart, this legal obligation imposed upon you is valid because of a superior norm, say the legislation which sets out the basis of particular taxes and how to assess them. This legislation will, in turn, be valid because of its source; as a duly enacted act of parliament. And what makes this act of parliament valid? This will be referred again to a higher norm, in this case most likely a constitution which stipulates the validity of parliamentary enactments as law. If we persist in such questioning we may trace the validity of the constitution back, says Kelsen, to a 'historically first' or original constitution. The matter then comes to a head: if there is no constitution prior to this one – that is, no higher constitutional or legal norm to which *it* can refer for its validity – then what makes *it* valid? This is where Hart and Kelsen differ. Hart, it will be recalled, had turned at this point to the conventional practices of officials and their 'internal point of view' on the rule of recognition. But Kelsen's answer is that every legal order must at this stage refer to a 'basic norm' – in German *Grundnorm* – which alone can infuse the whole legal order with validity.

What is this basic norm? For Kelsen it is a logical presupposition: 'that one ought to behave as the constitution prescribes.' It is therefore not a legal act, nor a matter of will: it is a matter of thought only – it has to be presupposed. But why does it have to be presupposed; and what purpose does it serve?

It has to be presupposed, argues Kelsen, because once we trace back the authority of legal norms to the historically first constitution, we cannot refer to another, higher, posited norm. We have, so to speak, run out of (positive, posited) legally authorised norms by reaching the historically first constitution. But given the conceptual gulf between facts and norms, no factual statement can provide validity to this constitution. We just have to assume it as valid in the following terms: 'Coercive acts *ought* to be performed under the conditions and in the manner which the historically first constitution, and the norms created according to it, prescribe' (Kelsen 1967, p 201, emphasis added). Only this presupposition can, as a matter of thought, answer the question of how legal validity is *possible*. It alone can answer the ultimate question of 'why the norms of this legal order ought to be obeyed and applied' (p 212). As MacCormick sums up, 'no positive, laid-down rule could confer upon constitution-makers the authority to do so. Everyone just has to act as if they had such authority' (MacCormick 2007, 45).

As to its purpose, 'the basic norm constitutes the unity of the multiplicity ... of all norms belonging to the same legal order' (p 205). In other words, the validity of a divergent range of legal norms is traceable through a hierarchy of legal authorisations which reaches its grounding in the basic norm. Where a particular claim cannot be so traced – like the demand of the robber for your money, or an unsigned

…side the validity-conferring system. Such a demand or wish … al to act in accordance with it. It is in this sense then that … tion of this basic norm is to found the objective validity of a … is, to interpret the subjective meaning of the acts of human … rms of an effective coercive order are created, as their objec- … 1967, p 202).

… wo points from this conclusion. First, Kelsen is clear that as a … must be *effective*: 'a minimum of effectiveness is a condition of validity … 1967, p 11). By effectiveness, Kelsen means two things: one, that legal norms are 'applied by the legal organs (particularly the law courts), which means, that the sanction in a concrete case is ordered and executed'; and two, that by and large individuals obey these norms: 'they behave in a way which avoids the sanction' (ibid). It is important to distinguish carefully between efficacy as a *condition* for validity, and the *reason* for the validity of a legal norm. The former is a *fact* (people, including officials, by and large *are obeying* the law), but as a fact it cannot be the reason for validity of legal norms. That reason, which alone creates objectively binding norms that people *ought* to follow, can only be another norm, whose validity is ultimately traceable, as we have seen, to the basic norm.

The second point is that legal validity is in no sense dependent upon any link to political or moral *values*. Again, that is not to say that we ought not to strive to make law fair or just or reasonable. As Kelsen notes, 'If the idea of justice has any function at all, it is to be a model for making good law and a criterion for distinguishing good from bad law' (Kelsen 1957, p 295). The problem is, however, that reasonable people (not to mention unreasonable people) disagree on what justice requires. Such 'subjectivity' – that justice depends on the point of view, interests or preferences of people – cannot be the source of objective legal meaning. Good law and bad law are still both law; and only the pure theory of law, freed from the subjective matter of what counts as 'good' or 'bad', can describe the objective existence of legally valid norms. But the consequence of such a view is stark: '*Any* kind of content might be law' (Kelsen 1967, p 198, emphasis added). That the *content* of legal norms – and whether they be considered as just or unjust, say – is entirely separable from their validity is seen by many as highly controversial. And whether there are limits on the form of what can count as law also raises crucial questions about the nature and exercise of political power in a society. It is to these two concerns that we now turn.

Legality and validity

Earlier we introduced the ideal of the rule of law and its relation to political and economic power, and we considered in more detail Lon Fuller's account of the inner morality of law. In this section and the next we look at two further invocations of this ideal, but in ways that deal more directly with how it impacts on the very possibility of identifying valid law. These two approaches engage with and critique the legal positivist views we have just considered, and do so in ways that have important bearing on how we think about what it means to be governed by law as opposed to other forms of rule and discipline.

According to Jeremy Waldron the legal positivist approach treats the rule of law (or what we may also call the principles of legality) as 'simply one of a number of ideals (such as justice, liberty, or equality) that we apply to the law, rather than anything more intimately connected with the very idea of law itself' (Waldron 2008b, p 59). On this account, it is possible, as we have just seen, to establish what the law is independently of political or moral values. Waldron argues that this view is incorrect. Instead, he says, 'we cannot really grasp the concept of law without *at the same time* understanding the values comprised in the Rule of Law' (ibid, p 10, emphasis added). Identifying valid law cannot therefore be done first, and then the question of the values of the rule of law be analysed and applied (or not, as the case may be) separately. The rule of law, writes Waldron, 'is an ideal designed to correct dangers of abuse that arise in general when political power is exercised, not dangers of abuse that arise from law in particular' (p 11). Choosing *law* as the way of checking or organising the exercise of political power – that is choosing 'governance through *law*' rather than through management or decree – means that law itself is 'prescribed as the remedy, rather than identified as the problem that a separate ideal – the Rule of Law – seeks to remedy' (p 11). The rule of law is not then an optional add-on to the question of legal validity, but is inextricably connected to what it means to be able to identify valid law at all.

To defend this approach, Waldron argues that we need to pay particular attention to the '*procedural* and *argumentative* aspects of legal practice' (p 5, emphasis added) that together connect what most people regard as the basic aspects of the rule of law with a richer account of the law's role in protecting and enhancing underlying values of human dignity and responsibility. To understand this better Waldron offers an analogy with the use of the term 'democracy'. The former East Germany called itself the German Democratic Republic. Yet what it was and what it called itself were two different things: no one, least of all its citizens, was taken in by the label 'democratic'. In order to *be* a democracy, certain standards have to be met, for example regularly held free and fair elections. In other words, there are certain conditions that provide independent criteria for identification of that practice as a democracy, regardless as to how it is self-described.

Is the same true of the use of the terms law and legal system? Are there criteria that must be met independently for their application to be legitimate? Waldron argues that there are, and is critical of legal positivists for being far too casual, too generous, in employing the term law to refer to any system of centralised order whose rules need only be efficacious and identifiable (in Hart's case, for example, by reference to an elite's rule of recognition). For Waldron, to qualify for the designation law, or legal system, requires something more than merely what legal positivists would have us believe, because 'to describe an exercise of power as an instance of law-making or law-application is already to dignify it with a certain *character*' (p 12, emphasis added). Such 'character' may or may not be actually present in a centrally organised order. So, just as a state that calls itself democratic may in fact not be, 'Not every system of command and control that calls itself a legal system *is* a legal system' (pp 13–14). We must go beyond the claims of legal positivists by understanding the *inseparability* of principles of legality and the existence of that which we dignify with the title law.

What then are the special features that are required to achieve the character of law and legal system? Waldron argues that there are five. First, there must be courts. By courts we understand not just institutions that apply the law to individual cases, but something much richer than this. Courts are bodies that apply the law in a particular way, providing an impartial third party to adjudicate between litigants. But most importantly, they do so under certain *procedural* conditions. For example, they hear and allow submissions from both sides, and they offer the opportunity for challenges to evidence and interpretation to both sides according to predetermined rules of evidence and procedure. Moreover, the examination and testing of the case is done in 'open court', and the reasons given for a decision likewise made publicly available (see Tomkins 2011). When we read about states where the rule of law is deemed under threat, a common reason for that threat is precisely because of a breakdown in or failure to instantiate those procedural guarantees that we associate with the existence of courts; for example, secret decisions of unknown officials where one party may not be able to find out what the evidence and rules being applied are. In such cases, we may not only criticise the fairness of the process, but ask whether the rulings of such bodies should be dignified with the title of legal at all.

The second characteristic identifies the need for 'general public norms'. The generality of norms was a factor we considered earlier when we looked at Fuller's work and Waldron shares his insights here, noting that law's generality makes an important contribution to instantiating the 'principles of impersonality and equality' (p 25) that are central to a conception of law. Waldron also gives special emphasis to the value of 'publicity'. Where it is lacking, for example where the creation and application of secret or unknowable directives is being used to discipline citizens, this might well involve the exercise of centrally organised power, but that is no reason for calling such an exercise of power law. For Waldron, unlike the mere coercing of human behaviour, or the herding of animals, people who are governed by law require to be made publicly aware of, or at least capable of finding out with assistance, the normative rules that apply to them. Only if this is the case are they being treated as responsible agents capable of understanding these rules *as* normative demands (things they ought to do but may not), and making decisions according to this knowledge. Taken together then, the first and second characteristics of law and legality combine firstly to respect people's 'dignity as beings capable of explaining themselves' and secondly to be 'respectful of persons as agents; it respects the dignity of voluntary action and rational self control' (p 28).

Waldron describes the 'positivity of law' as the third essential characteristic, but takes it to have more significance than that described by the legal positivists. Both share the idea that human law is posited (positive) law, and thus understand that as a 'mode of governance' it is made by people rather than discovered through some mystical or transcendental insights. But buried at the heart of this observation is something more fundamental. That law is humanly made means that it can change, by human means. That it could be different from what it is now means that the very 'idea of law, therefore, conveys an elementary sense of freedom, a sense that we are free to have whatever laws we like' (p 31). Of course, there may be many obstacles in the way of achieving this, some of which may be desirable, some not. But again where the rule of law is under threat, and where the exercise of power takes a non-legal form, it is precisely this very elementary aspect of freedom that is often denied.

Fourthly, Waldron identifies another aspect to 'publicness' in these terms: the fact that the law 'presents itself in a certain way – as standing *in the name of the public* and as *oriented to the public good* . . . [is] one of its defining characteristics' (pp 31–2, emphasis added). The matter of 'presentation' is important here, since any particular legal system or set of laws may not *in fact* deliver something that seems good for all. But that failure is different, says Waldron, from failing aspirationally to try to achieve or aim at the common good. We should not dignify as 'law' a set of orders or commands that simply seek to promote the interests of a few and which explicitly disavow the general and equal application of norms to all in the name of all. To qualify for the label of law, legal institutions and laws must therefore 'orient themselves in their public presence to the good of the community – in other words, to issues of justice and the common good that transcend the self-interest of the powerful' (p 31). Comparing Hart's claim, we might say that where many people in a society are treated in a sheep-like manner, and the sheep 'end in the slaughter-house' there is, on this principle, *every* reason for 'denying it the title of a legal system'.

The final characteristic Waldron calls 'systematicity'. Again this is a richer notion than that offered by the legal positivists' account of system validity. It invokes the sense in which the positive rules of the system all cohere. This is most commonly achieved through demanding a coherence of values that underpin the particular rules. It is perhaps most evident in common law judging (and we will turn to this with respect to judicial reasoning in Part II, and especially in the work of Dworkin and MacCormick) but it applies to legislation too. In positing new laws, legislation too should be understood as fitting in to an ongoing body of law that has coherence as a whole, often explicitly provided by tests of constitutionality. Systematicity in this sense is not just a matter of identifying valid law – though it also involves this – but includes a more profound value: 'It means that law can present itself to its subjects as a unified enterprise of governance that one can make sense of' (p 35).

For Waldron, having law, as opposed to other means of governing, requires seeing law as a common 'public resource' and while this requires a certain predictability it is, just as importantly, a resource for argumentation and contestation. This requires the procedurally guaranteed opportunity to debate the meaning not only of what the law ought to be but what the law actually is and requires. This 'arguable' character of law, as MacCormick calls it, is central to what we understand as legal practice, typified in the testing of arguments for and against particular propositions of law by advocates in court. And it is centrally in debates in legal argument over what the quality of coherence – or systematicity in this expanded sense – means that legal institutions again uphold the rationality and dignity of those subject to it. Legal positivists overlook this larger sense and so offer an impoverished account of law. This is the case not merely with respect to an aspirational quality, but to something that is descriptively essential to what it means to have governance through law at all: as Waldron puts it, 'Courts, hearings and arguments are aspects of law which are not optional extras; they are integral parts of how law works and they are indispensable to the package of law's respect for human agency' (p 60).

These five characteristics show, says Waldron, that a non-evaluative account of legal validity is descriptively wrong. To have valid law and a valid legal system requires knowing that governance through *law* means something different than just the deployment of centrally organised power. It means the working presence of procedural and institutional elements that the legal positivist account does not provide. It means understanding the congruence between these elements and legal validity in such a way that is not optional. In precisely the same way that holding regular free and fair elections is a non-optional requirement for having a democracy, the *concept* of law and ideal of the *rule* of law must be understood together and simultaneously; not separately and sequentially.

Injustice and invalidity

Our final understanding of the problem of identifying valid law turns directly to the question of the substantive *content* of the law. Most concisely, we can ask: is Kelsen correct to say that *any* kind of content can be law?

One of the most important negative answers to this question was given by the twentieth-century German legal theorist Gustav Radbruch. In response to the Nazi atrocities from 1933 to 1945, Radbruch gave an analysis that was profoundly critical of legal positivism's claims. His views influenced not only fellow legal theorists but lawyers and judges among whose tasks was to argue and decide cases which had to assess the validity or otherwise of Nazi-period enactments. Was it possible that a policy of mass extermination was also legal? Could those who were involved in the perpetration of mass slaughter defend their actions against accusers by saying that what they did was legally authorised at the time they did it? Did the legal positivist understanding that 'a law is a law' mean that there was nothing more to be said about the legal validity of such acts than that while they might be humanly abominable, they were nonetheless still lawful? Radbruch did not think so, and the German Federal Constitutional Court has endorsed his analysis in its own reasoning.

There is one kind of reason here that contains elements found in Waldron's analysis. It appears in an argument of an immediate post-war German prosecutor reported by Radbruch. The case concerned the prosecution of a man, Puttfarken, who had, as a clerk in the Justice Department during the Nazi period, informed on another man (Gottig) to the authorities for writing on a wall that 'Hitler is a mass murderer and to blame for the war'. Puttfarken's denouncement had led to Gottig's trial, conviction and execution. Standing trial himself now, as an accomplice to murder, could Puttfarken claim that what he had done was legal at the time? The Prosecutor comments: 'Anyone who informed on another during these years had to know – and did in fact know – that he was delivering up the accused to arbitrary power, not consigning him to a lawful procedure with legal guarantees for determining the truth and arriving at a just decision' (quoted in Radbruch, 2006/1946, p 2). This clearly resonates with Waldron's claim that the rule of law, and indeed, the law itself, requires certain procedural guarantees in order to qualify as legal. Where these disappear to be replaced by exercises of force, such as in Nazi Germany, then we are entitled, as the prosecutor urges, to no longer call this a legal system.

Puttfarken was found guilty and the problems of how to deal with informants, and indeed with the judges who had acted on the information in sentencing to death those like Gottig, was one that surfaced in a number of instances. But important as these were, they were of course not the worst of the atrocities associated with Nazi rule. The extermination of millions of Jews and others by the regime raised profound questions about the defensibility of actions under the supposed imprimatur of the state and its law. It was here that Radbruch's analysis about the *content* of law became most important.

Radbruch's 'formula', as it has become known, states that 'extreme injustice is no law': 'Where there is not even an attempt at justice, where equality, the core of justice, is deliberately betrayed in the issuance of positive law, then the statute is not merely "flawed law", it lacks completely the very nature of law.' In light of this, the Nazi state did not create bad, albeit still valid, law. In Radbruch's view it did not create law at all: 'it never attained the dignity of valid law' (Radbruch, p 7). As lawyers say in other contexts, it was void *ab initio*.

This is the core of the claim that political and moral values – centrally, justice and equality – *do* limit what counts as valid law. In the task of identifying valid law, for Radbruch there are certain contents that simply *cannot* be law.

Radbruch is careful to acknowledge that there are often complaints that positive law produces injustices or perceived immoralities, and that these complaints are often valid. And as a lawyer he maintains that in the vast majority of these cases, the validity of the positive law must still prevail, for reasons including the need to stabilise legal expectations. 'Any statute is better than no statute at all,' he argues, 'since it at least creates legal certainty' (Radbruch, p 6). But this cannot be conclusive of the matter of legal validity as such. There are other cases where 'the conflict between statute and justice reaches such an intolerable degree, [that] the statute, as "flawed law", must yield to justice' (Radbruch, p 7). Such cases of 'extreme injustice' cross the threshold of 'intolerability' in such a way that even instances of 'appropriately enacted and socially effective norms lose their legal character' (Alexy, p 17). Such enactments may be collectively organised forms of action which sanction conformity, but because of their content they are not merely politically or morally repugnant, they are legally invalid. These exercises of power, such as those carried out by the Nazis, might in fact 'serve as a basis for the "must" of compulsion, but [they] never serve as basis for the "ought" of obligation or for legal validity' (Radbruch, p 6). There is a limit in precisely that respect, which consists in the political-moral threshold test for validity.

But is what counts as 'extreme injustice' not liable to be open to dispute? Radbruch acknowledges that it may be, and that no clear defining line can be drawn here between extreme ('intolerable') and merely 'tolerable' injustice. But this does not of itself invalidate the formula, since the fact that one cannot identify a clear line does not mean that you cannot identify instances of extreme injustice. There can be little controversy over the fact that, as the Federal Constitutional Court expressed it, 'the attempt to destroy physically and materially certain parts of one's population, including women and children, in accordance with "racial" criteria' constitutes 'extreme injustice' (Alexy, p 33). That, at least, is a clear case.

This example, says Alexy, is decisive and shows that there is indeed a necessary connection between legal validity and moral and political values. And it is underpinned by the fact that, besides being socially effective and requiring procedural techniques for establishing how to make or change law, there is something more fundamental about law that necessarily determines the limits of its content.

This is what Alexy calls law's 'claim to correctness'. Imagine, he says, a new constitution being enacted by a state in which the majority is suppressed by the minority, and whose opening line is this: 'X is a sovereign, federal and unjust republic.' There seems to be something intuitively wrong with this. It is not simply that it is unconventional or that it might be politically imprudent. Nor even that it is morally problematic. There is a deeper flaw that is signalled by it seeming 'somehow crazy' (Alexy, p 28). The reason for its absurdity lies in the fact that it contains a profound *contradiction* because 'a claim to correctness is necessarily bound up with the act of giving a constitution, and in such cases it is above all a claim to justice' (p 29). There is a 'performative contradiction' in the constitutional provision in that a constitution or law that explicitly states its own injustice contradicts what we implicitly understand what constitutions and laws to be. Constitutions and laws claim, at least implicitly, to be correct or right – not wrong or unjust. It is this claim, concludes Alexy, that 'determines the character of law. It excludes understanding law as a mere command of the powerful' (p 28).

Radbruch's formula was deployed in post-war legal reasoning to invalidate many Nazi-era enactments. It also resurfaced in legal argument after the fall of the Berlin Wall in 1989. Several former East German soldiers were prosecuted for shooting those trying to cross the wall from East to West Berlin. Their defence was that their acts were legally authorised at the time. The Federal Court of Justice used Radbruch's 'intolerability' thesis in deciding that the acts were 'an offence to a higher order of law [and] manifested a patently gross offence to the fundamental tenets of justice and humanity', and so concluded that the Border Law the soldiers sought to rely on in their defence had 'from the outset no validity' (Radbruch, pp 21–2). (We consider the 'transitional justice' aspects of such issues further in Part I 2.5.)

This point about 'a higher order of law' is one that has a profound resonance throughout the natural law tradition. The idea that there are values, grasped through the exercise of reason, that transcend any particular state's laws, and that these values hold good independently of whether any state in fact recognises them, has been an important motivator of political ideas and practices, as well as in defences and critiques of the law. That their claimed reasonableness and universality has meant different things over time has also, perhaps ironically, been an essential part of the tradition. In their conservative mode, for example, they have at certain periods defended as natural the status quo of slavery and patriarchy; in their revolutionary mode – as natural or inalienable *rights* – they have inspired the overthrow of governments. And in their recent instantiation as 'universal human rights' they have held government acts up to scrutiny in light of principles deemed essential to what it means to be human. And it is the relation between fundamental values and positive law that has always, according to Finnis, been at the heart of answers to the central questions posed by natural law theories: 'How and why can law . . . give its subjects sound reason for acting in accordance with it? How can a rule's, or a judgment's, or an institution's legal ("formal" or "system") validity, or its facticity as a social phenomenon, make it authoritative in its subject's deliberations?' (Finnis 2007, s 1; we consider Finnis's work in more detail elsewhere.)

In light of this, it is specifically with respect to the *validity* of legal norms in the face of political and moral injustice that Radbruch's formula extends a tradition going back to St Thomas Aquinas and beyond which finds expression in the Latin phrase '*lex iniustia non est lex*'. This should not, argues Finnis, be taken to mean that 'an unjust law is not a law' in any simplistic sense. Rather it means that an unjust law is 'not straightforwardly or unqualifiedly a law'. That is, in noting that it is an unjust *law*, it is still recognised there is law but only in a distorted sense, in the same way we might say that 'an invalid argument is no argument' or a 'disloyal friend is not a friend' (Finnis 2007, s 4). In declaring a particular instance of law as being a distortion in this respect, there may be occasions where legal validity still overrides moral or political objections to its injustice, and where the proper question becomes: should, in conscience, this valid law still be obeyed? But there may be other instances, such as those Radbruch's formula identifies in the case of Nazi atrocities, where we say more than this: that in the 'extreme injustice' of its content, the law fails to create *legal* obligations since the enactment itself fails to be legally valid.

We noted earlier that it is improper to see natural law theorising as 'in opposition' to legal positivism. This must be borne in mind, particularly if we want to do justice to the former, lengthy, tradition of enquiry which in fact readily accepts (as we have seen Radbruch and Finnis acknowledge) the importance of recognising valid and socially effective law. Their point is, however, a different and deeper one that seeks to understand law and legal institutions as a central component of human societies and their political and moral values and organisation. A leading contemporary legal theorist has described legal positivism as a 'stagnant research programme' (Dyzenhaus 2000), but we need not endorse this charge still to see that the practical matter of when and how law endorses or repels certain political or moral positions rather than others, when and how its officials learn about distributive and procedural justice and their role in promoting or denying certain versions of it, and so on, issues which political and legal actors and theorists have contributed to in so many ways over so long, that all these are matters of immense importance to the vast majority of citizens; the technical academic disputes over the possibility of conceptual theoretical purity are not.

Reading

The theory of legal positivism has generated a large literature, both favourable and critical. The most important starting points for further reading are with the main twentieth-century proponents Hart (1961) and Kelsen (1957, 1967, 1992). A sympathetic treatment of Hart's work is provided by MacCormick (2008). Lacey (2006) offers a fascinating biography of Hart that situates his work well within the jurisprudential debates and social milieu of the period. Tur and Twining (1986) provide an important engagement with Kelsen's work. For a contextualisation of the sociological significance of questions about the nature of legal validity to the rise of legal modernity, see Part III 1.4.

D'Entreves (1951) and Finnis (1980) offer perhaps the best introductions, from quite different perspectives, to natural law thinking. Finnis (2007) is an excellent short introduction. Alexy's (1999) essay provides a succinct analysis of Radbruch's theory as well as engaging directly with a range of legal positivist critiques of his views.

References

Alexy, R, 1999, 'A Defence of Radbruch's Formula' in D Dyzenhaus (ed) *Recrafting the Rule of Law*, Oxford: Hart.
Austin, J, 1954/1832, *The Province of Jurisprudence Determined*, London: Weidenfeld and Nicolson.

Bangkok Declaration, 1993, 'Final Declaration of the Regional Meeting for Asia of the World Conference on Human Rights', available at http://law.hku.hk/lawgovtsociety/Bangkok%20Declaration.htm.

Baxi, U, 2008, *The Future of Human Rights*, 3rd edn, New Delhi: Oxford University Press.

Berlin, I, 1969, *Four Essays on Liberty*, Oxford and New York: Oxford University Press.

Craig, P, 1997, 'Formal and Substantive Conceptions of the Rule of Law', *Public Law* 466–87.

Craven, M, 1995, *The International Covenant on Economic, Social and Cultural Rights: A Perspective on its Development*, Oxford: Oxford University Press.

D'Entreves, AP, 1951, *Natural Law: An Introduction to Legal Theory*, London: Hutchinson.

Dworkin, R, 1985, *A Matter of Principle*, Cambridge, MA: Harvard University Press.

Dyzenhaus, D, 2000a, 'Positivism's Stagnant Research Programme' 20 *Oxford Journal of Legal Studies* 703.

Dyzenhaus, D, 2000b, 'Form and Substance in the Rule of Law', in C Forsyth (ed), *Judicial Review and the Constitution*, Oxford: Hart.

Finnis, J, 1980, *Natural Law and Natural Rights*, Oxford: Clarendon.

Finnis, J, 2007, 'Natural Law Theories', Stanford Encylopedia of Philosophy, http://plato.stanford.edu/entries/natural-law-theories/ (revised 2011).

Fuller, L, 1969, *The Morality of Law*, New Haven: Yale University Press.

Griffith, JAG, 1979, 'The Political Constitution', 42 *Modern Law Review* 1.

Hart, HLA, 1961, *The Concept of Law*, Oxford: Clarendon.

Hayek, F, 1944, *The Road to Serfdom*, London: Routledge.

Henkin, L, 1999, 'The "S" Word: Sovereignty, and Globalization, and Human Rights Et Cetera', 68 *Fordham Law Review* 1–14.

Hobbes, T, 1996/1651, *Leviathan*, Cambridge: Cambridge University Press.

Hume, D, 1978/1739, *A Treatise of Human Nature*, Oxford: Clarendon.

Kelsen, H, 1957, *What is Justice? Justice, Law, and Politics in the Mirror of Science*, Berkeley: University of California Press.

Kelsen, H, 1967, *Pure Theory of Law* (trans Max Knight), Berkeley: University of California Press.

Kelsen, H, 1992, *Introduction to the Problems of Legal Theory*, Oxford: Clarendon.

Lacey, N, 2006, *A Life of HLA Hart*, Oxford: Oxford University Press.

Laws, J, 1996, 'The Constitution: Morals and Rights', *Public Law* 622–35.

Locke, J, 1988/1690, 'The Second Treatise of Government' in P Haslett (ed), *Two Treatises of Government*, Cambridge: Cambridge University Press.

Loughlin, M, 2000, *Sword and Scales*, Oxford: Hart.

Loughlin, M, 2003, 'Ten Tenets of Sovereignty', in N Walker (ed), *Sovereignty in Transition*, Oxford: Hart.

MacCormick, N, 1982, 'Law, Obligation and Consent: Reflections on Stair and Locke', in N MacCormick, *Legal Right and Social Democracy*, Oxford: Clarendon.

MacCormick, N, 1989, 'The Ethics of Legalism', 2 *Ratio Juris* 184–93.

MacCormick, N, 1992, 'Law and the Separation of Law and Morals', in RP George (ed), *Natural Law Theory*, Oxford: Clarendon.

MacCormick, N, 1999, *Questioning Sovereignty*, Oxford: Oxford University Press.

MacCormick, N, 2005, *Rhetoric and the Rule of Law*, Oxford: Oxford University Press.

MacCormick, N, 2007, *Institutions of Law*, Oxford: Oxford University Press.

MacCormick, N, 2008, *HLA Hart*, 2nd edn, Stanford: Stanford Law Books.

Marks, S, 2000, *The Riddle of All Constitutions: International Law, Democracy and the Critique of Ideology*, Oxford: Oxford University Press.

Marshall, TH, 1992/1950, *Citizenship and Social Class*, London: Pluto Press.

Paine, T, 1961/1791, *The Rights of Man*, Garden City: Dolphin Books.

Pogge, T, 2002, *World Poverty and Human Rights: Cosmopolitan Responsibilities and Reforms*, Cambridge: Polity (2nd edn 2008).

Radbruch, G, 2006/1946, 'Statutory Lawlessness and Supra-Statutory Law', 26 *Oxford Journal of Legal Studies* 1.

Raz, J, 1979, 'The Rule of Law and its Virtue', in J Raz, *The Authority of Law*, Oxford: Clarendon Press.

Santos, B de Sousa, 2007, 'Human Rights as Emancipatory Script? Cultural and Political Conditions', in B de Sousa Santos (ed), *Another Knowledge is Possible: Beyond Northern Epistemologies*, London: Verso.

Shklar, J, 1986, *Legalism: Law, Morals and Political Trials*, Cambridge, MA: Harvard University Press.

Stammers, N, 2008, *Human Rights and Social Movements*, London: Pluto Press.

Sypnowich, C, 2000, 'Utopia and the Rule of Law', in D Dyzenhaus (ed), *Recrafting the Rule of Law*, Oxford: Hart, 2000.

Thompson, EP, 1977, *Whigs and Hunters*, Harmondsworth: Penguin.

Tomkins, A, 2011, 'National Security and the Due Process of Law', *Current Legal Problems* 1–39.

Tur, R and Twining, W, 1986, *Essays on Kelsen*, Oxford: Clarendon.

Vattel, E, 1883, *The Law of Nations or Principles of the Law of Nature Applied to the Conduct and Affairs of Nations and Sovereigns* (ed J Chitty), Philadelphia PA: T & JW Johnson & Co.

Waldron, J, 1987, *Nonsense upon Stilts*, London and New York: Methuen.

Waldron, J, 2008a, 'Positivism and Legality: Hart's Equivocal Response to Fuller', 83 *New York University Law Review* 1135.

Waldron, J, 2008b, 'The Concept and the Rule of Law', 43 *Georgia L Rev* 1.

Walker, N, (ed), 2003, *Sovereignty in Transition*, Oxford: Hart.

Walker, N, 2010, 'Out of Place and Out of Time: Law's Fading Co-ordinates' 14 *EdinLR* 13–46.

Cases

R v R (Rape: marital exemption) [1991] 4 All ER 481.

R v Secretary of State for Transport, ex p Factortame Ltd (No 2): C-213/89 [1991] 1 AC 603, [1991] 1 All ER 70, [1990] ECR I-2433, ECJ.

Stallard v HMA (1989) SCCR 248.

Chapter 2

Advanced topics

Chapter Contents

2.1	Justice	51
2.2	Constitutionalism and citizenship	65
2.3	Law, politics and globalisation	74
2.4	Law and the state of emergency	81
2.5	The rule of law in political transitions	88

2.1 Justice

Introduction

Few topics appear so central to thinking about the relationship between law and politics than the matter of justice. Yet according to David Hume, if there were adequate resources to satisfy people's needs and wants – such as there is with the abundant air we breathe – then the problems of justice would largely not exist. But where resources appear relatively scarce on the other hand, says Hume, human conventions of justice have developed to organise entitlements and distribution. Political questions then arise as to which principles ought to guide such organisation. Should people be left alone to determine their own sense of justice, individually or within particular groups? Or does some institution, such as the State, need to intervene to provide a common standard for all? If so, what would such a common standard require? Perhaps that people be treated equally? But given that people are not in fact equal – in abilities, say: they may be sick, or be children, or be unable to work – does justice require not equal but different treatment in recognition of these facts? And should people get what they need; or what they deserve; or what would be fair?

The proliferation of such questions signals that not only are the answers likely to be many and contested, but also that there is a wide range of contested questions too. For example: should all relations be considered as amenable to applying principles of justice: parenting, say, or the treatment of animals? Do citizens of one state owe duties of justice to citizens of another? Should law always be used to establish and regulate matters of justice? Can law do justice to justice? Or should talk about 'justice' even be superseded by alternative approaches? For is it not the case that ideas, and practices of proclaimed justice have readily co-existed with the reality of extensive exploitation and discrimination: against women, racial groups, the poor, and so on? Or is this observation precisely why we need to work harder at the problems – to do justice better?

In thinking about the relationship between law and politics, there are different senses in which we speak about justice. For example, *formal* justice is embodied in the principle of treating like cases alike and different cases differently. This is a central element of legal reasoning, including reasoning from precedent, and it is taken up in more detail in Part II. There are related aspects of *procedural* justice that are concerned with how institutions go about, or ought to go about, processing legal claims in a procedurally fair manner. (This was an essential element in Waldron's account of law and legality that we outlined in 1.5.) There is also a subset of instances where societies are called upon to 'do justice to the past' – commonly now identified as problems of *transitional* justice – where societies that have gone through major political and social upheaval are faced with special problems associated with coming to terms with acts of injustice perpetrated by predecessor regimes. Where there have been extensive human rights abuses, for example, questions of *corrective, retributive* and *restorative* justice often come to the fore in conflicting ways in assessing how best to deal with these abuses. (These problems are covered in more detail in 2.5.)

In this Advanced Topic, however, we will concentrate on questions of *distributive* justice. This concerns the just distribution of goods, benefits and burdens in a society. We will look at four approaches to distributive justice that have been influential in how modern societies organise themselves with respect to what they think are justice's best guiding principles. These are utilitarianism, libertarianism, liberalism and socialism. We will assess some of their central ideas though we necessarily have to be selective. (For fuller engagement with the topic, the further reading should be a starting point.) But we should note one thing at the outset: these are *normative* theories; not in the sense that they are concerned with describing legal rules which govern actions, but rather in the sense that they provide arguments concerning why the view they promote *ought* to be adopted. These theories conflict – hence their *political* nature – and you should consider which, if any, you find more persuasive and why.

Utilitarianism versus libertarianism

A *utilitarian* approach to justice seeks to maximise average welfare in a society. Jeremy Bentham and John Stuart Mill were two of the most prominent advocates of this approach. The most famous expression of it sees the goal of increasing overall utility as being to achieve 'the greatest happiness of the greatest number'. It is a *consequentialist* theory: it tests for justice by reference to consequences. There are two main variations. Act utilitarianism considers whether any proposed *action* will result in increasing the average welfare. Rule utilitarianism asks what *rule* is best instituted to increase such welfare. It is in assessing the outcomes of putting the proposed act, or rule, into effect that the morally best or just thing to do becomes clear. The outcome is not just because it was the right act to do, or rule to follow: it was the right thing to do, or rule to follow because the consequences were perceived to maximise average welfare; to produce the 'greatest happiness of the greatest number'.

Hypothetical examples are often used to make this approach clear. Here are two. A person is detained because police have reasonable grounds to suspect that he has planted a powerful bomb somewhere in a densely populated city. If such a device goes off it is likely to result in mass injury and deaths. The detainee refuses to speak. Is it justifiable to torture him to try to find out where the bomb is? Is it, in other words, permissible, as a matter of justice, to commit harm against one person rather than risk harm to a greater number?

From the point of view of *act* utilitarianism, we are essentially only concerned with the justice – that is, the consequences – of the act in this instance. From the point of view of *rule* utilitarianism, we are concerned with the consequences – or justice – of instituting a rule that would authorise such behaviour. In either case note what we must do in our deliberation: we must add up the pros and cons of the consequences of allowing or not allowing such an act, or instituting the rule. We assess the possible harms and benefits and then, as it were, put them on a set of scales in order to determine what act or rule would maximise overall welfare. Reading off the result from the scales we find out what justice requires. In this example, there might seem something intuitively plausible about the idea that justice demands acting in such a way as to minimise the aggregate harms when we weigh the harm done to the detainee against the potential harms done to a large number of innocents. Surely a greater injustice is allowed by failing to act in such a way that protects many innocents from harm?

But is this utilitarian approach the correct way of reasoning? Consider what is negated should torture be permitted: factually, an innocent person might be being

tortured: the detainee may be genuinely innocent because of a case of mistaken identity. This possibility is one reason why, in law, a presumption of innocence operates
according to which everyone is presumed innocent until proven guilty in a court of
law. Moreover, even on consequentialist grounds, applying torture is commonly seen
to be less a reliable way of procuring evidence than it is a measure of how much pain
a person can withstand. Does torture, that is, even get at the truth? And if the person
is willing to plant a bomb on this scale are they likely to confess the truth? And so on.
But perhaps the key, *non*-consequentialist objection to utilitarian reasoning here is
that a decent society respects the 'inalienable' human right *not* to be tortured regardless of the nature of the circumstances. Prohibitions on torture, or on 'cruel, inhuman
and degrading treatment', signal that 'To treat a person inhumanly is to treat him in a
way that no human should ever be treated' (Waldron 2005, p 1745) On this view, we
should in no circumstances even carry out a utilitarian calculation about outcomes: it
is wrong to torture *regardless* of the consequences.

Consider then another scenario: a member of your country's air force is shot
down while on a reconnaissance mission over a country with whom there are hostile
relations. The enemy captors have reasonable grounds to believe that he has knowledge of imminent air strikes, likely to result in major civilian casualties. But he
refuses to tell them what he knows about where the strikes are likely to be aimed. Is
it justifiable to torture him to try to find out the location of the strikes? Would it be
legitimate, as Harvard Law Professor Alan Dershowitz has suggested in the context
of detainees held by American forces, to use 'a sterilized needle inserted under the
fingernails to produce unbearable pain' (quoted in Waldron 2005, p 1685) in order
to get the information and so help to save lives? Should the utilitarian calculation of
harms and benefits allow such treatment? Even in the extreme circumstances of war,
the international standard on the treatment of prisoners of war declares that it should
not. Article 17 of the 1949 Third Geneva Convention states that 'No physical or
mental torture, nor any other form of coercion, may be inflicted on prisoners of war
to secure from them information of any kind whatever.' On this, widely respected
view, utilitarian calculations about claimed increases in aggregate welfare are *never*
to be entered into: detainee's rights, to use Ronald Dworkin's metaphor, automati-
cally trump any claims about possible consequences.

Consider now two additional concerns with a utilitarian approach to justice.
First, to what extent is it possible to measure utility? That is, how can we assess what
people's pain and pleasure consists in, in order then that we can calculate how it can
be increased? What if people have different understandings or experiences of what
for them counts as pleasure or pain? Moreover, are all desirable values – dignity,
say, or liberty – reducible to one single measure – 'happiness' – in order that they can
be weighed together and a clear solution reached? What our first two examples show
is that in some, extremely important, cases we may be either unable or unwilling to
make a commensurating calculation with values at all since it belittles notions of
dignity or liberty to reduce them to a process of measuring 'more or less' happiness.
This was a point noted by the Enlightenment philosopher Immanuel Kant, whose
work represents a strong challenge to utilitarianism. Dignity, he argued, is not something on which a price can be put and thus measured against other values, in the way
that we might calculate a market price on the value of cars or computers. He argued
that 'In the kingdom of ends everything has either a price or a dignity. What has a

price can be replaced by something else as its equivalent; what on the other hand is above all price and therefore admits of *no equivalent* has a dignity' (Kant 1993/1785, p 40, emphasis added). The difficulty of reducing a plurality of values to one single measure – the problem of the *commensurability* of values – therefore poses an important challenge to utilitarian thinking.

A second concern is with trying to figure out what in fact the consequences of any act – or, in the case of rule utilitarianism, what the consequences of instituting a particular rule – are going to be. Even if we were to assume that it is possible to compare competing values by weighing them on the scales of pleasure and pain, there may be conflicting ways of assessing which of the consequences matters most in the process of weighing. Consider another example. You are well-off and live comfortably in a wealthy suburb in a country which nonetheless has widespread unemployment, poverty and homelessness which afflict a majority of the population. The government has failed to remedy these problems. Is it justifiable for those with no shelter and little source of sustenance to enter properties in your neighbourhood and take what they need to live? On one reading of utilitarianism a net increase in aggregate welfare would suggest a positive answer to this. Protecting your property rights, and others similarly fortunate, seems to result in the consequence of failing to provide for the majority basic requirements for food and shelter and hence lowers the overall happiness of the society. Wouldn't the aggregate welfare of the society be increased – and therefore justice be better served – by letting a redistribution of property occur? But then another consequence of this may be that it leads to a state of anarchy, where no one, even when they managed to acquire for themselves food and shelter, would have any security in preserving it. As in Hobbes's state of nature, there would be no property, only possessions, and even those would be limited to what people just happened to be able to hold on to. The problem of weighing up, according to a single measuring scale, all these different possible consequences appears to be a further difficulty for the utilitarian approach.

Using the same example and applying non-consequentialist reasoning – of the type we touched on in our first two examples – you might argue that your *property rights* should take precedence over the claimed needs of those who have no food or shelter. This would hold that it is wrong to deprive you of the property you had lawfully acquired, and, just like in our first two examples, that this should hold true regardless of the consequences. In other words, the protection of property rights should take priority over a welfare-maximising redistribution, even at the cost of failing to meet the basic needs of the majority. But is this really what justice requires?

One of the most trenchant critiques of the utilitarian position comes in the form of an affirmative answer to this question. It is perhaps best exemplified in the work of Robert Nozick, who defends a *libertarian* account of justice. Briefly stated, Nozick argues that 'Individuals have rights, and there are things no person or group may do to them (without violating their rights)' (Nozick 1974, p ix). In our example, where you have acquired property, in wealth, land or goods, say, then it is unjust for others – including the government – to deprive you of that property unless you volunteer to do so. To coerce you into giving it up – for example through a system of compulsory taxation – is a violation of your rights and your freedom to do with it what you will.

To defend this position Nozick offers us an 'entitlement' theory of justice. He illustrates it with a story of Wilt Chamberlain, an outstanding basketball player who draws huge crowds to games. Suppose that in his contract with the club there is a clause that Wilt will receive 25 cents from the price of each ticket. The fans flock to see him, happy to pay the admission price knowing of Wilt's contractual provision. By the end of the season, Wilt ends up $250,000 richer. Assuming for the sake of argument that everyone started with an equal amount of money, it is now clear that Wilt is far richer than everyone else. Nozick asks: is this new distribution *unjust?* Or, conversely, would it not be unjust to *deprive* Wilt of any of the money he has gained from the voluntary transactions of the fans? Nozick argues that it would. He says that *re*distribution according to some preset pattern, of equality say, signals a violation in one of two senses: 'To maintain a pattern one must either continually interfere to stop people from transferring resources as they wish to, or continually (or periodically) interfere to take from some persons resources that others for some reason chose to transfer to them' (p 163). Either way, people's rights, and their liberty, would be violated.

At the heart of Nozick's theory is, therefore, the claim that 'Whatever arises from a just situation by just steps is itself just' (p 151). Three principles of 'justice in holdings' underscore this: first, that 'A person who acquires a holding in accordance with the principle of justice in *acquisition* is entitled to that holding'; second, 'A person who acquires a holding in accordance with the principle of justice in *transfer*, from someone else entitled to that holding, is entitled to the holding'; and third, where holdings have not been acquired according to the first two principles – they may have been attained by deception or coercion – then the 'principle of *rectification* of injustice' requires that they be returned to the rightful owner. In the case of Wilt Chamberlain then, even though we have gone from a position of equality to an unequal distribution of wealth, assuming that everyone had acquired their money justly, and that there has been no fraudulent activity, this resultant inequality is nonetheless just: the voluntary transfer of justly held property. Where a person, or a group, or even – perhaps especially – a government interferes with this process of just acquisition and transfer, it exceeds what is morally legitimate.

Drawing on the work of John Locke, Nozick argues that people have a right of self-ownership and so what they acquire through their own work is theirs as of right. For someone else to deprive them of this is not only to violate their justly acquired rights: it is 'to make them a *part-owner* of you; it gives them a property right in you' (p 172, original emphasis). The redistribution of wealth by the state outside the three principles of justice is therefore morally wrong. It is in this sense that Nozick concludes that the state's 'Taxation on earnings from labor is on a par with forced labor' (p 169). Accordingly, only a 'minimal' state is justified according to Nozick. This 'nightwatchman' state will be limited to certain core functions such as the 'protection against force, theft, fraud, [and] enforcement of contracts' (p ix). Beyond this no consequentialist reasoning can be invoked without, as we have seen, violating individual rights.

But returning to our earlier example, what about the claims of those without food or shelter that justice demands some fulfilment of their basic needs? On the libertarian account respect for individual rights, and indeed for individuals themselves, means not imposing any 'patterned', or 'end-state', redistribution when the cost is the violation of these rights. Even so, 'Isn't justice to be tempered with compassion?' asks Nozick. The answer is emphatic: 'Not by the guns of the state' (p 348).

Voluntary transfer of private property to those in need is legitimate; charity for the needy, in other words, is fine – forced 'giving' is not. As GA Cohen puts it, with a jaundiced eye, 'If children are undernourished in our society, we are not allowed to tax millionaires in order to finance a subsidy on the price of milk to poor families, for we would be violating the rights, and the "dignity" of the millionaires' (Cohen 1995, p 31).

We will return shortly to some criticisms of this account. To the extent that it is, as we have noted, one that is highly critical of utilitarianism in offering a defence of (a certain conception of) liberty, we turn now to another approach to justice that also extols the virtue of liberty but which does not do so at the expense of denying the value of *equality* in the sense of what Nozick called patterned distribution.

Liberalism: Rawls's justice as fairness

John Rawls's important book, *A Theory of Justice*, was published in 1971. It is often said by academic writers that political philosophy had been in the doldrums until rejuvenated by this work. This is patently false. Depression-era and post-Second World War reconstruction had seen a massive deployment of intellectual and material resources in attempts to build rights-respecting welfare states. These gave practical effect to philosophically grounded projects with enduring, if now sometimes waning, effects. To be blind to this academically seems to say more about the academic polit-ical philosophy community than it does anything else. (It appears to confirm the observation, attributed to Marx, that when the train of history turns a corner, all the thinkers fall off!) Nonetheless, Rawls's work has been more widely influential and has become a standard reference point for contemporary debates on justice.

For Rawls, 'justice is the first virtue of social institutions . . . [and] the primary subject of justice is the *basic structure of society*, or more exactly, the way in which the major social institutions distribute fundamental rights and duties and determine the division of advantages from social cooperation' (Rawls 1971, pp 3, 6, emphasis added). The basic structure includes 'the political constitution, the legally recog-nized forms of property, and the organization of the economy, and the nature of the family' (Rawls 1993, p 258). Given that individuals' views on what counts as good and valuable for them may reasonably differ, how should we best decide on the content to be given to the basic structure?

Rawls's answer is that we should endorse justice as fairness. Drawing on the social contract tradition, he suggests that we imagine a hypothetical situation – what he calls the 'original position' – through which we can debate and seek agreement on what he calls a 'first fundamental question about political justice in a democratic society, namely what is the most appropriate conception of justice for specifying the fair terms of social cooperation between citizens regarded as free and equal' (1993, p 3). We can use the original position as a technique of representation to work out how best to 'realize the values of liberty and equality' (p 5). To do so we should imagine ourselves, in the hypothetical situation, behind a 'veil of ignorance' as to what our own capabilities, social position, and opportunities might turn out to be. Additionally, we should imagine we do not know what gender, race, or ethnicity we might have. Using such a scenario our aim is thus to formulate what conception of justice would best achieve a cooperative scheme that would offer the opportunity for an 'overlapping consensus' given potential and actual differences. As Rawls puts it: 'The parties are trying to guarantee the political and social conditions for citizens to pursue their good and to exercise the moral powers that characterize them as free and equal' (p 76).

Before describing the principles of justice Rawls believes would emerge from such a thought experiment, one key question remains to be raised: according to what principle would it be legitimate for the outcome of these deliberations to result in a *coercive* political authority? For Rawls, where 'political power [is] the power of citizens as a collective body', its exercise is 'fully proper only when it is exercised in accordance with a constitution the essentials of which all citizens as free and equal may reasonably be expected to endorse in the light of principles and ideals acceptable to their common human reason' (p 137). This, he says, is the liberal principle of legitimacy.

Rawls argues that two principles of justice would be selected in the original position. The first principle is this: 'each person has an equal right to a fully adequate scheme of equal basic liberties which is compatible with a similar scheme of liberties for all' (Rawls 1993, p 291). These basic liberties will include freedom of thought, conscience, association, freedom of the person, and what he calls 'the rights and liberties covered by the rule of law' (ibid). While Rawls acknowledges that these basic liberties might conflict with one another, and hence one be limited for the sake of another, they have a special status which requires that they should *never* be compromised for the sake of utilitarian calculations about utility or efficiency. They must be secured *equally*, for all citizens, all the time. Using the distinction we employed earlier from Kant, Rawls argues that 'these liberties are beyond all price' and their inalienability is a core constituent of the basic structure of society (p 366).

The second principle is explained this way: 'Social and economic inequalities are to satisfy two conditions. First, they must be attached to offices and positions open to all under conditions of fair equality of opportunity; and second, they must be to the greatest benefit of the least advantaged members of society' (1993, p 291). It may seem surprising that in putting forward a theory of *justice*, there appears to be a central role for justifying *inequality*. But with respect to the first condition of the second principle, we can see that there are undoubtedly justifiable differences of authority and responsibility attached to different jobs or official roles that we can understand as reasonable: unequal powers, for example, associated with judicial or ministerial roles, or those required for doctors or social workers to carry out their work. The key point about this condition, however, is that, as a matter of fairness, no one is excluded from the equal opportunity to attain those offices or positions. They may not in fact attain them, but so long as the opportunity is not denied them (on the basis, for example, of legalised racial or gender-based criteria) then the process is fair. There can be inequalities, in other words, but they need not amount to injustices.

The second condition of the second principle of justice marks a decisive contrast with libertarianism. Rawls refers to it as the 'difference principle'. Unlike Nozick, Rawls acknowledges that even if we assume an original distribution of equal shares, *and* just procedures for transfer, the theory of justice should not stop there. The key reason for this, which we might think of by reference to the Wilt Chamberlain example, is that 'the upshot of many separate transactions will eventually undermine background justice' (1993, p 284). Therefore, we must incorporate, 'an ideal form for the basic structure in the light of which the *accumulated results of ongoing social processes are to be limited and adjusted'* (1993, p 281, emphasis added). This will include, for example, redistributive taxation on earnings and property holdings, and a range of other forms of state intervention. But for Rawls, because any such conditions can be clearly set out in advance and therefore be made predictable and foreseeable, they do not amount to the 'capricious interference with private transactions' (p 283) in the way Nozick described.

But again we might ask how, as a matter of justice as fairness, Rawls selects a second condition which justifies 'social and economic inequality'. The answer lies with the veil of ignorance in the original position. In imagining the society to come, we do not know if we will be rich or poor, talented or capable, or not. In these circumstances of ignorance, a rational stance would be to be reasonably risk-averse: imagine you were in the position of the worst-off in the community – what conditions would you reasonably assent to as those governing the community as a whole? In thinking this through we can deploy the 'maximin rule' that 'we are to adopt the alternatives the worst outcome of which is superior to the worst outcomes of the others' (Rawls, 1971, p 133). So, if you were to be in the worst-off position would you really prefer no distribution of wealth other than that offered from the charity of the wealthy, should they choose to be charitable? Would you be content to see agglomerations of wealth occur, albeit legally, to the point where a handful of rich citizens could monopolise access to political debate or employment opportunities? Would you choose the principle that it be the amount of private property you have – or do not have – that should determine the chances of you or your family gaining access to education or health care? From considerations such as these (and many others), from behind the veil of ignorance Rawls argues that the second condition of the second principle is one that all people *would* reasonably endorse. In this way, therefore, the 'difference principle' will be justified and will operate in this way: 'however great inequalities are, and however willing people are to work so as to earn their greater return, existing inequalities are to be adjusted to contribute in the most effective way to the benefit of the least advantaged' (Rawls 1993, p 7).

Given the legitimacy of these principles of justice as fairness, how do they relate to each other? According to Rawls, when it comes to *ranking* the principles among themselves there is a clear priority: the first principle – of equal liberties – takes primacy and should not be traded in for other supposedly equalising benefits, including, for example, increased material equality. Liberty may be restricted but only, as we have seen, 'for the sake of liberty'. This priority of the first principle lies at the heart of Rawls's theory as one of political *liberalism*. Subsequently, the first condition of the second principle – fair equality of opportunities – must also be satisfied first *before* any redistributive mechanisms can be invoked. That is, a fair society must guarantee equality of opportunity and should not gainsay this for the purposes of addressing other types of inequality. Any programme of wealth redistribution can, in other words, only be instituted to the extent that it is still consistent with the principles of equal liberties and opportunities. If it is not, it should be rejected.

Rawls's theory is therefore one that attempts to promote both liberty *and* equality. A liberal society would enact the principles of justice in establishing the basic structure of society, and it would identify and uphold those 'social values – liberty and opportunity, income and wealth, and the social bases of self-respect', that for Rawls constitute the 'social primary goods': the necessary social conditions required by individuals to pursue their own lives and goals (1993, p 307). Rejecting the versions of utilitarianism and libertarianism considered in the previous section, Rawls therefore defends a version of political liberalism that sees coercive state power as legitimate in upholding liberty, but also and only where it addresses equality in the form of justice as fairness.

Socialism

One of the most influential political theories from the nineteenth century onwards was socialism. From its inception and development in various versions, socialism was initially rooted less in abstract theorising than in observing the effects of exploitation, inequality and injustice experienced by so many people in a capitalist society. Responding to this experience, socialist thinkers and activists sought to understand and challenge the problematic features of the order which engendered such suffering, and they endeavoured to replace it with institutions that would no longer tolerate exploitation and injustice. The collective action that socialism pursued produced successes with respect, for example, to workers' rights, access to health care based on need, equality of educational opportunities and the like, reforms which were often historically opposed by liberals as well as conservatives.

We noted earlier how the doctrine of the rule of law and the liberties it can secure are nonetheless compatible with great social inequalities and injustices (see 1.3.) This observation may be recast as a problem of formal justice versus substantive (or material) injustice. Formal justice – the requirement of equal treatment before the law based on the principle that like cases be treated alike, and different cases differently – can, and often does, co-exist with widespread material injustice. Such injustice is also compatible with extensive liberties, at least where liberties are defined in a 'liberal' way such as in Rawls's first principle. Moreover, in upholding formal justice law not only allows material injustice to continue; it *legitimates* this continuance by reference to the claims of formal justice. This is part of law's ideological function and is taken up in more detail in Part III. But law also plays a more direct *coercive* function in maintaining material injustice. We do not need to draw on socialist writings for this, but find it already clear in the writing of Adam Smith, a founding thinker of modern capitalism. He observed that:

> When . . . some have great wealth and others nothing, it is necessary that the arm of authority should be continually stretched forth, and permanent laws or regulations made which may [secure] the property of the rich from the inroads of the poor, who would otherwise continually make incroachments upon it . . . Laws and government may be considered in this and indeed in every case as a combination of the rich to oppress the poor, and preserve to themselves the inequality of the goods which would otherwise soon be destroyed by the attacks of the poor, who if not hindered by the government would soon reduce the others to an equality with themselves by open violence.
>
> (Smith 1978, p 208)

That the poor need to be 'hindered by the government' from achieving equality acknowledges the direct relation between law, governmental coercion and material inequality. But socialists responded to this by seeking to address not only govern-mental power, but rather, and primarily, the material conditions and relations that produce wealth and inequality. And it is here that socialists differed most markedly from the liberal approach to justice. Liberals have traditionally been concerned with securing and maintaining liberties against the powers of *government* to intrude on people's lives. They are usually more concerned, that is, with political power and the dangers associated with the abuse of that power: hence the importance to them of political constitutionalism. They have traditionally been less concerned with other forms of power, and in particular economic power, arguing that freedom from government interference also requires leaving to the market or private realm economic activity. Socialists, by contrast, put the economy at the heart of their analyses of power and hence of any response to the inequalities in society.

Cohen thus sums up three essential elements of socialism as follows: 'instead of the class exploitation of capitalism, economic equality; instead of the illusory democracy of class-based bourgeois politics, a real and complete democracy; instead of the alienation from one another of economic agents driven by greed and fear, an economy characterized by willing mutual service' (Cohen 1995, p 253). Let us take each of these aspects – equality, democracy and community – in turn and compare them with the other models of justice we have considered.

Socialism has been criticised, along the lines of Nozick's argument, for taking away private property and individual freedom in the name of the community. The socialist response is two-fold: first, that under capitalism property and labour is *already* taken away from those who produce value. As Marx and Engels put it: 'Does wage-labour create any property for the labourer? Not a bit of it. It creates capital' (Marx and Engels 1977, p 232). Capitalism does *not* in fact protect what people labour to create; it protects the right of capitalists to make profit from the value of *other people*'s work. Secondly, to prioritise the rights and liberties of the individual to private property is to misunderstand the nature of production in society and indeed the nature of society itself. Socialists point out that the production of value through labour is *not* an individualistic process; it is an inescapably *social* one. To valorise individual rights, property and commodities as if they existed independently of social activity is to put, so to speak, the cart before the horse. To protect such rights is to protect something that has been created by social cooperation but which has been artificially separated off from it. Capital, said Marx, 'is not a thing, but a social relation between persons which is mediated through things' (Marx, p 932). The aim of the socialist then is not to get rid of property as such. It is to return to the collec-tive what is properly theirs through co-operative activity. It is to get rid of a form of property – private property under capitalist conditions – that in fact *deprives* the vast majority of people of that which they create. Hence it does not reduce individual liberty either but enhances it, granting people free access to the common wealth that would otherwise be fenced off from them.

Contrary to the liberal understanding then, under capitalism legally protected rights promote inequality and unfreedom. Moreover, the 'free market', far from being 'free', in fact requires constant government *intervention*. We can understand this in two senses. First, besides keeping the poor in line, as Smith noted, it also requires constant administrative supervision to maintain its supposed 'freedoms'. One need only think of the massive institutional effort required to maintain a 'free market' in the European Union to see the extent of intervention required. The bureaucracies, laws and policies, and enforcement mechanisms required to guarantee economic freedoms suggest that in practice the 'nightwatchman' state is likely to be nothing more than a fantasy. But it also requires intervention in a second sense. Historically, capitalism is subject to periodic but regular crises. When this happens, when the market 'collapses' as it did in the financial crisis that began in 2008 for example, the 'free market' requires an astonishingly high level of public intervention in the form of money in order to revitalise the possibility of making profit. In the recent crisis this required a massive redistribution of wealth: not from rich to needy, but from the vast majority of the people to the institutions necessary to sustain capitalist wealth. Intervention was required then to secure profit while those least responsible for the crisis had to pay: with their homes, pensions, jobs or public services. From a socialist perspective there can be few clearer examples of the way in which capitalism requires intervention in order to maintain relations of inequality.

At another level this may be understood as a problem of inequality of participation, and this takes us to the second aspect: democracy. In the political realm we expect political power to be legitimate only when those who are affected by it have an equal say in electing those who will exercise it. In a democracy we expect, in other words, to be both the subject and the author of political authority. As Rawls described it (above), political power is 'fully proper only when it is exercised in accordance with a constitution the essentials of which all citizens as free and equal may reasonably be expected to endorse in the light of principles and ideals acceptable to their common human reason'. And yet such a liberal principle of legitimacy in government does not apply in the economic realm. Here again, socialists diverge clearly from liberals. To address all the forms of power that sustain injustice in capitalist society requires attention not just to political power. It requires facing up to the way in which economic power works, and responding to it. Hence, just as liberals (and others) sought to make political power accountable through democratic means, it seeks to remedy economic power by making *it* democratically accountable.

This leads us to think about how socialism seeks to rectify the problems it describes. Now socialist thought comes in many different forms, but we might usefully distinguish here between *affirmative* and *transformative* redistributive remedies to socio-economic injustices. Affirmative remedies are 'aimed at correcting inequitable outcomes of social arrangements without disturbing the underlying framework that generates them' (Fraser 1995, p 82). These may include certain aspects promoted by Rawls's difference principle, but will usually go further than this due to a clearer understanding of the social nature of the production of value. Hence they may be less concerned with the primacy of liberty and more concerned with securing equality across a full range of social needs and so aim to ameliorate the worst excesses of a market society by ring-fencing the fulfilment of certain needs from the predations of private wealth and the profit motive. But in essence affirmative approaches deal with *effects* of the problem, rather than striking at the causes.

Transformative redistributive remedies by contrast strike directly at the *causes* of socio-economic injustice. They aim to restructure socio-economic arrangements in a more fundamental way. They commonly include a combination of the following policies: 'universalist social-welfare programmes, steeply progressive taxation, macroeconomic policies aimed at creating full employment, a large non-market public sector, significant public and/or collective ownership, and democratic decision-making about basic socioeconomic priorities' (Fraser, p 85). These latter two policies in particular correspond directly to the need to make economic relations and practices democratically accountable. But more than this, transformative remedies demand that attention be paid to other structural causes of injustice that do not so readily appear, if indeed they appear at all, in the individualism of the liberal approach to justice. We highlight two here that are of key importance for the transformation of society: *gender* and *race*.

The centrality of these two factors to socio-economic injustice lies in the fact that each of them is a 'basic structuring principle of the political economy'. First, with respect to gender, Fraser notes how 'it structures the fundamental division between *paid* "productive" labour and *unpaid* "reproductive" or domestic labour, assigning women primary responsibility for the latter' (Fraser, p 78, emphasis added). Hence the 'naturalisation' of domestic labour as a lesser form of labour both justifies it being unpaid while simultaneously providing a 'free' (and exploitative) basis for the practices of paid labour. On the other hand, *within* paid labour, gender structures the division 'between higher-paid, male dominated, manufacturing and professional occupations and lower-paid, female dominated "pink-collar" and domestic service occupations' (ibid). It also structures discrimination within paid employment with respect to pay and conditions. Because these gendered injustices tend to continue even where legislation has been enacted to prohibit direct and indirect discrimination, it suggests that such affirmative remedies have clear limits in terms of their inability to abolish the gendered division of labour between unpaid and paid labour and within paid labour itself.

Secondly, race plays a structuring role in capitalist societies. The roots of this ongoing problem lie in the history of colonialism and slavery, racial segregation and discrimination. It is important to note in this regard that these practices, abhorrent as they are to many liberals, were not independent from the rise of political liberalism in the powerful Western nations, nor were they 'lawless' but commonly proceeded under the auspices of the law. As Mike Davis has written of the policies of British imperialism in the context of famines in nineteenth-century India and elsewhere, 'Millions died not outside the "modern world system", but in the very process of being forcibly incorporated into its economic and political structures. They died in the golden age of Liberal Capitalism' (Davis 2001, p 9). This historical trajectory plays a significant role in the persistence of racialised socio-economic injustices. Thus there continue to be extensive racialised divisions and hierarchies *within* paid employment, and race also has an influential role with respect to access to, or exclusion from, official labour markets themselves. Hence, as well as class-based divisions there continue to be ' "race-specific" modes of exploitation, marginalization, and deprivation' (Fraser, p 80). Once again the effectiveness of ameliorative remedial programmes may be questioned where racialised injustices continue to pervade even the best-intentioned affirmative policies and laws. A transformative socialist response therefore requires, says Fraser, 'abolishing the racial division of labour' (ibid).

With respect to the structural causes of injustice there is one further level that socialists necessarily engage with and it is one that has differentiated their approach from most mainstream theories of justice for some time. If the injustices of capitalism are to be overcome, then any remedies must track the nature of how these injustices are produced. Where capitalism is, and has been for some time, a mode of exploitation that spreads across the globe, then it would be wrong and artificial to stop the analysis of justice and remedial action at the territorial borders of any one state. Under conditions of globalisation, 'People in relatively affluent countries act within a transnational system of interdependence and dense economic interaction, which has systemic consequences for the relative privilege and disadvantage that people experience in different parts of the world or within particular locales' (Young 2004, p 372). This transnational system includes forms of power – transnational corporations, trading organisations and treaties, and so on – all of which are not readily captured in a liberal model of individual entitlement or fairness. But more importantly these constellations of wealth and power, and the interdependencies of the global economy that constitute contemporary economic practices, mean that questions of justice and remedial transformation can no longer plausibly be addressed solely at the level of any one individual state's policies and their political processes. In fact, to act as if they could is to perpetuate a further, if often less visible, injustice, one that Fraser identifies as *misframing*. As she puts it: 'By partitioning political space along territorial lines, [the state-territorial principle] insulates extra- and non-territorial powers from the reach of justice. In a globalising world, it is less likely to serve as a remedy for misframing than as a means of inflicting or perpetrating it' (Fraser 2005, p 81). This larger frame has therefore to be accessed in a way that addresses and overcomes the nature of practices of global injustice today. In terms of remedies the socialist arguments for economic democracy within a framework and tradition of internationalism may be offered as a resource for transformative remedial action.

We come to our third and final aspect, community. As we noted at the start of this section, the essence of the socialist position lies in observing the fundamentally destructive nature of subjecting human lives to the principle of profit that drives capitalism. To deploy Kant's distinction, human relations, we might say, can be valued according to either a price or a dignity. For socialists a community that adequately respects human dignity cannot be built on the foundations of price. People cannot live free and equal lives when the basis of their social lives are grounded in the 'fear and greed', the inequality and unfreedom, that capitalism compels. Even something like Rawls's difference principle comes, so to speak, too late: it accepts capitalism and inequality and then asks how it might be ameliorated. For socialists, however, just as there is no common good – no 'good community' to speak of – between master and slave, or lord and peasant, neither can there be a proper community of dignity among equals built on capitalist social relations. As Alasdair MacIntyre noted, in such conditions 'It becomes impossible for workers to understand their work as a contribution to the common good of a society which at the economic level no longer has a common good, because of the different and conflicting interests of different classes' (MacIntyre 2006, pp 147–8). Moreover, given the underlying exploitative relationship – the *conditio sine qua non* of capitalism – even increased material prosperity is 'irrelevant as a rebuttal' (ibid, p 149). In fact, says MacIntyre, the incentives capitalism requires and deploys (in particular *pleonexia*, the vice of seeking more and more), corrupt the materially *wealthy* as much as anyone. For socialism, therefore, there is an elementary contradiction in seeking to build equality on inequality, or expecting that from relations of exploitation a community of genuine human solidarity could be realised. As one early, pre-capitalist, account famously put it: it is easier for a camel to go through the eye of a needle than for a rich man to enter the kingdom of heaven (Matthew 19: 24).

Reading

Nozick (1974) and Rawls (1971) and (1993) should be the first place to start with their ideas. They have both spawned a huge amount of commentary. Two of the best collections are, respectively, Paul (1982) and Daniels (1975). Wolff (1991) also provides an extensive engagement with Nozick, as does Cohen (1995). Cohen (2000) is a lively engagement with Rawls's theory of justice from a socialist perspective, while the title of Cohen (2009) raises the question the book answers.

Fine (1984) offers a critical analysis of the rule of law from a Marxist perspective, and Sypnowich (1990) provides an extensive treatment of socialist law. You should also consult the relevant topics in Part III of this book for an analysis of Marx's work.

References

Cohen, GA, 1995, *Self-ownership, Freedom, and Equality*, Cambridge: Cambridge University Press.

Cohen, GA, 2000, *If You're an Egalitarian How Come You're So Rich?*, Cambridge, MA: Harvard University Press.

Cohen, GA, 2009, *Why Not Socialism?* Princeton: Princeton University Press.

Daniels, N, ed., 1975, *Reading Rawls*, New York: Basic Books.

Davis, M, 2001, *Late Victorian Holocausts*, London: Verso.

Fine, B, 1984, *Democracy and the Rule of Law: Liberal Ideals and Marxist Critiques*, London: Pluto.

Fraser, N, 1995, 'From Redistribution to Recognition? Dilemmas of Justice in a "Post-Socialist" Age', *New Left Review* 68.

Fraser, N, 2005, 'Reframing Justice in a Globalizing World', *New Left Review* 69.

Kant, I, 1993/1785, *Groundwork for the Metaphysics of Morals* (trans JW Ellington), 3rd edn, Indiana: Hackett.

MacCormick, N, 1982, *Legal Right and Social Democracy*, Oxford: Oxford University Press.

MacIntyre, A, 2006, 'Three Perspectives on Marxism: 1953, 1968, 1995', in A MacIntyre, *Ethics and Politics: Selected Essays*, vol 2, Cambridge: Cambridge University Press.

Marx, K, 1976, *Capital*, vol 1, Harmondsworth: Penguin.

Marx, K, and Engels, F, 1977, 'The Communist Manifesto', in *Karl Marx: Selected Writings* (ed D McLellan), Oxford: Oxford University Press.

Nozick, R, 1974, *Anarchy, State and Utopia*, Oxford: Blackwell.

Paul, J, 1982, *Reading Nozick*, Oxford: Blackwell.

Rawls, J, 1971, *A Theory of Justice*, Oxford: Oxford University Press (revised edition 1999).

Rawls, J, 1993, *Political Liberalism*, New York: Columbia University Press.

Smith, A, 1978, *Lectures on Jurisprudence*, Oxford: Clarendon.

Sypnowich, C, 1990, *The Concept of Socialist Law*, Oxford: Clarendon.

Waldron, J, 2005, 'Torture and Positive Law: Jurisprudence for the White House', 105 *Columbia Law Review* 1681–750.

Wolff, J, 1991, *Robert Nozick: Property, Justice and the Minimal State*, Cambridge: Polity.

Young, IM, 2004, 'Responsibility and Global Labor Justice', 12(4) *Journal of Political Philosophy* 365–88.

2.2 Constitutionalism and citizenship

The paradox of constitutionalism

The 'paradox' of constitutionalism can be approached in terms of the tension between 'democratic will' and 'constitutional reason', that is, between *voluntas and ratio*. Or, more abstractly, it can be seen in terms of the tension between constituent power and constituted power, or in its original formulation going back to the French Revolution, as between *pouvoir constituant* and *pouvoir constitué*. Either way, what creates the paradoxical situation is this: that the two terms of the opposition, the two antagonistic imperatives, must articulate because they are both significant dimensions of 'constitutionalism'. And yet that articulation of the two terms can lead neither to a reconciliation of their opposition nor to an overcoming of the tension between them.

Let us see, more gradually, why.

Constitutional theorists have variously described the difficulties of reconciling reason and will. American constitutional lawyers in particular, return and return again to the 'counter-majoritarian paradox', the 'federalist' dilemma, the 'Thayerite objection', the clash between self-rule and law-rule, and what – in numerous other formulations – boils down to roughly this: how can we justify our commitment to democracy and thus to the right of a sovereign citizenry to determine the terms of public life and at the same time curtail that right in the name of constitutional rights? Every answer to this appears to stumble on paradox.

In their important recent book, *The Paradox of Constitutionalism* (2007), Martin Loughlin and Neil Walker quote Maistre's famous dictum: 'the people are a sovereign who cannot exercise sovereignty' and explain the puzzle in this way: 'the power [the people] possess can only be exercised through constitutional forms already established' (2007, p 1). And 'who then is "the people" at the centre of the paradox?' they ask (2007, p 2). And how are we to make sense of the 'authorizing moment' that brings them to presence? (2007, p 3) Constituent power is always already implicated with constitutional form, the instituting already coupled with the instituted. Political power *must* present itself as conditioned, and with it the highest power of a political community is, so to speak, sovereign only under conditions that it is *not*. Because to be validly exercised, constituent power must be imputed to the constitution that establishes the conditions under which the popular will can be expressed *as* sovereign. Law and democracy are reconciled only via the suppression of a paradox that impacts on constitution-making as never, inevitably, fully democratic.

The paradox is real, fascinating and persistent. While suspending for a moment the question of foundation and of the identity of the 'sovereign people, we look at constitutional solutions to the problem of the clash between will and reason, politics and law. These have broadly taken two forms; we can call them 'dualist' or 'monist'. Monist 'solutions' involve either subordinating reason to will or subordinating will to reason. Both are worth exploring. If these might be called 'monist' solutions, the dualist is less a 'solution' and more an invitation to live with the paradox.

In the *dualist* line of thinking, fundamental rights theorists argue that our political culture incorporates both rights and democracy as of fundamental value. Western democracy has accordingly developed a commitment to upholding fundamental rights as an inherent and constitutive feature and it is its dual commitment to both ideals that characterises our political systems. But to argue with the dualist that constitutionalism accommodates both will and reason is problematical because it passes off description for explanation. It elides the problem that the two ideals are mutually denying, and therefore it becomes impossible to have a coherent system of constitutional law that might give solutions to the many difficult cases when these clash. It is not an exaggeration to say that such cases have dominated constitutional jurisprudence across Western constitutional jurisdictions.

'Monist' solutions to the paradox, as mentioned, attempt to dissolve the tension through an act of subordination of reason to will, or of will to reason. Some of the attempts are quite remarkable here. Let us begin with Kant from whom comes the idea of the subordination of will to reason.

> For in order for the people to be able to judge the supreme political authority with the force of law, they must already be viewed as united under a general legislative Will; hence they can and may not judge otherwise than the present chief of State wills.
>
> (Kant 1965/1797, p 318)

Kant tells us this in an argument about why 'there is no right to sedition, much less a right to revolution'. The argument against revolution is a conceptual one. It pivots on representation. The general will is represented by the government; to oppose the decisions of the government is thus to oppose the general will. And to oppose the general will, says Christine Korsgaard in an intriguing paper on Kant (1997), is to dissolve the *juridical condition* among human beings and thus to return to the state of nature. It is this dissolution of *the juridical condition as constitutive of the general will* that concerns us crucially here as we explore the logic of this monist subordination of the will to legal reason. For Kant there can be no general will outwith the procedural rules for ascertaining it as contained in the Constitution. Any representation of the will is contained and exhausted in such procedure, the procedure itself the very vehicle for the expression of the will, not some fallible device for ascertaining it. The people cannot speak *as* a people until they have a voice. In this argument then there can be no democratic (or general) will if there is no prior constitutional means to give it expression. Reason comes first in every sense.

The other '*monist*' line of argument subordinates constitutional reason to the will. John Ely is usually hailed as the first major exponent of this orientation. Judicial review exists, according to Ely, to 'unblock stoppages in the democratic process' (Ely 1981, p 117) and maintain open the channels of political change, by, for example, facilitating the representation of minority interests. By securing political freedoms, judicial review secures what is integral to the function of 'an open and effective democratic process' (p 104). Ely's path-breaking work could, thus, more broadly be seen as suggesting that democracy provides a kind of master-narrative that gives content and meaning to provisions about rights and lends the perspective through which rights may be interpreted. As Neil MacCormick puts it:

> The advantage of insisting on rights as constitutionally derivative is, as we now see, that this leaves them in the end subject to democratic processes . . . It is to the people as a whole that belongs the decision about the exact specification of those rights, and about the other essential elements of constitutional structure and

distribution of constitutional authority. In this way democracy acquires a self-referential character.

(MacCormick 1993, p 143)

Representation and foundation

It might be useful to visit the 'paradox' of constitutionalism by picking up a different thread, that connects it back to the founding act of 'a people'. Let us thus approach it, with Hannah Arendt, through the notion of 'the act of foundation'. Arendt says:

> To the extent that the greatest event in every revolution is the act of foundation, the spirit of revolution contains two elements which to us seem irreconcilable and even contradictory. The act of founding the new body politic, of devising the new act of government involves the grave concern with the stability and durability of the new structure; the experience on the other hand, which those who are engaged in this grave business are bound to have, is the exhilarating awareness of the human capacity of beginning, the high spirits which have always attended the birth of something new.

(Arendt 1963, p 223)

Exhilarating indeed. So much so that even Kant finds the French Revolution 'thrilling'. '[T]his revolution finds in the hearts of all spectators . . . a wishful participation which borders on enthusiasm, the very expression of which is fraught with danger' he says (Korsgaard 1927, p 299).

How will the constitutional moment, Arendt's concern with 'the structure of stability and durability' reconcile itself to the 'general will', that of Rousseau or Robespierre, which needs only to will in order to produce law? The general will becomes the revolutionary will which is expressed as revolutionary law and thus the revolutionary process becomes a law unto itself, impossible to contain. This, as Kant would have it (see above), is a general will that *cannot* be, since 'the people' are not constituted as such and thus cannot will at all, at least on his reading of social contract theory. Compare Jefferson's passionate preoccupation that the Constitution might stifle what Arendt later called the 'lost treasure of the revolutionary tradition'. Arendt talks of his 'outrage about the injustice that only his generation should have it in their power "to begin the world over again"'. The 'unchangeability' and 'unalienabilty' of the rights of man for Jefferson included – paradoxically and explosively – the right to rebellion and revolution. The act of foundation – the framing of a constitution – cannot be at the expense of freedom in 'its most exalted sense' as freedom to act. 'God forbid', says Jefferson, 'that we should ever be twenty years without such a rebellion' (Arendt 1963, p 233).

The French experience did, of course, force him to reconsider. In his later writings, Jefferson is more concerned to provide in the Constitution itself 'for its revision at stated periods', and the concern behind it is to allow each generation to determine for itself the terms 'most promotive of its own happiness'. The tension here comes to a head: the frustration with which Jefferson struggled involves grappling with the impossibility of arresting the revolutionary moment without betraying it, of containing the act of freedom within a lasting institution, *of expressing the active will through constitutional reason.*

Thus understood, the time of 'foundation' does not of course confine itself to the time of revolution but spreads over continuous time. There survives in non-revolutionary times a tension between constitutional reason and democratic will, a will that must – in normal rather than revolutionary times – be expressed *within* the confines of that reason. This enduring and very 'ordinary' paradox finds its most urgent expression in the suspect legitimacy of constitutional review or, as Alexander Bickel put it, in the fact that judicial review remains a 'deviant institution' in demo-cratic thinking (Bickel 1962, p 18). Because how can it be consistent with the demo-cratic imperative that any Constitutional Court should be able to invalidate in the name of constitutional rights the decision-making capacity of *We the People*, as expressed through democratic legislation? Even if we accept that sovereign power straddles both *pouvoir constituant* and *pouvoir constitué* we still need to work out how *both* are kept at play *at once*, constituting (as democratic will) what presupposes itself as already constituted (constitutional reason).

But the stakes are even higher: this paradoxical articulation of will and reason underlies the concept of popular sovereignty and thus the identity of 'the people'. In other words: if the articulation of reason and will is what underlies sovereignty, the identity of the people as sovereign subject is the emergent property of that relation-ship. The difficulty is of course that as emergent property of a paradoxical articula-tion, the identity itself is thrown into turmoil. What comes to the forefront now in need of explanation is the inter-dependence, in fact inter-constitution, of this triad: will, reason and what is represented: the identity of a sovereign people. With this we return to the triangular relationship that we began with and with the stakes raised: the question is now that of the identity of a people that *must, yet apparently cannot*, be represented. That this replicates the initial paradox (and not a different one) in a further dimension is because of the internal connection between democracy and collective identity: a sovereign people can establish their identity by negotiating and deciding their constitutive commitments; democratic will substantiates the polity, it expresses who we are. Constitutionalism is the name for an intersection of law and politics. Viewed from the point of view of popular sovereignty and thus also from the point of view of the identity of the people assumed sovereign, constitutionalism balances identity on a difficult juncture. Because if we conceive of the demos as a dynamic ever-changing entity – and how could it be otherwise? – what conclusions are we to draw about the containment of its forever renewed will in constitutional reason that is overwhelmed by the need to institutionalise and thus to still, to induce permanence, to reduce contingency and mutation? The identity of the people must meet the exigencies of containment in the ideals of fixity, predetermination, stasis or not be represented at all. What is truly unsettling is that the paradox now pushes against the limits of representation.

Constitutional 'moments'

If there is one theorist who is closest to Jefferson in his concern with the injustice that 'only one generation should have it in their power to begin the world over again', that is Bruce Ackerman. His theory of 'constitutional moments' is a theory that spreads the act of 'foundation' over the entire scope of US constitutional past and future. (Indicatively, Ackerman, 1984 and 1991) Like Arendt's 'act of foundation', a 'constitutional moment' feeds off an ambiguity: these are moments of constitutional reason yet moments where democratic will re-embeds itself in constitutional reason, retrieving from within the constitution the recourses to express itself as *pouvoir constituant*, as foundational act. Constitutional moments are moments when the *will* breaks through, yet where *reason* serves as vehicle and guarantor. Intriguingly these are moments of reasserting an identity; they are moments that allow the citizens to experience and fulfil their identity as '*We the People*', which is the title that Ackerman gives to his three-volume US constitutional history.

The notion of 'constitutional moment' was introduced by Bruce Ackerman in his 1984 Storrs lectures (Ackerman 1984) and elaborated in much of his subsequent work. Against a liberal 'levelling' understanding of democracy Ackerman pits his own republican understanding of an elevated constitutionalism. The liberal 'leveller' fails to distinguish two quite distinct levels of political conduct, says Ackerman. The leveller's 'impoverished constitutional vocabulary' does not give form to those 'constitutional moments' in a people's history when 'the people sacrifice their private interests to pursue the common good in transient and informal political association' (1984, p 1020). It is during such moments that the true voice of 'the people' is heard. It is in such moments that citizens act in their capacity as sovereign populace. What is a constitutional moment? According to Ackerman's definition, it is an occasion upon which 'the people' exercise deliberative, 'considered judgements' regarding 'the rights of citizens and the permanent interests of the community' (Ackerman 1991, pp 240, 272–4). The appeal to the common good 'ratified by a mobilized mass of . . . citizens expressing their assent through extraordinary institutional forms' (1984, p 1042) defines Ackerman's republican vision. He is prepared to concede that these moments of exceptional politics occur rarely and 'should become pre-eminent only under well-defined historical situations'. During these moments of profound rupture, citizens re-claim their delegated sovereignty through direct popular action. Because the constitutional provisions do not license these moments of creativity, the amendment that the constitutional moment carries is not, legally speaking, demo-cratically licensed. Yet they are democratic in a more fundamental sense as exercises of political sovereignty. These moments are moments of 'constitutional creativity' (1991, pp 314ff) and 'democracy reborn' (1991, pp 295–6), in the sense that the popu-lace as sovereign periodically instigates transformations of such depth that they can be credibly claimed to have resituated the meaning of freedom, democracy and self-determination. Ackerman puts it in terms of the idea of a constitutional conversation, to which we will return:

> While established Constitutional Law did not always resolve America's deepest crises, *it has always provided us with the language and the process within which our political identities could be confronted, debated and defined* – both during the periods of normal politics and on those occasions when Americans found themselves called, once again, to undertake a serious effort to redefine and reaffirm their sense of national purpose.
>
> (1984, p 1072)

There are certain problems that beset the theory, most importantly the identification of instances that do fulfil the conditions that Ackerman stipulates for his ideal type of a 'constitutional moment'. Doubts, for example, can be expressed even for the moments that Ackerman has in mind as paradigmatic. The first moment, the moment of foundation of the independent Republic in Philadelphia, is an act of insurrection that qualifies as a *constitutional* moment only *ex post facto*; it is not the sovereign undertaking of a sovereign people at the time; in fact it is, at the time, a seditious act of subjects of the British Crown. Speaking of Ackerman's other 'moments' such as the New Deal and the civil rights movement in America, historically it was overwhelmingly the case that they were initiated and pursued by active minorities of the population who have come up against and managed to curb the 'normal-political' attitude of large indifferent majorities. The case of the extension of equal rights to all Americans, identified by Ackerman as the moment of confluence of popular mobilisation (civil rights movement) and judicial decision-making (*Brown v Board of Education*) was not really a moment at all, since confluence implies simultaneity, and *Brown* significantly predated the eruption of the civil rights movement. In any case, even if there is disagreement over the conditions and the facts, the idea of a constitutional moment breaks the 'paradox' of the antagonism between will and reason: they are moments of popular mobilisation and expression of the will, of a people who use the resources of the constitution to reach new constitutional understandings. The two key notions are found here not in an antagonistic relationship but in one of mutual enablement.

Because of this, Ackerman's theory and insights have generated a spectacular constitutional optimism and have travelled across time and jurisdictions to furnish 'discoveries' of 'constitutional moments'. As such one finds described the creation of the EU, the various extensions of its powers, referendums, the establishment of universal jurisdiction for certain crimes, even international organisations' declaration of principles (e.g. the International Labour Organization (ILO)'s declaration of its four 'core' principles in 1998).

Citizenship: liberal and republican

A republican account of citizenship, whether couched in the language of 'constitutional moments' or not, whether it looks at foundational or exceptional moments primarily, or whether it spreads across normal periods too, opposes the liberal conception that we identified at the outset as 'dualist'. For the liberal conception of citizenship rights and democracy remain antagonistic, and rights delineate the sphere proper for democratic decision-making as that which does not infringe rights. Rights, here, serve as 'trumps' against democratic and policy decisions.

Where in liberal constitutionalism the Constitution is primarily a framework of constraint for politics, in the republican variant the Constitution becomes the springboard for politics. Republicanism is a theory about how political sovereignty finds expression in law. Law, claim the republicans, substantiates popular sovereignty by lending it constitutional provisions as a vehicle or 'home' of political deliberation. Of course in an important, if limited way, liberal and republican constitutionalism are at one: both seek a home for political deliberation in the Constitution. But the republicans attribute far more decisive functions to constitutional political deliberation, and the aspiration of 'community' is central to their theory. Republicanism's aspiration is for an intimate, mutually nurturing relationship between law and politics. But that is not all. Republicanism is not simply a theory about how law and politics emerge in a new synthesis – it is also a theory about retrieving the 'self' in the process. The citizen actively participates in forming the political future and this active involvement, in turn, feeds back and situates the self-in-community.

There are strong resonances in this opposition of liberalism and republicanism in the important discussion that dominated political philosophy in the 1980s and 1990s between liberals and communitarians. It concerns the relationship, also key to our discussion, between law, politics and community. The communitarian target in this debate was the liberal 'thin' theory of the self. The most eloquent account draws its inspiration from Michael Sandel. The liberal image of the individual, says Sandel, is one of the 'unencumbered self' (Sandel 1982), whose values and convictions – as attributes of the self – become relegated to the external and the contingent, as features of one's condition rather than as constituents of one's person. In this way liberal theory misconstrues communities that generate value and commitment because it remains blind to the intricate ways in which these values and beliefs impinge upon the very constitution of the self. For liberals, already constituted selves 'enter' the community they inhabit in the same way that they would enter a voluntary association. Sandel contrasts this with his 'constitutive' conception of community whose members understand it as describing 'not only what they have as fellow citizens but also what they are, not a relationship they choose but an attachment they discover, not merely an attribute but a constituent of their identity' (1984, p 150). The recourse to communitarian theory allows republicanism to confront liberalism first and foremost on an epistemological basis. This in turn allows them to argue the fundamental importance of participation in politics as constitutive of both communities and selves.

For the advocates of a republican form of citizenship, constitutionalism is about self-determination and sovereignty, and sanctions the processes where the sovereign democratic will is formed. To counter the liberal world-view they argue that what needs to be resisted is the liberal/pluralist understanding of politics as a bargaining process where interests battle for recognition and superiority. According to the republicans, the liberal/pluralists view the public sphere as a *political market* that functions on the lines of the economic market. (This picture is typically associated with OW Holmes, who conceived the 'marketplace of ideas' as the medium of competition of ideas and the mechanism of striking a balance.) Here, individual preferences and interests seek a mechanism to best accommodate their competition. Groups are nothing more than organisational forms through which individuals pursue their individual interests more effectively. What wins the competition is conceived as approximating public interest, and the market logic underpinning the political process guarantees democracy's self-correcting capacity. What the republicans most oppose is this conception of the political actor projected from within the logic of the *homo economicus*, because this conception destroys any possibility of conceiving an objective public interest in politics that transcends individual and group interests. The republicans are very sceptical of the pluralist commitment to the sovereignty of associations and their superiority over state sovereignty, because this would erode the fundamentally *integrative* role of the democratic deliberative process and the production of authoritative public norms. Their important organising hypothesis is that membership in the political community is not as means to an end, the pursuit of partisan choice, but instead it is in the very process of participation as its own end that perspectives engage with one another and conceptions of a *good* that is *common* are shaped. And such pursuit of the common interest by and large supersedes the liberal 'absolute' defence of individual entitlements.

But if politics is the site where communities strive for self-determination, the constitution, claim the republicans, hosts the political process. In this context the republican rebuttal of pluralism is a rebuttal of a misconception that understands law as external to politics and community. The Constitution is misconstrued as a mechanism of checks and balances for – but external to – the bargaining process that is politics. Instead, republican theory claims that the Constitution provides the possibility of politics and the substantiation of community. The legal–institutional connection is the significant one: what characterises the republican thesis is the centrality of law both to politics and to the moulding of collective identity.

How do the republicans establish that the Constitution comes to underpin the community's politics? In its more sophisticated recent expressions, the answer that they give is that the constitution *contains* the deliberative practice of a community, the dialogue of all about all. There is here the double articulation that concerns us. Firstly that of law and politics, because by participating in the dialogic–deliberative practice, citizens engage in politics. During the communicative exchange principles to guide public life are hammered out. Secondly that of law and identity, because the participation in the public realm in turn feeds back in a way which 'calls forth' the individual as a political actor. The entry into the public sphere through citizenship – the legally backed capacity to partake in the political dialogue – mediates the assumption of political identity. In Frank Michelman's influential paper 'Law's Republic' (1988), for example, the argument for the *intrinsic* value of citizenship is attributed to the fact that 'the self is constituted by, or comes to know itself through, such [political] engagement'. And the republicans can now celebrate having established a connection between the embedded *self*, where the form of that embeddedness is participation in a dialogue, that at once both constitutes the realm of *politics* and substantiates *community*, and finally *law* as enabling the dialogue in the constitutional forum.

The background to the republican theory of citizenship is a tradition of political thought with roots in Aristotle's *Politics*, Cicero's *Res Publica*, Macchiavelli's *Discourses*, a tradition renewed by Hannah Arendt and Leo Strauss, all of who conceive society as a politically constituted system. This tradition envisages man as a 'political being', who could only realise his *telos* in a *vivere civile*, a republic. The debt to these theorists runs deep. Arendt's own definition of politics sounds very apposite: 'The realm of politics', she says in *On Revolution*, 'is the organisation of the people as it arises out of acting and speaking together, and its true space lies between people living together for this purpose'. The most important element here – and in the new republicanism – is that membership in the political community is not seen – as the liberals and pluralists would have it – as a means to an end, the pursuit of partisan choice, but instead it is in the very process of participation as its own end that perspectives engage with one another and conceptions of a good that is common are shaped. The theory professes to fulfil the promise of what Jürgen Habermas calls a 'constitutional patriotism' or even the more elusive one of social solidarity, which, as Michael Walzer once put it, is the patriotism of the Left. Whereas in the liberal/pluralist world-view politics is about promoting diverse goods, and thus relies on bargaining within a framework of rules neutral to the bargaining parties, the republican picture of politics is one of the pursuit of the common good. In their account, the heterogeneity of interest associated with liberalism gives way to the heterogeneity of perspective. Bargaining gives way to arguing, and this shift allows the republicans to claim 'civic virtue' for their politics, a tenet so central as to be characterised as the 'animating principle' of republicanism. In recent continental political theory, notably in the vein of the hugely influential theory of Habermas, the synthesis that unlocks the deadlock between will and reason, democracy and rights, is the republican thesis about the *co-originality* of law and democracy and of private and public autonomy (Habermas 1996).

Reading

For the conceptual and historical puzzles associated with the 'paradox of constitutionalism', see the essays in Loughlin and Walker (2007) and Dobner and Loughlin (2010). On the concept of representation see Lindahl (1998).

Ackerman's theory of 'constitutional moments' is outlined in (1984) and developed in (1991) and subsequent volumes of 'We the People'.

See Sandel's 'The Unencumbered Self' in Sandel (1984) for the classic statement of the communitarian attack on liberalism's conception of the person. See, also, Taylor (1989), 'Cross-Purposes: The Liberal-Communitarian Debate' and MacIntyre's exceptional *After Virtue* (1981).

For the theories that see democracy and constitutional rights as complementary or co-original, see Ely (1981), and Habermas (1996), especially the 'postscript', which provides a good summary.

For a republican reading of constitutionalism in the UK the classic text is Griffith (1979), and for a recent restatement Tomkins (2005), ch 1.

In the US context see especially Michelman (1986), and Michelman (1988) for one of the most interesting republican accounts of constitutional interpretation that engages questions of democracy, community and self-determination.

References

Ackerman, B, 1984, 'The Storrs Lectures: Discovering the Constitution', 93 *Yale L J* 1013.

Ackerman, B, 1991, *We The People: Foundations*, Cambridge, MA: Belknap.

Arendt, H, 1963, *On Revolution*, Harmondsworth: Penguin.

Bickel, A, 1962, *The Least Dangerous Branch: The Supreme Court as the Bar of Politics*, Cambridge, MA: Harvard University Press.

Dobner, P and M Loughlin, 2010 (eds), *The Twilight of Constitutionalism*, Oxford: Oxford University Press.

Ely, JH, 1981, *Democracy and Distrust*, Cambridge, MA: Harvard University Press.

Griffith, JAG, 1979, 'The Political Constitution', 42 *Modern Law Review* 1.

Habermas, J, 1992, 'Citizenship and National Identity: Some Reflections on the Future of Europe', 12 *Praxis International* 1–19.

Habermas, J, 1996, *Between Facts and Norms*, Cambridge, MA: MIT Press.

Habermas, J, 1999, *The Inclusion of the Other*, Cambridge: Polity.

Kant, I, 1965/1797, *The Metaphysical Principles of Justice*, New York: MacMillan.

Korsgaard, C, 1997, 'Taking the Law Into Our Own Hands: Kant on the Right to Revolution' in Reath (et al) (eds) *Reclaiming the History of Ethics: Essays for John Rawls*, Cambridge: Cambridge University Press.

Lindahl, H, 1998, 'The Purposiveness of Law: Two Concepts of Representation in the European Union', 17 *Law & Philosophy* 481–507.

MacCormick, N, 1993, 'Constitutionalism and Democracy', in R Bellamy (ed), *Theories and Concepts of Politics*, Manchester: Manchester University Press, 124–47.

MacCormick, N, 1999, *Questioning Sovereignty*, Oxford: Oxford University Press.

MacIntyre, A, 1981, *After Virtue*, London: Duckworth.

Michelman, F, 1986, 'Foreword: Traces of Self-Government', 100 *Harvard L R* 4.

Michelman, F, 1988, 'Law's Republic', 97 *Yale L J* 1493.

Rosenblum, N, 1994, 'Democratic Character and Community', 1 *The Journal of Political Philosophy* 67.

Sandel, M, 1982, *Liberalism and the Limits of Justice*, Cambridge: Cambridge University Press.

Taylor, C, 1989, 'Cross-Purposes: The Liberal-Communitarian Debate', in N Rosenblum (ed), *Liberalism and the Moral Life*, Cambridge, MA: Harvard University Press, 159–82.

Tomkins, A, 2005, *Our Republican Constitution*, Oxford: Hart.

2.3 Law, politics and globalisation

Globalisation and the reconfigured State

In the modern era, the State has been central to debates in law and politics. The main prize for political parties was to gain control of national legislative and executive institutions, with the power to make national laws and policies seen as the means of implementing their policy agenda. This framework remains influential: much political activity is still directed towards national parliaments and governments, and the study of law largely consists of learning rules of the national legal system where the student resides. However, this traditional focus on the State is coming under pressure from claims that we live in a time of globalisation. Globalisation stands for the idea that national borders are becoming less important to the conduct of social life. For example, arguments about the emergence of global patterns of economic organisation, or global forms of culture, have been advanced to show that we are living in a significantly more interconnected world, often in relation to the spread of liberal capitalism and Western-style consumerism.

We can identify three ways in which the idea that the Nation-State is the sole, or principal, location of political authority is coming under pressure in the global era. First is the relocation of power from the national level to supranational entities such as the European Union (EU) and the World Trade Organization (WTO). While the original impetus for this was often framed in relatively narrow terms, such as setting common customs duties, the deliberations of these bodies now affect a wide range of public policy matters, such as agriculture, health, trade and social policy.

Other developments that should be included here are the rise of regional and international mechanisms supervising the protection of human rights. The legal instruments issuing from these bodies often have a higher formal status than national laws, and disobedient states can face the threat of sanctions.

Political authority can also be seen to be escaping downwards as well as upwards. Claims for greater devolution of power within existing states are themselves something of a global phenomenon, whether in Canada, the UK, Spain, Germany, Italy or former Soviet States. These present a further challenge to the Nation-State by redistributing political authority to the sub-national level, often constitutionally guaranteed against encroachment from the centre. In contrast to this emphasis on new institutions above or below the State, a third challenge highlights the dispersal of power beyond the State. This argues that political authority is now exercised in multiple settings, for example, new forms of decision-making within supranational organisations, or networks of international agencies or in the actions of multinational corporations.

As a result, the State is being significantly reconfigured. Some of its former core functions are being performed elsewhere, whether by global regulatory bodies or privatised utilities. Those functions it retains are often subject to new restraints, for example, that they follow market-based ideas such as efficiency and effectiveness. Some argue that it is important to place these developments in geopolitical context, and that the worldwide trend to adopt neoliberal economic policies, that is reduced taxation, fiscal restraint, deregulation, privatisation, free trade and unrestricted currency flows, necessarily leads to a weakened State. The other processes listed above can also be seen to accentuate State weakness: supranational economic and human rights regimes can limit the scope for national policy innovation, while subnational entities have even less power to resist the prevailing global consensus.

Some capture the complexity of contemporary patterns of political authority with the idea of multilayered governance. Where once political activists may have sought to lobby MPs or government ministers, there are now a host of potential actors who may require their attention, whether members of devolved or regional assemblies, Members of the European Parliament (MEPs), non-governmental organisations (NGOs), international agencies, social movements or boards of directors. In some cases, it may be unclear as to who are the responsible actors. The result is to remove the State from any preordained position at the centre of the legal and political universe. As Martin Loughlin has put it, '[t]he success of the modern state over the last two hundred years has been based mainly on its ability to promote economic well-being, to maintain physical security and to foster a distinctive cultural identity of its citizens' (Loughlin 2000, p 145). This account is now being called into question by globalisation.

Sovereignty after globalisation

In an earlier section, we characterised sovereignty as a contested concept. If anything, debates over sovereignty have intensified in the context of globalisation. The departure point for these debates is the demise of the Nation-State, understood in terms of a homogeneous people exercising self-governance through a single set of public institutions. In this traditional model, sovereignty was seen as an expression of a State's political autonomy. This political autonomy had an internal and external dimension:

internal authority over a particular community, and external independence vis-à-vis other States. We can identify two strands of debate that call this account increasingly into question. One addresses principally the first two developments listed above, that is the rise of new sub- and supranational institutions, while the other considers the consequences of globalisation writ large, that is, the rise of the global economy. Each approach brings a quite different perspective to the questions of what sovereignty is, where it resides and how far it has to be reconceptualised as a result of globalisation.

If we take first the new institutional structures that operate across and within borders, some theorists, such as Neil MacCormick, suggest that in an era of multi-layered governance, sovereignty may have outlived its usefulness as a concept. Focusing on the development of the EU, MacCormick argues its Member States do not possess unfettered constitutional power to make laws as this can be overridden by EU law. Furthermore, as a result, these states no longer enjoy unrestrained political power in their external relations. However, this does not mean sovereignty has been transferred to the EU as it does not possess political or legal independence apart from its members. Accordingly, notions of ultimate authority fail to capture the nature of contemporary legal and political relations. Thus as we have seen, MacCormick believes the supposedly sovereign State may well be a transient historical phenom-enon, and that we are now in an age of 'post-sovereignty'. This is posited as a prefer-able framework for the study of law and politics: once we reject the idea of absolute sovereignty, this better tailors discussion about democracy to the reality of a plural legal and political order, for example by acknowledging that sometimes citizens' needs are best met at a smaller level of government, other times at a larger.

Other commentators argue that rather than seeing the appropriate response to globalisation as dispensing with the concept of sovereignty, it is better to consider how it is being transformed. They note that despite calls to abandon the language of sovereignty, it persists in political debate, for example, to resist further European integration. Neil Walker describes the present as a period of 'late sovereignty', to signify that we have not achieved a complete conceptual break with the past. For Walker, the key to overcoming the limits of the Westphalian approach is to shift from describing sovereignty as some objective measurement of power to regarding it as a 'claim concerning the existence and character of a supreme ordering power for a particular polity' (Walker 2003, p 6), whose practical importance depends on its plausibility to key actors in the political system.

The context for Walker's analysis is the growth of non-State entities, such as the EU, as rivals to states in claiming sovereignty. However, what is distinctive about this phase of sovereignty is that these claims are no longer being viewed in absolute terms. This arises because supranational bodies tend not to exercise authority over all matters within a particular territory, but only in respect of certain functions. For example, while the EU claims to be the highest legal authority over matters such as agriculture or fisheries, competences remain with Member States. Accordingly, we can no longer link claims of ultimate authority to territorial exclusivity. Walker argues that this picture of multiple and overlapping – including State and supra-State – claims to authority gives us a better explanation of the emerging global legal configuration. For him, this also has a prescriptive dimension, and provides the guiding ethic that law and politics should be based upon the mutual recognition of different authority claims.

Other theorists regard talk of 'post' or 'late' sovereignty as premature. Loughlin finds the original conceptual underpinnings of sovereignty highly relevant today (see Loughlin 2003). For him, sovereignty expresses a political relationship between rulers and ruled. This relationship combines two facets of sovereignty in the modern State: competence, which refers to its formal legal authority, and capacity, which denotes where political power actually resides. Once this is grasped, he suggests that developments such as the establishment of the EU should not be seen as eroding sovereignty. While Member States may agree to share jurisdictional competence with the EU, this does not amount to a sharing of sovereignty (which in Loughlin's view is conceptually impossible). This is because questions of sovereignty are not determined by new institutional arrangements, but are essentially matters of political capacity. He suggests that the test of continuing sovereignty is whether Member States can withdraw from the EU. Loughlin argues that in the exceptional state of crisis that this scenario envisages, there is little doubt that states retain the right to leave, and for him this shows that they still possess ultimate power and authority.

The debates so far canvassed have focused on public institutional developments, but what of the growth of private political authority beyond the State? An alternative approach is advanced by Saskia Sassen (1996 and 2007) who sees the relevant challenges to sovereignty as grounded in changes in global political economy. In this connection, she posits a 'new geography of power' whose key sites include supranational organisations, but also global capital markets, transnational legal firms, international commercial arbitration, international human rights codes and electronic economic activity. These combine to reconfigure the interface between territory and sovereignty. For example, for some, New York City is a municipality that runs local services such as rubbish collection, while for others it is a centre for international bond agencies, whose credit ratings can veto national economic policies. In this way, the new geography leads to a partial displacement of economic activity from national territory.

Loughlin acknowledges that these developments may present a stronger challenge to sovereignty as capacity because the power ceded to global markets is not readily recoverable by issuing edicts through formal legal authority (Loughlin 2004). But this raises important questions about the relationship between law and politics: if, as Loughlin suggests, sovereignty ultimately depends on political capacity, is there a point at which the exercise of power by private actors translates into legal competence? Sassen answers this in the affirmative, and highlights new legal regimes that operate outside the public institutional setting, but are located in the activities of multinational corporations. These regimes are important in explaining the rules and procedures that apply, for example, to regulating the internet or intellectual property, or aspects of international trade such as insurance and the maritime industry.

Within the supranational debate, there is a strong tendency to attribute sovereignty to expressions of public power, and remove consideration of the private or economic sphere from the discussion. But in the changing landscape of governance painted by globalisation, distinctions such as that between public and private may now appear outmoded and unhelpful. This casts some of the debates outlined above in a different light. If, as Loughlin tells us, sovereignty is an expression of a political relationship, some of the most important relationships in the global age may be those between individuals and the corporations whose decisions affect the quality of their lives in significant ways, or those that arise from the complex interaction between State, supra-State and non-State forms of normative ordering on which the residual effectiveness of State law may now depend. Or if, as Walker tells us, sovereignty is now better understood as a claim, should sovereignty be restricted to those making self-conscious claims, or should we expand it to cover those private actors who remain silent, perhaps because they do not wish to attract unwanted scrutiny to the political authority they exercise? Accordingly, adverting to broader processes of globalisation potentially represents a more radical conceptual rupture with the traditional understandings of sovereignty.

Constitutionalism beyond the State

The diffusion of political authority as a result of globalisation raises important questions about how power is held to account. Traditionally, constitutions have provided the institutional and normative framework for discussing questions of law and politics, and in particular the question of the legitimate exercise of power. In modern times, a constitutionally legitimate regime has come to be understood as one that embodies the values of democracy. As with sovereignty, our conceptual apparatus of constitutionalism initially developed with reference to the Nation-State. Thus in its ideal condition, constitutionalism was the means by which a sovereign people within national borders could exercise control over those who governed them, by subjecting politics to the rule of law. But in an age of globalisation, State-centred approaches to constitutionalism may address only part of a broader constellation of political authority. For example, while constitutions safeguard free and fair elections to national parliaments, they generally provide for negligible or no popular participation in decisions of supranational bureaucracies or multinational corporations despite the impact that the decisions of these bodies have on people's lives. Accordingly, globalisation can be seen to provoke a legitimation crisis, as national constitutions can no longer guarantee citizens effective democratic control over their rulers.

There has been considerable interest recently in ideas of constitutionalism beyond the State (Walker, 2008). Walker (2003) argues that constitutionalism – which he sees as the vocabulary for the mutual articulation of law and politics – is intrinsic to the polity understood as the setting for the conduct of politics. In the period of late sovereignty, the polity is not confined to the State, and so we should now associate constitutions with bodies such as the EU or WTO. Walker suggests that we need to understand how some of the traditional functions of national constitutions, such as delineating a formal hierarchy of laws or specifying the rights of citizenship, are now carried out at the supranational level. The extent to which any supranational entity can be characterised in constitutional terms, though, is a matter of degree. In this regard, Walker finds that the EU (where the supremacy of EU law is accepted by Member States) is further down the path of constitutionalisation than the WTO (which has no equivalent doctrine).

Supranational constitutionalism does not simply reproduce national constitutional forms on a broader scale. It is in many respects qualitatively different as these new polities, unlike states, are limited in their jurisdictional scope, and do not aspire to provide a comprehensive legal order within hermetically sealed borders.

Accordingly, the task of translating State-based constitutional concepts to the supra-national level is not straightforward, as the above discussion of the various attempts to adapt sovereignty to the global age demonstrates. However, for Walker the key to accomplishing this is to understand that State constitutional orders have not disappeared, but necessarily exist in relation to non-State sites of constitutionalism, whose purpose is often to influence or direct national legal systems. Accordingly, he suggests we now live in an era of 'constitutional pluralism' (Walker 2002).

For Walker, recovering the language of constitutionalism at the supranational level is important because the often contentious issues which animated traditional constitutionalism, such as the nature of representation and how institutional power should be structured and regulated, remain relevant and important, but have been relocated in the contemporary age. A powerful objection to this project is that it may confer an undeserved legitimacy upon supranational bodies. Given the strong positive connotations of constitutionalism with democracy, to speak, for example, of the WTO as a constitutional entity may suggest a capacity to exert democratic oversight over world trade, which may be absent. Walker's response is that the values and practices of constitutionalism (suitably adapted) are the best available means for engaging in debates over the legitimate exercise of power, and that rather than providing inappropriate closure, they keep dialogue open over how the democratic credentials of the emergent sites of supranational constitutionalism can be improved.

An alternative approach to constitutionalism beyond the State comes under the rubric of 'the new constitutionalism'. According to Stephen Gill, the new constitu-tionalism is a ' "global economic governance project" designed to "lock-in" the power gains of capital on a world scale' (Gill 2000, pp 6, 11). The context for this project is the rise of neoliberal economic policies (such as privatisation and low taxation) since the 1980s, which, Gill argues, seek to discipline national governments so that they do not interfere with the free market. New constitutionalism supports this by placing barriers in the way of more redistributive forms of constitutionalism (which might, for example, promote social democratic goals of lowering material inequality) through legal and political measures that are difficult to reverse. Supranational legal forms are also highlighted here, whether it is the WTO imposing sanctions on states that deviate from the global economic consensus, or bilateral treaties that may require domestic constitutional reform in order to be eligible for inward investment. Less formal mechanisms are also important, for example, the pressures exerted by corporations on states to lower taxation or reduce domestic regulatory standards if they wish to attract their factories and jobs (resulting in what critics describe as a 'race to the bottom').

The question at the heart of the new constitutionalism is whether economic pro-cesses should be regarded as relevant for constitutional analysis. How we answer this has an important implication for how we link constitutionalism and democracy in the global age. In traditional terms, economic actors, like individual persons, were seen as subject to the constitutional jurisdiction of the State. Thus any problems posed to democracy by the growth of private power in the global economy can be addressed by making appropriate adjustments to existing constitutional mechanisms. In this connection, it is argued that developing constitutionalism on a supranational scale may provide the better opportunity for establishing democratic oversight over the forces of the global economy.

But from another point of view, this separation between the economic and the political can no longer be sustained in an era where corporations can be richer and more powerful than many States. For example, comparing annual sales to national gross domestic product (GDP), General Motors has a higher annual turnover than Denmark, and Sony is bigger than Pakistan. If corporations should now be seen as important political actors whose actions and decisions have a direct impact on the lives of millions, this implies that political power (or the polity) not be limited to the public institutional setting of states and supranational organisations. It follows that, according to the new constitutionalism, questions about the location of sovereignty and the exercise and accountability of power now have to consider the relation not just between State and supranational, but also non-State sites of constitutionalism. Moreover, the latter may in practice be the most important, so focusing our attention on the first two sites alone may be of limited utility if our objective is to establish some degree of constitutional regulation over the market. This suggests that it may be necessary to craft innovative solutions, which do not adapt, but replace, current constitutional practices. For some, the only means for effective governance over the global economy is to establish a truly global polity – for example, with global (not international) representative institutions – while for others, the answer lies in bottom-up, not top-down, approaches such as the development of new forms of law and politics in global social movements. What seems clear is that in a time of globalisation many long-standing assumptions about law and politics may have to be revisited and rethought.

Reading

For an introduction to the idea of multilayered government, see Ilgen (2003). Loughlin's distinction between right and capacity, or the normative and empirical conceptions of sovereignty is discussed in Loughlin (2000, ch 10). MacCormick's theory of 'post-sovereignty' is concisely set out in MacCormick (1999, ch 8). For Walker's account of 'late sovereignty', see Walker (2003), and also the responses by Loughlin (2004) and MacCormick (2004). For an application of the ideas of 'constitutional pluralism', and an elaboration of the constitutional attributes of the EU and the WTO, see Walker (2001). For an application of ideas of the 'new constitutionalism' (Gill 2000) in the context of contemporary investment regimes, see Schneiderman (2008, ch 6).

References

Cutler, AC, 2003, *Private Power and Global Authority*, Cambridge: Cambridge University Press.

Gill, S, 2000, 'The Constitution of Global Capital', accessed 14 March 2007, www.theglobalsite.ac.uk/press/010gill.pdf.

Held, D and McGrew, A, 2003, 'The Great Globalization Debate: An Introduction', in Held and McGrew (eds), *The Global Transformations Reader*, 2nd edn, pp 1–50, London: Polity.

Ilgen, TL, 2003, 'Reconfigured Sovereignty in the Age of Globalization', in TL Ilgen (ed),
Reconfigured Sovereignty: Multi-Layered Governance in the Global Age, Aldershot:
Ashgate.

Loughlin, M, 2000, *Sword and Scales: An Examination of the Relationship Between Law
and Politics*, Oxford: Hart.

Loughlin, M, 2003, 'Ten Tenets of Sovereignty', in N Hart Walker (ed), *Sovereignty in
Transition*, Oxford: Hart, pp 55–86.

Loughlin, M, 2004, *The Idea of Public Law*, Oxford: Oxford University Press.

MacCormick, N, 1999, *Questioning Sovereignty*, Oxford: Oxford University
Press.

MacCormick, N, 2004, 'Questioning Post-Sovereignty', 29 *Eur L Rev* 852.

Sassen, S, 1996, *Losing Control? Sovereignty in an Age of Globalization*, New York:
Columbia University Press.

Sassen, S, 2007, *A Sociology of Globalization*, New York: W.W. Norton.

Schneiderman, D, 2008, *Constitutionalizing Economic Globalization: Investment
Rules and Democracy's Promise*, Cambridge: Cambridge University
Press.

Walker, N, 2001, 'The EU and the WTO: Constitutionalism in a New Key', in G De Burca
and J Scott (eds), *The EU and the WTO: Legal and Constitutional Issues*, Oxford:
Hart.

Walker, N, 2002, 'The Idea of Constitutional Pluralism', 65 *Modern Law Review* 317–53.

Walker, N, 2003, 'Late Sovereignty in the European Union', in N Walker (ed),
Sovereignty in Transition, Oxford: Hart.

Walker, N, 2008, 'Taking Constitutionalism Beyond the State', 56 *Political Studies*, 519.

2.4 Law and the state of emergency

Emergency, derogation and the 'war' on terror

Inter arma silent leges: 'laws fall silent during armed conflicts'. How relevant is this statement today to explain the situation we find ourselves in, where talk of 'war' of a novel type, the 'war on terror', is everywhere and legal regimes routinely suspend the rule of law and fundamental rights to deal with situations of alleged emergency? Is it enough to reply that we do now acknowledge laws of war and Geneva Conventions on Prisoners of War and against Torture? Or do these new challenges and novel types of conflict both circumvent and erode even those, rudimentary, guarantees?

Action against persons suspected of participation in terrorist activity has been severe, with a string of measures adopted by the US, the UK and a large number of other states, both independently and under the auspices of the UN Security Council. We have become increasingly accustomed to the deployment of the language of 'emergency' and extreme measures such as extraordinary rendition, interrogation techniques amounting to torture, judicially unchallengeable asset-freezing, fast-tracked deportations, incarcerations with or without a guilty verdict, without representation, without a chance to confront accusers, without a trial at all or after a 'secret' trial; all of these have come to be alternately tolerated or sanctioned by governments, normalised, even routinised. Notoriously in the so-called 'Camp Delta', maintained by the United States at Guantanamo Bay, the US government deemed those it held in detention to be 'unlawful combatants', not prisoners of war;

it accordingly also considered that the normal legal constraints of domestic and international law did not apply. When in February 2006 the UN Commission on Human Rights issued a report declaring that the US had committed acts amounting to torture at Guantanamo Bay, and called for it to close its holding pen for suspected terrorists, the response of the US authorities was to dispute the Commission's understanding of the law and to deny the evidentiary basis of the report. The denial that inmates there were suffering torture turned on the claim that ordinary definitions of torture could not be applied during such a conflict as the war on terror. Hence the Commission's findings that the circumstances of solitary confinement and other aspects of the detention at Guantanamo amounted to 'inhuman and degrading treatment' could be dismissed. The classification of detainees as 'unlawful combatants' is represented as entailing that the rules of the Geneva Convention on Prisoners of War do not apply, and rights that would belong to prisoners of war cannot be asserted in favour of these detainees. The Obama administration has since closed Guantanamo Bay and moved its detainees to other sites. But the so-called 'war on terror' continues unabated, with the mushrooming of new detention centres, practices of 'extraordinary rendition', asset-freezing and extensive police powers.

In the UK, the Labour government in one of its early reforms made the European Convention on Human Rights (ECHR) applicable as a part of domestic law, by the **Human Rights Act of 1998** and the **Scotland Act** of the same year. Within three years, however, in the light of the events of '9/11' and emergent threats to the UK, the government had lodged a declaration *derogating* from the provisions against detention without trial (Art 5, ECHR). It had, further, obtained Parliament's approval for legislation to facilitate detention without trial of suspected terrorists who were foreign nationals, but who could not be deported on account of the risk of being tortured or put to death were they to return to their country of origin. It had become embroiled in controversy concerning the possible use of evidence obtained by torture in foreign countries with the complicity of the British security forces. Legal constraints thus appeared to be slipping in two of the oldest and most stable democracies, and emergency conditions led to evermore sweeping emergency powers.

The British judiciary had an opportunity to test the Executive's use of its emergency powers in a number of cases, most notably in *Rehman* and *A v Secretary of State for the Home Dept*, referred to in the literature as the *Belmarsh* case. In the first case the House of Lords showed complete deference to the Executive on matters of national security, in effect rendering judicial review unavailable (non-justiciable) due to the political nature of the judgement over security. In the important *Belmarsh* decision, to which we briefly turn, they revisited the line of reasoning in *Rehman* concerning detention without trial.

Five days after the 2001 Act came into force, eight men had been taken from their homes in the early hours and taken to high security prisons where they were detained as category A prisoners. According to Keith Ewing, who relies for this account on solicitors' statements, 'the men were immediately locked up in solitary cells for 22–23 hours a day'; for some 'it took about 3 months just to get access for family visits and telephone calls'; the men 'were not taken to a police station for questioning and were not questioned by anyone, they did not have any allegations put to them and they were not told the reasons for their internment'. Over the following few months another nine people were rounded up, and all 17 were kept in conditions not dissimilar to Camp Delta, 'with internees spending so much time locked up in tiny cells they seldom saw daylight' (Ewing 2010, pp 228–9).

A challenge to the detention finally[1] reached the House of Lords where a Bench of nine judges was, unusually, assembled to hear the case. The judges had to decide whether the **2001 UK Anti-terrorist Act** which gave the government the power to detain indefinitely non-nationals (where to deport them would risk their being tortured or put to death in their country of origin) was lawful, in other words whether the UK government could lawfully derogate from its obligations under the **Human Rights Act 1998** that forbids indefinite detention. The detainees argued the case on two grounds: (i) that there was no 'national emergency threatening the life of the nation' such that would allow the derogation; and (ii) that the detention provisions discriminated against them on 'grounds of national origin'. The House of Lords upheld the challenge on the basis that it was indeed discriminatory and disproportionate. The majority however also conceded that it was not for the court to decide whether there was an emergency, and deferred to the government to determine the matter. It is worth quoting here the Attorney-General's submission as summarised by Lord Bingham in his opinion: '[I]t is for Parliament and the executive to assess the threat facing the nation, so it [is] for these bodies and not the courts to judge the response necessary to protect the security of the public. These [are] matters of a political character calling for an exercise of political and not judicial judgement.' (Lord Bingham at 110)

The decision is important not just because the court stood up to the government, or for the powerful rhetoric of Lord Hoffmann ('the real threat to the life of the Nation . . ., comes not from terrorism but from laws like this'), but also because of the careful way in which the lines between politics and law were drawn, the careful delineation, that is, of what were properly the political and what the legal issues. What is at stake in the decision is the relationship of what is 'political' (the determination of the emergency), what 'legal' (what is justiciable) and how the Constitution – the supreme law of the land that is understood as giving *legal form* to the exercise of *political power* – is understood in situations of 'emergency'. It would be a mistake, of course, to read in this decision anything like the 'final word' on the issue, and in what Ewing refers to as the subsequent 'round two of the battle between the government and the Courts on this issue', the courts did indeed appear to 'beat a retreat from the apparently bold position' adopted in the *Belmarsh* decision. It did nonetheless provide an important and revealing legal pronouncement on the complex and hugely important issue of the legal containment of political decision-making, as well as how the two 'converge' in the logic of sovereignty.

Situations of emergency are situations where the 'convergence' of law and politics, which we usually associate with the idea of 'constitutionalism', comes undone, and law is *subordinated* to politics. On the one hand we have the extraordinary

---

1   The Court of Appeal had already upheld the derogation from the Convention, on grounds that, as per Lord Woolf, 'the emergency which the government believes to exist justifies the taking of action which would not otherwise be acceptable' (*A v Home Secretary* [2002] EWCA Civ 1502 (Lord Woolf)).

violation of the rule of law, involving the indefinite detention of individuals on the authority of the Home Secretary (not a judge), without notice of the case against the individual, without a hearing in advance and, of course, without having been found guilty of any offence. On the other hand we have a *collapse of the division of powers*: the parliament enacts the emergency legislation, the executive implements it and the judges either wash their hands of it or defer to the executive: all three branches of government are involved in a game of mutual facilitation with a single political purpose, rather than engaged in a system of checks and balances which underwrites and justifies the constitutional order.

Under the eloquent title 'Permanent emergency and the Eclipse of Human Rights Law' Ewing argues that:

> [t]hese exceptional powers bite deeply into constitutional principles and civil liberties. They entail extensive State powers to ban political organisations, powers which are not subject to judicial review; the use of secret evidence against people who are stripped of financial resources; and the arbitrary and excessive deployment of law to interfere with freedom of movement and freedom of expression. All this has the stamp of judicial approval, again sometimes at the highest level . . . In the process there are now grave challenges to core freedoms – freedom of association, of assembly and of expression – that few could have anticipated ever arising in this country.
>
> (Ewing 2010, p 221)

And he concludes:

> But for all the courage and the cheers of the judges' many admirers, one question is always overlooked. Looking back, precisely what benefit did these legal 'victories' secure for those interned in Belmarsh in 2001? The utility of human rights law is to be judged not by what happens in the court-room, but by what happens in the prison-cell, or (in this instance) what happens in the living room of a dingy one-bedroom flat liable to invasion by the State at any time, and under constant surveillance somewhere in Britain.
>
> (p 262)

Carl Schmitt: sovereignty and the exception

In one of the most fascinating, if controversial, understandings of sovereignty, the constitutional lawyer, Carl Schmitt, identified the 'sovereign' as the one who decides on 'the state of exception' (1985a/1922, p 1). A leading scholar of the Weimar Republic, Schmitt entered public life initially as an adviser to the government on constitutional matters, and was later to become closely affiliated to the National Socialist Party after Hitler's rise to power. Notwithstanding the taint of his association with the Nazi Party, his theoretical contributions (particularly during the Weimar period) have proved difficult to ignore and have become increasingly influential. Among the most famous of his dicta remains the aforementioned opening sentence of the first of his four essays in *Political Theology*: 'Sovereign is he who decides on the exception.' As *a state of exception* Schmitt understands, following 'continental' constitutional parlance, an instance of political turmoil that involves a suspension of rights and other constitutional guarantees under conditions of *necessity* (in Anglo-Saxon theory the relevant descriptions would be *martial law* or *emergency powers*). It originates in the French Constituent Assembly's decree of a 'state of siege' (which is the French equivalent term) in 1791; as an extraordinary 'police measure' to cope with internal turmoil and sedition, it has taken many forms since, but it is important, Schmitt reminds us, that it finds its origin in the democratic–revolutionary tradition. The essence of sovereignty, he argues, is revealed in those 'limit situations', under conditions where politics necessitates a suspension of law; in the process law yields to politics, which, for Schmitt, is governed by the ever-present possibility of conflict between friends and enemies. His point was that in ordinary times it can be unclear who has the ultimate power in a State, especially where some form of separation of powers is in operation. But times can be extraordinary – there can be security crises, such as that triggered by Al Qaida. For Schmitt, a crisis is 'more interesting than the rule', because 'it confirms not only the rule but also its existence, which derives only from the exception.'

The most important point to understand is Schmitt's emphasis on the *decision* as underlying the legal system, and as informing not just the suspension of the Constitution as such, but also as pervading the application, of law. About the latter let us say very briefly this: that for Schmitt, the very essence of judgement is the fact that *there can never be absolute declaratory judgements*. Whenever we move from a general premise to a particular application *a decision* is involved to apply *that* norm rather than another to the case at hand. This is a discussion, however, that will take us beyond our concern with constitutionality and emergency. For that let us return to the first and most fundamental of such 'moments of decision', the decision, that is, whether to suspend the constitutional order as such, or not. Surely, one might argue, one cannot define an order through a highly exceptional moment; and furthermore to argue that one has to look at *decisions* rather than *norms* to understand the constitutional order must be distorting. Hans Kelsen, for example, whose theory we discussed earlier, argued that the legal system consisted of norms all the way back to a first Constitution, authorised in each case as valid by a superior norm, authorised in turn by a *Grundnorm*, and certainly not a decision. If decisions were to count as legal they would need to be authorised as such, and in that sense they were decisions only in a weak sense, because the decider had no freedom or authorisation other than to apply the norm within the weak discretion afforded him or her.

Contrast Schmitt to this Kelsenian picture of norms which are authorised all the way back to a 'first Constitution'. The decision to apply the exception, to suspend the Constitution, may indeed be rare – though perhaps even Schmitt may have been surprised with the frequency of its suspension these days and at how unexceptional 'exceptionality' has become. But Schmitt would argue that the *normal* situation may also be understood as the product of a decision of the sovereign *not to suspend*. And that decision is informed not by legal but by political criteria, typically that order and stability have been restored, that no significant danger exists, and therefore that the 'normal' constitutional disposition can be afforded or risked. As Schmitt says, 'for a legal system to make sense, a normal situation must exist, and he is sovereign who definitely decides whether this normal situation actually exists'. In all, to steady the ship of state, measures by way of exceptions to normal constitutional propriety may be called for. Emergency powers have to be exercised. So who decides about this? Whoever decides, and makes that decision stick, said Schmitt, is truly the sovereign. All ordinary law really depends on this sovereign, whose presence may be unknown and unsuspected outside of emergency times. The exception not only proves the rule, it proves *the ruler* as well, as Schmitt might have said. For ultimately, the decision is the ruler's to make: it is by definition not governed by objective, legal criteria. There could be no legal tests about when the conditions of emergency apply; the concept of necessity is entirely *subjective* in that sense. It is a matter of political judgement, informed by considerations and criteria of dangerousness and of the efficiency of the response, that arise in the forcefield of politics and are aligned to the logic of conflict.

This is in some ways a tempting doctrine, seemingly well-fitted to the exceptional times that have prevailed since 2001. Yet it is worth noticing where it leads. It points to the conclusion that, despite appearances and theoretical constitutional limits, law is always in the last resort subordinate to politics, and politics is in the last resort a matter of raw power. Such power is doubtless enhanced through successful manipulation of law and legal institutions, but it is never constrained by law except on a strictly voluntary basis, that is, as a matter of appearance, but never of underlying reality. There is always, in this view, a residue or 'trace' of violence behind the civil mask of the most ostensibly consent-based State.

Let us conclude by linking what Schmitt says about the exception to the House of Lords decisions we discussed at the outset. Remember the reluctance of the judges to venture into this 'no man's land' between the political risk, fact and judgement on the one hand and constitutional law on the other. For Schmitt the state of exception was a total suspension, cancelling the separation between powers and subsuming all power to that of the sovereign. Unlike the situation in Weimar where the legal order was suspended in its entirety, the tendency in Western democracies has been to generalise security regulation to the point where effectively the constitutional protection of citizens is removed. In both cases the effect is similar. Is it not the case that when the judges refrain from a judgement as to whether there exists a threat to the nation and what should be done about it, that they approximate Schmitt's analysis over the logic of exceptionality and the submission of law to politics, and the Constitution, whose guardians the judges are, is reluctant to provide any guarantees to rein in political power? The alternative view that we saw in the initial sections of the 'general themes', above, conceptualised law and politics as genuinely distinct and genuinely interactive. The political activity of governing a state successfully can be carried on under the rule of law, and ideally is. There can be effective, if never complete, institutional arrangements for separation of powers, with resultant checks and balances, which check the tendency of power-holders to seek absolute power, and anyway normally prevent anyone from achieving it. Is it the case that crises and emergencies betoken an *absence* of law, rather than give an insight into law's essence? This is the question that Schmitt identifies as significant, and one that it is becoming increasingly urgent to address, as the so-called 'war' on terror forces us to rethink, assess and even defend the historical achievement that is the Constitution.

Reading

For works by Schmitt see in particular Schmitt (1985a/1922), especially the first essay for his account of sovereignty and the exception. For his conceptualisation of the political on the basis of the friend/enemy distinction see Schmitt (1996/1927). For the most complete account of his legal theory in English see Schmitt (2004/1932), and for his critique of liberal parliamentarianism Schmitt (1985b/1923), especially pp 22–32. His important early lectures on Constitutional law, the *Verfassungslehre*, have now also appeared in English Schmitt (2010/1928):

From the increasing secondary literature on Schmitt, see, in particular, Dyzenhaus's comprehensive and critical account in Dyzenhaus (1997), pp 38–101. Ewing (2010) explores questions of constitutionalism and rights in times of emergency; it looks at the corrosion of civil liberties between 1997 and 2010 and the difficulties that beset efforts to deploy legal rights to restrict the power of executive government. From a radical democratic perspective, see Mouffe (1999) (especially the articles by Mouffe, Hirst and Zizek), and for a historical account see Muller (2003). See also MacCormick (2007) ch 10 s 6, and Paul Kahn (2011). For an excellent discussion of the contrasting theories of Schmitt and Kelsen, see Lindahl (2007).

On questions of constitutionalism and emergency see Finn (1991); for its origin in the democratic–revolutionary tradition, and for an insightful, but demanding analysis, see Agamben (2005). For a detailed and thorough constitutional analysis of emergency, see Dyzenhaus (2006), in which he defends the rule of law as capable of responding even to those situations that place the legal and political order under great stress.

References

Agamben, G, 2005, *State of Exception*, Chicago: Chicago University Press.

Dyzenhaus, D, 1997, *Legality and Legitimacy*, Oxford: Clarendon.

Dyzenhaus, D, 2006, *The Constitution of Law: Legality in a Time of Emergency*, Cambridge: Cambridge University Press.

Ewing, K, 2010, *The Bonfire of the Liberties*, Oxford: Oxford University Press.

Finn, JE, 1991, *Constitutions in Crisis*, Oxford: Oxford University Press.

Kahn, P, 2011, *Political theology: Four new chapters on the concept of sovereignty*, New York: Columbia University Press.

Lindahl, H, 2007, 'Constituent Power and Reflexive Identity', in M Loughlin and N Walker (eds), *The Paradox of Constitutionalism*, Oxford: Oxford University Press.

MacCormick, N, 2007, *Institutions of Law*, Oxford: Oxford University Press.

Mouffe, C, 1999, *The Challenge of Carl Schmitt*, London: Verso.

Muller, J-W, 2003, *A Dangerous Mind: Carl Schmitt in Post-War European Thought*, New Haven: Yale University Press.

Schmitt, C, 1985a/1922, *Political Theology: Four Chapters on the Concept of Sovereignty*, Cambridge, MA: MIT Press.

Schmitt, C, 1985b/1923, *The Crisis of Parliamentary Democracy*, Cambridge, MA: MIT Press.
Schmitt, C, 1996/1927, *The Concept of the Political*, Chicago: Chicago University Press.
Schmitt, C, 2004/1932, *Legality and Legitimacy*, Durham, NC: Duke University Press.
Schmitt C, 2010/1928, *Constitutional Theory*, Durham, NC: Duke University Press.

Cases

Secretary of State for the Home Department v Rehman [2002] All ER 123.
A v Home Secretary [2002] EWCA Civ 1502.
A v Home Secretary [2004] UKHL 56.
A v Secretary of State for the Home Department [2005] 1 WLR 87.

2.5 The rule of law in political transitions

Dilemmas of the rule of law

Over the last 20 years a theme has come to prominence in legal studies concerning the role of law and legal institutions in political transitions. Under the title of 'transitional jurisprudence', scholars have paid close attention to the various ways in which law has been involved in facilitating countries – from as far apart as Central and South America to Africa – in moving from non-democratic forms of political organisation to democratic ones. With the fall of the Berlin Wall and the so-called 'velvet revolutions' of the early 1990s, Europe also saw a burgeoning of jurisprudential reflection on problems of 'how to deal with the past'. What made these recent transitions so interesting – and so important – was due, in part, to the kind of problems thrown up for new governments who wanted to instil a faith in the belief that they would uphold the rule of law. Yet these governments were simultaneously faced with many competing demands to hold to account those who had perpetrated 'historic injustices' under the previous regime. As many people saw it, this produced a kind of rule of law dilemma: on the one hand, as we have already seen, the rule of law means (among other things) securing legal certainty by upholding legal expectations as they have been set out, in advance, by legislatures, courts and constitutions. On the other hand, many of the despotic policies of the previous regimes had been carried out by governments acting under the guise of the laws they had established. Now if the ideal of the rule of law as the upholding of legal expectations was to be respected and aspired to by the new regime, this would mean recognising the laws and legal expectations established by the previous regime, no matter how much suffering they might have caused. For example, in the well-known cases of the East German border guards, soldiers who had shot at escapees were to be prosecuted under the reunified German legal process for the shootings, which were deemed to be criminal offences; yet, the soldiers argued, these actions had been carried out under legally sanctioned orders at the time of their actions and for which they had been rewarded under the East German regime. Would it be legal or fair to find them guilty of criminal acts? Was this not a breach by the new democratic regime of the rule of law (and basic human rights) principle that no one should be punished for an act that was not a crime at the time of its commission? This, in a nutshell, was the dilemma: how to respond to prior injustices of a regime that claimed to be legal at the time. And it presented itself not only in criminal law, but in public and private law too (for example, as claims to restitution in property law). Moreover, bringing in another dimension to this, if reconciliation is important as an ideal for the emerging nation, what are the best approaches to justice and the rule of law in that regard and, significantly, might legal adjudication in these matters not in fact undermine the promise of and conditions for reconciliation, for example, between victims and former oppressors or between victims and current beneficiaries? At the very least we can note that how issues of reconciliation are presented will impact on jurisprudential questions in ways that are not experienced in non-transitional situations.

In this section we will explore in a little more detail some of the jurisprudential issues arising out of such 'transitional' problems. But it should be noted at the outset that although they have become, and remain, highly relevant to contemporary societies throughout the world, these problems are not entirely new. People have always had to deal with the issues of despotic governments and the consequences of their injustices, with problems of coming to terms with the aftermath of wars, civil conflicts and liberation from colonial rule (whether in America in the 1770s, Africa in the second half of the twentieth century, or post-Second World War Europe), and writers and political and legal actors have always had to engage with these problems. The social contract tradition, for example, most vivid in the work of such key thinkers of the modern era as Hobbes, Locke, Kant and Rousseau, was itself centrally concerned with how to establish legitimate government in a transition from what they described (in their different ways) as the state of nature. In that sense, problems of transitional justice are not new. Arguably what is new, though, is the legal and international backdrop against which recent transitions have taken place. In a context where the rule of law, democracy and human rights are deemed to establish fundamental values that place limits on the actions of governments, and where – potentially in tension with this – an increasingly powerful and legally established global capitalist economy attempts to set the terms of national and international relations and commerce, the nature of political transitions is itself, we might say, in transition. The point has been reached, it could be argued, where it is law and legal norms in a global setting, rather than simply local politics or violence, which sets the terms of engagement for societies going through radical social and political upheaval. Where this is so, special attention needs to be paid to how the involvement of law and legal mechanisms operate either to limit or create possibilities for genuine social transformation.

In order to make some headway in this broad area of enquiry, we will identify a few key thematic issues in the area of transitional jurisprudence. Mainly, we are concerned here with highlighting the kinds of jurisprudential problems raised, rather than trying to address them in detail.

Difficulties in establishing accountability and responsibility

Where a country has experienced despotic government and injustice resulting in widespread harms, and that regime has now been replaced by a democratic one, one of the key questions faced is how to establish accountability for the harms suffered; that is, who, or which institutions, are to be held to give an account for causing the harms? Establishing accountability in this sense is the first step towards assessing the nature and extent of responsibility for the harms. While at first glance this might appear reasonably straightforward, in countries where this question is asked, a number of problems – some common, others unique to a particular place and time – make it less easy than it may at first seem. When atrocities have occurred on a massive scale, for example, in the commission of genocide or crimes against humanity, establishing accountability and responsibility requires analysing the complex causes, which together facilitated the commission of the harms, and for which conventional criminal law categories may not be adequate. Hannah Arendt, in her famous study of the 'banality of evil', quoted the judgment of the Israeli court in the trial of Adolf Eichmann for his role in the perpetration of the Holocaust:

> in such an enormous and complicated crime as the one we are now considering, wherein many people participated, on various levels and in various modes of activity – the planners, the organizers, and those executing the deeds, according to their various ranks – there is not much point in using the ordinary concepts of counsel-ling and soliciting to commit a crime. For these crimes were committed en masse, not only in regard to the number of victims, but also in regard to the numbers who perpetrated the crime, and the extent to which any one of the many criminals was close to or remote from the actual killer of the victim means nothing, as far as the measure of his responsibility is concerned.
>
> (Arendt 1965, pp 246–7)

It is the extent of the harms, the difficulty of establishing exactly who is to be called to account, and which social institutions (for example, the military or government or the court system) might do this, that make establishing responsibility for them commonly such a daunting task. Despite this, however, there is the desire to see that some kind of justice is done and that impunity – that is, blanket immunity from being held responsible – does not prevail.

Forms of justice

But what kind of justice? Here we encounter different possibilities. One is a form of *retributive justice*, which holds that those who committed or ordered the crimes ought to suffer proportionate punishment for the harm they have caused, that is, they ought to be held criminally liable – assuming they are found guilty by a duly constituted court – and punished accordingly. This was the model adopted post-Second World War in the Nuremberg trials. Again, however, prosecutors and courts face an invid-ious task. They must establish in the first case the relevant jurisdiction over the offences and the accused, and they must establish that the alleged offences exist as crimes. (In the case of Nuremberg, one of the key crimes to be established was 'crimes against humanity'.) Otherwise, there may be a tendency, rightly or wrongly, to see the prosecutions as merely victors' justice, amounting to the imposition of retroactive laws on the defeated and overlooking offences committed by the victorious side. (This is a common argument, which arises in transitional contexts, most recently, for example, in the prosecution of the former Iraqi leadership.) Moreover, given the further problems of identification and capture of offenders, the potentially vast number of accused, and the difficulties surrounding evidence adequate to the high standard of the criminal trial, the very real possibility exists that only a few people will be brought to justice. Thus in some contexts there may be a sense that some people are being treated as scapegoats, and that a few convictions will work to expiate the crimes or complicity of many others who remain free, while in other contexts it may be perceived that the 'foot soldiers' rather than the senior political agents behind the policies of the regime are singled out unfairly for prosecution. In many such situations, then, courts have to engage with the identification of actual perpetrators under conditions in which the 'normal' operation of criminal law seems to be unsettled, since it is often the case that in such scenarios 'the degree of responsibility increases as we draw further away from the man who uses the fatal instrument with his own hands' (Arendt 1965, p 247).

This problem of unequal or uneven treatment is another element of the rule of law dilemma – whether and who to prosecute and for what – and it plays out particularly in the context of criminal law. If the new regime wants to establish its credentials as a rule of law State, then it must be seen to be objective, procedurally proper and not politically biased in its stance towards the prosecution of crime.But in transitional settings, which are often still highly unsettled, it is almost impossible to establish the conventional distance between politics and the criminal law. Would the establishment of the International Criminal Court (ICC) help in dealing with these questions? This is debatable. Even with the establishment of this Court, these doubts and difficulties do not disappear. Moreover, not all states have accepted its jurisdiction – perhaps most problematically the United States of America – and even those that have may well argue that prosecutions are liable to be politically skewed.

These are perhaps some of the reasons why alternative means of holding to account have arisen in the context of recent political transitions. Under the broad banner of *restorative justice*, there has been an acknowledgement of the limits – though not the complete redundancy – of criminal law as a means of dealing with past injustices, and so attempts have been made to provide a different sense of doing justice to past injustices. Restorative justice is centrally concerned with restoring dignity to victims of injustice, and is also based on a concern that the community itself is in some need of restoration. One of the ways in which this has been promoted is through the use of different forms of tribunal which break the link between a finding of responsibility and punishment. Here, it is argued, it is necessary still to hold to account and find responsible those who committed atrocities, but due to a sensitivity to the conditions of the transition it is deemed desirable, for the sake of social reconciliation, both to establish the truth and give the victims and community a role in ways that criminal trials would not be able to achieve, and to understand the consequences of findings of responsibility in a way that goes beyond punishment and promotes social healing.

Perhaps the most prominent contemporary example of this is the Truth and Reconciliation Commission (TRC), established in South Africa in 1995 after the end of apartheid. The TRC was given the task of finding out the nature and causes of the offences committed under the apartheid regime, and one of its most important mechanisms for doing so was to provide amnesties for those who came forward and gave full disclosure of offences committed that were associated with the conflict between the apartheid government and anti-apartheid resistance. Thus, in order to establish the truth about past injustices, and so to begin to promote the possibility of reconciliation in a deeply divided society, it was seen as necessary to sever the link between a finding of responsibility and punishment.

This was controversial, and a number of victims of apartheid policies objected that it failed to take seriously the gravity of the offences, and denied them the right to have justice – of the criminal or tortious variety – established by a court. If wrongs had been committed, they argued, then justice and the law demanded that they be prosecuted. The TRC responded, and the South African Constitutional Court upheld, that unlike blanket amnesties that give no form of accountability for past offences, amnesty of this conditional form was not a denial of justice, but rather provided for an alternative form of justice. This was legitimated by the TRC performing the difficult balancing act between victims' grievances and the need to determine the truth of the past in order to begin to overcome its divisions. This type of conditional amnesty – amnesty on condition of truth-telling – was seen as instrumental to the goal of seeking a shared and peaceable future. Of course, there is a paradox to amnesties in this form: from the same root as 'amnesia' they are about forgetting at least the legal consequences of past acts; but in order to forget, one must first know what to forget, that is, it is necessary to establish the truth about the past. In this tension lies what has been called the 'risk of reconciliation': exposure of too much truth about the past may undermine the restorative process, yet a complete covering over of the past fails to take seriously the injustices of the past and risks ongoing social disharmony and trauma for that reason.

Both these forms of justice in transitional scenarios have, however, been criticised from a third perspective. Where there is a focus on criminal law sanctions, or on amnesties and reconciliation processes, it has been argued that there tends to be inadequate attention paid to a third form of justice, namely *distributive justice*. Distributive justice is concerned with the distribution of goods, opportunities and liabilities in society. After the fall of the old regime, one of the important sets of decisions to be taken is the extent to which the new democratic regime will upset the distribution of such goods and opportunities as were established prior to the transition. For example, questions will be raised about whether or not to maintain the existing regime of property rights or relations, and the extent to which the effects of systemic discrimination against racial or ethnic groups ought now to weigh heavily in favour of redistribution. We might compare, say, the very different approaches taken to land distribution in Zimbabwe and South Africa after white minority rule came to an end in these countries.

In these instances the new government, or, as is often the case, the courts, will face another version of the rule of law dilemma: on the one hand, to uphold legal expectations rooted in the already extant law, and on the other, to deal with the fact that these laws legitimated distributively unjust patterns which, if left in place, would merely continue the legacy of the prior regime. This problem usually reaches its height with regard to property law. Where the right to property is enshrined in the new democratic constitution then those holding property at that time could – again according to a principle of the rule of law – reasonably expect to have their legal rights secured and their property protected. But since this fails to address the problem of material injustice on behalf of the victims of the prior regime, competing claims emerge that challenge the *status quo ante* and demand that redistribution based on redressing past injustice trump the right to property.

One of the important jurisprudential aspects of this involves consideration of what might be called a 'temporal' dimension to justice. This raises the question of whether the existence of *prior* injustice is relevant to doing justice now. Consider the following two arguments. One is that if there is a group in society who is at the moment disadvantaged, this means they should have a valid claim in distributive justice to address their needs now, and, that this is so, regardless of how their disadvantage has historically arisen. In that sense, doing justice to their needs is no different from any other group in a society. By way of contrast, the other argument suggests that the disadvantaged group has a *special* claim in distributive justice, based in the nature of their experience in the past, that is, that their claim should be treated differently from others, because the historical causes of current disadvantage need to be taken into account in order that a full understanding and response to contemporary injustice be made meaningful.

Think, for example, of the case of those in the United States who seek reparations for the effects of slavery. Many argue that the historical injustice that was slavery creates special obligations to descendants of that institution that ought to be taken into account in addressing their needs in the present.

Among other things, they argue that were the existence of current disadvantage *not* in fact to take into account the prior injustice that was slavery, then there would be a failure to fully understand and grapple with the nature of the current social and economic inequalities suffered by many descendants of slaves. Of course, we would encounter questions of identity and causation across times that are not easily addressed in legal categories. And for that reason, among others, many suggest that the disadvantages suffered by many contemporary African-Americans should be dealt with merely as a matter of contemporary distributive justice, oriented to current need, irrespective of why or how that need came about. These are urgent debates that often require difficult choices over priorities in the distribution of resources and goods.

Hence the rule of law dilemmas in political and social transitions show up across a range of areas of legal practice, such as criminal, property and human rights law. But they also encounter more fundamental questions, in two senses: first, that these areas of law themselves may conflict as to their demands and benefits and that negotiating such conflicts may overload the legal categories themselves with political or moral pressures, which, in turn, may undermine the claim to any impartial or objective rule of law; second, as such, the value of the rule of law itself may well turn out to be only one factor among many competing social forces and so not only will the benefits of the rule of law itself be unable to negotiate the making of compromises, but that it too may need to be compromised in order to ensure a relatively stable transition.

These deeper problems are ones that are commonly taken to have been settled in stable societies. But it is one of the benefits of thinking about the rule of law in transitional periods that they expose to the light what exactly these 'settled' assumptions are. And this should constantly remind us that, despite them having receded into the background, they never entirely disappear, and this is particularly so in circumstances where past injustices may rear their head again for consideration, or where contemporary conditions may be deemed to be entering a period of insecurity or instability.

Reading

For a good analysis of several of the main themes see Teitel (2000), or Teitel (1997). For more extensive empirical analyses see Kritz (1995) and McAdams (1997).

Dyzenhaus's review article of several books on this topic gives a good introduction to the literature in this area and some of the central issues it raises: see Dyzenhaus (2003). For his work on the Legal Hearings in the South African TRC, see Dyzenhaus (1998). For a comparative study of truth commissions see Hayner (2002).

For a legal philosophical development of these themes, see the essays in Christodoulidis and Veitch (2001), especially – on South Africa – chapters by Dyzenhaus and du Bois. The South African Constitutional Court's validation of the amnesty process in the context of the truth and reconciliation process can be found in *AZAPO v The President of the RSA* (1996) judgment by Mahomed DP. See also *South African TRC Report* (1998), especially vol 1 ch 5 'Concepts and Principles'.

There is a wealth of literature on restorative justice; for an introduction, see Johnstone (2003).

On the border guards cases see the essays by Alexy and Rivers in Dyzenhaus (1999). For the cases themselves, see *K-HW v Germany*, and for the military superiors, *Streletz, Kessler and Krenz v Germany,* both decisions of the European Court of Human Rights.

For a thoughtful essay on problems of justice and identity in periods of transition, see Ignatieff (1998), final chapter.

The *International Journal of Transitional Justice* provides an excellent resource for contemporary developments in the field.

References

Alexy, R, 1999, 'In Defence of Radbruch's Formula', in D Dyzenhaus (ed), *Recrafting the Rule of Law*, Oxford: Hart.

Arendt, H, 1965, *Eichmann in Jerusalem: A Report on the Banality of Evil*, Harmondsworth: Penguin.

Christodoulidis, E and Veitch, S, 2001 (eds), *Lethe's Law: Justice, Law, and Ethics in Reconciliation*, Oxford: Hart.

Dyzenhaus, D, 1998, *Judging the Judges, Judging Ourselves*, Oxford: Hart.

Dyzenhaus, D (ed), 1999, *Recrafting the Rule of Law*, Oxford: Hart.

Dyzenhaus, D, 2003, 'Review Essay: Transitional Justice', 1.1 *International Journal of Constitutional Law* 163–75.

Hayner, P, 2002, *Unspeakable Truths: Facing the Challenge of Truth Commissions*, London: Routledge.

Ignatieff, M, 1998, 'The Nightmare from Which We are Trying to Awake', in M Ignatieff, *The Warrior's Honor*, London: Chatto & Windus.

Johnstone, G, 2003, *A Restorative Justice Reader: Texts, Sources and Context*, Cullompton: Willan.

Kritz, N, 1995, *Transitional Justice: How Emerging Democracies Deal with Former Regimes*, Washington DC: Institute of Peace Press, 3 vols.

McAdams, A (ed), 1997, *Transitional Justice and the Rule of Law in New Democracies*, Notre Dame: University of Notre Dame Press.

Rivers, J, 1999, 'The Interpretation and Invalidity of Unjust Laws' in D Dyzenhaus (ed), *Recrafting the Rule of Law*, Oxford: Hart.

South African TRC Report, 1998, 5 vols, Cape Town: Juta Press.

Teitel, R, 1997, 'Transitional Jurisprudence: The Role of Law in Political Transformation', 106 *Yale Law Journal* 2009–80.

Teitel, R, 2000, *Transitional Justice*, New York: Oxford University Press.

Cases

Azapo v President of the RSA (1996) 4 SA 671 (CC).

K-HW v Germany, Judgment of the European Court of Human Rights, 22 March 2001 (Application no. 37201/97).

Streletz, Kessler and Krenz v Germany, Judgment of the European Court of Human Rights, 22 March 2001 (Application nos. 34044/96, 35532/97 and 44801/98).

❖ **TUTORIAL 1**   Legality and the rule of law (1): Fuller

Read pp 33–44 and 145–162 of Lon Fuller's *The Morality of Law* (Fuller 1969).

For the purposes of the tutorial you should be ready to explain and evaluate his approach to law. Consider in particular the following questions:

- In what sense is Fuller's theory an 'inner morality' of law? How does this differ from an 'external morality' of law?

- Are any of the eight ways of making law more important or persuasive than others?

- Do the eight principles of legality constrain in any way the substantive content of laws? If so, what examples can you think of?

- Does Fuller's analysis have any impact on how *judges* do or should go about justifying their decisions?

- What values do you believe the doctrine of the rule of law upholds? How are these the same or different from Fuller's eight principles of legality?

- Fuller states that 'there is a kind of reciprocity between government and the citizen with respect to the observance of rules' (Fuller 1969, p 39). In light of his 'principles of legality', how do you understand Fuller's claim? (Select two or three principles by way of example.) Do you find Fuller's analysis persuasive? Why/not?

Corresponding Sections: Part I General Themes 1.3 and 1.5.

❖ **TUTORIAL 2**   Legality and the rule of law (2)

1 According to Roberto Unger, the idea of constraining power by an impersonal rule of law in liberal societies rests on two assumptions,
both of which, he says, turn out to be fictitious: first that the 'most significant sorts of power can be concentrated in government', the second, that 'power can be effectively constrained by rules' (Unger 1976,
pp 178–179). How do you understand these criticisms of the modern idea
of rule of law? To what extent are they correct?

2 '... formal equality before the law is in conflict, and in fact incompatible, with any activity of the government deliberately aiming at material
or substantive equality of different people, and any government policy
directly aiming at a substantive ideal of distributive justice must lead
to the destruction of the Rule of Law' (Hayek 1944, p 59). Explain what
Hayek means by this claim. Is he correct? Why/not?

3 To what extent might certain features of our modern rights culture
in the administrative welfare state, and if so, which ones, operate to undermine the values of the rule of law in practice?

Corresponding Sections: Part I General Themes 1.3 and 1.4.

❖ **TUTORIAL 3**   Law and politics (1)

Part 1

The province of Cloude, politically a part of the state of Ukania, is an island. Those who believe in independence for Cloude – claiming the right to self-determination – are involved in an armed separatist struggle against Ukania. The separatist movement has major support, gains funds, and espouses its cause mainly from the United States of Amerigo. The government of Ukania – claiming the right to self-defence – is threatening air strikes against and invasion of those countries suspected of 'harbouring terrorists', including Amerigo.

As a jurisprudentially informed expert, you have been asked to comment on the following issues for a radio programme:

1   What would be the differences between a legal and a political solution to the problems raised by these events? What are the conditions of success for each, and what are the possible consequences?

2   The Cloudean separatists claim they are freedom fighters; the Ukanian government claims they are terrorists. Who is correct, and why?

3   Are there any legal limits on what can be done in the name of politics? Should there be?

Part 2

In response to the perceived worsening of events the Ukanian Parliament declared that the situation amounted to an emergency threatening the peace and security of the State and passed an Act authorising the indefinite detention without charge or trial of those suspected of promoting or carrying out terrorist activities. After the detention of a number of suspects under this Act, its legality was challenged in the Ukanian Supreme Court. The judges were referred to a House of Lords decision that includes the following passages:

A (FC) and others (FC) (Appellants) v Secretary of State for the Home Department (Respondent)

LORD BINGHAM

[29] [The] Home Secretary, his colleagues and Parliament [. . .] were called on to exercise a pre-eminently political judgment. It involved making a factual prediction of what various people around the world might or might not do, and when (if at all) they might do it, and what the consequences might be if they did. Any prediction about the future behaviour of human beings

(as opposed to the phases of the moon or high water at London Bridge) is necessarily problematical. Reasonable and informed minds may differ, and a judgment is not shown to be wrong or unreasonable because that which is thought likely to happen does not happen. It would have been irresponsible not to err, if at all, on the side of safety. As will become apparent, I do not accept the full breadth of the Attorney General's argument on what is generally called the deference owed by the courts to the political authorities. It is perhaps preferable to approach this question as one of demarcation of functions or what Liberty in its written case called 'relative institutional competence'. The more purely political (in a broad or narrow sense) a question is, the more appropriate it will be for political resolution and the less likely it is to be an appropriate matter for judicial decision. The smaller, therefore, will be the potential role of the court. It is the function of political and not judicial bodies to resolve political questions. Conversely, the greater the legal content of any issue, the greater the potential role of the court, because under our constitution and subject to the sovereign power of Parliament it is the function of the courts and not of political bodies to resolve legal questions. The present question seems to me to be very much at the political end of the spectrum.

LORD HOFFMANN

[95] But the question is whether such a threat is a threat to the life of the nation. The Attorney General's submissions and the judgment of the Special Immigration Appeals Commission treated a threat of serious physical damage and loss of life as necessarily involving a threat to the life of the nation. But in my opinion this shows a misunderstanding of what is meant by 'threatening the life of the nation'. Of course the government has a duty to protect the lives and property of its citizens. But that is a duty which it owes all the time and which it must discharge without destroying our constitutional freedoms. There may be some nations too fragile or fissiparous to withstand a serious act of violence. But that is not the case in the United Kingdom. When Milton urged the government of his day not to censor the press even in time of civil war, he said:

> 'Lords and Commons of England, consider what nation it is whereof ye are, and whereof ye are the governours'.

96. This is a nation which has been tested in adversity, which has survived physical destruction and catastrophic loss of life. I do not underestimate the ability of fanatical groups of terrorists to kill and destroy, but they do not threaten the life of the nation. Whether we would survive Hitler hung in the balance, but there is no doubt that we shall survive Al-Qaeda. The Spanish people have not said that what happened in Madrid, hideous crime as it was, threatened the life of their nation. Their legendary pride would not allow it. Terrorist violence, serious as it is, does not threaten our institutions of government or our existence as a civil community.

97. For these reasons I think that the Special Immigration Appeals Commission made an error of law and that the appeal ought to be allowed. Others of your Lordships who are also in favour of allowing the appeal would do so, not because there is no emergency threatening the life of the nation, but on the ground that a power of detention confined to foreigners is irrational and discriminatory. I would prefer not to express a view on this point. I said that the power of detention is at present confined to foreigners and I would not like to give the impression that all that was necessary was to extend the power to United Kingdom citizens as well. In my opinion, such a power in any form is not compatible with our constitution. The real threat to the life of the nation, in the sense of a people living in accordance with its traditional laws and political values, comes not from terrorism but from laws such as these. That is the true measure of what terrorism may achieve. It is for Parliament to decide whether to give the terrorists such a victory.

Questions

1   How do the two judges differ in terms of assessing whether or not there is a state of emergency?

2   Which institution – the court or the Parliament – has the ultimate right to determine whether there is a state of emergency?

3   How, in your view, should the judges decide the case before the Ukanian Supreme Court?

Corresponding Sections: Part I General Themes 1.1, 1.2 and Advanced Topic 2.4.

❖ **TUTORIAL 4**   Law and politics (2)

Part 1

The oppressive government of the state of Ukania was toppled by a democratic revolution in 1997. The new government seeks to act in line with sound constitutional and legal principles such as might be found in European Conventions. One of these principles is that there should be no punishment without a law, while another is that no law is to be retrospective in its effect. The new constitution states that those suspected of gross violations of human rights must be brought to trial. It also states that citizens have the right to have justiciable disputes settled by a court of law.

In its final days the old Parliament passed an Act, it was claimed for reasons of maintaining peace and stability in the transition to the new regime, which gave immunity from criminal and civil liability to all functionaries of the former government.

Three cases are now being brought before the courts.

1   Two victims of torture are bringing a civil suit for damages against their torturer.

2   A prosecutor has decided to bring to trial the former head of the security services and the former Home Secretary for conspiracy to murder 83 political opponents who died as a result of security operations.

3   A former border guard is being prosecuted, despite his claim merely to have been following legitimate orders, for shooting two people who tried to escape the country.

You are the Minister of Justice and have been asked by the Cabinet for your opinion on these cases.

Part 2

The Pinochet 'episode' in British legal history is remarkable: not only did it place the House of Lords at the centre of a national and international political debate about the role of courts, but also because it generated a debate about the relationship between national and international legal orders and most importantly, for our purposes too, the nature of the relationship between law and politics.

In 1973 General Pinochet assumed power in Chile after a military coup that saw the overthrow of the democratically elected government of Salvador Allende; he became President of the governing Junta and assumed the title of President of the Republic. During his headship of the Chilean State, around 4,000 individuals were killed or disappeared. In 1978 he granted an amnesty to all persons involved in criminal acts since the coup, and thus absolved himself of any violation of human rights committed during the time. In the final of his many official visits to the UK, during which he was always accorded diplomatic courtesies and became a 'close friend' of Margaret Thatcher and other Tories, he was arrested pursuant to a warrant issued under the **Extradition Act 1989**. Judge Garzon in Madrid had issued an international warrant requesting that Pinochet be extradited to Spain to face the charges of genocide, mass murder and hostage-taking, among other crimes. Pinochet made an application to quash the warrant, claiming that he was entitled to immunity as a former Head of State from criminal and civil process in the English courts; his application succeeded before the Divisional Court. We pick up the story at this point, in the House of Lords decision over, arguably, the most significant question as certified by the Divisional Court: 'the **proper interpretation** and scope of the immunity enjoyed by a former Head of State from arrest and extradition proceedings in the UK in respect of acts committed while he was Head of State'.

Compare and contrast the following extracts:

LORD LLOYD of Berwick

It would be unjustifiable in theory and unworkable in practice, to impose any restriction on Head of State immunity by reference to the number or gravity of the alleged crimes.

On the issue [of Head of State immunity at common law] I would hold that Senator Pinochet is entitled to immunity as former Head of State in respect of the crimes alleged against him on well established principles of customary international law, which principles form part of the common law of England.

. . .

The answer is the same at common law or under statute [the **State Immunity Act 1978**]. And the rationale is the same. The former Head of State enjoys continuing immunity in respect of governmental acts which he performed as Head of State because in both cases the acts are attributed to the state itself.

LORD SLYNN of Hadley

The Rome Statute of the International Criminal Court provides for jurisdiction in respect of genocide . . . but in each case only with respect to acts committed after the entry into force of this statute.

There is no doubt that States have been moving towards the recognition of some crimes as those which should not be covered by claims of State or Head of State. . . . It has to be said, however, . . . that some of those statements read as aspirations, as embryonic. . . . Nor is there any jus cogens in respect of such breaches of international law which require that a claim of State or Head of State immunity, itself a well established principle of international law, should be overridden.

. . .

[I]f States wish to exclude the long established immunity of former Heads of State in respect of allegations of specific crimes, or generally, then they must do so in clear terms. They should not leave it to National Courts because of the appalling nature of the crimes alleged.

LORD NICHOLLS

It hardly needs saying that torture of his own subjects, or of aliens, would not be regarded by international law as a function of a Head of State. All states disavow the use of torture as abhorrent . . . Similarly [with] the taking of hostages. International law recognises, of course, that the functions of a Head of State may include activities which are wrongful, even illegal, by the law of his own state or by the laws of other states. But international law has made plain that certain types of conduct, including torture and hostage-taking, are not acceptable conduct on the part of anyone. This applies as much to Heads of State, or even more so, as it does to everyone else; the contrary conclusion would make a mockery of international law.

. . .

[Since] a resolution passed unanimously in 1946 by the UN general assembly . . . no Head of state could have been in any doubt about his potential personal liability if he participated in acts regarded by international law as crimes against humanity.

LORD STEYN

[For the immunity to obtain] the acts must have been performed by the defendant in the exercise of his functions as Head of State. . . . The Lord Chief Justice observed that a former Head of State is clearly entitled to immunity from process in respect of some crimes. I would accept this proposition. Rhetorically the Chief Justice then posed the question: 'Where does one draw the line?' . . . it is inherent in this stark conclusion [the Chief Lord Justice's and Collins J's] that there is or virtually no line to be drawn. It follows that when Hitler ordered the 'final solution' his act must be regarded as an official act deriving from the exercise of his functions as Head of State.

Why should what was allegedly done in secret in the torture chambers of Santiago on the orders of General Pinochet be regarded as official acts? Why should the murders and disappearances allegedly perpetrated on his orders be regarded as official acts? . . . In none of these cases is the essential requirement satisfied, viz. . . . that these acts were part of the functions of a Head of State. The normative principles of law do not require that such high crimes should be classified as acts performed in the exercise of the functions of the Head of State.

Questions

1 When Lord Steyn, in the quotation above, talks of the 'normative principles of law' is he relying on a Natural Law argument? Is he relying on a political rather than a legal argument?

2 Is it the business of courts to argue for what rightly falls under the function of a Head of State and what doesn't?

3 Does an allegation of torture 'trump' a plea of immunity, an issue raised by Lord Lloyd?

4 In your opinion is the fact that Lord Hoffmann was at the time a Director of Amnesty International a valid reason to 'vacate' the decision and rehear the appeal?

Corresponding Sections: Part I General Themes 1.1, 1.2 and 1.4, and Advanced Topics 2.1, 2.4 and 2.5.

Advanced

 **TUTORIAL 5**   Law, justice and disobedience

Part 1

Whether we think it a law or not we still have to decide what to do. Saying it is immoral and therefore not a law would have the same practical effect as saying it is a law but immoral and therefore we must not obey it. Does the distinction matter?

Reflect on the following two theses:

Thesis 1: The strict separation between law and morality cannot be upheld: An unjust law is not valid law. Or at least there is a threshold beyond which a law is too evil to count as law. Those who enforced the apartheid regime in South Africa, the soldiers who shot at Germans trying to flee East Berlin during the Cold War, the officials of the Nazi regime *cannot* claim to have acted according to the law. Some acts – including torture and genocide – should be punished regardless of any prior prohibition.

Are these merely cases of objectionable law, or are they actually cases of invalid law? If the latter, who is to draw the threshold (every citizen for herself?) and where (does sentencing someone to death row – to the extent that that amounts to torture – invalidate law?)

Thesis 2: The strict separation between law and morality cannot be upheld: there is an important internal link between law and morality but it is to be sought in the *purpose* of law. To explain this: One cannot describe a social institution like law unless one has an idea of what is good for human persons and thus the point of the institution. From there we can see if various laws in the empirical world measure up. To the extent that they do, we can call them laws or, if they do not, approximation of laws. Take a parallel case. We can have two ways of deciding what a university is. We might say that a university is an institution that the State has allowed to be called a university and there may be good universities and bad universities. We might, on the other hand, not look at it in this neutral way, but first of all have some idea of the essence and point of a university. We would say then that the purpose of the university has something to do with the pursuit and dissemination of knowledge and only an institution committed to that aspiration is properly called a university. Then we could look at all the institutions the State calls a university and see whether they measure up. We can call some universities, some not universities at all and some approximating, but not quite universities. What was said about universities can be said about law. The latter is approximately they way Fuller and Finnis would look at it, the former is more the way positivists would go at the problem.

1   In your opinion, is this argument persuasive in demonstrating that the definition of law necessarily imports value judgements?

2   A member of the British armed forces has objected to going to fight in the Iraq war because he believed it to be illegal on the grounds that it violated the fundamental value of law that it should protect human life. He is now being court-martialled for disobeying orders. He has asked you for your advice as to whether there are any jurisprudential grounds for supporting his defence. What do you advise?

Part 2

Read one of the following texts, summarise their arguments, and relate them to the questions outlined in the context set out below.

Dworkin (1986), pp 101–108 and 172–175
Dyzenhaus (1998)
Christodoulidis (2004)

All South African lawyers who opposed apartheid had to answer the question whether *law could be used to resist law*. Etienne Mureinik was a South African scholar whose work consists of articles which relentlessly criticised the Appellate Court for failing to fulfil its role in considering the *legality* of executive decisions and action taken to sustain apartheid. It may be worth pausing for a moment to consider what questions this injunction throws up for us. In this context, to put it polemically: what would we make of Finnis's argument that law, as an instance of practical reason, by providing the possibility to live under its authority is necessarily a good worth protecting? Of Dworkin's argument that coherence matters; and that we should thus resist taking decisions strategically (to protect the discriminated?) if the coherence of past decisions demands that any current decision must command a *fit* with the legal record of our community?

The case of South Africa under apartheid does of course appear particularly problematic in this respect. It is uncontroversial that laws instituting racial segregation were wicked laws. The question whether the common law gave judges a genuine resource to interpret statute law in ways that modified the oppressive intent of the legislators or whether it became itself infected by this wickedness is one that has troubled legal theorists writing on South Africa. But let us for the sake of argument limit the question to statute, to the laws enacted to implement the principle of separate development, provisions that sought to exclude judicial review for illegality, the security laws that buttressed apartheid and the abundance of subordinate legislation that laid out policy in fantastic detail along lines of race. Altogether these provisions and 'canons' form a weighty, complex and detailed body of statutory law. Integrity does not call us to experiment with latent, subordinate and subversive interpretative options, but calls for fidelity to what becomes entrenched as institutional record, in other words with *what carries the interpretative weight of that record*. And if it is iniquity that entrenches itself legislatively, what is the moral judge to do? What hand does Dworkin deal him? How would Finnis's analysis help solve this problem?

1 Can a legal system of this kind command allegiance for Finnis or Dworkin?

2 To what extent can one use the law to overcome iniquity? Or does morality, instead, call one to abandon the law since the very categories of its understanding and action are always compromised?

Corresponding Sections: Part I General Themes 1.4 and 1.5, and Advanced Topic 2.2.

❖ TUTORIAL 6   Rights culture

Part 1

What are the normative justifications for the following rights?

(a)   The right to life

(b)   The right to property

(c)   The right to a fair and public hearing within a reasonable time by an independent and impartial tribunal established by law

(d)   The rights to work and to strike

(e)   The right not to be discriminated against on grounds of sex, age, race, disability or sexual orientation

Read Waldron 1990, ch 5.

Part 2

Read Loughlin 2000, ch 13.

1   What, according to Loughlin, are the principal characteristics of our contemporary rights culture?

2   Are there any reasons to be concerned about rights discourse and its cultural impact?

3   In particular, are there any problems about the role and power of the judiciary, and the doctrine of the rule of law?

Part 3

From the *Guardian* newspaper, 3 February 1999:

'A New York Judge yesterday put Americans' constitutional rights to free speech ahead of shielding children from pornography on the Internet. Judge Lowell Reed blocked a law to prevent website operators from making sexually explicit material available to under-17s.'

He said in his ruling: '[p]erhaps we do minors in this country harm if First Amendment protections which they will with age inherit fully are chipped away in the name of their protection.'

Anne Beeson, a civil liberties union lawyer, said: '[t]he Court was able to cut through a lot of very complicated evidence and focus on what this case is really about: first amendment speech.'

Do you agree that this is a victory for civil rights?

Could a liberal consistently argue for rights and defend the protection of children from pornography on the net?

Corresponding Sections: Part I General Themes 1.4 and Advanced Topics 2.2 and 2.3.

❖ **TUTORIAL 7** Aspects of justice

1   Consider the three examples used in Advanced Topic 2.1, section 2.1.2 (i.e. on torture of terrorist suspects; torture of prisoners of war; and the demands of others' needs against your property rights). In each case analyse the relative strengths of the utilitarian and libertarian positions. Which do you think is more defensible in each example?

2   Does justice require redistribution, and if so, according to what criteria should redistribution be made?

3   Given that we live in a globalised economy – one that links us through vast networks of production and consumption – do we owe duties of justice and redistribution to people beyond our own borders from whose cheap labour we benefit? Why or why not?

Corresponding Sections: Part I Advanced Topics 2.1 and 2.3.

References

Christodoulidis, E, 2004, 'End of History Jurisprudence: Dworkin in South Africa', *Acta Juridica* 64–85.
Dworkin, R, 1986, *Law's Empire*, London: Fontana.
Dyzenhaus, D, 1998, 'Law as Justification: Etienne Mureinik's Conception of Legal Culture' 14 *SAJHR* 13.
Fuller, LL, 1969, *The Morality of Law*, New Haven: Yale University Press.
Hayek, F, 1944, *The Road to Serfdom*, London: Routledge.
Loughlin, M, 2000, *Sword and Scales*, Oxford: Hart.
Unger, RM, 1976, *Law and Modern Society*, New York: Free Press.
Waldron, J, 1990, *The Law*, London: Routledge.

Cases

A (FC) and others v Secretary of State for the Home Dept [2004] UKHL 56.

Part II

Legal reasoning

| 1 | General themes | 113 |
| 2 | Advanced topics | 148 |

Chapter 1

General themes

Chapter Contents

1.1	Introduction to legal reasoning	114
1.2	Legal formalism	117
1.3	American Legal Realism	123
1.4	Rules, 'open texture' and the limits of discretion	131
1.5	Law as a practice of interpretation	137
1.6	Critical legal studies	142

1.1 Introduction to legal reasoning

Consider the following scenario. A woman gives birth to conjoined twins. Unless some attempt is made to separate the twins, both, according to medical opinion, will die a short time after birth. The couple has travelled from the island of Gozo, off Malta, to Manchester seeking medical assistance unavailable in Malta. While medical intervention to separate them is possible, and while it might keep one twin alive, the other would necessarily die. Of the two, the weaker twin, Mary, was only alive due to the supply of oxygenated blood from her sister, Jodie, without which she would have died anyway and could not have been resuscitated. The parents, guided by their religious beliefs, are opposed to any medical intervention, refusing to contemplate, let alone authorise, that one of their children should die to let the other survive. The doctors, on the other hand, are under a professional duty to try to save life and a legal duty to act in the best interests of the children. But what are the best interests of the children, in the *plural*, when one can live at the expense, and only at the expense, of the other? In the face of the parents' unwillingness to have them undergo an operation, the doctors apply to a court to have the legal authority granted to them to go ahead with the operation. How should the court decide? Can they decide on the basis of moral beliefs about life? Are these to play any role at all? Is the cost of treatment a relevant factor at all to be considered? Or must they follow existing legal rules? But what happens in a situation where there are, or seem to be, no pre-existing rules?

The judges of the Court of Appeal, in this case, after agonising over it, *decided* in favour of lawful separation but on the basis of very different lines of reasoning. The surgical operation was performed and, as expected, Mary died and Jodie lived.

Take a second case. Five days after the **2001 UK Anti-terrorist Act** came into force, eight men were taken from their homes in the early hours to high security prisons where they were detained as category A prisoners. They were immediately locked up in solitary cells for 22–23 hours a day; and for some it took about three months just to get access for family visits and telephone calls. The men were not taken to a police station for questioning and were not questioned by anyone, they did not have any allegations put to them and they were not told the reasons for their internment. Over the following few months another nine people were rounded up, and all 17 were kept in conditions not dissimilar to Camp Delta, at Guantanamo Bay. The Court of Appeal having allowed the detention on grounds that 'the emergency which the government believes to exist justifies the taking of action which would not otherwise be acceptable', a challenge to the detention finally reached the House of Lords before a Bench of nine judges. The judges had to decide whether the 2001 Act, which gave the government the power to detain indefinitely non-nationals, was lawful; in other words whether the UK government could lawfully derogate from its obligations under the **Human Rights Act 1998** that forbids indefinite detention. The detainees argued that there was no 'national emergency threatening the life of the nation' such that would allow the derogation; and that the detention provisions discriminated against them on 'grounds of national origin'. While the court upheld the challenge on the basis that it was indeed discriminatory and disproportionate, the majority also conceded that it was not for the court to decide whether there was an emergency, and deferred to the government to determine the matter. It is worth quoting here the Attorney-General's submission as summarised by Lord Bingham in his opinion: '[I]t is for Parliament and the executive to assess the threat facing the nation, so it [is] for these bodies and not the courts to judge the response necessary to protect the security of the public. These [are] matters of a political character calling for an exercise of political and not judicial judgement.' (This case is discussed at length in Part I 2.4.)

The aim of this part of the book is to describe the kind of arguments that are employed in legal reasoning, and the normative theories behind them, which focus on what kinds of arguments are *appropriate* to legal reasoning.

Of course, we cannot argue about what kinds of arguments are appropriate in legal reasoning unless we have some idea of what law is. If, for example, we think that all that law is is a system of rules, then we might argue that legal argumentation involves merely the 'mechanical' application of those rules to cases that fall within their ambit. But then we might find it difficult to explain what it is that makes some cases so hard, and why it is that top lawyers and judges routinely disagree about what the law requires. If, alternatively, we believe that law is to be understood as an argumentative practice that necessarily engages questions of morality and politics, then that belief will incline us to reach very different conclusions about how legal argumentation is to be best understood and carried out. Or again, if we treat law as essentially an open-ended practice, where policies of 'social engineering' or conserving the status quo are the determining factors, then we will have a different view of the nature and purpose of adjudication. And so on.

We will look in this part at how theorists and judges approach and answer these questions in different ways, and what they say about the nature of legal reasoning, the nature of law, and the connection between the two. If legal argument is about justifying the application of the law in terms of principles and values, then the judges may be right in engaging with moral and political justifications, or wrong to artificially exclude them. Conversely, we may be unwilling to grant judges the power to invoke moral and political argument without understanding how their reasoning may be influenced by factors they do not explicitly engage with: their professional or class background, or issues of gender or political bias.

How we answer the more general and abstract questions on the nature of law and legal reasoning bears directly on what we argue is the right solution in each and every case in law. It is in this sense that practices of adjudication and reasoning with law, their underlying features, rationality, or biases, are absolutely central to an understanding of the operation of law, and are therefore in need of closer, critical, examination.

As lawyers and students of law we do of course look *to the law* for answers. It is not, so the assumption goes, for us as lawyers to look to politics, religion and other normative orders, or to look into our conscience to find the right legal answer. And to look to the law means fundamentally to look to the *sources of law*. There are a number of sources of law, including in some cases custom, in some others international treaties that are binding and generate obligations, in some cases even authoritative writings like those of Blackstone or Hume. But in most cases, as far as the common law is concerned the main sources of law are *statute*, the laws enacted in our parliaments, and *precedent*, prior binding decisions of our courts. Where the sources provide contrasting determinations, there are rules that tell us how to sort out the clash: more recent law repeals older law; constitutional law prevails over ordinary law and so on. All these sources *exist* as a matter of fact: they are enacted as laws, decided as cases, agreed as treaties, observed as custom. So if clear rules originating in the sources of law provide the solutions to questions of law and, in cases where these solutions conflict, provide solutions for that conflict in terms of formal tests (of repeal and constitutionality), what is there to disagree about in legal argument and how (and why) do morality and politics bear on legal argument? Is it not the case that while they do of course inform the kinds of debates we have over what law we want to enact, after that discussion is over and a decision is made (typically in our parliaments), the political disagreement ends at the point at which the law comes into being?

It is no less than the key organising principle of our constitutional systems, the separation of powers, that is at stake here. If political disagreements of the kind that are proper to Parliament, as the democratic forum, are not contained there but instead 'spill over' into arguments in courts, then the separation between the political enactment of law (in Parliament) and its legal application (in courts) is compromised. The fundamental principle of the rule of law, as we will see, is also jeopardised. Is this 'spill-over' or continuity between political and legal argument something that *can* and *should* be avoided, or might there be reasons why we might welcome it?

These are difficult but unavoidable questions, questions that frame the practice of legal reasoning even when they are not always at the forefront of our engagement with the law when we read, interpret and apply it. So before we move to these deeper questions that frame and inform the practice of legal reasoning, whether it is undertaken by judges, other state officials, teachers and students of law, or lay persons as they reason about their rights and duties under the law, let us distinguish analytically, in the way it is ordinarily done, between two moments of legal reasoning – that of reasoning about 'facts' and that of reasoning about 'rules'.

It is of course often the case that what gives rise to a dispute is a disagreement over facts. 'Fact-finding' impacts on legal reasoning, and gives rise to difficult questions over the processes and instruments we have in law for establishing what can be taken as evidence that a fact has occurred, what counts as proving that it has, according to what principles of admissibility and what standards of proof, and distribution of 'burdens' – what party, that is, carries the 'onus' of proving what. While much of this belongs to the branch of law called 'evidence' and will not be directly of concern to us here, it also of course impacts directly on what comes into view as the 'factual situation' that calls for legal response. To that extent it is of direct relevance to legal reasoning and we will discuss issues of 'fact-finding' in this part. But legal reasoning is of course also crucially concerned with the 'rules', how one reasons from the 'rules' that the sources of law provide, and how to understand the *interface* between the two: reasoning about facts and reasoning about rules.

When it comes to understanding the 'rules' and how to deal with cases where they are not clear, judges often resort to certain 'rules of thumb': the 'literal rule', the 'golden rule' and the 'mischief rule'. The first of these prescribes that judges first of all opt for the 'literal' meaning of a rule, and it involves judges taking to the dictionary to resolve ambiguities of terms. If this exercise at retrieving the 'literal' or 'ordinary meaning' of the rule yields unreasonable results, then the 'golden rule' tells them to deviate from it or, in extreme cases, to ignore it; then the 'mischief rule' is meant to kick in and direct the judge to identify the 'mischief' that the rule was enacted to rectify, or to give effect to the law in the light of the purpose that guided its enactment.

For all their wide use these rules are obviously of limited value, either circular or, ultimately, question-begging. Only briefly, the 'golden rule' begs the question what counts as 'unreasonable' enough to trump the 'literal' interpretation; the 'literal' rule, in turn, misses the basic insight that what is the 'ordinary' meaning of any statement can only count as that *given a context*, and that the meaning of any statement that may be deemed 'ordinary' in some contexts is only relevant in those contexts. The 'purposive' rule either states the obvious – that a rule is enacted for a purpose which should inform its meaning – or points to very difficult questions over the 'original' intention of legislators or 'teleological' approaches to law, that a simple reference to 'purpose' merely elides. It is remarkable then that, as Francis Bennion puts it:

> Consult even the latest edition of almost any other book on statutory interpretation and you will find the same old parrot cry trotted out: 'the interpretative criteria consist of the literal rule, the mischief rule and the golden rule, and the court chooses between them.' It amounts to a serious breakdown in communication.
>
> (Bennion 2001, p 2)

He concludes:

> There is no golden rule. Nor is there a mischief rule, or a literal rule, or any other cure-all rule of thumb. Instead there are a thousand and one interpretative criteria. Fortunately, not all of these present themselves in any one case; but those that do yield factors that the interpreter must figuratively weigh and balance. That is the nearest we can get to a golden rule, and it is not very near.
>
> (Bennion 2002, pp 3–4)

In what follows we will look at theories of law and legal reasoning that have provided very different answers to the question of how one deals with 'hard' cases in law and in fact how the very distinction between hard and easy cases is drawn. It is these kinds of questions that theories of legal reasoning are concerned with, and to which we will now turn.

1.2 Legal formalism

What is formalism?

Formalism in an extreme form presents a picture in which law *is* and *should be* an entirely self-determining system, where judges are never faced with choices or alternative interpretations of a kind that would be resolvable only through extra-legal considerations, such as moral or political values. For a formalist, therefore, such considerations never enter into the determination of legal outcomes.

Many lawyers and statesmen in nineteenth-century Europe took the project of constructing such systems as a serious ambition. On the Continent, the great codes in

Germany (the BGB) and in France (the Code Civil) brought together what was to be called the 'jurisprudence of legal concepts' – abstract, conceptual and logical legal scholarship in the exegetical tradition – and a revival of Roman law. (The work of German sociologist Max Weber analysed the historical development of this (see Part III).) In Britain, Jeremy Bentham argued the case for codification as part of his general attempt to reform the law in an enlightened, liberal fashion. In both cases, codifying the law was seen as a safeguard against arbitrariness in the courts and interference by the executive in the legal process. The idea of the importance of the separation of powers and the ideal of a democratic society resulted in a picture of the law which saw judges as mere executors of the legislature's will, applying the law mechanically. The image of law that emerges as particularly powerful in the nineteenth century, both in codified legal systems on the Continent and among common lawyers, might be summarised as follows: the more nearly we could come to constructing a legal system of clear and coherent rules, containing precise and 'scientifically' analysed terms, elaborated out of perfectly analysed and synthesised concepts, the concepts being unvaryingly used in the same sense throughout the whole body of law, the more we may succeed in producing a gapless, highly formalised and thus properly rational system of law, capable of guaranteeing 'the rule of law'.

It is above all the idea of a self-contained system of norms that defines the aspiration of formalism. A system, we might describe it, that already contains the answers to legal questions within it. Roberto Unger, to whose critique of formalism we will return later, defines formalism in this way:

> Formalism is a commitment to, and therefore also a belief in the possibility of, a method of legal justification that contrasts with open-ended disputes about the basic terms of social life, disputes that people call ideological, philosophical or visionary. Such conflicts fall far short of the closely guarded canon of inference that the formalist claims for legal analysis. . . .
>
> A second distinctive formalist thesis is that only through such a restrained, relatively apolitical method of analysis is legal doctrine possible. . . . Doctrine can exist, according to the formalist view, because of a contrast between the more determinate rationality of legal analysis and the less determinate rationality of ideological contests.
>
> (Unger 1983, pp 1–2)

The 'pure theory of law' and the notion of self-containment

Already in Part I, in our discussion of legal validity, we discussed Hans Kelsen's important statement of the 'pure theory of law'. We can see formalism as an expression, in legal reasoning, of Kelsen's aspiration to set out a pure science of law. The making of judicial decisions that apply to individual cases is, for Kelsen, the making of individual legal norms. Nothing significant separates norm-creation from norm-application, and both fall under the sign of validity. For Kelsen, the application of law is a moment of *juris-diction* (the stating of the law) by officials of the legal system authorised to do so. What does this mean? It means that in reaching the individual decision, that passes a sentence on a wrongdoer, or that deems a specific contract void, or that annuls a marriage or that allocates custody for child, *whatever* the content of a decision may be, the official of the system follows precisely the same logic of authorisation that has guided the production of norms in general: the logic, that is, of validity. The production of the individual legal norm is authorised by a superior norm that establishes the jurisdiction of the court and provides for the content of a judgment in terms of the abstract norm that is given concrete expression in the case at hand, in the same way as the norm-creating capacity of a governmental agency is authorised by the statutes that set it up and determine its powers. And this, again, occurs in the same way as the enactment of statutes by parliaments is authorised and circumscribed by constitutional norms. It is the same logic of validation at work, of an inferior norm by a superior norm, simply at different points of the scale, of more accurately in Kelsen's theory, the hierarchy of norms.

Here is Kelsen, describing how the objective meaning of law attaches to the subjective behaviour of individuals, in *The Pure Theory of Law* (1967/1934):

> [Let us] analyse any condition of things such as is law – . . . [e.g.] a judicial ruling. We can distinguish two elements. The one is a sensible act in time and place, an external process, generally a human behaviour; the other is a significance attached to or immanent in this act or process, a specific meaning. . . . A man, clothed in a gown, speaks certain words from an elevated position to a person standing in front of him. This external process *means* a judicial sentence. . . . These external circumstances, since they are sensible, temporospatial events, are in every case a piece of nature and as such causally determined . . . indeed not legal matter at all. That which makes the process into a legal (or illegal) act is not its factuality, nor its natural, causal existence, but the objective significance that is bound up with it, its meaning.

And Kelsen will conclude:

> The Pure Theory of Law, as a specific science of law, considers legal norms not as natural realities, not as fact in consciousness, but as meaning-contents. And it considers facts only as the content of legal norms, that is only as determined by the norms. Its problem is to discover the specific principles of a sphere of meaning.

What Kelsen is offering here is a radical account of the self-containment of law, which, as we saw, is the essence of formalism. Law comes about as a separate sphere of meaning by vesting events in the world with the objective meaning of law, that is, for Kelsen, through the prism of validity. Why does the behaviour of the 'man, clothed in a gown' *mean* the passing of a sentence? Because the law lends it objective significance through rules that determine the conditions under which it is validated as a legal act. It is then bound up with the notion of *jurisdiction* and the chains of authorisation link the speech act of the judge back to the body of law of which it is an instantiation. The judge thus speaks the law. And his voice is the voice of the law, not of his personal conscience, not of morals, or religion. That is why Kelsen writes:

> What is here chiefly important is to liberate law from the association which has traditionally been made for it – its association with morals. This is not of course to

question the requirement that law ought to be moral. That requirement is self-evident. What is questioned is simply the view that law, as such, is a part of morals and that therefore every law, as law, is in some sense and in some measure moral.

Formalism and deduction

The promotion of the values of objectivity, impartiality and neutrality are all linked to the formalist concern with determinate rule application. Neil MacCormick has vividly portrayed this:

> A system of positive law, especially the law of a modern state, comprises an attempt to concretize broad principles of conduct in the form of relatively stable, clear, detailed and objectively comprehensible rules, and to provide an interpersonally trustworthy and acceptable process for putting these rules into effect. That process is especially visible in cases where there is some interpersonal dispute or where social order or justice have been held to require the organization of public agencies to police and enforce observance of rules that might not otherwise be voluntarily obeyed. In these situations, the private complainer or public rule-enforcer must bring forward some assertions about the state of facts in the world, and attempt to show how that state of facts would call for intervention on the ground of some rule that applies to the asserted facts. Accordingly, the logic of rule-application is the central logic of the law within the modern paradigm of legal rationality under the 'rule of law'.
>
> (MacCormick 1994, pp ix–x)

Put at its simplest, the model at work here, says MacCormick, can be written as the following formula:

R + F = C or 'Rules plus facts yields conclusion'

or, in perhaps its more familiar depiction, as the separation between a major premise containing the rule and a minor premise containing the facts. According to this formulation:

(1) $X_1, X_2, X_3, X_4 \ldots X_n \rightarrow P$

(2) $x_1, x_2, x_3, x_4 \ldots x_n$
_____

(3)   P

Statement (1) is called the major premise of the syllogism and it appends the 'operative facts' to a sanction. These operative facts are the necessary and sufficient conditions for the legal sanction to take effect. Necessary because they all have to be met; sufficient because the law requires no further condition except these. Think of all the conditions, for example, that the law stipulates in order for a will to be valid. These will pertain both to the mental state of the testator, and to external, objective conditions (the existence of witnesses for example). These will be stated in the major premise exhaustively, $(X_1, \ldots, X_n)$ and the law's 'sanction' (P) (the creation of a valid will) will be conditional on their all being fulfilled.

Statement (2) is called the 'minor premise' of the syllogism, and it concerns establishing that the required conditions stipulated in the major premise have in fact occurred as a matter of empirical evidence. To establish the minor premise litigants and the court will engage in 'fact-finding', in establishing what happened as a matter of fact.

If there is established a coincidence between statement (1) and statement (2), if, that is, all operative facts stipulated by the law in the major premise are established as a matter of fact in the minor premise, then the 'sanction' of the law, (P), follows as a matter of logic. No further legal argument is required. The subsumption of S (2) under S (1) yields the legal outcome as a matter of course. *Modus ponens*, this method of reasoning that relies on deduction, is at the heart of the formalist picture of law. The material or relevant facts as established through the use of rules of evidence are then subsumed under the rule. Legal formalism argues that establishing legal conclusions is therefore a process of rational justification, not one of evaluative or subjective judgement. This is important since it limits the discretion of judges, and also provides for certainty, predictability and objectivity in the law.

The legal rule that is laid out in the major premise S (1) may have as its source either a *statutory* provision or a rule based on a *binding* precedent. It may also have as source custom, an international treaty or institutional writings. Whatever the source of S (1), the formalist aspiration that one can discover the law simply by subsuming facts to laws rather than through any creative intervention, does not come undone due to possible difficulties in establishing the content of S (1). Such difficulties, of establishing the exact content of the major premise, become clearly evident when it is the outcome of a previous judicial decision, where the 'rule' that informs the decision and which it establishes as binding for the future, does not appear in a clear-cut and unambiguous statement. Not every word uttered by the judges in the previous case is relevant or binding; instead the *ratio decidendi* of the precedent case will need to be identified, separated off from what are mere *obiter dicta* of a case, and established by being stated in the form of a rule. Of course, there is no agreed statement of what the *ratio* is or how to find it in any given case. But that, argues MacCormick, is not a reason to doubt the possibility of extracting it from a decision. 'When a Court gives a ruling on a point of law which it conceives to be necessary to its justification of its particular decision, it would seem not unreasonable to regard that ruling as the *ratio* of the case' (1978, p 83).

Formalism, as we have sketched it, assumes a connection of legal reasoning with deductive logic. Here is an example of deductive logic in practice, exemplified in the form of syllogistic reasoning used in the presentation of legal determination. In *Daniels* the plaintiffs, having suffered poisoning from drinking a lemonade heavily contaminated with carbolic acid, sued the manufacturer for damages in compensation for their illness, treatment expenses and loss of earnings while ill. Here is the syllogistic translation:

(i)   'In any case if goods sold by one person to another have defects unfitting them for their only proper use but not apparent on ordinary examination, then the goods sold are not of merchantable quality.

(ii)   In the instant case, goods sold by one person to another had defects unfitting them for their only proper use but not apparent on ordinary examination.

(iii)   Therefore in the instant case the goods sold are not of merchantable quality.'

(MacCormick 1994, p 22)

As we saw, sentences (i) and (ii) here are the 'premises', while (iii) is the 'conclusion' of this argument: (i) is the 'major premise', the Rule; (ii) is the 'minor premise', the Fact; (iii) the Conclusion. Together this constitutes the argument form called a 'syllogism'. The argument is a deductive argument, where the conclusion is deduced from the premises. The important thing about syllogistic deduction is that the validity of the argument depends purely on its logical form. So long as the premises are true, the conclusion must also be true; one could not assert the premises and deny the conclusion without self-contradiction. The form of this deductive argument can be expressed formulaically as follows:

All M are P	e.g. famously:	All men are mortal
S is M		Socrates is a man
S is P		Socrates is mortal

In legal rules, the major premise usually takes the form of a conditional statement: an 'if – then' sentence. For example: 'if a person agrees to do any act which tends to corrupt public morals, [then] that person is guilty of a crime at common law'; or 'if ["where"] the seller sells goods in the course of a business, [then] there is an implied condition that the goods supplied under the contract are of merchantable quality' (**Sale of Goods Act 1979**, s 14(2)2). In order for the syllogism to work, as we discussed at some length above, the material facts of the present case must match the 'operative' facts as stipulated in the major premise. In this way the conclusion – the 'then' component of the sentence – comes into effect as a legally – and logically – justified conclusion. While judges will seldom literally use logical formulae in their judgments, this itself does not negate the 'essential truth', says MacCormick, of the form $R + F = C$ in legal reasoning.

We have sketched a view of formalism as embodying a vision of legal rationality operating in the sphere of legal adjudication. Law is understood as a system of known general rules – presumed to be clear and, ideally, capable of a purely literal interpretation – that are deductively applied by judges to factual circumstances to yield a conclusion. Correspondingly, the facts of cases must be presentable in readily identifiable typical situations, admitting of simple and uncontroversial application of legal rules. In these circumstances, the legal conclusion necessarily follows and is justified according to the operation of logic. According to MacCormick, so far as legal systems include rules that it is mandatory to apply in every case to which they clearly refer, observance of the requirements of deductive logic is a necessary element in legal justification.

The promise of formalism

There is both a descriptive and a normative side to the formalist theory and ideal. Formalism is a theory about how law *does* contain within its formal, systematic structure all answers to the questions that can be posed in law and legal argument, and at the same time claims that this containment is a good thing, in that it separates off questions of what law is from what one might see as questions of justice or of politics. That does not mean that the formalist would not wish law to be just. It simply means that whether it is just or not does not impact on its being law, and that keeping those two questions distinct is a good thing for the reasons that we saw Hart arguing the case earlier. The emphasis, with formalism, is on the dynamics, we might say, of that containment of all legal answers within the body of law. The more we succeed in this, the more the law will comprise a set of general – and logically consistent – rules capable of being 'deductively' applied to every relevant case of proven facts. The more this is so, the more certain, predictable and uniform will be the law.

Formalism is a realisation of the rule of law ideal in which 'government in all its actions is bound by rules fixed and announced beforehand – rules that make it possible to foresee with fair certainty how the authority will use its coercive powers in given circumstances and to plan one's individual affairs on the basis of that knowledge' (Hayek 1944, p 54). With this statement, it is important to note the political stance of the formalist position. That is, legal formalism is not just a theory about how judges do or should decide cases that come before them; it is also an approach that seeks to uphold and promote certain political and moral ends too. This may seem paradoxical. Yet, a belief in the virtues of formalism is bound up with taking a specific stance on the doctrine of the rule of law, the separation of powers, on personal, political and economic autonomy, and to judicial accountability in the political system (see Part I).

Reading

For a short and clear defence of the rule-based account of legal reasoning, read Neil MacCormick's 'Foreword' to MacCormick (1994), and for his reconstruction of *Daniels* in terms of a series of purely deductive syllogisms, see chapter 2 – 'Deductive Justification' – of that book.

With regard to the formalist analysis of the application of statutes, see MacCormick and Summers (1991), ch 13, 511–25. For an analysis of formalist reasoning from case law, see MacCormick (1994) 19–29.

For Kelsen's exceptional, if demanding, analysis of the pure science of law, as an account of the systematicity of law and its containment within the formal structure, see Kelsen (1967).

For a defence of formalism as a normative ideal see Hayek (1944) in particular ch 6.

1.3 American Legal Realism

The formalist image of law has never gone unchallenged, and the earlier part of the twentieth century saw throughout the Western world various forms of what may even be called a 'revolt' against formalism. This was not simply a revolt against an ideal-ised deductive model of rule application, but was critical of even the more nuanced forms of formal justification. This critique was frequently associated with new approaches in the sociology of law and 'sociological jurisprudence', involving people such as Roscoe Pound in the US, Francois Geny in France, Rudolf von Jhering, Eugen Ehrlich and various proponents of *Freirechtsfindung* ('Free law-finding') in Germany.

The American Legal Realists comprised a loose grouping of legal academics and practitioners (such as Llewellyn, Frank, Oliphant, Holmes, Rodell, etc). They were not concerned to offer a theory of law or even a theory of legal reasoning. They were concerned with changing legal education, legal practice and court processes, so as to bring into the open the policy issues involved in law-making by judges. This was seen as important first, for the training of lawyers and judges; second, for an improvement in the predictability of judicial decisions; and third, for the flexibility that judges should show in updating the law to deal with changing social conditions. The ideas of these thinkers were influenced by pragmatism in philosophy (John Dewey and William James) and by a belief in the role that scientific experts could play. They were not rigorous philosophers or social scientists, but they had a profound effect on American legal education and practice and a delayed and patchy influence in Britain.

The critique took the form of arguing that formalistic interpretation was not in fact the only available (or commonly used) approach to legal doctrines and codes, and arguing that formalism involved ignoring the social interests on which law was truly based and by reference to which it ought to be interpreted and developed. The revolt against formalism was particularly vigorous in the US in the 1920s and 1930s, at the time of the early conflict between Roosevelt's 'New Deal' and the conservative constitutional activism engaged in by the US Supreme Court Judges who would systematically strike down redistributive policies on constitutional grounds. The most typical example of this was the Supreme Court's 1905 decision in *Lochner v New York* (198 US 483 (1905)) that came to define an era of Supreme Court constitutional jurisprudence ('Lochnerism'); the question the Court answered in the affirmative was whether the US Constitution's protection of liberty forbade laws aimed at social protection and the control of the operation of markets. Vigorous theoretical debate ensued, over formalism and the relation of law to politics, and gradually, over the next few decades there arose something akin to a 'movement' in legal theory that came to be known as 'legal realism' – the doctrines of its main proponents amounting to various forms of more or less extreme scepticism about all aspects of legal formalism.

The attack on formalism as scepticism over whether rules are capable of determining outcomes was coupled with a strong political programme of 'social engineering', that is the idea that law can be used as an instrument of policy and a belief that scientific expertise can make a real difference to how societies can be 'run' with the help of the law. What brings together the two aspects – the critique and the programme – is a new agenda to study 'law in action', not, that is, as it is presented 'in the books' as containing certain constitutionally unchallengeable, because a-contextual, commitments to the protection of liberty and property, but as institutionally embedded, and harnessed to the pursuit of social and welfare aims.

It is interesting here to note Roscoe Pound's earlier attack on the Anglo-American common law system, whose 'individualist spirit agrees ill with a collectivist age', and which arouses resentment by turning great social and economic issues into private legal disputes, encouraging 'petty tinkering where comprehensive reforms are needed' (1960, p 185).

An influential account of the 'common points of departure' of the main Realist scholars is provided by Karl Llewellyn in his (1931) defence of Realism against Roscoe Pound. These consist of:

(i)   the conception of law in flux, moving law, and of judicial creation of law;
(ii)   the conception of law as means to an end, and therefore the interpretation of law as relevant to its purpose and assessment as to its effect;
(iii) the notion of society in flux, where the rate of change is faster than the law, therefore the need for law to keep up;
(iv)   the 'temporary' separation of 'is' from 'ought' for purposes of the study of law;
(v)   'distrust in traditional legal rules and concepts insofar as they purport to *describe* what either courts or people are actually doing';
(vi)   distrust that the rules as expressed in the form of legal doctrine 'are the heavily operative factor in producing court decisions';
(vii) belief in the worthwhileness of grouping cases and legal situations into narrower categories than has been the case in the past;
(viii) an insistence on evaluating the law in terms of its effects;
(ix)   insistence on 'sustained and programmatic attack' on legal problems in these various ways. (1931, pp 55–7)

'The Path of the Law': law as prophecy

Some of these theses are already present in the much earlier address by Oliver Wendell Holmes, 'The Path of the Law' (1897), that remains one of the seminal pieces of legal writing. In this piece, Holmes, a forerunner of the American Legal Realists, argued that the reality of legal decision-making should not be concealed by the pretence that law is a system of known rules applied by a judge to produce logical outcomes – the 'myth of legal certainty'. The life of law, Holmes stated, is not logic, but experience: 'the felt necessities of the time, the prevalent moral and political theories, intuitions of public policy, avowed or unconscious, even the prejudices which judges share with their fellow-men, have a good deal more to do than the syllogism in determining the rules by which men should be governed' (Holmes 1897).

'The Path of the Law' contains a number of surprising claims, perhaps none of them generating such controversy as Holmes's invitation to the student of law to adopt the 'bad man's point of view':

> If you want to know the law and nothing else, you must look at it as a *bad man*, who cares only for the material consequences which such knowledge enables him to predict, not as a good one, who finds his reasons for conduct, whether inside the law or outside of it, in the vaguer sanctions of conscience. . . . Take the fundamental question, 'what constitutes the law?' You will find some text writers telling you that it is something different from what is decided by the courts of Massachusetts or England, that it is a system of reason, that it is a deduction from principles of ethics or admitted axioms or what not, which may or may not coincide with the decisions. But if we take the view of our friend the bad man we shall find that he does not care two straws for the axioms or deductions, but that he does want to know what the Massachusetts or English courts are likely to do in fact. I am much of his mind. The prophecies of what the courts will do in fact, and nothing more pretentious, are what I mean by the law.
>
> (1897, pp 460–1)

The object of the study of law, then, is for Holmes nothing but *'prediction'*, or as he puts it *'prophecy'*: '[A] legal duty so called is nothing but a prediction that if a man does or omits certain things he will be made to suffer in this or that way by judgment of the court; and so of a legal right. The number of our predictions when generalized and reduced to a system is not unmanageably large.' Elsewhere he says: 'I wish, if I can, to lay down some first principles for the study of this body of dogma or system-atized prediction which we call the law, for men who want to use it as the instrument of their business to enable them to prophesy in their turn.' He takes the example of contract to illustrate the point: 'Nowhere is the confusion between legal and moral ideas more manifest than in the law of contract. Among other things, here again the so called primary rights and duties are invested with a mystic significance beyond what can be assigned and explained. The duty to keep a contract at common law means a prediction that you must pay damages if you do not keep it, – and nothing else.'

For Holmes it is 'experience', not 'logic' that dictates outcomes. It is in this respect, he says, that 'a second fallacy' comes in:

> The fallacy to which I refer is the notion that the only force at work in the develop-ment of the law is logic. . . . The danger of which I speak is not the admission that the principles governing other phenomena also govern the law, but the notion that a given system, ours, for instance, can be worked out like mathematics from some general axioms of conduct. . . . This mode of thinking is entirely natural. The training of lawyers is training in logic. The processes of analogy, discrimination, and deduction are those in which they are most at home. The language of judicial decision is mainly the language of logic. And the logical method and form flatter that longing for certainty and for repose which is in every human mind. But certainty generally is illusion, and repose is not the destiny of man. Behind the logical form lies a judgment as to the relative worth and importance of competing legislative grounds, often an inarticulate and unconscious judgment, it is true, and yet the very root and nerve of the whole proceeding. You can give any conclusion a logical form.

'I cannot but believe,' says Holmes, 'that if the training of lawyers led them habitu-ally to consider more definitely and explicitly the social advantage on which the rule they lay down must be justified, they sometimes would hesitate where now they are confident, and see that really they were taking sides upon debatable and often burning questions. So much for the fallacy of logical form.'

1.3.2 Rule-scepticism

Two of the forms of realist scepticism that have attracted much attention will be outlined here: rule-scepticism – the doctrine that rules do not and cannot play the determinative part in legal decision-making that formalism credits to them; and fact-scepticism – the idea that 'facts' are not so much independent entities that legal processes discover, but rather propositions about a supposed reality that is generated by legal processes.

The reality is, it is argued, that judges typically cannot decide cases simply by following rules and precedents because these rules are never totally determinate.

Again, Holmes stated the position unambiguously: 'no case can be settled by general propositions . . . I will admit any general proposition you like and decide the case either way.'

According to an early helpful analysis of rule-scepticism provided by Wilfred Rumble (1968), judges face interpretative choices for a number of reasons including, though not limited to, the following:

- The ambiguity of legal language means cases and statutes are open to different interpretations.
- The avalanche of precedents: You can find a precedent for either side and for almost any view.
- Multiplicity of techniques for describing what a precedent established. How is the *ratio decidendi* determined?
- How broad is the scope of a given precedent? How do you decide between broad and narrow implications? How can you tell in an unprecedented situation whether an old rule was supposed to cover it or not?
- The potential for distinguishing: no two cases are ever identical. Which are the important differences of law or fact for the purposes of decision?
- The potential for comparison: cases that once might have seemed quite separate may come to seem similar in some important respect.

Thus rule sceptics find various ambiguities both in statutory interpretation and in the use of precedent. Laws do not take the form of clear, general unambiguous rules, but are radically indeterminate. The idea of treating like cases alike poses radical problems about likeness and difference. Consequently, there is always room for some factor other than the legal rule that conditions the decision – factors ranging from the influence of prejudice to attention to policy. Such factors may operate randomly or they may offer alternative regularities and predictabilities of law that do not derive from the rules as such.

Realist critiques may thus take different forms. At the level of legal denunciation, realism seeks to unmask hypocrisy and double standards by showing that formalism licenses prejudice and arbitrary decision-making cloaked in the form of authority and judicial deference to the rules. At another level, it involves the more everyday observation that predicting judicial outcomes may depend more on knowing about factors that have nothing to do with the rules as such ('Know your court', as lawyers often say).

In any case, the Realists argued, when judges consider a case, they do not work 'forward' from general rules but backwards from the type of outcome that seems appropriate. So any syllogistic logic manifest in the final presentation of a judicial opinion can be contrasted to the logic by which the decision was actually reached.

The issue raised then, in mainstream jurisprudence at least, has been understood primarily in terms of the questions it raises about judicial decision-making. Judicial creativity is seen as a challenge to the doctrine of separation of powers and hence the rule of law ideal. Rule-scepticism clearly presents a problem for any theory that claims law can be described purely as a system of rules. Yet in response it might be argued that the Realists conflated, on the one hand, the process of thinking about or reaching a decision (the 'discovery' of the decision) with, on the other hand, the way in which it is justified. Drawing an analogy with the physical sciences, 'discovery' is identified as the moment when a judge has an idea about what the outcome should be, a process that may well be non-syllogistic, involving hunches, personal views and possibly extra-legal considerations, including views about policy (just as great scientific discoveries may be unpredictable and inspirational – in 'eureka' fashion). But such insights have to be tested to see if they fall within the relevant sphere of legal truth, and only if they do can they be justified. Syllogistic reasoning only comes in at the second stage of testing and presenting the rationale. Jurisprudence is interested only in the justification process. So long as a decision may be justified by reference to an existing rule of law, then the judiciary has not exceeded their consti-tutional powers. But arguably this merely postpones the problem. Is this justificatory reasoning itself rational and determinate? The Realist criticisms apply here too.

Fact-scepticism

It has been argued that not only formalists, but also rule sceptics ignored the difficul-ties associated with facts in adjudication. The facts are an essential element in the application of the law, but to what extent is it the case that courts – judges, or lawyers, or juries – actually get at, or even can get at, the 'truth'? Much of a court's, and thus the lawyers' time, is spent on ascertaining or arguing over the facts, yet this has often been neglected when considering processes of justification in legal decision-making. Among Realists, it is the 'fact sceptics' who turned their attention to such matters.

They argued that we should look at the challenges that come from the world of the lower courts. From this perspective, the grand debates about legal interpreta-tion appear remote and academic. This 'appeal court jurisprudence' concentrated on prestigious and intellectually stimulating 'hard cases', but thereby ignored many salient if more mundane aspects of the everyday life of the courts. So Jerome Frank, writing in the 1940s–1950s, chastised his fellow legal Realists: rule sceptics concen-trated on a very limited aspect of the law in action, whereas most cases were decided on their facts. Like his fellow sceptics, he was extremely dubious about the predict-ability of legal outcomes. Moreover, the possibility existed that the facts as found by judge and jury did not correspond to actual facts.

At its simplest, Frank's scepticism can be understood in terms of the psychology of fact-finding. Witnesses' observations and memory may be extremely hazy, but they will be pressed to produce clear and confident statements in court. Pre-trial interviews with lawyers may even amount to a form of witness coaching in which the witness gets an idea of which version of the facts would best suit prosecution or defence stories. Then, under cross-examination they will be subject to many tech-niques of double-checking and discrediting. By the end of this process, which began in uncertainty in the first place, we may be many degrees from the truth. Ironically, even witnesses who are sure of the truth, and tell it as they saw it, may be 'bad' witnesses. In jury trials these psychological problems are compounded by the jury's complex reactions to witnesses and their capacity to be swayed by the oratory of the lawyers. Yet the jury is supposed to be the 'master of facts'. Even judges in this setting may be less than rational in their reactions and their influence on juries is not inconsiderable. This aspect of Frank's position has been developed subsequently by social psychologists' studies.

To counter such psychological instabilities of truth-finding, Frank called upon the expertise of psychology itself. Experts could be brought in to examine witnesses for the accuracy of their perceptual apparatus and their propensity to lie (with reference to standards of reliability and credibility). Juries should be abolished altogether but, failing that, there should be training in jury duties at school, and jury experts to accompany and advise the jury in the court. The confusing and emotional panoply of costumes and ritual should be eliminated. And judges should undergo psychoanalysis to control their projective tendencies.

Frank focused primarily on the adversarial process, which he likened to a trial by combat with each side's champions trying to do down the others – a 'fight' method of proof. While this may have made sense in the past, when we believed that God was on the side of justice and truth, it is not appropriate to the age of secular rationalism. Instead he proposed an inquisitorial system, which would include better training of legal officials, impartial government officials to dig up all the facts, specialisation of judges and state administrators to deal with the complex facts of modern society, and increasing use of expert witnesses.

Today, Frank's belief in the value of scientific expertise, free proof and managerial legal officials may seem naive, costly and politically worrying. But Frank's basic points have had considerable influence in disturbing the formalist presumption that 'law' divides neatly from 'facts' and that the jury can easily master them. Put polemically, the present system of proof seems self-contradictory. On the one hand, it is based on a presumption that ordinary people can assess and make inferences from the facts as disclosed. On the other hand, legal methods of getting at facts are far from everyday standards of perception or making sense of the world (and, for many, should be). Whether or not legal proof and procedure is as incoherent as Frank would argue, legal virtue and legal vice – confusion and protection, ordeal and ideal – are often embedded in the same legal rules and procedures.

The faith in science

With the knowledge provided by the social sciences, including what we might call today socio-legal studies, it would be possible for the law to be deployed rationally in the pursuit of specific goals: social protection, social inclusion, crime control and the multitude of other policy aims that drive regulatory states in the efforts to enhance social welfare.

It is worth quoting from 'The Path of Law' at some length here, from a passage of Holmes where the faith that law can learn from science (and the opposition to its learning from its history!) is unequivocally expressed:

> For the rational study of the law the black-letter man may be the man of the present, but the man of the future is the man of statistics and the master of economics. It is revolting to have no better reason for a rule of law than that so it was laid down in the time of Henry IV. It is still more revolting if the grounds upon which it was laid down have vanished long since, and the rule simply persists from blind imitation of the past.

> What have we better than a blind guess to show that the criminal law in its present form does more good than harm? I do not stop to refer to the effect which it has had

in degrading prisoners and in plunging them further into crime, or to the question whether fine and imprisonment do not fall more heavily on a criminal's wife and children than on himself. I have in mind more far-reaching questions. Does punishment deter? Do we deal with criminals on proper principles?

I look forward to a time when the part played by history in the explanation of dogma shall be very small, and instead of ingenious research we shall spend our energy on a study of the ends sought to be attained and the reasons for desiring them. As a step toward that ideal it seems to me that every lawyer ought to seek an understanding of economics. The present divorce between the schools of political economy and law seems to me an evidence of how much progress in philosophical study still remains to be made.

As Yntema puts it in a retrospective article (1960), American Legal Realism took for granted the conception of law as an applied science. 'This imported, on the one hand, consideration of the ends to be subserved by the legal order, or in other words the policies and values that it connotes, and on the other hand, examination of its technical efficiency and more especially its effects' (Yntema 1960, pp 322–3).

Finally, the Realists argued that judges were faced with crucial policy questions. Formalism was being used as a cloak for hiding innovations and policy decisions, even, conservatively, to deny the need for change. Remember their commitment was to a form of legal scholarship that would provide guidance for 'social planning and perspective' in the wake of the catastrophe of the 1929 Wall Street stock market crash and the ensuing depression. Recognising that law had become a policy battleground, Realists espoused judges openly taking a stand. Thus they supported the adoption of a form of explicit 'substantive rationality' (see Part III, on Weber) in the search for just and appropriate solutions to particular cases or types of case. Taking a stance was unavoidable, and the judges' cloaking of their decisions behind the façade of legal neutrality was merely an ideological move hiding their endorsement of the status quo. As Joseph Singer (1988, p 482) puts it well:

[American] legal realists criticized the idea of a self-regulating market system which was immune from state involvement or control. They challenged the [traditional] distinction between public and private spheres. The realists asserted that state and society could not be completely separated either logically or experientially. Once the state had been created, it altered (or was intended to alter) the distribution of power and wealth in society. [E]ven by failing to intervene in 'private' transactions, the state effectively altered contract relations; it delegated to the more powerful party the freedom to exercise her superior power or knowledge over the weaker party. Thus, the state determined the distribution of power and wealth in society both when it acted to limit freedom and when it failed to limit the freedom of some to dominate others.

From this perspective, a free market system could not be distinguished in a significant sense from a regulatory system. All market systems distribute power, and thus constitute regulatory systems. The rules in force have the effect of privileging the interests of some persons over the interests of others. It is impossible for a legal system not to so distribute power and wealth. Any definition of property and contract rights necessarily requires the state.

However, Realist arguments about policy should not be interpreted too contextually, as a specific response to the idiosyncratic developments of the American legal system. Rather, they reveal one of the underlying tensions between the 'justice' and 'instrumental' aspects of modern law. Since policies are by definition oriented to factors outside the legal system (the social rather than systemic context), how far can a theory of legal interpretation require that judges have to blind themselves to such goals? If the law is deliberately framed with a view to social policy, it seems bizarre to restrict the ways in which such considerations may enter into the application of law.

Realism has had an enormous impact on subsequent arguments about law and legal reasoning. It has inspired the growth of socio-legal studies that attempt to look at the range of non-rule factors influencing the legal process, and to examine the internal perspective of the judicial community. In its more radical Marxist versions – or in Critical Legal Studies (CLS), as we shall see shortly – the Realist strain is taken to mean not only that the rule of law in its formalist guise is unattainable, but that it is an important myth legitimating an inherently oppressive system, a symbolic/ideational device to make injustice seem morally acceptable to its victims.

Reading

For an early, highly influential piece and a classic text in the Realist tradition, read Holmes (1897). Cotterrell (2003) in *The Politics of Jurisprudence*, 2nd edn, chapter 6, provides an excellent discussion of 'sociological Jurisprudence' as expounded by Roscoe Pound and the points of convergence and divergence with the American Legal Realists. See in particular the section on 'Llewellyn's constructive doctrinal realism', pp 187 ff.

For magisterial historical accounts of currents in American legal history see Horwitz (1992) and Duxbury (1995).

For Frank's account of fact-scepticism see Frank (1949a) especially pp 418–23 and Frank (1949b) 'Introduction'. See also Jackson (1995) for an updated and illuminating account of the 'psychology of fact-finding', issues of reliability of witnessing, advocacy techniques of cross-examination, and the construction of narratives. For further development of these issues see Part II 2.3.

For Hart's critique of American Legal Realism see Hart (1983) and (1961, ch 7).

1.4 Rules, 'open texture' and the limits of discretion

HLA Hart and the 'open texture' of legal language

In his article, 'The Legal Nightmare and the Noble Dream', HLA Hart (1983) responded to the Realist picture by presenting a dichotomy between formalism or 'absolutism' (the 'noble dream') and the picture of total legal anarchy he attributes to rule sceptics. In *The Concept of Law* (1961), while making certain concessions to Realism, Hart suggested that Realists were 'disappointed absolutists', who have grossly exaggerated interpretative leeway because they secretly sought a utopian version of the rule of law ideal.

Hart argues that while the vast majority of cases where legal rules are applied are straightforward, easy cases, there is inevitably an element of judicial discretion in legal reasoning because of the necessarily 'open texture' of law. Drawing on the work of Wittgenstein, he argues that the indeterminacy of natural language makes it impossible for meaning to be somehow 'stilled' and contained in determinate form in rules. Words and phrases may have a 'core' of settled meaning, but there is always a 'penumbra' of doubt and this always leaves room for interpretation and disagreement. Second, there exists a relative ignorance of fact. We cannot predict what 'fact situations' the future may generate and, in that sense, how our attempts to capture future eventualities through general categories today may be challenged. We cannot predict whether our current legal designations will be adequate in the future, although it is precisely future behaviour and situations that we are forever at present trying to regulate. Third, there exists an indeterminacy of legal aim in the legislative process: rules cannot, nor should they aim to, cover all eventualities.Such openness is not a weakness, but may be considered desirable, since it allows the law to be developed to meet changing or unforeseen circumstances. Moreover, the law uses general standards, which themselves necessarily introduce indeterminacy (or at the very least an under-determinacy): standards such as 'reasonableness' ('the reasonable man test', 'reasonable foreseeability', etc), 'proximity' (in negligence), 'fairness', 'good faith', 'equitable', and so on, all inevitably allow for leeway in interpretation. These legal standards are not formal rules in the way that we would think of arithmetic rules – they are open to, and demand, interpretation in the instant case.

In addition to this, we know that valid rules or principles in our law come into conflict with each other: the right, for example, to free speech claimed by a newspaper publishing details of a celebrity's private life may conflict with that celebrity's right to privacy. Often in these cases there is no simple way of rendering the legal rule as clearly as the formalist position might claim; interpretation – or a balancing of the competing valid rights claims – is required.

Finally, it will also be the case that in legal systems based on precedent, the assessment of the *ratio decidendi* of a precedent case is itself a source of indeterminacy. Even in a single judgment, or especially in an appeal court decision where there may be different majority opinions to analyse, there will be room for interpretation in ascertaining what the rule is. This difficulty is magnified where there exists, as often there will, a series of cases in a particular area of law, many of which may be treated as providing potential precedents, and at least some of which may themselves conflict.

Against both the formalists and, as we have seen, the Realists, Hart argues that legal rules cannot function as simple predictions of what judges will do, since they are rules of adjudication. Thus in Hart's view, formalism and rule-scepticism (the claim, as we have just seen, that rules do not and cannot do the work legal formalists say they do) are both exaggerations. Rules can have a clear meaning in legal cases and here formal interpretation works unproblematically. In fact, arguably much of our dealing with the law corresponds to this paradigm.

But where, for any number of the reasons mentioned, the law is not clear, says Hart, there are inevitably going to be hard cases. Here the judge must use his or her discretion to adapt the pre-existing rules to new cases as they arise. Since the law as established does not supply a clear answer to the case in hand, necessarily the judge must work out a basis for the decision by reference to substantive (and therefore not simply formal, deductive) extra-legal moral or political considerations. Yet while in such 'hard' cases judges may have strong discretion, it is never total discretion. No matter how the judge reaches his or her decision as a matter of thinking the problem through, they must publicly give reasons for their decision in the form of arguments about justice, social policy, morality, and so on and show how these arguments are best weighed up in justifying the decision which they give.

On this view then, law is a system of rules supplemented by law-creating exercises of judicial discretion, where adjudication is best thought of as being a middle way between purely formal legal rationality and overstress on substantive rationality after the style of the Realists.

But if it is the case that there are these systematic sources of indeterminacy (of the kind both Hart and the Realists drew attention to), and if it is also true that judges – at least in 'hard' cases – have a great deal of discretion in deciding, would this not be a cause for concern? Would this not tend to undermine the values of judicial objectivity and neutrality, and the predictability offered by the formalist approach? Are there no more substantive constraints on how judges reason, or no more to say on how these substantive constraints might operate when we think about how we expect judges to justify their decisions?

We know that lawyers do argue about the meaning or the application of a particular rule of law, and that sometimes even our most senior judges, often by writing dissenting opinions, disagree about what a legal rule requires or how it applies to the facts of the case before them. Given this, we might ask two sorts of questions. First, are there any common types of reasons why reasonable disagreement about the meaning and application of law occurs in a legal system? If so, what are these factors, and how should we understand the role they play? Second, given the fact of disagreement, does this mean that formalism as an approach to legal interpretation is neither in practice, nor even as an ideal, defensible; or, to put it even more strongly – is legal formalism at the end of the day simply a myth? And if it is, what interests would be served by promoting such a myth? Alternatively, is legal formalism – as an approach to how legal decisions are justified – true, but only to an extent, and in practice in need of being supplemented by a range of other justificatory techniques? If so, what are these techniques and how should we understand how they operate? In the next unit we consider three different contemporary approaches to these questions.

Neil MacCormick: the defence of an 'extended formalism'

Drawing on and expanding Hart's theory, Neil MacCormick attempts to develop an account of adjudication, which shows clearly what substantive constraints exist in legal reasoning and how they work. As we have already seen, he seeks to show the

– very important – place of established valid legal rules as normally applicable by simple deduction or 'subsumption' in clear cases. Now we can turn to how the underlying logic of legal argumentation in its non-deductive phases or elements works. Picking up on the insights of Hart on the open texture of law, MacCormick offers an 'extended formalism' in which the analysis of legal reasoning is true to both common-law reasoning and the justificatory arguments that constrain freewheeling substantive reasoning. This is an account that, he argues, is based on what judges actually do in practice. It is, in other words, a descriptive account. But it is a normative one too: that is, it is one that argues that the forms of justification he identifies in judicial decision-making should be looked on as good practice.

Before looking further it may be helpful to clarify three types of problems judges or lawyers will encounter in interpreting legal rules. These are: problems of relevancy, problems of interpretation and problems of classification.

- Relevancy refers to the question: what is the relevant legal rule? Can it be properly established that the case as averred can be warranted by reference to a valid rule?
- Interpretation refers to the problem: given that there is a relevant legal rule, how should it be interpreted?
- Classification refers to whether or not the case as averred can be properly classified as of the type which would fall under – be subsumed under – the relevant legal rule.

In easy cases, where the rule can be established and interpreted clearly and the facts classified without difficulty, the case can be subsumed as an instance of the rule and the legal ruling can be established uncontroversially. Hard cases, by contrast, are those in which problems of any of the three types identified may arise individually or in combination, and so raise the question of how the judge should act to apply his or her discretion where the relevant ruling is not immediately obvious. Problems of relevancy might mean that we identify a 'gap' in the law, or a clash of laws, or a lack of 'fit', or that we allow analogy to do too much work in establishing similarity between cases even where the latter may be somewhat strained. Problems of classification might mean that the case before the judge may not be immediately subsumed under a single legal rule. Problems of interpretation may arise where there is some doubt or contest over whether a condition stipulated in the major premise can be interpreted to include the instance within its ambit. How, then, is the ruling to be given in the case at hand?

In response to these problems, MacCormick identifies a number of constraints in legal reasoning – conditions that any suggested ruling must meet to qualify as a legal ruling. The first is 'universalisability', which, he argues, is and should be a part of all judicial decision-making. Indeed, he says, it is of the essence of justification as such. That is, to give an adequately justified decision, a judge must make a ruling that deals with the particular case before the court as an instance of a general or universal class. MacCormick suggests that what judges do is to consider whether a proposed decision is capable of universal application. For example, in *Donoghue v Stevenson*, the issue of liability was not simply about this specific manufacturer's negligence towards Mrs Donoghue. Rather, as Lord Tomlin put it (quoted in MacCormick 1978, p 57):

> I think that if the appellant is to succeed it must be on the proposition that every manufacturer or repairer of any article is under a duty to everyone who may thereafter legitimately use the article . . . It is logically impossible to stop short of this point.

The stress on 'every manufacturer', 'any article', 'everyone' in this passage exemplifies the criterion of universalisability and, MacCormick argues, it is necessary for this to be met if a decision is to be properly justified. Putting the argument that justification is not based on the merits of the particular case, but rather on a universal or general treatment of it, he concludes:

> I cannot for the life of me understand how there can be such a thing as a good reason for deciding any single case which is not a good generic reason for deciding cases of the particular type in view, that is to say, the 'merits' of any individual case are the merits of the type of case to which the individual case belongs.
>
> (MacCormick 1978, p 97)

Universalisability is an extension of the requirement of formal justice. This requires us to treat like cases alike and different cases differently. Justification through univeralisation is therefore linked to doing justice to all members of a class in the same way. MacCormick describes this as follows:

> One who has to do justice among other persons, and one who seeks this or that as a matter of justice, is committed at least to the principle that like cases are to be treated alike and differences of treatment to be grounded in difference of relevant factors in a situation. In so far as we have reason to wish that our public agencies act in relation to citizens in a rationally comprehensible and predictable way, we have reason to wish that they act in accordance with this conception of formal justice.
>
> (MacCormick 1979, p 110)

Formal justice therefore requires that for a decision to be justified, it must treat the instant case in the same way as any other similar case. If there are sufficient relevant differences, then distinguishing this case from another can be justified. (We will see later how this process is in fact less than straightforward, and indeed is contested at a number of different levels.)

While applying these criteria may be sufficient to dispose of the case at hand, it may be that two competing understandings of the law can be found to be both universalisable and justified by reference to formal justice (treating like cases alike). Thus for example, in *Donoghue v Stevenson*, both the majority and minority opinions – the one holding manufacturers liable according to the principle of negligence, the other denying it by reference to the lack of a contract – may be justified in precisely these ways.

In these circumstances then, universalisability can act as a control on consequentialist calculations, which may be used to test the competing propositions of law. According to MacCormick, 'Among the consequences of a ruling [are included] both (i) the logical implications of the ruling, viewed by reference to the range of hypothetical cases it covers; and (ii) the results of practical outcomes which will or may ensue given the existence of a rule showing those logical implications' (MacCormick 1979, p 116).

Here, what is properly to be evaluated is not the individual ad hoc decision between parties – it is the consequences of the ruling about the point(s) in issue which matter. What will be the case if this or that among the rival propositions of law proposed by rival parties prevails? How do such consequences square with justice, common sense, public policy, and so on? Consequentialism may commonly be seen in legal judgments in the form of 'floodgates' arguments, and usually as a form of suggesting why liability, say, should not be extended. But those are by no means the sole instances, and in fact MacCormick here would include criteria of value ranging from 'justice', to 'common sense', 'public benefit' and 'convenience'.

Thus in the senses indicated, substantive reasoning in law appears to involve consequentialist argument under the constraint of formal justice, which requires universalisability of grounds of decision. The explicit or implicit ruling by the court on the question(s) before it ought therefore to be tested and justified in terms of the court's evaluation of its consequences. But if a decision is justifiable on the basis of consequentialist argument, does it follow that judges can act on the basis of any ruling whatever, which they represent as having advantageous or highly acceptable consequences? Are there no other constraints beyond those already identified? MacCormick argues that there are two other important constraints.

The requirement of *consistency* in law: rulings must not be inconsistent with pre-existing laws, in the sense of not directly contradicting some binding or authoritative rule. If we discover, that is, that the candidate ruling that has met the criteria of 'universalisability' and has the most desirable consequences, contradicts nonetheless a valid rule of the legal system, then it fails as a legal solution and must be ruled out of the competition. If that were not so, the idea of legal systems as being or including systems of valid, binding rules would be necessarily false.

The requirement of *coherence* in law is similar to consistency, yet there is an important difference between them. While consistency is a negative property, consisting in the absence of contradictions, coherence is a positive property. To fulfil its requirements, judges must decide cases only in accordance with rulings that are in keeping with the existing body of law, and supported by it. And this is primarily achieved by reliance on principles in legal argument. The ruling in a hard case must be shown to be justifiable by reference to some legal principle, and thus 'coherent' with already settled law. While consistency is an either/or quality, coherence is a matter of degree. For MacCormick 'general principles are to be understood as expressing values which are held to be significant in and for the legal system. They are broad normative generalisations under which more concrete rules and rulings of the system can be subsumed. Hence "coherence" is secured by observance of general principles in legal argumentation, to the extent that sets of rules are made to make sense by being geared together to the pursuance of some supposed value or values' (MacCormick 1981, pp 118–19).

Another important aspect of 'coherence' is manifested in argument by analogy. Arguments from analogy are not formally valid in any sense. Rather they work by being more or less persuasive. In cases that are partially similar and partially different, an analogy may support without compelling the decision in the case. For example, on the face of it, there is nothing similar between a snail in a ginger beer bottle and a pair of itchy underpants; but on another reading the latter is analogous to – or 'just like' – the former, in that a consumer suffered harm caused by a defective product (*Grant v Australian Knitting Mills*).

Judges use analogies reasonably often. And while they do not count as a formal justification, they can often have a direct impact on how the judge treats the case and the light in which s/he expects others to see it. For example, in the case of *In re A (Conjoined Twins)*, the case that provides the fact situation described in the first paragraph of this part, Ward LJ wrote:

> In my judgment, parents who are placed on the horns of such a terrible dilemma simply have to choose the lesser of their inevitable loss. If a family at the gates of a concentration camp were told they might free one of their children but if no choice were made both would die, compassionate parents with equal love for their twins would elect to save the stronger and see the weak one destined for death pass through the gates.
>
> (Ward LJ, *Re A Children* 1009–1010)

To summarise: MacCormick finds that judges and lawyers use – and can be expected to use – certain *kinds* of argument that on the one hand go beyond deductive reasoning, yet on the other work to constrain how they may justify their decisions. In this sense where judges do have to make value choices in interpreting the law, particularly in hard cases, these choices are limited by systemic or substantive constraints (see MacCormick 1993, p 18). As such, legal reasoning is best thought of as centrally about rule application and where the formal application is contested, one that remains nonetheless a process of rational justification.

Reading

For a fascinating account of how analogy works in the common law, with specific reference to the notion of dangerousness in delict as a moving classification system, see Levi (1948) sections I and II, pp 501–19.

The 'conjoined twins' case provides the focus of several essays in Bankowski and MacLean (2006), which also deals in greater depth with issues of universality and particularity in legal reasoning.

For a concise summary of MacCormick's analysis, see MacCormick (1979). For fuller treatment, see MacCormick (1978, 1994 2nd edn, chs 5–9).

1.5 Law as a practice of interpretation

Dworkin on 'hard' cases

Since his earliest writings, Ronald Dworkin has consistently maintained that every judicial decision requires discretion understood as the exercise of judgement, as interpretation, and yet none requires discretion of an unrestricted type. Dworkin's attack on formalism – and its core concept of law as a system of rules – is a powerful one and is oriented to its delimitation of the category of hard cases. We neither discover the right legal answer by looking up the right rule, says Dworkin, nor do we 'hit upon' a hard case when we have merely 'run out of rules' in some sense – because, for example, there is a 'gap' in the law, or because of the 'open texture' of the rules (see Hart). Because how would we know that we have run out of rules? Dworkin's famous examples (*Riggs v Palmer, MacPherson v Buick, Brown v. Board of Education*) are highly convincing attempts to force the 'rules + discretion' model into impasses, because in none of these cases is it obvious that we have indeed 'run out of rules'. These were cases where the formalist model appeared to give an answer, and yet judges argued passionately about whether it was in fact the right legal answer. Their disagreement, for Dworkin, captures precisely what the 'stuff' of law as an argumentative practice is about. They sought the right legal answer by constructing a justification (that subsumes the rule under it) in terms of discussing principles embodied in the law. Hard cases in effect are not hard for the reasons formalists would have it: either because of problems of the correct application of the rule or because, in line with how we have described the formalist position, of semantic ambiguities in the language of the specific rules. Hard cases cannot be 'read off' rules in this way. Discerning and arguing a hard case involves a theoretical disagreement about law, involving principles, standards and purposes embodied in the law; in effect, Dworkin sees hard cases not as pathologies that call for a more or less arbitrary decision to be made, but as pivotal, pointing to the law's essential contestability that calls for decisions that are, as he will call them later, always interpretive.

Let us take things more gradually. The theories of Hart and MacCormick, while accepting some of the Realist claims, maintain that law provides rational constraints to substantive reasoning and that these constraints have to do with the predominantly formalist nature of legal reasoning. It involves a supposition that judges should always seek to make rulings on disputed points of law, should do so consistently with the pre-established law, and should aim at coherence with established law through seeking always to make their judgments conform with legal principles. Such principles, they argue, stand in a rational, justificatory relationship to the valid rules of law. Ronald Dworkin criticises these views because of their acceptance of discretion, judicial law-making and retrospectivity. If their view of law-as-a-system-of-rules is correct, according to Dworkin, then rules have an all-or-nothing quality and so, once they run out, there is nothing left in law to appeal to and hence they must give judges a kind of strong discretion that is indeed unrestricted by law, given that law comes only in the form of rules, and hard cases that require discretion are hard precisely because there is no rule governing the case. The rules have in a crucial sense 'run out'. (Compare Hart's presentation of and attack on the Realists.) For Dworkin this inevitable concession is unacceptable. It is unacceptable descriptively, because that is not how judges understand the exercise of legal judgment; if they struggle and agonise over the answer in a hard case, it is not because they think that there is no law to be found covering it and that they therefore need to decide it purely in political or ethical terms. No, it is still the exercise of legal judgment that they are involved in. But formalism (and 'extended' formalism) has it wrong prescriptively too, for Dworkin, because it is an unacceptable violation of the values of law and democracy, as they find expression in the rule of law ideal, to concede that judges should in hard cases usurp the role of the legislator.

The discretion that judges have in a legal system, says Dworkin, is only discretion in the 'weak sense', but this is not MacCormick's 'weak sense', which for Dworkin is still a strong discretion, weakened only in that it is 'rationally' constrained. For Dworkin, the discretion that judges have is, and should be, weak in a different sense. Of course as an exercise of judgement, its outcome is never determinable in advance. But this does not mean that there are not right and wrong ways to exercise judgement. He gives the example of an army officer who is given the instruction 'to choose five men' for a mission. The strong discretion he is given in that instruction differs crucially from the weak discretion he would have been given had the instruction been: 'choose the five best men for the mission'. Obviously the latter instruction gives the officer discretion too, but it consists not in the freedom of choice, but in the exercise of informed judgement as to what 'best' means in terms of the requirements of the mission. It is this kind of discretion that judges are given. For Dworkin there are always relevant legal standards that will inform the outcome even though, unlike the case of merely deductive reasoning from rules, how to apply them is not always clear and always requires the exercise of judgement. This is difficult to do and often controversial, but there is ultimately a right answer. The judge's task is not to legislate new law. It is to apply existing law. The crucial point is that existing law contains more than the positive rules of law.

In his major work, *Law's Empire* (1986), the insight is integrated in a theory of law as interpretive practice. Much has been made of the differences between earlier approaches and that of this book, and although it is fair to say that emphases have been shifted, the later work integrates the earlier insights in a theory of law-as-interpretation, fundamentally enriched by the notion that the law is a practice and that it occurs in a community of interpreters. With this move Dworkin shifts the understanding of the nature of law from text to practice, from settled fact to ongoing revision. In contrast to the concept of law as a matter of past official decisions (positivism), for Dworkin, law is an interpretive concept, the meaning of every law an exercise in interpretation, the very distinction between a hard and an easy case always an interpretive choice. This exercise in interpretation is impossible unless we appreciate that law is a practice and involves us as participants in arguing its meaning. Borrowing from the hermeneutical tradition, Dworkin claims that an understanding of a social practice requires turning to the meaning it has for participants. The meaning of the law, as is the case with every practice and concept, can only be retrieved from within a shared context, a shared form of life, a community. As a community of interpreters of the meaning of our legal practice, we share a context of its possible meanings. We can begin to appreciate its demands not because we hold fast to some rigid list of rules, but because we can take the 'internal' point of view of the participant and interpret its point or purpose and how that might inform what it requires of us in each case. So arguing for the best among possible understandings involves us participants in an argument over the purpose or point of the practice. To discover what the law requires, each and every time, we must attempt to see the institution in its best light and to understand its requirements in the light of what would most fully realise its implied purpose. This exercise in (what Dworkin calls) 'constructive interpretation' must be performed on objective grounds; not, that is, by imposing upon the practice outside moral or personal purposes, but by retrieving purpose from within the practice, as it is intelligible to the people participating in it.

The 'right answer': law as integrity

This is as true of all social practices as it is for law. Interpretation is always justification for Dworkin: one understands a practice – here legal practice – by justifying what it is about; but this imputation of justificatory principle or purpose needs to be one that is already embodied in the practice, one that we retrieve from the best understanding of the practice, not that we impose on it. We may, for example, find that the best justification for awarding damages for delicts is the fair distribution of risks or even the protection of vulnerable members of society. But if that is not what makes sense of the practice of awarding compensation in our legal system, because, for example, the justification for holding people responsible has to do with whether they, could have foreseen the injury rather than whether they can pay for it, then however attractive one might find one's own justification, it is not the principle or justification that can be read off the practice; it is imposed not retrieved. And therefore it does not 'see' the practice under scrutiny in its best light because it does not fit the practice, but instead reconstructs it as something different. The enterprise of 'constructive interpretation' carries great complexity into legal practice and the business of reaching decisions in law. Competing interpretations in law are different rationalisations of the history of the practice competing on the terrain of 'fit'. Justifications command certain 'fits', 'fits' delimit certain justifications. It is a kind of reflexive equilibrium between the two that will allow the best balance of the two – a balancing undertaken against the background of the whole body of the law – to read as the legally right answer.

The 'right answer' for Dworkin, is an answer where weight matters. And what weight means, in this respect, is the gravitational pull of principles that need to be deployed to rationalise rules and decisions into coherence. The judge who is guided by integrity will decide on the morally most attractive principle, that is, a principle that best fits, or carries the most weight within that order, having been entrenched in previous decisions. What does this mean in practice? Take an example: someone is before the court having successfully incited a crowd to perform an illegal act. Can we extend criminal liability to her? Perhaps the 'morally most attractive' justification, the principle that the interpreter of law most values, is that all speech needs to be immune to prosecution; our political activist should be let off. But testing it against the legal practice of his community, the interpreter may find that it is not the case that this principle 'fits' the practice. The law curtails all kinds of speech acts: from threats to forms of advertising. On the other hand the justification might be over-inclusive; perhaps one should limit it to cases of 'political speech', arguing that the best reading of our legal practice demands that political speech acts be protected. In that case, perhaps, the requirement of 'fit' has been met, although it may also, perhaps, now stumble on something different: does the act in question, the incitement of the crowd, fall under the protected category, that is, is it an instance of 'political speech' or has the better 'fit' rendered the justification under-inclusive?

Dworkin calls his prescription for the right answer in law 'Integrity'. Integrity means consistency in principle with past decisions and requires retrieving that principle in precedent as the justification that best fits the institutional record. Dworkin tellingly contrasts integrity to pragmatism, which is the name he gives to his main theoretical adversaries, the CLS movement. A pragmatist's recourse to political principles only serves his/ her own pursuit of an ideal. There is no commitment to working out common schemes of principle embodied in the law; principles are imputed strategically in order for 'judges [and lay participants] to make whatever decisions seem best for the community's future' (Dworkin 1986, p 95). Unlike pragmatism, '[i]ntegrity demands that the public standards of the community be both made and seen, so far as this is possible, to express a single, coherent scheme of justice and fairness in the right relation' (ibid, p 219). Although every decision about what the law is can be debated as to what the principle to be read into text and precedent ought to be, integrity, unlike pragmatism, does not leave the question open. It insists, as we said, that the operative principle should fit the most coherent scheme of justice that can be envisaged for the past history of legal decisions and morally justifies that practice. Integrity demands that the rationalising principle of the decision at hand be part of a pattern that coheres as a whole and shows it in its best light.

To bring the connection between interpretation and coherence forcefully home, Dworkin uses the metaphor of the chain novel in which judges assume the roles of the consecutive co-authors. In adding his/her chapter, the author must both assure it reads as a whole as well as the best in its genre; in the same way the judge, if his/ her decision is to respect law as integrity, will reconstruct the practice as a meaningful whole, thus sustaining the unity of community by giving coherence to the understanding of its practice of law in which people argue their conceptions of what justice requires. This is for Dworkin, aspirationally, what law is about and he entrusts the momentous task to his imaginary judge Hercules. Although every decision about what the law is can be debated as to what the principle to be read into text and precedent ought to be, integrity does not leave the question open, but provides Hercules with a guiding ideal that will yield the answer; it insists that the operative principle should fit into the most coherent scheme of justice that can be envisaged for the past history of legal decisions. Integrity demands that the rationalising principle of the decision at hand be part of a pattern that coheres as a whole. And that is the crux of Dworkin's restatement of the right answer thesis. Integrity yields the right answer and thus sustains the rule of law ideal.

Reading

The concept of 'integrity' is developed in Dworkin (1986) ch 7, where it is usefully contrasted with other prevalent views on legal interpretation. For a concise summary of his theory of legal interpretation, see Dworkin (1990).

Dworkin (1995) is a valuable collection of a series of important analyses and interventions.

For an application of the theory of integrity to the question of the protection of free speech in the Scottish context, see Christodoulidis and Finnie (1995) and in the context of South African apartheid law Christodoulidis (2004).

For Dworkin's attack on law-as-system-of-rules, see Dworkin (1977). For his use of the above cases to 'test' the formalist model, see Dworkin (1986) ch 1. Dworkin's formulation of 'rights as trumps' was developed in Dworkin (1977), but downplayed in his later work.

Although *Law's Empire* (1986) remains Dworkin's most important statement of his theory of law, he has developed key ideas further in (2000) and (2006).

1.6 Critical Legal Studies

In 1976, a new academic movement was formed when a group of scholars met to form a network called the 'Conference on Critical Legal Studies'. Despite considerable opposition in the legal academy, the group's influence grew, drawing together a variety of left-wing radical stances towards law into an umbrella movement and giving an institutional unity to those who opposed 'legal orthodoxy'. Picking up the radical moment in American Legal Realism (above), the CLS movement argue that taking legal doctrine seriously means revealing rather than concealing contrary aspects of law (even teaching law through them). With the Realists they argue against formalism that rules do not fix unambiguous meanings; the text of law can be 'deconstructed', they argue, to reveal its inherent ambiguities (see 2.5 below on 'law and deconstruction'). Emphasising 'contradictions' means highlighting the choices and possibilities present in law that allow legal scholars, practitioners and judges to tap the resources the law itself makes available in order to argue the case for those who find themselves systematically disempowered by the way legal orthodoxy operates. This ties in with the CLS's second objective – to explore, criticise and eventually reverse the manner in which legal doctrine, legal education and the practices of legal institutions entrench advantage, disempower the vulnerable and sustain the status quo of a pervasive system of oppressive relations in society.

Although it would be wrong to see the CLS movement as a 'monolithic' movement, it is also not untrue to the variety it harbours to discern certain common themes. The first has to do with the claim that the law is riddled with real (not apparent) contradictions. The second has to do with how power operates in law to conceal these. Both of these moments – the tensions in law and the importance of power and hierarchy – are evident in the way CLS analyses law by stressing the various paired master oppositions that resolve cases in opposite and incompatible ways: mechanically applied rules/situation-sensitive ad hoc standards, values as subjective/values as objective, human action is willed/human action is determined by environment, private/public, individual/group, law/policy, reason/*fiat*, freedom/coercion. Such pairs are hierarchically structured in that one side of the opposition is dominant, the other subordinate and supplementary. The dominant side sustains the status quo; the subordinate, in exceptional cases, allows us to question it.

While critical legal analysis in the US has been developed in a number of fields of law (Karl Klare in labour law, Duncan Kennedy in torts, David Kennedy in international law, etc) in the remainder of this section we will focus on only one, if highly influential, figure in the CLS movement – Brazilian activist, minister in the Lula government, and Harvard Professor, Roberto Unger – and approach the complexity of his work, straddling legal, political and social theory, through one of his less demanding examples. Unger contends that because the content of our legal past is inherently indeterminate, it can be made to make sense in different ways depending on the principle we impute each time. He illustrates this with the example of contract law, reading the doctrine alternately through 'individualistic' and 'communitarian' spectacles, or more accurately, by imputing alternately the principle of freedom of contract and the counter-principle of fairness of contract. Both, he will conclude, yield coherent accounts of precedent. He sees in the unleashing of the counter-principle a potential for fresh legal interpretations of the law of contract.

Unger's argument runs something like this:

1   For every rule, there is an exception.
2   The rule represents the dominant principle; the exception stands for a counter-principle, subordinate but still present in law.
3   Different social visions are in contest in law – individualism vs altruism – and these underlie the rule/dominant principle and the exception/counter-principle.

Applied schematically to the law of contract these yield the following threefold pairing of oppositions:

Rule	Exception
Pacta sunt servanda	Except when contract is void or voidable
[contractual obligations must be upheld]	

Principle	Counter-principle
Freedom of contract: both as to contractual partner(s) and terms	Fairness of contract: agreements are struck down where:
	(i) terms are unfair
	(ii) communal aspects of social life are subverted
	(iii) parties acted unconscionably

Value	Counter-value
Individualism/Autonomy	Solidarity, protection of the vulnerable, community values

This is of necessity schematic. However, the basic point, as emphasised by Unger, is that the possibility is present in law to argue a case as falling under the rule (*pacta sunt servanda*) or the exception (doctrine of duress, undue influence, unreasonable terms, impossibility, unconscionability, protection of good faith and reliance on less formal representations, etc); that this opposition at the level of doctrinal interpretation reflects a deeper opposition of competing principles; and that in that opposition of principles a further deeper and legally irresolvable opposition is in turn played out, between two politically irreconcilable value systems – liberal individualism and socialism. The point is not merely that the law provides a wealth of possibilities for lawyers to argue any case either way, but that in fact our legal system acts both as passive enforcer of private transactions and in a paternalistic, active role as protector of vulnerable parties against economic predators. The law does not contain 'right answers' waiting to be discovered. Instead, the law's oppositions correspond to competing normative visions of human association present within law and that the presence of such clashing perspectives should be discussed openly, not least because the suppressed side of law's oppositions are taken to be the more politically progressive. Thus law is to be taken seriously as a means of effecting radical social transformation.

In subsequent work Unger (1987) has gone even further and spoken of the need to institutionalise further categories of rights, including 'solidarity rights'. Although very little is said about the precise content of these rights, one can assume on the basis of Unger's other writings that the content would be retrieved through playing up princi-ples already present – if suppressed – in existing law. The mechanism and logic of this has been elaborated above. In 'Legal Analysis as Institutional Imagination' (1996) he renewed his call for a 'selective probing of institutions' through the 'dialectical exercise of mapping and criticism'. Unger's suggestion in all of this is for an interpretative method of reasoning that draws on and exploits strategically existing, if latent, institutional possi-bilities. In the case of solidarity rights, reconstruction would proceed from the protection of solidarity in existing law – of contract and delict basically – such as the protection of reliance and the protection of the disadvantaged party, general clauses of good faith and of abuse of rights, and so on, 'by which private law supports communal relations while continuing to represent society as a world of strangers' (Unger 1987b, p 537).

Hugh Collins describes a further model for deploying legal analysis in what he describes as a horizontal rather than the above vertical manner (Collins 1987b). According to the orthodox view of how law functions in society, one can discern broadly three spheres of social life with law applying differently to each. There is the sphere of public life and here our public law provides citizens with robust protection (in the form of civil rights) against the might wielded by the State, and organises the democratic system by guaranteeing political rights. Here the law acknowledges a certain asymmetry in the relations of citizen to State and thus affords the vulnerable party protection and guarantees. The second sphere is that of exchange and work. In this sphere liberal law typically treats parties as equal, providing the language and the categories to sanction their dealings with each other, but remaining neutral in the process. Finally there is the third sphere, the sacrosant private sphere of family and intimacy in which the law intervenes minimally in order to maintain it free of State intervention and secure privacy understood as negative freedom.

There are good, political reasons, claims the CLS movement, why this frozen picture of social life needs to be challenged as maintaining oppression rather than guaranteeing freedom, entrenching advantage rather than opportunity. Family rela-tions, if not put under legal scrutiny, are free to harbour abuse, patriarchal privilege, domestic violence, violation of trust. The sphere of work and exchange is emphatic-ally not a sphere where equal parties strike their deals, but instead where corporate giants manipulate individual workers and where economic predators prey on vulner-abilities of contractual partners.

Unger's agenda for radical political change to counter advantage uses law to renego-tiate the boundaries between spheres, and manipulate the fragilities and porous nature of those boundaries to stir up social change. More precisely, the horizontal application of 'deviationist doctrine' here, of critical legal doctrine, depends again on tracing the paired opposition of principle and counter-principle within each sphere and arguing the case for treating the counter-principle as significant. What gives particular credence to this argumentative strategy here is that what counts as counter-principle in one sphere is indeed dominant in another. For example: while in the sphere of public life we may have freedom to expose corrupt authority and to associate to pursue our claims, the very same rights are denied in the sphere of exchange. The very same activities draw very different legal responses in this sphere: 'whistle-blowing' is not protected and secondary picketing is criminalised. But the logic of this differential legal response is completely flawed and self-contradictory. The sphere of exchange is not a sphere of equality; corporations act increasingly in corrupt ways and their activities need to be exposed to scrutiny, particularly in an era where there are corporate actors who indeed wield much greater power than even Nation-States do; employees are one of the most vulnerable categories in the face of ruthless new management techniques and the threat of unemployment. So why not use the resources the legal system affords us in the form, here, of the protection of rights, and cross the boundaries between spheres, the autonomy of which is becoming increasingly unconvincing, imaginatively to deploy legal argumentation traditionally incongruent to any particular area of social life?

Unger's work is suggestive and radical, both as to its vision for the possibilities of legal analysis and its careful mapping of the ways in which the logic of law can be deployed to stretch those limits. Against an understanding of law as striving for the right answer on the basis of imputation of the one best principle, like Dworkin, CLS propounds the possibility of political choice through the imputation of 'counter-principle'. Hence the debate between Dworkin and the CLS movement is best understood against a background of political theory. CLS are attempting to feed the possibility of transformative political action into law. If law is indeterminate and has to be 'rationalised' each time, then it is a malleable vessel for political vision. What legal answer we see as appropriate is relevant to our politics. What reason is 'right' depends on our political choice of what political principle underlying it is right. Dworkin's project is motivated by a typically liberal concern to keep law clean of politics. He professes a theory that will elevate choices from the battleground of politics to the legal forum of principle. On Dworkin's account of it, law provides the politically neutral means of mediating between politically competing positions, so that what one perceives as the right answer in law does not necessarily identify with what one conceives to be politically desirable. The CLS movement on the other hand not only views it as impossible to avoid political choices in legal debate, but sees Dworkin's attempt to settle this as itself a political move.

Reading

For Unger's critique of 'formalism' and 'objectivism', see Unger (1983), pp 5–14. For a comprehensive introduction to the emergence of the CLS movement in its various strands, see Kelman (1987). For an accessible summary, see Altman (1993) ch 1.

References

Altman, A, 1993, *Critical Legal Studies*, Berkeley CA: University of California Press.

Bankowski, Z and MacLean, J (eds), 2006, *The Universal and the Particular in Legal Reasoning*, Aldershot: Ashgate.

Bennion, F, 2001, *Understanding Common Law Legislation*, Oxford: Oxford University Press.

Bennion, F, 2002, *Statutory Interpretation*, 4th edn, London: Butterworths.

Christodoulidis, E, 1996, 'The Inertia of Institutional Imagination: A Reply to Roberto Unger', 59 *Modern Law Review* 377.

Christodoulidis, E, 2004, 'End of History Jurisprudence: Dworkin in South Africa', in *Acta Juridica*, 64.

Christodoulidis, E and Finnie, W, 1995, 'How the Ace of Trumps Failed to Win the Trick', *Res Publica* 131.

Collins, H, 1986, *The Law of Contract*, London: Weidenfeld and Nicolson.

Collins, H, 1987a, 'The decline of privacy in private law', 14 *JLS* 91.

Collins, H, 1987b, 'Roberto Unger and the Critical Legal Studies Movement', 14 *JLS* 387.

Cotterrell, R, 2003, *The Politics of Jurisprudence*, 2nd edn, London: Butterworths.

Cross, R, 1995, *Statutory Interpretation*, 5th edn, London: Butterworths.

Cross, R and Harris, JW, 1991, *Precedent in English Law*, 4th edn, Oxford: Clarendon.

Duxbury, N, 1995, *Patterns of American Jurisprudence*, Oxford: Clarendon.

Dworkin, RM, 1977, 'The Model of Rules', extracted in Dworkin (ed), *The Philosophy of Law*, Oxford: Oxford University Press, and expanded in chapters 2 and 3 of *Taking Rights Seriously*, Cambridge, MA: Harvard University Press.

Dworkin, R, 1985, *A Matter of Principle*, Cambridge MA: Harvard University Press.

Dworkin, R, 1986, *Law's Empire*, London: Fontana.

Dworkin, R, 1990, 'Law, Philosophy and Interpretation [the Kobe lecture for Legal and Social Philosophy]', *ARSP* 1.

Dworkin, R, 2000, *Sovereign Virtue*, Cambridge, MA: Harvard University Press.

Dworkin, R, 2006, *Justice in Robes*, Cambridge, MA: Harvard University Press.

Frank, J, 1949a, *Courts on Trial: Myth and Reality in American Justice*, Princeton: Princeton University Press.

Frank, J, 1949b, *Law and the Modern Mind*, London: Stevens.

George, R, 1994 (ed), *Natural Law Theory*, Oxford: Clarendon.

Griffith, JAG, 1977, *The Politics of the Judiciary*, London: Fontana.

Hale, R, 1923, 'Coercion and Distribution in a Supposedly Non-Coercive State', 38 *Pol Sci Q* 470.

Hale, R, 1943, 'Bargaining, Duress, and Economic Liberty', 43 *Col L Rev* 603.

Hart, HLA, 1961, *The Concept of Law*, Oxford: Clarendon.

Hart, HLA, 1983, 'The Legal Nightmare and the Noble Dream', in ch 4 of *Essays in Jurisprudence and Philosophy*, Oxford: Clarendon.

Hayek, FA, 1944, *The Road to Serfdom*, London: Routledge & Kegan Paul.

Holmes, OW, 1897, 'The Path of Law', 10 *Harvard Law Review* 457.

Horwitz, M, 1992, *The Transformation of American Law, 1870–1960: The Crisis of Legal Orthodoxy*, New York: Oxford University Press.

Jackson, B, 1995, *Making Sense in Law*, Liverpool: DC Publications.

Kelman, M, 1987, *A Guide to Critical Legal Studies*, Cambridge, MA: Harvard University Press.

Kelsen, H, 1967/1934, *Pure Theory of Law* (trans Max Knight), Berkeley: University of California Press.

Levi, E, 1948, 'An Introduction to Legal Reasoning', 15 *University of Chicago LR* 501.

Llewellyn, K, 1931, 'Some Realism about Realism', reprinted in Llewellyn, 1962, *Jurisprudence: Realism in Theory and Practice*, Chicago: University of Chicago Press.

MacCormick, N, 1978, *Legal Reasoning and Legal Theory*, Oxford: Clarendon.

MacCormick, N, 1979, 'The Artificial Reason and Judgement of Law', *Rechtstheorie* 105.

MacCormick, N, 1981, *H.L.A. Hart*, London: Arnold.

MacCormick, N, 1989, 'The Ethics of Legalism', *Ratio Juris* 184.

MacCormick, N, 1993, 'Argument and Interpretation in Law', *Ratio Juris* 16.

MacCormick, N, 1994, *Legal Reasoning and Legal Theory*, 2nd edn, Oxford: Clarendon.

MacCormick, N and Summers, R, 1991, *Interpreting Statutes*, Aldershot: Dartmouth.

McLeod, I, 2005, *Legal Method*, 4th edn, Basingstoke: Palgrave Macmillan.

Pound, R, 1960, 'The Causes of Popular Dissatisfaction with the Administration of Justice', reprinted in R Henson (ed), *Landmarks of Law*, New York: Harper.

Rumble, WE, 1968, *American Legal Realism*, Ithaca, New York: Cornell University Press.

Singer, J, 1988, 'Legal Realism Now', 76 *Cal L Rev* 465.

Twining, W, 1984, 'Some Scepticism about Scepticisms', 1 *Journal of Law and Society*, 137–71.

Unger, RM, 1983, *The Critical Legal Studies Movement*, Cambridge, MA: Harvard University Press.

Unger, RM, 1987a, *Social Theory: Its Situation and Its Task*. Vol 1 of *Politics: A Work in Constructive Social Theory*, Cambridge, MA: Cambridge University Press.

Unger, RM, 1987b, *False Necessity: Anti-Necessitarian Social Theory in the Service of Radical Democracy*. Vol 2 of *Politics: A Work in Constructive Social Theory*. Cambridge, MA: Cambridge University Press.

Unger, RM, 1996, 'Legal Analysis as Institutional Imagination', 59 *Modern Law Review* 1.

Yntema, H, 1960, 'American Legal Realism in Retrospect', 14 *V and L Rev* 317.

Cases

Brown v Board of Education 347 US 483 (1954).

Daniels & Daniels v R White & Sons [1938] 4 All ER 258.

Donoghue v Stevenson [1932] UKHL 100.

Grant v Australian Knitting Mills [1936] AC 85.

In re A (Conjoined Twins) [2000] 4 All ER 961.

Lochner v New York 198 US 483 (1905).

MacPherson v Buick 111 NE 1050 (NY 1916).

Riggs v Palmer 115 NY 506 (1889).

Chapter 2

Advanced topics

Chapter Contents

2.1   Justice, natural law and the
      limits of rule-following   149

2.2   Equality, difference and domination:
      feminist critiques of adjudication   154

2.3   Trials, facts and narratives   159

2.4   Judging in an unjust society   168

2.5   Law and deconstruction   174

2.1 Justice, natural law and the limits of rule-following

Moral reason and hard cases

In an important House of Lords judgment on the controversial issue of 'wrongful conception', Lord Steyn made the following remark:

> [J]udges ought to strive to give the real reasons for their decision. It is my firm conviction that where courts of law have denied a remedy for the cost of bringing up an unwanted child the real reasons have been grounds of distributive justice. That is, of course, a moral theory. It may be objected that the House must act like a court of law and not like a court of morals. That would only be partly right. The court must apply positive law. But judges' sense of the moral answer to a question, or the justice of the case, has been one of the great shaping forces of the common law. What may count in a situation of difficulty and uncertainty is not the subjective view of the judge but what he reasonably believes that the ordinary citizen would regard as right.
>
> (*McFarlane and Another v Tayside Health Board* [1999] 4 All ER 961, per Lord Steyn at 977–8)

A debate has long existed in jurisprudence over how best to characterise the role of morality in the practice of law. While some authors (legal positivists) claim there is no necessary connection between law and morality, many others suggest the interplay between law and morality is more complex and nuanced than this suggests. As this issue is particularly vexed in the case of legal reasoning, it demands our attention here. We need to consider whether and how legal reasons and justifications can meaningfully be insulated from moral reasons and justifications, and whether it makes sense to do so; moreover, what is actually at stake in our assessment of these questions? In order to explore these issues, we will focus on another landmark medical law case that has been interpreted by John Finnis, who argues against the legal positivists' position by claiming that the case he discusses exemplifies how legal reasoning is best understood as an instantiation of general practical reason. This is the case of *Airedale National Health Service Trust v Bland.*

Anthony Bland had suffered severe injury in the Hillsborough Stadium disaster. He never recovered consciousness and remained in a persistent vegetative state (PVS). Medical experts judged that he had no prospect of recovery or improvement. The Trust applied for a declaration to remove all of the treatment, including feeding, which was keeping him alive. The House of Lords granted the declaration.

In this case, several stark and central issues of morality are at play. Is the outcome morally justified? Is it justified by the state of the law? And more specifically – is it worse directly to intend someone's death than it is to foresee that his or her death will definitely occur? Is it worse to kill than it is to let die? Are either of these distinctions morally significant? How are we to assess the boundary between life and death? Is quality of life an issue with which the courts should concern themselves in these cases?

The House of Lords struggled with these issues and one question that we might want to ask in this context, revealingly, is whether their quandary was a moral or a legal one or even whether the legal answer they gave was one that was morally acceptable (and vice versa). Witness Lord Browne-Wilkinson's agonising over the decision (quoted in Finnis 1993, p 329):

> The conclusion I have reached will appear to some to be almost irrational. How can it be lawful to allow a patient to die slowly, though painlessly, over a period of weeks from lack of food but unlawful to produce his immediate death by a lethal injection, thus saving his family from yet another ordeal . . .? I find it difficult to find a moral answer to that question. But it is undoubtedly the law.

Why was it 'undoubtedly the law' for the Lords? The position in common law is that a failure to act, an omission that causes the death of a 'stranger' (that is, a person to whom one owes no statutory or contractual obligations) is unlawful where, inter alia, there is a duty of care, as in the case of a doctor–patient relationship. The duty of care demands that doctors act in the best interests of their patients. What Bland established as the juridical position was that discontinuance of life-sustaining measures is a duty of physicians who consider 'invasive' life-sustaining measures to no longer be in the patient's 'best interests'. But is it rational to distinguish between two courses of action – a commission of an act (administering a lethal injection) and an omission of an act (withdrawing nutrition and hydration), both undertaken by the same actor and both undertaken with the same intention of ending the patient's life? Is it not 'morally and intellectually misshapen' (per Lord Mustill) to establish the distinction between murder and duty of care on that basis? And is it rational to argue that it is in someone's 'best interests' to cease to have interests?

John Finnis and the morality of the law

A good way to introduce Finnis's approach is to discuss his opposition to the realist view. Finnis objects to Holmes's aspiration to 'wash with cynical acid' all idealistic fancies about the law, of which, presumably, Finnis's would be one of the more powerful versions. Holmes argued that 'the test of legal principles' is 'the bad man's point of view'. We saw above what the notion of legal duty meant to a 'bad man' for Holmes. 'Mainly, and in the first place, a prophecy that if he does certain things he will be subjected to disagreeable consequences by way of imprisonment or compulsory payment of money.' 'So much' comments Finnis for 'the widest concept which the law contains – the notion of legal duty' (Finnis 1980, pp 322–4).

To argue against Holmes, Finnis takes the example of contract: according to Holmes, 'the duty to keep a contract at common law means a prediction that you must pay damages if you do not keep it, – and nothing else'. More precisely: 'the only universal consequence of a legally binding promise is, that the law makes the promisor pay damages if the promised event does not come to pass. In every case it leaves him free from interference until the time for fulfillment has gone by, and therefore free to break his contract if he chooses' (ibid). For Finnis, this way of viewing it is misconceived. For him, 'the virtually universal legal interpretation of contracts and contractual obligation has its significance as an indication that contracts are upheld by the law for the sake of the common good, which is positively enhanced (i) by the co-ordination of action, and solution of co-ordination problems, made possible by performance of contracts . . . and (ii) by the continued existence of a social practice which actively encourages such fully co-ordinate performance and discourages non-performance. Even without collapsing the clear distinction between law and morals, it is possible to see and say that the law's ambitions are higher than this, and its distinctive schemata of thought quite different' (ibid, p 324). But according to Finnis, Holmes failed to see that contractual obligation, like legal obligation in general, can be explained as the necessity of a type of means uniquely appropriate for attaining a form of good 'otherwise attainable only imperfectly, if at all'. He failed to see that the social importance of law (as of the practice of promising) derives not only from its ability to mould the 'bad man's' practical reasoning, but also 'from its capacity to give all those citizens who are willing to advance the common good precise direc-tions about what they must do if they are to follow the way authoritatively chosen as the common way to that good' (ibid, p 325).

For Finnis, although the law can be seen as a system, it is not from its pedigree that it gets its normativity, but from its function of bringing about the common good. Its normativity comes from the fact that we recognise it as the right thing to do since it instantiates basic values. What are these basic values? Finnis lists seven such values: life, knowledge, play, aesthetic experience, friendship, practical reasonable-ness and religion (Finnis 1980, pp 85–90). All other values and virtues are subordi-nate. They are models of realising or participating in basic goods. The basic goods are goods in themselves. For Finnis, law advances the common good by instantiating the basic goods. Much has been written about his analysis of the basic goods, but this is not the place to visit that discussion. What is more important, for current purposes, is the role of law as providing an instance of practical reasoning and thus an instan-tiation – *a determinatio* – of the goods. This is a difficult idea and we need to unpack some of its components.

On the one hand, legal reasoning, as a form of practical reason, expresses and substantiates the basic goods. Reasonable and sociable beings must recognise their need for community with others as the necessary context for pursuing the good. The creation of a condition in which all members of a community have full opportunity to participate in the good (to use their practical reasonableness in realising other goods) is the realisation of a good shared by all members of the community. Law facilitates this pursuit. A condition of achieving the common good is a concern for justice, and the example of contract, as we have just seen, illustrates this well.

The second thing that has to be remembered in Finnis's analysis is his emphasis that what any healthy community requires is some common authority. Unless we all in common accede to the authority of some common code of conduct we cannot live together in community at all. And the implementation of any common code of conduct requires the institutionalisation of some agency or agencies, which adjudicate upon breaches of the common code. The more complex a political society becomes, the more rich and varied are the opportunities it presents for diverse manifestations of the good. But the more that is so, the more we face problems of co-ordination, each with another. Hence the more sophisticated are the common public agencies we need for adjudication, administration, enforcement and amendment or enrichment of our common and authoritative code of social conduct.

This, finally, links to another significant point about legal reasoning. Finnis employs Aquinas's idea of *determinatio* (as adapted from Aristotle) to express how the very abstract requirements of the good acquire specific form and present us with concrete moral imperatives. The flourishing of life, of knowledge, and so on, as basic goods, is pitched at too abstract a level to give guidance in practical dilemmas, which require the mediation of practical reason and, paradigmatically in this context, of legal reason. As occupying the middle space between what drives human endeavour (common goods) and concrete situations calling for regulation, legal reasoning, for Finnis, establishes itself, necessarily, as a species of practical reason and this, again necessarily, ties it to morality.

Clear analytical thinking, object positivists, demands that we separate the 'is' and the 'ought', questions of what the law is from questions of what it ought to be. Picking up a thread from Aristotle, Finnis rehearses a powerful argument that theorists from Aquinas to Leo Russell have used against the positivist injunction. In Finnis, it takes the form of an argument about 'focal meaning'. He argues his methodological commitments at the beginning of his *Natural Law and Natural Rights* (1980). Every attempt, he says, to define an institution, must elevate certain criteria as significant, and this choice necessarily carries an element of evaluation. Why are these – whatever they might be – the criteria that matter? The 'is' and the 'ought' fuse in a zone of indistinction.

But if analytical clarity is our priority, Finnis would insist, how do the positivist judges in *Bland* purport to seriously maintain the distinction between an ethical response and 'what is undoubtedly the law'? Is it really rational to distinguish between two courses of action (one 'legal', the other 'illegal') that are undertaken by the same actor (the medical profession) with the same intention and having the same result (the termination of Anthony Bland's life) because one is performed through a commission of an act (lethal injection) and the other the omission of an act (starving him to death)? Finnis is of course arguing that a 'basic good', life, should under no rationale – moral or legal – be terminated; we may agree or disagree on the ethics of that. But has he not pointed out in the 'irrationality' of that distinction a certain irrationality of a legal decision – Lord Browne-Wilkinson's 'what is undoubtedly the law' – that is at pains to keep itself pure of ethics, establishing its credentials on what is properly legal?

There are, of course, important counter-arguments to 'natural' law, and these inevitably turn on and into normative questions surrounding legal reasoning. At stake here is the possibility of insulating law from ethics and presenting it as a domain with its proper criteria and methods for reaching outcomes that do not necessarily already engage us in a discussion about ethics. Given the nature of ethical discussions as deeply divisive, indeterminate and subjective, it is no wonder that positivists insist on the need of the 'separation thesis' and advocate its importance for establishing pure, objective and publicly ascertainable legal bases for decisions. It is because the stakes are so high that this discussion matters.

To reflect on this consider the following: in his early work *The Unity of Law and Morality* (1984), another natural lawyer, Michael Detmold, gives us another argument about the 'necessary connection' of law and morality. It gives us a different angle altogether as we close this discussion for now. Imagine, says Detmold, a judge who is passing sentence on a person guilty of treason. Treason has been established beyond reasonable doubt and carries a mandatory death sentence. Our judge believes that the taking of life is wrong under any circumstance. His dilemma whether to pass sentence is an ethical one; over his duty in law he has no choice. He may decide to fulfil his role as a judge and pass sentence because he might decide that the duty to uphold the law outweighs his personal choice, which his conscience dictates. Or he may decide to step down because he cannot bring himself to send a man to his death. Either way, however, the clash between legal and ethical duty is played out on the ethical plateau. No legal reason can transcend the dilemma: it is and remains, irreducibly, ethical, and in that sense the ethical retains its priority over the legal.

Reading

For Finnis's definition of law see (1980) pp 276–90. His methodological stance on the evaluation and description of law, and focal meaning is developed in ch 1 of Finnis (1980). For the full discussion of *Bland*, see Finnis (1993), and for a concise account of the relation of natural law to ethics, see Finnis (1999). Finnis's work has now been collected in a series of five volumes (Finnis 2011). See especially vol IV.

On the positivist/natural law divide that has dominated analytical jurisprudence, see, in particular, Hart in Dworkin (1977) and MacCormick (1984) and others in the volume edited by George (1994).

References

Detmold, M, 1984, *The Unity of Law and Morality*, London: Routledge & Kegan Paul.
Dworkin, R (ed), 1977, *The Philosophy of Law*, Oxford: Oxford University Press.
Finnis, J, 1980, *Natural Law and Natural Rights*, Oxford: Clarendon.
Finnis, J, 1993, 'Bland: Crossing the Rubicon', 109 *LQR* 329.
Finnis, J, 1999, 'Natural Law and the Ethics of Discourse', 12 *Ratio Juris* 354.
Finnis, J, 2011, *The Collected Essays of John Finnis*, vols I–V, Oxford: Oxford University Press.
George, R (ed), 1994, *Natural Law Theory*, Oxford: Clarendon.
MacCormick, DN, 1994, 'On the Separation of Law and Morality', in R George (ed), *Natural Law Theory*, Oxford: Clarendon.

Cases

Airedale National Health Service Trust v Bland [1993] 2 WLR 316.
McFarlane and Another v Tayside Health Board [1999] 4 All ER 961.

2.2 Equality, difference and domination: feminist critiques of adjudication

Initial challenges

Some of the most consistently challenging critiques of legal reasoning over the last few decades have come from feminist writers. These critiques are inspired not just by academic analysis, but by an understanding of the very real and detrimental effects of law and its reasoning processes on women's lives. The history of law in Westernised societies is the history of laws written by men. It would not be at all surprising, then, that women's voices and status have been excluded or denigrated, and that processes of legal reasoning have been profoundly implicated in this. While there is a range of divergent positions within feminist analysis, certain strands have emerged that may be considered as critiques – on the one hand of the substance of law, and on the other of the form of law itself.

For many feminist writers, notably those writing earlier in the feminist tradition, the aim was to establish formal legal equality between men and women as a matter of the substantive content of the law. Such work inspired – and continues to inspire – much thinking behind anti-discrimination legislation and its application, whose intention is to ensure that men and women have formally equal standing and rights in law. Prominently, for example, in the arena of employment law, women struggled to establish the principle of equal pay for equal work and equal access to employment opportunities, pensions, and so on, which could be established in legislation that enshrined the universal principle of non-discrimination on the basis of sex. From this perspective, laws that directly discriminated against women undermined equality under the rule of law. If law's self-image valorised its fairness and impartiality, then those same standards demanded that men and women be treated equally in the eyes of the law. In other words, the principle of formal equality among all citizens should be given full, not partial, effect. Sometimes referred to as 'liberal feminism', this approach argued that women's freedom to participate as equals in society meant holding law to its self-professed standards. Hence already-existing principles of law and legal reasoning could be used to develop full and equal rights for women, in both legislation and adjudication.

This belief in the law's ability to include women, where once they had been excluded, came to be seen as having a number of shortcomings. That is, despite claims to formal equality having been heard, legal interpretation nonetheless still drew on a male perspective in the definition or application of general categories. On this account, the interpretation of equal rights or standards contained within them biases that meant women continued to be discriminated against. So, for example, with regard to the criminal law defences of provocation or self-defence, the application of the relevant law to cases that did not fit the (masculine) image of an immediate retaliation worked to exclude situations where women responded to male abuse over a long period of time. And, in anti-discrimination law itself, women, in order to find an appropriate comparator against which the question of discrimination could be addressed, had always to compare themselves to a man in the equivalent situation. Hidden here was that the male standard was always assumed to be the norm, and it was deviation from that which was written through the law's assumptions about equality. The general point here is summed up by Naffine (1990, pp 136–7): 'while the law may appear to offer roughly equal rights to men and women, in truth the law organises around a particular individual who is both male and masculine. The legal person is still very much a man, not a woman, and the law still reserves another place for women: as the other of the man of law.'

Conventional techniques of legal reasoning meant that even where equality was announced in law, the question 'Equal to what?' tended to be answered by treating male standards as the unproblematised and universal ones. As Naffine (p 144) continues, the underlying question was really this: 'Why can't a woman be more like a man?' In deciding what aspects of the broader social understandings of roles, relationships and expectations were highlighted or downplayed, judges (who are overwhelmingly male) filled in, more or less consciously, the content of abstract legal categories such as legal personality or formal equality by importing male assumptions of these to inform the law's response, while simultaneously legitimating them as expressing equality. In so doing, women's experiences were devalued, or failed to register, in giving content to the law.

Critiquing the *form* of legal reasoning

These insights raised deeper problems with the liberal feminist approach, which went to the very form of law and legal reasoning itself. The values associated with the formalist position – objectivity, neutrality, universality, formal justice – have all been subjected to criticism by feminist authors. Why would these values be seen as such a cause for concern? The essence of the argument is that while these values purport to treat people equally, they nonetheless operate to do precisely the opposite. There are two kinds of arguments here.

The first is that the very idea of trying to be objective, impartial, neutral, and so on, in fact embodies a male perspective on social relations. There are two divergent interpretations of how this impacts on legal reasoning. One argues that men and women have different styles of reasoning. Drawing on analyses of moral reasoning, psychologist Carol Gilligan (1982) found that men tended to emphasise abstract, individualistic and universal or rule-driven approaches to moral problems, while women emphasised connectedness and more particularised or contextualised reasoning. The former she associated with an ethic of justice, the latter with an ethic of care. Moreover, Gilligan noted, the 'justice' style of reasoning was traditionally seen as more 'developed' or 'advanced', and hence the notions of objectivity and impartiality given priority, ahead of those associated with 'care'. Thought of in the legal context, it might be seen that the values of legal formalism replicate such a hierarchy, and in so doing implicitly embody a more male-centred account of what is deemed the most appropriate, 'just', way of approaching legal interpretation. In all this, women's essential experiences could be downplayed, and their 'different voices' excluded from processes of understanding and reasoning.

Such an interpretation has been widely criticised with regard to law and social relations generally. According to Catharine MacKinnon, a feminist legal author, this approach 'essentialises' what is really a matter of contingent power between the sexes, not one of natural differences. Caring, suggests MacKinnon, is just what men want women to do. Rather, she argues, it is not difference but dominance that explains sexual relations in contemporary society. While, as we have seen, treating men and women equally means using the male as comparison, different treatment, she argues, is not the result of real differences, but of domination through social practices writ large. Moreover, where exceptions have been made in attempts to recognise 'difference', these are open to the charge of further entrenching male stereotypes and power. Thus even where supposedly well-intentioned judges sought to protect women's differences, 'as a result of their very womanhood', the results could be a form of paternalism that undermined any putative freedom. MacKinnon gives a particularly graphic example of this: where a court decided that it was legitimate to exclude women from a contact job in an all-male prison because they might be raped by inmates, MacKinnon suggests the court took 'the viewpoint of the reasonable rapist on women's employment opportunities' (1989, p 226).

MacKinnon's critique is that the values associated with legal formalism – objectivity, neutrality, impartiality – are themselves suspect since they constitute the basic ways of organising social power to the detriment of women. Central to these are the State – its legislative and adjudication processes – and the doctrine of the rule of law itself when thought of in these terms: 'The state is male in the feminist sense: the law sees and treats women the way men see and treat women. The liberal state coercively and authoritatively constitutes the social order in the interests of men – through its legitimating norms, forms, relation to society, and substantive policies' (ibid, pp 161–2). The notion of objectivity, for example, so central to the formalist account, does the work in fact of objectifying – that is, turning into objects – women. Hence for MacKinnon, 'Formally the state is male in that its objectivity is its norm . . . The state is male jurisprudentially in that it adopts the standpoint of male power on the relation between law and society' (ibid, pp 162–3).

As such, understandings of legal interpretation must pay more attention to the form of law, and not just its substantive content; or, rather, it must pay attention to the way in which the power of law's form operates to determine its content. And this is true across the whole range of legal regulation: as Finley argues, 'Legal reasoning and its language are patriarchal . . . Privileged white men are the norm for equality law; they are the norm for assessing the reasonable person in tort law; the way men would react is the norm for self-defense law; and the male worker is the prototype for labor law' (Finley 1989, p 893). It is significant that Finley emphasises the linguistic element in legal reasoning since it shows up both the power of language to normalise social relations of inequality, but also, importantly, its limits; that is, that merely changing to non-sexist language in the law – the reasonable person, rather than the reasonable man in negligence, for example – will not necessarily lead to gender equality where underlying structures of inequality remain unaddressed. It is these observations that point to the intimate links between legal language, formalist values and social domination. As Finley puts it: 'Universal and objective thinking is male language because intellectually, economically, and politically privileged men have had the power to ignore other perspectives and thus to come to think of their situation as the norm, their reality as reality, and their views as objective. Disempowered, marginalized groups are far less likely to mistake their situation, experience, and views as universal' (ibid, pp 893–4).

Questions remain however, about the extent to which it is persuasive to treat all women's experience as uniform, and whether such accounts tend to downplay other social dynamics such as race, class or culture, across which women's experiences may differ greatly (Fraser 1995, pp 68–93).

Comparing approaches

Let us return to some of the aspects of legal reasoning as identified by MacCormick, earlier, and consider them now in the context of feminist critiques (see above, Part II 1.2.3). It will be recalled that MacCormick considered three central problems associated with legal reasoning: those of relevancy, interpretation and classification. Now, each of these is open to evaluation according to different ways of thinking about how gender bias may be involved.

First, relevancy: what is the relevant legal rule? This is one of the key areas in which contestation has occurred. Let us take one example: the question of whether the principle of equal pay for equal work should apply to domestic labour – labour that continues to be carried out predominantly by women. By excluding such work from being recognised within the field of paid employment (and hence attracting the benefits or obligations that may go with it), women's work is devalued in line with what Fraser (1995, p 78) sees more generally as a gendered social hierarchy: gender, she writes, 'structures the fundamental division of labour between paid "productive" labour and unpaid "reproductive" labour, assigning women primary responsibility for the latter'. When considered in addition to discrimination existing across the field of paid employment itself, the result, she concludes, 'is a political-economic structure that generates gender-specific modes of exploitation, marginalisation, and deprivation' (ibid). At this most basic level – the production and reproduction of social goods – the question of relevancy clearly plays a crucial role in being able to recognise and respond to – or, as is more often the case, failing to recognise and respond to – the structured injustices of contemporary gender relations. Establishing the 'relevancy' of a particular law to a particular harm is therefore a crucial way of asserting the applicability of hitherto ignored claims.

Interpretation refers to the problem: given there is a relevant legal rule, how should it be interpreted? Again, here we encounter a whole range of interpretative matters, which can be opened to challenge by feminist encounters with the law. In particular, we might note how certain binary oppositions (or 'dualisms'; see Olsen 1990) operate to construct and naturalise the assumptions within which interpretation takes place. The distinction between public and private is one such opposition, and has a substantial history in legal thought and feminist critiques of it. Here, it has been argued, much of women's experience has been traditionally placed in the 'private' realm into which general legal norms have been only reluctantly applied in order, in theory, that the State respect as fully as possible the autonomy of individuals in their private lives. The effect of this, however, is often to normalise the violence or abuse that may occur in the domestic setting, actions that again impact primarily on women and which would be less likely to be countenanced if they happened 'publicly'. As Lacey points out:

> the practical consequence of non-regulation is the consolidation of the status quo: the de facto support of pre-existing power relations and distributions of goods within the 'private' sphere . . . the ideology of the public/private dichotomy allows

> government to clean its hands of any responsibility for the state of the 'private' world and depoliticises the disadvantages which inevitably spill over the alleged divide by affecting the position of the 'privately' disadvantaged in the 'public' world.
>
> (Lacey 1998, p 77)

Although challenging this distinction has been fruitful in raising consciousness – according to the slogan 'the personal is political' – and exposing the failures of legal interpretation to live up to its professed standards, it has also been seen more recently as being descriptively inaccurate and normatively questionable. As legal norms – such as in family or social security law – increasingly regulate or intervene in areas traditionally seen as private, the distinction between the two becomes less clear. Moreover, as Lacey points out, there is an important difference between saying that the 'private' realm should be repoliticised, and that it should be legally regulated. Yet despite this, the language and stereotypical associations of the public/private distinction may still operate in an ideological way. Lacey's analysis shows how generally, as well as in the context of legal interpretation, 'what happens in this kind of rhetoric is that the labels "public" and "private" are used in question-begging ways which suppress the normative arguments which they actually presuppose. This means that the debate sounds commonsensical rather than politically controversial' (Lacey 1998, p 78). It is the importance of that last observation – that what appears as 'common sense' in legal reasoning is itself the result of contingent political victories – that holds the key to understanding the importance of conflicts over interpretation, especially to the extent that these are involved in continuing sexual discrimination.

Finally, classification refers to whether or not the case can be properly classified under the relevant legal rule. One of the most controversial examples of this concerns the debate over pornography. Should pornography be classified as an actionable harm perpetrated by men against women, or rather as an exercise in free speech or expression and thus be protected by the law? As MacKinnon puts it, 'as a social process and as a form of "speech", pornography amounts to terrorism and promotes not freedom but silence. It promotes freedom for men and enslavement and silence for women' (MacKinnon 1987, pp 129–30). The classification of it under the protection of free speech laws merely confirms her observation that the State and its laws are complicit in the reproduction of domination and sexual violence against women. Contrarily, it has been argued that the rights to freedom of speech and expression should be held as paramount, policed only and at the fringes, by obscenity laws. Here, problems of classification clearly refer not to some internal logic of the law or working through of the law's principles, but to how we should understand harm in the context of expressions or violations of sexuality and the extent to which objective, neutral, or impartial accounts of this are possible or indeed desirable, since the very assumptions they make may be part of the problem.

In all these examples, it is clear that attention needs to be paid to the ways in which interpretative leeway and/or the claimed 'naturalness', impartiality or objectivity of legal reasoning may operate to obscure and legitimise gender divisions in the law. This may be referred to as part of the law's ideological role. But it should not be inferred from this that such interpretive leeway is either haphazard, or that its assumptions are set in stone. Rather, the types of arguments presented here suggest that gender discrimination is more or less clearly patterned, that legal categories and interpretive modes of reasoning are implicated in this, but that these forms of exploitation can, and should, be challenged through more creative forms of legal intervention.

Reading

Several of the important statements are set out in the references below. For a general overview, Olsen (1995) provides a helpful starting point. For an interesting collection of feminist engagements with the law see Munro and Stychin (2007). Important studies are being carried out across a variety of branches of law, for example, Buss and Manji (2005) and Cowan and Hunter (2007).

Hunter *et al*, 2010, provide an innovative recent engagement with legal doctrine.

References

Buss, D and Manji, A (eds), 2005, *International Law: Modern Feminist Approaches*, Oxford: Hart.

Cowan, S and Hunter, R (eds), 2007, *Choice and Consent: Feminist Engagements with Law and Subjectivity*, London: Routledge-Cavendish.

Finley, L, 1989, 'Breaking Women's Silence in Law: The Dilemma of the Gendered Nature of Legal Reasoning', 64 *Notre Dame LR* 886.

Fraser, N, 1995, 'From Redistribution to Recognition? Dilemmas of Justice in a "Post-Socialist" Age', 212 *New Left Review* 63.

Gilligan, C, 1982, *In a Different Voice*, Cambridge, MA: Harvard University Press.

Hunter, R, McGlynn, C and Rackley, E (eds), 2010, *Feminist Judgments: from Theory to Practice*, Oxford: Hart.

Lacey, N, 1998, *Unspeakable Subjects: Feminist Essays in Legal and Social Theory*, Oxford: Hart.

MacKinnon, CA, 1987, *Feminism Unmodified: Discourses on Life and Law*, Cambridge, MA: Harvard University Press.

MacKinnon, CA, 1989, *Toward a Feminist Theory of the State*, Cambridge, MA: Harvard University Press.

Munro, V, and Stychin, C (eds), 2007, *Sexuality and the Law: Feminist Engagements*, London: Routledge-Cavendish.

Naffine, N, 1990, *Law and the Sexes*, London and Sydney: Allen & Unwin.

Olsen, F, 1990, 'Feminism and Critical Legal Theory: An American Perspective', 18 *International Journal of the Sociology of Law* 199–215.

Olsen, F, 1995, *Feminist Legal Theory: Foundations and Outlooks*, New York: New York University Press.

2.3 Trials, facts and narratives

The legacy of fact-scepticism

We saw earlier when discussing the American Legal Realists, that one of the main preoccupations of those we called 'fact sceptics' was to argue that the usual critique of law concentrated on a very limited aspect of the law-in-action, whereas most cases were decided on their facts. Jerome Frank, for one, pointed to the likelihood that the facts as found by judge and jury did not correspond to actual facts. While a number of writers had already pointed out that 'the personal bent of the judge' affects his decisions, this was seen as a factor only in the selection of new rules for unprovided cases. This, for Frank, is only a small part of the story. In his own words:

> In a profound sense the unique circumstances of almost any case make it an 'unprovided case' where no well-established rule authoritatively compels a given result. The uniqueness of the facts and of the judge's reaction thereto is often concealed because the judge so states the facts that they appear to call for the application of a settled rule. But that concealment does not mean that the judge's personal bent has been inoperative or that his emotive experience is simple and reducible.
>
> (Frank 1970, p 162)

We saw earlier that much of Frank's scepticism revolved around what could be called the psychology of fact-finding. Witnesses' observations and memory may be extremely hazy, but they will be pressed to produce clear and confident statements in court. Pre-trial interviews with lawyers may even amount to a form of witness-coaching in which the witness gets an idea of which version of the facts would best suit prosecution or defence stories. Then, under cross-examination, they will be subject to many techniques of discrediting. Jackson examines in some detail the two-tier processes whereby witnesses attempt to make sense of what they say and courts and jurors attempt to make sense of the witness's act of testifying (1995, pp 357–62). Processes of perception are involved in eyewitness testimony, memory and recall, identification evidence, confession and expert statements. In all this, 'to observe a witness testifying in Court is not merely to make sense of what is said . . . The role of the lawyers is not limited to questioning the witnesses; they also initiate and frame the narrative in their opening and closing statements and provide a running commentary of the acceptability of the performance of the witnesses' (1995, p 15). In fact cross-examination serves as much to reveal as to obscure the 'truth'. One of the prevailing images of our age is that of Milosevic at The Hague, aggressively examining one of the survivors of the atrocious act of ethnic cleansing at Srebrenica to the point at which the witness broke down and was unable to recall the details of his aggressors' actions. The pattern has been repeated in numerous political and other trials.

By the end of this process, which began in uncertainty in the first place, we may be many degrees from the truth. In jury trials these psychological problems are compounded by the jury's complex perception and reaction to the facts as narrated. But it is not just witnesses and juries that Frank has in mind:

> Of the many things which have been said of the mystery of the judicial process, the most salient is that decision is reached after an emotive experience in which principles and logic play only a secondary part. The function of juristic logic and the principles which it employs seems to be like that of language, to describe the event which has already transpired. These considerations must reveal to us the impotence of general principle to control decision . . . The reason why the general principle cannot control is because it cannot inform . . . It is obvious that when we have observed a recurrent phenomenon in the decisions of the courts, we may

appropriately express the classification in a rule. But the rule will be only a mnemonic device, a useful but hollow diagram of what has been. It will be intelligible only if we relive the experience of the classifier.

(Frank 1970, pp 159–60)

What Frank is stressing here is the subjective and active character of decision-making that only ex post facto is vested in terms of classification and rule-following. This says a great deal about the articulation of rule and fact, though perhaps what Frank is mostly concerned with is the active character of the intervention that is the decision. And to counter such psychological instabilities of truth-finding, Frank called upon the expertise of psychology itself. Experts could be brought in to examine witnesses for the accuracy of their perceptual apparatus and their propensity to lie (with reference to reliability and credibility). Juries should be abolished altogether but, failing that, there should be training in jury duties at school, and jury experts to accompany and advise the jury in the court.

More crucially, Frank's argument is not just about psychological reactions and human fallibility. Rather, the unreliability of fact-finding is a direct result of the institutional process of fact-finding itself. For him, the very rules of proof and procedure are antithetical to truth. The whole trial process, as developed over the centuries, is less a unified, scientific and rational method of getting at the truth and far more an archaeological site where successive systems have all left their traces. Archaic legal forms jostle with slightly less archaic forms. Frank focuses primarily on the adversarial process, which he likened to a trial by combat with each side's champions trying to do down the others – a 'fight' method of proof. While this may have made sense in the past, when we believed that God was on the side of justice and truth, it is not appropriate to the age of secular rationalism. The jury is thus an archaic element whose original task was not to judge facts and individuals they had never come across before, but to deal with a fellow member of the community.

Other writers have made related points. Weber described methods of proof by combat, ordeal and oracle as formally irrational – there was no logical connection between the facts and the outcome (means–end). Substantive irrationality was found in systems of 'khadi' justice typical of traditionalism, individualised decisions pronounced with the wisdom of Solomon or the common-law magistrate (see Part III). For Weber, such formal and substantive irrational elements still persisted particularly in the lower courts. Britain had developed what he saw as a 'two-tier' system of justice, legal and rational at the higher level where the powerful (notably capitalists) were seeking to find clear and predictable rules for commercial dealings, yet irrational and summary where the less powerful (notably workers) had their crimes assessed. Other writers have described the Roman-canon system, which replaced trial-by-combat-and-ordeal with elaborate rules of evidence (and confession as the centrepiece), maintaining a horror of circumstantial and hearsay evidence and a grading of witnesses by their status credibility. On the Continent at least, the use of torture was seen as a small price to pay for the certainty of confession: in replacing absolute divine knowledge with human sources, only the highest standards were acceptable. Modern methods of extracting confessions from suspects, and ranking the credibility of witnesses (the doctor the highest, the unchaste woman the lowest), show that the past is far from superseded. In fact the use of torture has reappeared on the agenda in the context of the West's waging the so-called 'war' on terror. The use of torture in practice (typically the West's practice of 'extraordinary rendition') and the discussion over its 'justifiability' in theory have made a spectacular, and spectacularly alarming, reappearance in the last few years.

As we have become more willing to accept inferences and indirect human knowledge, we have also increased the number of protections against error and injustice by introducing strong corroboration rules (especially in Scotland) and exclusionary rules concerning admissibility of evidence, for example, of bad disposition, and so on. Of course for Frank, as for Bentham in the nineteenth century, this series of reforms, undertaken in the very name of fairness and rationality, merely compounds the problem. The whole lot should be swept away in the name of modern scientific rationalism. Such protections could be abolished, he said, if the remnants of the archaic past were totally eliminated and we adopted an inquisitorial system of free proof in which the judge was an investigating magistrate and the jury was no more. Frank's inquisitorial system would include better training of legal officials, impartial government officials to dig up all the facts, specialisation of judges and State administrators to deal with the complex facts of modern society, and increasing use of expert witnesses.

It may well be that today Frank's belief in the value of scientific expertise, free proof and the managerial legal official may seem naive, costly and politically worrying. But Frank's basic points have had considerable influence in disturbing the formalist presumption that 'law' divides neatly from 'facts' and that the jury can easily master them. The incorporation of facts in narratives, the possible limitations of legal procedures, the intelligibility of legal language, the aspiration that the courtroom may function as the forum for the establishment of the truth and of genuine communicative exchange, are all deeply contested issues in legal theory. It is to these issues, also at the core of legal reasoning, that we now turn.

Trials and perceptions of fact: language and narrative in the courtroom

The law of evidence provides the structure within which facts may be 'found' and established as legally relevant. There is of course much that is filtered out in the process. There are rules about the admissibility of evidence, ruling out evidence that is unreliable because, for example, it is 'hearsay', and there are rules about the criteria for the allocation of the burden of truth and the threshold – 'beyond reasonable doubt' – that establish what has to be proven as true. Judgments as to whether something counts as relevant or as to whether the case has been proven occur 'within this outline structure', as Jackson (1995, pp 390ff) characterises it, and at the point where that judgment must be made, 'common sense' is called to complement 'legal sense', judges often explicitly instructing juries to use it. At that point of confluence of the two, of 'legal' and 'common-sense' construction of meaning, neat analytical distinctions become blurred in practice. Inferences and intuitive judgements come to play a crucial role in the reconstruction of the story and it is different criteria from those stipulated in the rules of evidence that take centre stage.

In his important work in legal semiotics, Jackson (1988, 1995) surveys linguistic, semiotic and psychological accounts of sense construction in some depth. For present purposes it suffices to raise only a few of the basic arguments, in each case stressing the constructive – rather than given – elements in the perception of facts and of how that perception is translated in enunciation in the courtroom. Semiotics alerts us to the dimension of 'signification' – how meanings are constructed within contexts of interaction. Indicatively:

> Judgements as to the truth of the evidence of witnesses, made by jurors who have no direct or personal knowledge of the events, is based in part on the plausibility and coherence of the stories told by the witnesses: such plausibility is a function of the relative similarity of the rival accounts to narrative typifications of action already internalised by the jurors.
>
> (Jackson 1995, p 392)

What are these 'typifications' and in what sense do they determine perception and allow selective communicability? Let us take a step back here to look at the kind of stock narratives or stock stories, which, as ordering structures, allow us to rationalise or make sense of how things 'hang together', as it were, as meaningful wholes. In *Rethinking Criminal Law* (1978) Fletcher made use of the term 'collective images', which serve as a kind of 'paradigm': the collective image for an offence against property is the 'thief', and 'collective image' of the thief is the nocturnal burglar. These paradigmatic images collect and orient understanding and allow also a certain sharing of understandings (hence 'selective communicability' above). The crucial thing, of course, is that all collective images are temporally and culturally contingent, and, even where those contingencies are shared, often class-specific. This may explain why jurors will be more attuned to picking out certain elements of a situation before them on this basis. This may explain why certain forms of offences against property in their eyes are 'privileged' (housebreaks) and others command lesser 'fit' (forms of fraud), why jurors may be keener to see certain offences punished more than others in the sense that they feel more vulnerable to them (to breaking and entering, for example, rather than fraudulent undertakings in financial circles), or, in extreme cases – like the jury in the Rodney King trial in which a community of peers acquitted police officers for a grave assault on a black man in the aftermath of the violent riots in Los Angeles – why they are willing to leave offences unpunished. Collective images, obviously, while allowing selective understanding, carry tacit evaluations. Jackson's notion of action typifications can be understood on the same continuum: they provide the necessary and sufficient conditions for recognition of fact situations; they allow recognition of what lies within and what outside the situation; they come laden with evaluation; and they are relative to 'semiotic groups', whether these are determined along class, professional, cultural or other social lines (1995, pp 141–63, and for the discussion of examples, pp 163ff). Knowledge is not conveyed in some 'unmediated' way, but through the narration and behaviour of those who present the case in court. We add 'behaviour' here because signification and meaning are not of course limited to what is said, but to a wealth of other factors (body language, signs of sincerity, reliability, nervousness, pace, etc) to which we attach meaning. Going back to our discussion of truth-telling, these images, typifications, 'frames', 'schemas', or whatever we want to call the narrative frames that 'collect' sense-data as information for us, determine the ways in which we decide who is telling the truth, when and under what circumstances.

In their pioneering early work on narratives in the courtroom, Bennett and Feldman analyse the form of stories in terms of central (a 'setting-concern-resolution' sequence) and peripheral action. Battles in court are about who can define the central action successfully and – they claim – success in this matter depends on:

- narrative strategies by prosecution and defence (definitional, inferential and validational; defence also uses challenge, redefinition and reconstruction as rhetorical strategies);
- the cognitive and social functions stories play in everyday life in organising complex information and codifying normative value. Apart from being used in 'narrativising' practices, juries also have stock stories that prosecution or defence may appeal to. Stories thus mediate between law and social life.

Thus, unlike MacCormick for example, they see social bias as a potential element in constructing narrative coherence – but this is no crudely realist account of prejudice distorting law from the outside (for example, gut reactions to individuals on the basis of class, race, sex and stereotypes). Rather, bias is structured into stories in terms of 'plausible' action.

Bennett and Feldman also look at another important aspect – *narration* – the way the story is told, particularly the success of witnesses in getting 'their' story across. They draw here on the work of sociolinguistics. From Bernstein (1971), they take the distinction between elaborated codes used in (middle class) formal languages and the restricted codes of (working class) public language. Elaborated codes involve many abstract terms with defined meanings and alternative words to convey and explain; the object of discussion is clearly specified (context-independent). Elaborated codes are thus more mobile in that everything in principle can be explained and defined. They are also more inner-oriented and individualistic. Restricted codes are seen as closed, inflexible and context-bound because they have a fixed vocabulary where knowledge of meanings often depends upon being a member of a particular group (for example, slang) and hence use of this code is also status-oriented. Supposedly, the language used in court by legal professionals is an elaborated middle-class code and working-class witnesses are therefore disadvantaged ('linguistically incompetent') in the courtroom. (But *is* law really an elaborated code? Perhaps a better use of Bernstein would be to see law as a restricted code.) Bennett and Feldman also draw a contrast between 'narrative' and 'fragmented' testimony styles – the extent to which the witness is permitted utterances long enough to constitute an independent narrative string, as against mere responses to questions, and find psychological evidence that the first style is more persuasive and successful.

There lies implicitly, and sometimes explicitly, in these theories of the trial a more radical, philosophical, objection to correspondence theories of truth that presuppose some single truth 'out there' waiting to be discovered, perhaps distorted by story forms and linguistic incompetence. For our writers, it is a naive realism that does not recognise that facts are constructed by and within different discourses and thus do not have an independent status. If witnesses suffer cognitive dissonance between their understanding of the facts and the law's understanding, then this is a clash between legal and everyday discourses. Writers from varied perspectives (and not just relativists and postmodernists) challenge the whole notion that there is a distinction between law and fact, arguing that legal norms already determine what can count as legally relevant and indeed how that fact is defined. However, does this necessarily mean that law is a totally closed-off, sealed system? There still seems some plausibility in the idea that stories in the courtroom are mediating between legal and social discourses. Or, as Jackson argues (1988, pp 94–7), that there may be narrative structures that occur in both: he cites a judgment of Lord Denning's (*Miller v Jackson*) involving cricket and analyses, following Greimas, the story involved in terms of paradigms (community) and oppositions (young/old) and narrative sequence in which tradition is disrupted by newcomers. The narrative involves 'value-laden associations [which] are not legally relevant, yet they are inextricable from the narrative understanding of the situation'.

Trials, regulation and justice

Let us finally, in this section, take a step back from the level of interaction in the courtroom to the function of the trial and look at how the imperatives of State regulation have affected the character of the trial. The question that becomes central from this perspective is this: Is there a growing conflict between the bureaucratic organisational form and due process? For Weber, describing late-nineteenth-century State bureaucracies, there was not a conflict but a fruitful convergence between bureaucratic structure, the spread of formal rationality and the rule of law. These provided a social and administrative guarantee of formal justice and control of the judiciary. The hierarchy of supervision and division of labour was also the most efficient way to handle cases. The uniform and regular application of rules was an effect of the institutional structure. Conversely, however, this guarantee may turn into a threat to the rule of law, for the connection between efficiency and due process is only contingent. If the situation of the administration changes – for example, through increased volume of work – then formal rationality may cease to be the most efficient form of administration. The guarantee has no inherent stability.

Many contemporary analyses of legal administration have thus focused on a general trend towards mechanical regulation and bureaucratic goal displacement. Internal administrative goals conflict with due process. The increasing volume of work and decreasing resources put the legal system under severe pressure to increase productivity or even to maintain level 'throughput' in processing cases – 'conveyor belt justice'. The response is, on the one hand, to increase the pitch of the bureaucratic logic of standardisation where due process has to be observed in the trial and pre-trial decisions and, on the other hand, to seek ways of avoiding contested trials:

1 simplification techniques: no-fault liability; reducing the need to investigate the mental element in crime; standardising sentencing tariffs;
2 diversion techniques: pre-trial and post-trial diversion; decriminalisation; plea-negotiation; substantial shifts in decision-making powers to the 'paralegal' sphere – police, procurators-fiscal, social workers involved in production of social enquiry reports.

Critics argue that legal decision-making thus becomes almost a parody of formalism since legal outcomes will be increasingly uniform and predictable, while leaving the rule of law an empty shell. Legal rationality has no simple protection against this trend since the form of law still remains the 'general application of known [administrative and legal] rules' – the form of the rule of law. Yet simplification techniques mean that crimes and delicts are increasingly put into meaningless categories; for example, the pressure to lose the concept of fault is a major shift away from traditional views of responsibility. Transfer of responsibility to paralegal spheres means decisions are increasingly being made on an extra-legal basis and hence are discretionary in the sense of not being controlled by strictly legal rules. (Their source is no longer internal to law.) Moody and Tombs argue that, in the Scottish prosecution service, this does not mean an increase in individual discretionary powers, but rather an increase in bureaucratic rigidity, control and form-filling, which they characterise as 'extra-legal formalism' and a loss of external accountability.

The second trend associated with the growth of the modern State converges with the first in involving an alleged increase in discretionary powers and a shift away from rights-based law to social management. State bureaucracies have increasingly involved themselves in substantive ethical and policy issues associated with a welfare interventionism. This often involves legal formulations that take an overtly discretionary form, thus requiring judges to bring in open-ended considerations. This expansion of judicial discretion is associated with:

- the increasing abstractness or open-endedness of statutory provisions and standards, whereby inherently discretionary concepts such as 'the best interests of the child' replace fault-based legal actions;
- therapeutic and hence offender-specific calculations in respect of sentencing and the consequent reliance on paralegal judgements of social workers;
- the increase in short-term government-of-the-day policy uses of law – the use of criminal law provisions in industrial disputes, 'football hooliganism', drug abuse, and so on;
- the blurring of the boundaries between broad policy, administrative and narrowly legal aspects of legal administration, in the expansion, for example, of welfare law, or the use of equal opportunities legislation. Judges are increasingly expected to adjudicate in fields of expertise – social and economic policy – that lie outside their competence. Increasing use is made of tribunals and regulatory agencies, such as the Equal Opportunities Commission, that rely on informal procedures. Conciliation procedures are increasingly important in family law.

Weber suggested that the features of law that dominated its liberal era – formality and neutrality – would pervade future development. Neutral rules, thought Weber, were particularly conducive to the workings of bureaucracies and they would persist and expand to new ground without challenge, due to their apparent indispensability to the logic of bureaucratic organisation. While post-liberal law has shifted significantly from legislatures to administration, its form remains what Weber predicted it would remain, formal rational. But that of course is only part of the story. Let us say that between bureaucratisation and welfarism in law there is both a tension and a convergence. Tension because bureaucratic law is rational law, its form that of general abstract rules, while welfarist regulation is substantive, particular and casuistic. Convergence because often welfarist concerns key in with bureaucratic ones, for example, the welfarist shift away from fault (as socially inappropriate) meets with the efficiency demand of bureaucracy, the speedy processing of cases thus far inhibited by the requirement to explore *mens rea*. Other tensions and compatibilities may be traced.

Let us then briefly identify some of these here. First, the 'materialisation' of law marks the tendency towards particularised legislation: the movement towards breaking up the general categories into subcategories towards which law applies differentially. The grand category of the legal person gives way to a specification of categories, and the formal equivalence of the legal subject gives way to a proliferation of different legal statutes: consumer (consumer law), worker/trade union member, employee, welfare recipient, business franchisee. In each case the law addresses the legal subject under that more specific description and there is a move from the formal to the material. But further: natural and artificial persons, grouped together under liberal law become differentiated for specific legal purposes, so that, for example, the privacy of the natural person is protected where that of company is not (access to data, freedom of information). Second, the separation of powers, that other lynchpin of liberal law, is eroded, for example, once courts are called upon to determine whether a government has acted in the public interest; equally, when the legislature delegates responsibility for fixing the terms of what appear as general directives because the executive state machinery has the resources to do the job better. Finally, formal equality is eroded by 'reverse discrimination' or 'affirmative action', that is, a reverse preference to a disadvantaged group becomes institutionalised in law in order to redress existing inequalities.

Reading

See Cotterrell (1992) for a concise account of the changing forms of regulation (pp 161–6). For an in-depth, comprehensive semiotic approach to narrative construction, see Jackson (1995) and generally for the role of narratives in trials, see Burns in Duff *et al* (2004). For an analysis of juries, see Redmayne and Schafer and Weigand in Duff *et al* (2005). On the relationship between truth, standing, participation and due process in the trial, see Duff *et al* (2007).

For one of the most striking examples of the use of cross-examination for political purposes see Bilsky (2001) on the Kastner trial, and Boas (2007) on the Milosevic trial. On the political uses of the courtroom see Koskenniemi (2002) and the classic (though still untranslated into English) Vergès (1968).

References

Bennett, W and Feldman, M, 1981, *Reconstructing Reality in the Courtroom*, New Brunswick: Rutgers University Press.
Bernstein, B, 1971, *Class, Codes and Control*, London: Routledge and Kegan Paul.
Bilsky, L, 2001, 'Justice or Reconciliation? The Politicisation of the Holocaust in the Kastner Trial', in E Christodoulidis and S Veitch (eds), *Lethe's Law*, Oxford: Hart.

Boas, G, 2007, *The Milošević Trial: Lessons for the Conduct of Complex International Criminal Proceedings*, Cambridge: Cambridge University Press.

Cohen, LJ, 1977, *The Probable and the Provable*, Oxford: Clarendon.

Cotterrell, R, 1992, *Sociology of Law*, 2nd edn, London: Butterworths.

Duff, A, Farmer, L, Marshall, S and Tadros, V (eds), 2004/5, *The Trial on Trial*, vols 1 (2004) and 2 (2005), Oxford: Hart.

Duff, A, Farmer, L, Marshall, S and Tadros, V, 2007, *The Theory of the Trial*, Oxford: Hart.

Fletcher, G, 1978, *Rethinking Criminal Law*, Boston: Little, Brown & Co.

Frank, J, 1970, *Law and the Modern Mind*, Gloucester, MA: Peter Smith.

Jackson, B, 1988, *Law, Fact and Narrative Coherence*, Liverpool: DC Publications.

Jackson, B, 1995, *Making Sense in Law*, Liverpool: DC Publications.

Koskenniemi, M, 2002, 'Between Impunity and Show Trials', *Max Planck Yearbook of United Nations Law* 1–35

Moody, S and Tombs, J, 1982, *Prosecution in the Public Interest*, Edinburgh: Scottish Academic Press.

Vergès, J, 1968, *De la Stratégie Judiciare*, Paris: Minuit.

Case

Miller v Jackson [1977] All ER 338.

2.4 Judging in an unjust society

Systematic and profound racial discrimination may occur in societies that are committed to principles of formal equality, democracy and the rule of law. It is necessary to try to understand how the operation of basic principles of conventional legal reasoning may be complicit in this situation by operating to entrench injustices, both of the past and present. Australia provides one such contemporary example, and in this section we will look at the High Court decision in *Mabo v The State of Queensland (No 2)* (1992) (hereafter *Mabo*, paragraph references in parentheses). The *Mabo* decision is important and interesting for many reasons, among which, in the current context, are what it tells us about the very assumptions within which legal reasoning takes place, and about the limits of law in addressing its colonial past and present.

Australia was colonised by the British in 1788. Sovereignty over the territory was claimed under the doctrine of *terra nullius*. According to this doctrine – which means literally 'no man's land' – land that was uninhabited could be acquired for the colonial power – in this instance, technically the British Crown – upon being 'settled'. Of course, the Australian continent was not uninhabited; European 'settlers' encountered the presence of an extensive Aboriginal population and, often, their resistance to invasion. In such instances, however, an 'enlarged' doctrine of *terra nullius* could still be applied by the colonising power, if the following assumption was made: that 'the indigenous inhabitants were not organized in a society that was united permanently for political action' (33). In essence, this involved an assessment by the imperial power, as the Privy Council put it in *In re Southern Rhodesia* in 1919 (quoted in *Mabo*, 38) that, 'Some tribes are so low on the scale of social organization that their usages and conceptions of rights and duties are not to be reconciled with the institutions or the legal ideas of civilized society. Such a gulf cannot be bridged.' In other words, the inhabitants of *terra nullius* and their form of society were seen, from an openly racist understanding, as inferior: as Brennan CJ put it: 'The indigenous people of a settled colony were thus taken to be without laws, without a sovereign and primitive in their social organization' (36).

In *Mabo*, the High Court of Australia was asked to adjudicate a claim on behalf of the Meriam people living on the Murray Islands in the Torres Strait that they had native title to their land, which survived the acquisition of sovereignty by the British Crown. This claim involved the Australian High Court re-evaluating the nature and consequences of this original racist assumption on which Australia was founded, and which had, for over 200 years, denied in law the existence of any such title. As Brennan CJ wrote:

> According to the cases, the common law itself took from indigenous inhabitants any right to occupy their traditional land, exposed them to deprivation of the religious, cultural and economic sustenance which the land provides, vested the land effectively in the control of the Imperial authorities without any right to compensation and made the indigenous inhabitants intruders in their own homes and mendicants for a place to live.
>
> (28)

However, continued Brennan CJ:

> Judged by any civilized standard, such a law is unjust and its claim to be part of the common law to be applied in contemporary Australia must be questioned.
>
> (28)

Accordingly therefore, he saw that there was:

> a choice of legal principle to be made in the present case. This Court can either apply the existing authorities and proceed to inquire whether the Meriam people are higher 'in the scale of social organization' than the Australian Aborigines whose claims were 'utterly disregarded' by the existing authorities or the Court can over-rule the existing authorities, discarding the distinction between inhabited colonies that were terra nullius and those which were not.
>
> (39)

According to Brennan CJ, overruling the precedent cases was necessary since otherwise their authority:

> would destroy the equality of all Australian citizens before the law. The common law of this country would perpetuate injustice if it were to continue to embrace the enlarged notion of terra nullius and to persist in characterizing the indigenous inhabitants of the Australian colonies as people too low in the scale of social organization to be acknowledged as possessing rights and interests in land.
>
> (63)

On the one hand, therefore, Brennan CJ acknowledged that:

> Their [Aboriginal] dispossession underwrote the development of the [Australian] nation.
>
> (82)

On the other, however, he argued that:

> . . . the peace and order of Australian society is built on the legal system.
>
> (29)

and that the court was:

> not free to adopt rules that accord with contemporary notions of justice and human rights if their adoption would fracture the skeleton of principle which gives the body of our law its shape and internal consistency.
>
> (28–29)

In other words, the clash of principles to be adjudicated involved confronting the foundational act that dispossessed Aboriginals of their lands, while simultaneously understanding that that act was the very condition of the ongoing existence of the Australian nation. How then could the racist founding of Australia be dealt with in accordance with contemporary principles of justice and equality when that founding was itself the one which gave the Australian State – and hence the law and the High Court – its authority?

The court's solution to this problem involved making a key distinction between the acquisition of sovereignty and the consequences of that acquisition. The former, it said, is not subject to review by the court; that is, the sovereignty established by the initial act of colonisation is not justiciable in the Australian courts – it is that very sovereignty that gives the court its jurisdiction to hear this case. Were the matter to be justiciable – and the answer given that the act of sovereignty was invalid – then the court would undermine its own authority to make precisely such a decision.

However, it was open to the court to review the consequences of the acquisition of sovereignty. And here was where their interpretative leeway entered. The court decided that although sovereignty had been acquired under the doctrine of *terra nullius*, this did not mean the Crown also acquired 'full beneficial ownership' (that is, a complete property right) to the whole territory. Rather, using a doctrine going back to feudal times, it had only a 'radical' (or ultimate or final) title, according to which it was entitled to grant full property rights under it, even though it did not itself own the land. 'What the Crown acquired was a radical title to land and a sovereign political power over land, the sum of which is not tantamount to absolute ownership of land' (55). Radical title therefore meant the Crown had sovereign jurisdiction to create property rights, but where no grant of ownership rights had been made to another party, then since the Crown did not own the land it was possible for native title to it to continue to exist 'as a burden' on the radical title. It was in this space, so to speak, between radical title and full beneficial ownership that the possibility for a native title claim could exist that survived the British acquisition of sovereignty.

In this way, where native title had not been extinguished by Crown grants of land, it was open for Aboriginal communities to show that their continued association with the land, from the time of colonisation, qualified them as entitled to native title rights on that land, despite the acquisition of sovereignty by the Crown. For the first time then – and overruling precedents to bring Australian law in line with principles of non-discrimination – the common law was able to redress the racist implications of the doctrine of *terra nullius* and recognise native title to land.

We might consider two very different types of interpretation of this ruling. The first is congratulatory, and celebrates the much-vaunted virtues of the flexibility of common-law styles of reasoning. According to one commentator, the decision reflects the virtues – the 'genius' and 'spirit' – of the common law, in its ability to uphold basic standards of human rights and to respond in a pragmatic way to 'social, economic and political considerations' (Bartlett 1993, p 181). It also shows something more fundamental, namely how the law can embody – or fail to embody – fundamental human values. On this view, what the *Mabo* decision offered, for the first time in Australia, was the recognition of a full humanity that had hitherto been denied indigenous people by the law and that had in turn played a role in legitimating a broader social and political racism. Moreover, it was only once this full humanity was properly recognised that the further questions of policies directed towards alleviating the suffering that Aboriginals continued to experience could be addressed. Drawing attention to this distinction, Raimond Gaita wrote:

> Fairness is at issue only when the full human status of those who are protesting their unfair treatment is not disputed . . . The justice done by *Mabo* is deeper than anything that can be captured by concepts of equity as they apply to people's access to goods. It brought indigenous Australians into the constituency within which they could intelligibly press claims about unfair treatment.
>
> (Gaita 1999, pp 81–2)

But there is a contrary view. Kerruish and Purdy (1998) make three important observations. First they note that common-law reasoning involves the application of general principles, chief among which in the *Mabo* decision were equality and formal justice (treating like cases alike). But legal equality, they argue, is intimately connected to the concept of the 'legal person'. It is this idea of modern Western law that provides a key legitimating role insofar as it operates according to the idea of treating persons as 'free and equal subjects of the law's address'. According to Kerruish and Purdy, this freedom has two aspects:

> First they are free (in the sense of stripped) of all their actual characteristics (from names to locations within basic social relations). Second they are supposed to have the capacity for choice or free will. Equality at law inheres in this dual freedom; that is, all those who come before the law are equally stripped of their actual characteristics and equally presumed to be responsible for their own actions.
>
> (Kerruish and Purdy 1998, p 150)

There are two criticisms we might draw from this. First, treating people as equal before the law – referring them to or measuring them by the same standard – is in fact to treat them differently by ignoring characteristics about their identity or the context (in this instance violent colonisation) that might be relevant under some other descriptive or normative standards. Moreover, this operation of formal legal reasoning does not in fact attribute no identity to the legal person; rather it imposes its version as an identity, in fact as the only available identity, against which there is no appeal or recourse. As Aboriginal lawyer Irene Watson noted, the *Mabo* decision 'failed to recognise difference in [the] construction of native title so as to make it fit within a western property paradigm' (Watson 2002, p 257). And this point informs the second criticism: that the idea that those who come before the law are responsible for their own actions is not in fact self-determined, but rather is prescribed and defined by law itself. But to the extent that this misdescribes the historical reality, it does so in a way that nonetheless provides legitimacy for overlooking this fact.

Second, as we have just seen, the sovereignty established by the initial act of colonisation was not justiciable in the Australian courts, because it is that sovereignty that gives the court its very jurisdiction to hear this case. Such apparently watertight logic marks the limitations of the court's power. But the effect of this is, however, that by refusing to engage with the acquisition of sovereignty, the original act of dispossession and its legitimacy based in racist doctrines remains intact as the founding act, not removed. This continuity – that Aboriginal dispossession 'underwrote the development of the nation' – is now legally set in stone, but is legitimated in the present by the claim that the common law is acting in a non-discriminatory manner. Thus *Mabo* in fact whitewashes responsibility for the damage caused by the invasion of Australia since, again in Watson's terms, 'doctrines of state supremacy conjure a magic, which absolves centuries of unlawfulness and violence against indigenous peoples' (ibid, p 265).

Finally, the common-law condition for recognition of native title requiring an ability to demonstrate continuous association with the land since the initial colonisation involved serious drawbacks. Many Aboriginals, because of government policies, had been removed from their traditional lands either to other places or to the cities and towns, which meant that not only would connection with the land be in most cases impossible to show (because of these very colonial practices, but also because, even in those few cases where connection might be shown, the standards of proof required by the common law rely heavily on documentary evidence, which they know to be unavailable because Aboriginal culture was an oral one), but that this very fact of dispossession is now legitimated by the common law's decision in the case. These dispossessed indigenous people are now treated by the law equally as Australian citizens, their dispossession failing to register in law. As Kerruish and Purdy conclude, therefore, 'the Australian common law has now managed to strip those Aboriginal people whose connection with the land has been broken of the identity at law of native inhabitants of Australia. It is a further act of colonisation that compounds dispossession by non-recognition of Aboriginal identity' (1998, p 162, emphasis added).

From these observations, we witness the power of common-law reasoning in legitimating – on the very grounds of equality, freedom, and formal justice – ongoing dispossession and discrimination. This is the power of legal reasoning in a colonial context, even where democratic and non-discriminatory principles are espoused. In other words, while the damage and inequalities that exist in Australia for Aboriginal people are ongoing, the integrity of the common law remains intact.

Thus we might finally reflect on both the power and the limits of modern legal thought, by asking whether and to what extent principles of modern law and legal reasoning (of the type we saw in earlier sections) are able to redress the effects of colonial and deeply discriminatory practices, when these very principles have been and continue to be themselves complicit in the legitimation of these discriminatory practices.

Reading

Brennan CJ's judgement in *Mabo v The State of Queensland (No 2)* is the best starting point for the legal and historical matters raised here. An early symposium on the *Mabo* decision can be found in Bartlett (1993). Ten years on, a critical symposium can be found in 13 *Law & Critique* (2002).

For questions about 'judging in an unjust society' with special reference to Ronald Dworkin's theory of legal reasoning and applied to the context of South Africa, see the special issue of *Acta Juridica* (2004) devoted to that theme. See also Mureinik (1988) for a critique of Dworkin. Also in the context of South Africa see Dyzenhaus (1991) and Abel (2010). For an interesting discussion of the role of the judiciary in Nigeria, see Yusuf (2010), as well as the essays collected in Christodoulidis and Veitch, *Lethe's Law* (2001) and Kritz (1997). Ruti Teitel (1997) is widely regarded as having set the terms of the debate regarding the role of the judiciary in 'transitional justice'.

References

Abel R, 2010, 'Law Under Stress: The Struggle Against Apartheid in South Africa, 1980–94 and the Defense of Legality in the United States after 9/11', 26 *South African Journal on Human Rights* 217.

Bartlett, R, 1993, '*Mabo*: Another Triumph for the Common Law', 15:2 *Sydney Law Review* 178–86.

Christodoulidis, E and Veitch, S (eds), 2001, *Lethe's Law*, Oxford: Hart.

Dyzenhaus, D, 1991, *Hard Cases in Wicked Legal Systems: South African Law in the Perspective of Legal Philosophy*, Oxford: Clarendon.

Gaita, R, 1999, *A Common Humanity*, Melbourne: Text Publishing.

Kerruish, V and Purdy, J, 1998, 'He "Look" Honest, Big White Thief', 4:1 *Law.Text. Culture* 146–71.

Kritz, N (ed), 1997, *Transitional Justice: How Emerging Democracies Reckon with Former Regimes*, 3 vols, Washington: USIP Press.

Mureinik, E, 1988, 'Dworkin and Apartheid', in H Corder (ed), *Law in Social Practice in South Africa*, Cape Town: Juta.

Teitel, R, 1997, 'Transitional Jurisprudence: The Role of Law in Political Transformation,' 106 *Yale LJ* 2009.

Watson, I, 2002, 'Buried Alive', 13 *Law & Critique* 253–69.

Yusuf, H, 2010, *Transitional Justice, Judicial Accountability and the Rule of Law*, London: Routledge.

Case

Mabo v The State of Queensland (No 2) (1992) 175 CLR 1.

2.5 Law and deconstruction

Deconstruction is a mode of philosophical thinking, literary criticism and socio-political critique associated with the work of the French philosopher Jacques Derrida. The *Cardozo Law Review* published a long essay by Derrida in 1990 under the title 'Force of Law: The "Mystical Foundation of Authority" ' (Derrida 1990). Derrida's work had enjoyed the attention of legal scholars long before 'Force of Law' appeared, but the publication of this essay marked the beginning of a period of legal theoretical scholarship during which the work of Derrida received widespread attention among legal theorists, especially in English-speaking countries. This legal theoretical engagement with Derrida's work ranged from strong enthusiasm and endorsement, on the one hand, to serious scepticism, on the other. However one might feel about the reception of deconstruction in legal theory today, a contemporary text book on jurisprudence can hardly claim to be a comprehensive engagement with the prominent trends in this field of scholarship without paying due attention to the implications of deconstruction or Derridean thinking for legal theory.

Thirteen years after the publication of Derrida's essay in the *Cardozo Law Review*, the Italian philosopher Giorgio Agamben published a little book of which the English translation appeared two years later under the title *State of Exception*. In this book he commented on the continuing failure of legal theorists to arrive at some cogent interpretation of the title of Derrida's essay 'Force of Law: "The Mystical Foundation of Authority" ' (Agamben 2005, p 37). Agamben then proceeded to articulate his own understanding of the title of Derrida's essay in which he linked it to states of exception in which the *force of law* is suspended for the sake of maintaining or sustaining the law. Agamben's interpretation of Derrida's essay is forceful and convincing in many respects. Constraints of space preclude an engagement with this interpretation in what follows. Suffice it to observe in this regard Agamben's crucial insight that Derrida's essay and deconstruction in general is concerned with *a state of exception in which the law is observed but not applied* (Agamben 2005, pp 35–40). Why this state of exception concerns *'the foundation of authority'* and why these foundations can be described as *mystical* are questions that Agamben nevertheless addresses only indirectly or implicitly. The engagement with Derrida's essay 'Force of Law' and with his work in general that follows here endeavours to address these questions expressly and directly so as to explain and scrutinise the possible significance of Derridean thinking for legal theory. Derrida's invocation of the mystical foundation of authority in the essay is taken from an observation of Pascal regarding the 'the mystical foundation of law' to which the law cannot be traced without annihilating it (Derrida 1990, pp 938–9). It is this annihilating source or foundation of law that legal theory must come to understand should it wish to respond to Agamben's challenge.

A meaningful engagement with Derrida's work requires considerable background knowledge. It is impossible to come to grips with Derrida's thinking without some understanding of the way core thoughts of those such as Martin Heidegger,

Edmund Husserl, Ferdinand de Saussure, Sigmund Freud, Karl Marx, Friedrich Nietzsche and Emmanuel Levinas impacted on his work. The short engagement with Derrida's thinking that follows here cannot pay attention to all these influences, but some of them will become evident in the course of the discussion. It is instructive, however, to highlight the influence of Heidegger's work on Derrida (arguably by far the strongest of the influences mentioned here). Derrida would take over from Heidegger a critique of Western philosophical thinking as a thinking that invariably and predominantly gives priority to the stable presence of the *existence* (*Being*) of all things (*beings*) at the expense of a regard for the way *existence* concerns the primordial and temporal *emergence* of things from 'origins' or an 'origin' that cannot be described in terms of presence or present existence. *Being*, for Heidegger, 'is', then, the non-present (which is not the same as absent) origin of all things (beings) that eventually become present.

The philosophical disregard for the temporal emergence of all things, argued Heidegger, is the defining characteristic of the long tradition of Western philosophical thinking that, according to him, started with Plato and Aristotle and continued right up to and into Nietzsche's identification of the *will to power* as the source of all things. This whole history of philosophy, he maintained, pivoted on the disregard for the way things are never simply *infinitely present* but the outcome of a *finite event of disclosure*. Heidegger accordingly referred to this long tradition of Western thinking as the history of the *metaphysics of presence* and he presented his own philosophical endeavour as a *destruction* of this metaphysics of infinite presence for the sake of recovering the regard for temporal and finite emergence or disclosure of things that, according to him, was still evidently prevalent among the pre-Socratic Greek philosophers. These essential themes in Heidegger's work emerged from a vast oeuvre to which more specific references are not necessary for present purposes. (For more specific bibliographical references to these thoughts and a more comprehensive engagement with Heidegger's work from a legal theoretical perspective, see Ben-Dor 2007 and Van der Walt 2011.)

Heidegger's selection of the word *destruction* for purposes of recovering the sense for the way things are not simply present and do not simply exist but come to presence and emerge into existence played a crucial role in Derrida's characterisation of his own thinking as *deconstruction*. For Derrida too, *deconstruction* concerned the recovery of the regard for the way things come to presence and are not simply present. It is not only crucial for philosophers and theorists who wish to engage more fully with Derrida's thought to understand this aspect of his thinking incisively. It is also crucial for legal theorists who may only want to engage with Derrida's thoughts about law or the implication of his thinking for law. This is so because the concern with the finite and temporal emergence, as opposed to the stable and infinite presence of existence, goes to the heart of Derrida's thoughts on justice and the law, as will soon become clear.

The emergence of existence, for Derrida, concerns a *textual event*. According to him, dominant texts structure the prevailing forms of consciousness and understanding of an era. Fundamental texts (for instance religious and philosophical works or political documents like constitutions, international treaties, human rights declarations, classic literary works, etc) constrain the variety of present possibilities of human existence and hold them in place. They maintain *the presence* in which any given era of human existence unfolds and proceeds; hence his provocative assertion that 'there is nothing outside the text' that met with much opprobrium among literal-minded philosophers who did not share Derrida's affinity for probing rhetorical phrases that often capture penetrating thoughts more economically and effectively than laborious prose. What Derrida meant by this assertion 'there is nothing outside the text' concerned an insight that would, in the wake of the work of especially Ludwig Wittgenstein, become common cuurency in contemporary theories of language. In contrast to earlier analytical theories of language, which pivoted on the idea that accurate language mirrors and reflects in the human mind a world that is already in place outside the mind, post-Wittgensteinian theories of language, as especially articulated in the work of Donald Davidson, turn on the insight that language does not reflect or refer to a world that exists independently outside language and outside the human mind. Language *constructs* the world in which human beings live. Already in an early work that is still closely associated with the picture, correspondence or reflection theory of language elaborated above, Wittgenstein observed that 'the limits of my language mean the limits of my world' (Wittgenstein 1922, 5.6). There may well be things or obstructions 'out there' against which humans bump into mutely, uncomprehendingly, and often disastrously (violation of human dignity and environmental pollution were surely 'around' for some time before definitive language introduced it into our normative and physical worlds), but these 'things' or 'obstructions' do not become part of the human world until such time as they become integrated into a coherent and comprehensible human environment. And the work of integrating coherent and comprehensible human environments is done by language. Pre-Wittgensteinian legal philosophical sentiments may still want to object that this work of integration is done by human individuals *with the help* of language. In doing so they would be clinging to the idea of language as a mere tool with which the human being's subjective experience of objective reality can be ordered and integrated so as to render it coherent and integrated. They would be suggesting that both the subjective and the objective pillars of the subject–object reality come first and that language comes second. Their suggestion would be that human beings (subjects) first live in the world (objective environment) and then resort to language to make better sense of themselves and their environments. With this suggestion, however, they would be ignoring something that takes place 'right under their noses', so to speak, namely, the way they rely on already available and constraining language to describe the very notion of subjectivity, objectivity and the whole array of linguistic tools with which the former can 'reflect the latter accurately' or 'through which everything can be integrated into a comprehensive and comprehensible whole'. Heidegger had already observed that the human being does not speak. Language speaks; humans only answer to the speaking of language. Humans are not capable of a single or first thought without language making that thought possible in the first place. And one might add: humans are not humans before the articulation of the first thought that language makes possible for them.

One cannot understand Derrida's thought and more specifically his assertion that 'there is nothing outside the text' without due consideration of these developments in twentieth-century philosophy of language and the way this philosophy of language came to understand the human world as *constructed* by language. Derrida's concern with *deconstruction* must be grasped as a concern with the *de-construction* of the world or worlds *constructed* by language. Deconstruction is the textual event under the sway of which new worlds, new possibilities of observation and new modes of assertion become possible. Deconstruction, broadly definable as the picking at the seams of dominant texts that hold existing worlds in place, seeks to solicit the textual event through which new worlds may emerge. It is a picking at the textual seams that sustains present realities in the hope that they may unravel, come apart, and begin to release new ways and new forms of understanding. A regard for this funda-mental point also allows one to grasp a remarkable twist that Derrida's thought would bring about in the development of contemporary theories of language outlined above. Having realised that all words and all linguistic signs are arbitrary denotations that bear no unique, necessary or non-conventional relations to the things they denote, mainstream analytical philosophers of language started to emphasise the *stabil-ising* linguistic practices (conventional rules of grammar, exigencies of contextual coherence, etc) that secure linguistic meaning despite the arbitrariness of linguistic signs. Derrida, quite to the contrary, focused microscopically on the dynamics of language for purposes of discovering and emphasising the *destabilising* potential of this dynamics. What was his motive for doing so?

The answer to this question lies in the concern with the *emergence* or *disclosure* of existence that Derrida took from Heidegger. To get to the point quickly, let us repeat two sentences on which we have already relied above: the emergence of exist-ence, for Derrida, concerns a *textual event*. According to him, dominant texts struc-ture the prevailing forms of consciousness and understanding of an era of history. The concern with the emergence or disclosure of existence can evidently not be or not only be a concern with the stabilising dynamics of the texts that construct prevailing modes of consciousness in any given era or epoch; it is also and predominantly a concern with the ways in which dominant texts of an era or epoch become unstable. Deconstruction is a concern with the way dominant texts of an era become unstable and, thus, susceptible to the inauguration of unprecedented modes of consciousness and understanding. And this points to the second twist that Derrida's thought would bring about in contemporary philosophy of language. Derrida may have underlined and emphasised along with and not against his major contemporaries that the world is constructed through language and that 'there is nothing outside the text' constructed by the dominant language or languages of a particular era of history, but the fact that he was concerned with the deconstruction of the text constructed by dominant languages points to an acute concern with the outside of that text, the *nothing outside* that text. In other words, deconstruction is acutely concerned with that which is *not constructed* by the text, that which is *excluded* from the text.

One might say deconstruction suffered from semantic claustrophobia. It expe-rienced the worlds of readily available linguistic meaning as suffocating. It gasped for a breath of fresh 'meaning' that is not yet contaminated, or not yet fully contami-nated, with the stale air of recirculated linguistic meaning. Provided one does not read into it a suggestion that Derrida returned to a reference theory of language that scrutinised the conditions for accurate referential relations between language in the world, one can risk the following suggestion: in a very surprising and different way (different from referential theories of language), Derrida was much more of a 'realist', much more concerned with some independent 'reality' that exceeds the worlds of linguistic construction, than were most of his contemporaries. Strictly speaking, this 'reality' cannot be named at all. It can hardly be alluded to. This is so because all naming and all allusion take place within language, within the constraints that existing languages impose on knowledge and understanding. The 'reality' at issue here cannot be named from within language and can only be alluded to *indirectly* from within language, because it concerns the very emergence of language that precedes whatever naming or allusion may take place from within established language and established linguistic practices.

Derrida knew the bounds of the metaphysics of presence, the bounds of languages that define things, give meaning to things and render them present as some or other established form of existence, human or animal, animal or vegetative, organic or inorganic, spiritual or material, and so on, that cannot be crossed or transgressed. He was well aware that these are the bounds of the typical binary oppositional ways in which humans constructively understand their worlds. He knew that there is no escape from these bounds. There is nothing beyond the metaphysics of presence. Language allows for no escape and no transgression. He would emphasise this repeatedly throughout his career. And yet, his whole philosophical endeavour obsessively and relentlessly scrutinised possibilities of alluding, at least indirectly or obliquely, to the emergence of language to which no direct allusion is possible. For this purpose his writings experimented, over a period of four decades (starting in the 1960s and ending with his death in 2004), with a number of key concepts such as *différance, trace, supplement, event, coming* (the irreducibly *coming* or *arriving* nature of things), *spectre, hospitality* and *justice*. Let us very briefly look at the first three of these concepts. We return to the last four later.

Derrida's insight into the arbitrariness of linguistic signs was not instilled by Wittgenstein or post-Wittgensteinian philosophy of language, as might well have been the case. It derived from his engagement with the work of structural linguists, especially that of Ferdinand de Saussure. And it is in response to especially De Saussure's work that Derrida would develop the concepts of *différance* and *trace*. De Saussure had already articulated the insight into the lack of any necessary relation between the signifier and the signified, that is, between the linguistic sign and the object or product of its signification. The signified, De Saussure argued, was a product of differential relations between signifiers. It was the outcome of how linguistic signs related to one another. It was not an outcome of any referential relation to any specific signifier. Meaning, argued De Saussure, is the outcome of interaction between signifiers; it was an outcome of interplay between acts of signification. It is against the background of this insight that Derrida would argue that language turns on the dynamics of *différance*. The word *différance* was a neologism (like the word deconstruction, it is no longer is one) with which Derrida denoted the double dynamic of *differentiation* and *postponement*, that is, of *differing* and *deferring*. This dynamic suggested that meaning never enjoys any anchorage in some or other positive and present signifier. The meaning of any present signifier is always the product of its difference from other signifiers (*a* is *a* because it is not *b* and *c*, etc; cat is cat because it is not dog or fish or monkey, etc). As a result of this incircumventible differentiation from other signifiers, the meaning of any one signifier is always deferred or postponed. The meaning of any one signifier only comes to the fore once other signifiers have also been in play. And considering this basic dynamics of interminable differentiation and deferring, argued Derrida, positive meaning is never positively present at any given point in time. Meaning is nothing but the inter-lacing of *traces*.

The remarkable reversal at stake here must be noted. The *trace* is not the lingering remainder of any nodal point or chunk of fully present meaning that happened to have disappeared just recently, as the common understanding of the word 'trace' would suggest. Quite to the contrary, any nodal point of present meaning is nothing but the effect of an interlacing of traces that never were anything but traces. The same dynamic is evident in the phenomenon of the *supplement* and *supplementation*. Close analysis of the practice of constructing texts into main parts and supplements led Derrida to a similar insight into the reversed dynamics between main and supple-mentary parts of texts. To the extent that they are acts of significant or pertinent *supplementation*, supplements *alter* and *re-organise* main bodies of texts. If they do not do this, they serve no real purpose and may just as well be omitted from the text. This again leads to the remarkable insight that textual meaning is the product and result of supplementation. It does not precede the supplement. The supplement becomes the origin which, in turn, has its origin elsewhere. (For Derrida's elabora-tion of these themes, see especially Derrida 1982, 1973, 1978.)

Meaning thus never has any solid purchase in any present reality. It is the product of spectral events of differing, deferring, tracing and supplementation. The concern with *spectres* and *ghosts* and *haunting* would come to mark a later phase of Derrida's thinking and most expressly so in his engagement with Marx (Derrida 1994). He suggested in this regard that philosophy should replace *ontology*, the study of exist-ence, with *hauntology*, the study of ghostly haunts. But his acute regard for the way fully fleshed 'present' realities derive from a spectral play of ghostly realities that defy the categories of both presence and absence, is already abundantly evident in his early engagement with structural linguistics and the notions of différance, trace and supplementation that he developed in these earlier works. The brief engagement with these key concepts in Derrida's early works should nevertheless make clear that the haunting 'reality' with which deconstruction might be said to be concerned does not entail something or *some thing* beyond language. It simply concerns the spec-tral event or events and the primordial or early structuration that sustain language. The deconstructive analysis of this primordial structuration – Derrida also called it *arche-writing* – is the closest that language can move to its ineffable outside, the closest that it can come to saying something about its outer limits without falling into utter incomprehension.

Wittgenstein famously observed that language must remain silent with regard to that which it cannot articulate (Wittgenstein 1922, 7). Considered from this Wittgensteinian position, the outer boundaries or outsides of language fall within this ineffability because language would have to reach beyond itself to articulate the film or membrane of its outer limits. And the moment it would do so, it would no longer be able to articulate anything. Unlike Wittgenstein, or perhaps only in a different way, Derrida nevertheless pressed on with a relentless endeavour to say something about the limits of language, to say the unsayable. As will become clearer in the next paragraph, the linguistic engagement with the unsayable is not as such a Derridean invention. It has been the mark of mystic contemplation and poetry that is as old as language itself, and Wittgenstein, too, was not impervious to this mystic concern with origins that cannot be articulated (Wittgenstein 1922, 6:552: 'There are things indeed that cannot be put into words. They make themselves manifest. They are what is mystical'). And as we shall see in the next paragraph, the mystic concern with ineffable origins can plausibly be said not to be the exclusive inclination of unique individuals. It is plausible to say that language itself posits, alongside the register of clarity and clear communication the register of an irrepressible curiosity regarding the mists and mysteries from which its clarity emerges.

These reflections on language and the deconstructive concerned with the bound-aries of language provide a telling clue to what Derrida may have wanted to express with the title of the essay 'Force of Law: The "Mystical Foundation of Authority"'. We shall presently turn to this essay, but one more observation is important before we do so. Careful readers of everything said above might still want to raise the objection that *someone* is experimenting here; *someone* is picking at the seams of texts; *someone* is intervening to solicit the textual event; *someone* is doing deconstruction and using language or experimenting with language to do so. The old subject–object constel-lation of the metaphysics of presence, in terms of which language is nothing but the tool of a pre-existing subject, is still conspicuously present in all of this. Derrida's reply to this objection would be ambivalent. He would concede that this is correct to the extent that the language of the metaphysics of presence indeed holds us captive and constrains us to repetitions of its essential linguistic schemas. The philosophy of deconstruction, to make its point, also has to resort to language that is largely conven-tional and common. We have already mentioned this. There is indeed no transgression possible, not even for deconstruction and deconstructionists. But the language that holds us captive in this way remarkably also allows for, grants, and even solicits, the experimentation and exploration that resist this captivity. Deconstruction is not some extra-textual philosopher's brainchild. It is not just a smart idea or thought that one of the ingenious thinkers of our time plucked from his undoubtedly highly productive and creative mind. Derrida knew that deconstruction is the product of a language or languages that has and have been around long before him. His entire oeuvre consisted of painstakingly following and tracing leads already followed by other thinkers before him. He knew that his own creativity was a textually *provoked* creativity, a creativity *solicited* by the creative possibilities that the language of his predecessors (especially, as mentioned above, Heidegger, Husserl, De Saussure, Freud, Nietzsche, Marx and Levinas) offers. Deconstruction is an event of language, an event in which language gives itself, as it has done for ages, to the possibility of an impossible resistance to its own constraints. That this resistance of language to itself is as old as language itself is attested by ancient instances of mystic poetry, philosophy and theology that sought to explode or transgress language for the sake of a direct, or at least more direct, experience of existence. It has always been evident whenever significant poetry resisted conventional ways of saying in order to say what has hitherto remained unsaid. Heidegger found a telling instance of this mystic resistance to language in Parmenides' poetic probing of a thinking that would be close enough to existence to become *boundless* and to warrant the assertion of the *oneness of thinking and exist-ence*, the oneness of *thought* and *Being* (Heidegger 1982). He also found this resist-ance to be evident in the work of several poets, especially in the poetry of Friedrich Hölderlin (Heidegger 1971). Derrida found and explored this resistance in the writings of the medieval mystic theologian/poet Angelus Silesius (Derrida 1995), and in the poetry of Paul Celan (Derrida 1986b), among many others.

The mystic and poetic resistance of language to itself has indeed all along been a regular feature of language, a regular feature of significantly innovating philosophy, theology and poetry. Might this mystic and poetic resistance of language to itself also be evident in, or pertinent for, legal theory and thinking about law? This is the question that Derrida's essay 'Force of Law: The "Mystical Foundation of Authority"' added to the concerns of contemporary legal theory. The lively response and wide acclaim that this essay found in contemporary legal theoretical scholarship would suggest that this is a worthy legal theoretical and jurisprudential concern. Is this so, or has a considerable contingent of contemporary lawyers and legal theorists just succumbed to the allure of something that is completely foreign to law and should have remained foreign to legal theory? Might one not argue that the concerns of legal theory are circumscribed by the clear language of law? Should legal theory therefore not confine its concerns to the register of clear communication and, at that, to a very clearly defined sub-category of this communication that complies with the even higher levels of linguistic clarity exacted by the demands of law and the ideal of the rule of law? Has the legal theoretical reflection upon the social and political origins of law in the course of the twentieth century (legal realism, sociological theories of law, critical legal studies, etc) not already bitten off more than it can chew by venturing much too far beyond the proper province of jurisprudence? Has it not already moved much too far beyond clear primary rules of legal obligation backed up by clearly defined secondary rules of legal recognition, application and change (Hart)? Has this introduction of political and sociological impurities not polluted the concern with pure law enough; has it not already introduced enough troubled water into the transparency of pure law, the transparency of legal norms that are clearly validated by higher norms and ultimately by a clearly defined foundational norm that insulates the law from all extra-legal impurities (Kelsen)? And if this circumscription of the domain of jurisprudence is perhaps too narrow, should one not then let the matter rest with the respectable and relatively transparent integration of some fundamental moral considerations into law and legal theory (Dworkin)?

The concern with a well-circumscribed domain of jurisprudence or legal theory that is reflected in these questions must surely turn into dismay when the question of deconstruction's relevance for legal theory comes to the fore, for deconstruction is not just concerned with the political, sociological and moral origins of law. As if these origins are not already worrying enough, deconstruction is concerned with the origins of these origins; the origins of the social, the political and the moral; the origins of social, political and moral languages. It is concerned with origins of origins, moreover, that can never be pinned down anywhere but are ever again displaced, suspended, deferred or supplemented by other originating moments; origins that are mere traces of traces that are lost in the mists of linguistic differentiation. No rule of recognition stands a chance here. No foundational norm and no moral principle can hope to arrest the abyssal chaos of the primordial event of language.

Had it not been for Agamben's challenge, one might not have needed to elaborate the matter to this extent. The mystic curiosity of deconstruction is mentioned right up there in the title of the essay that catapulted deconstruction into the concerns of twentieth-century legal theory – *the mystical foundation of authority*. Derrida was upfront and considerate enough to state the concern of the essay straight away. Anyone for whom the foundation of legal authority begins and ends with a rule of recognition,

foundational norm, fundamental moral principle or considerations of social legitimacy, and so on could have turned away immediately. But the essay 'Force of Law'
made its mark on legal theory and continues to do so. Why is this?

The essay is in the first place an engagement with Walter Benjamin's essay 'The
Critique of Violence'. We cannot do justice here to the richness of either Benjamin's
text or Derrida's engagement with it. Suffice it to highlight some of the key themes
of Derrida's essay. The first theme concerns Benjamin's analysis of the law in terms
of a recurring cycle of two forms of authority and violence (the German word *Gewalt*
which Benjamin employs denotes not only authority, but also violence), law-*founding*
authority and law-*preserving* authority. This analysis is in itself already interesting
to Derrida because of the way it reflects the split origins of law. It reflects the fact
that the authority or violence required to found the law (for instance during a popular
revolution) is never enough. The resulting order of law or rule of law does not ter-
minate the authoritarian and violent origins of law so as eventually or subsequently
to inaugurate what might be called non-violent and non-authoritarian governance
or non-violent authority. The rule of law repeats the authoritarian violence of its
origins incessantly in the form of law-conserving violence (Derrida 1990, especially
pp 948 ff). Derrida also discerned and highlighted the split and repetitive origins
of law in the relation between the initial drafting and ratification of the American
Constitution. The initial draft was unlawful for it was not yet mandated by law and
only became law as a result of ratification. But the ratification necessarily remains
haunted by a lack of law, for the unlawful cannot be ratified without contaminating the
lawful with the unlawful (Derrida 1986a). What, after all, ratifies or legitimises the
act of ratification? The ultimate foundations of law and legal authority can evidently
never be pinpointed with reference to a single and clearly definable origin that is in
itself sufficiently authoritative. The foundation of authority is mystical because it
is never fully present. As is the case with the materialisation of linguistic meaning
that we described above with reference to Derrida's early works, authority always
emerges from split origins, repetitions, traces and supplementations. It emerges
from the mists and mysteries of multiple moments of law-making of which no single
moment is authoritative. Authority is therefore also always significantly extra-legal or
non-legal. Regular legal authority itself thus always involves, in significant respects,
a state of exception.

The second theme in Benjamin's essay that interests Derrida is Benjamin's invocation of a third kind of violence that breaks completely with law-founding and law-
conserving violence. Benjamin calls this third kind of violence *divine violence* to
contrast it with law-founding and law-conserving violence, both of which Benjamin
subsumes under the category of *mythical violence. Divine violence* differs from *mythical violence* because it has no relation to law. It neither founds, nor conserves, law.
Benjamin identifies the possibility of such divine violence in the revolutionary practice of the *general strike*. Derrida's interest in Benjamin's analysis should be evident
when one keeps in mind deconstruction's concern with the outer limits of language
or the *outside of the text* that we outlined above. Benjamin's notion of *divine violence*
evidently seeks to articulate a source of authority or violence that transcends the law
and the language of law. Benjamin's concern with *divine violence* is a concern with
absolute transgression and the absolute outside of law; something one might want to
call *divine justice.* Derrida's regard for the impossibility of complete transgression

and the impossibility of transcending the limits of language, irrespective whether this language is legal, political, moral, revolutionary, theological or poetic, nevertheless renders him highly critical of Benjamin's idea of *divine violence*. The last part of the essay turns, in fact, into a sharp critique of Benjamin. One might comment in this regard that Derrida had a mystical curiosity regarding the ineffable foundations from which things emerge, but he had little tolerance for any mysticism that would hold these foundations accessible.

This brings us to the third theme of the essay: law is not justice, justice is impossible. The insight that legal authority is interminably caught up in cycles of law-founding and law-conserving authority/violence precludes the law from any claim to justice. The law cannot be just. Not only is the law not just, justice is impossible. The insight that language and legal language preclude direct access to divine authority and divine justice demands the recognition that justice between humans is impossible. No legal rule and no application of a legal rule can be just because all law is always caught up in some form of authoritarian violence or violent authority and no revolutionary destruction of law can save or deliver us from law and the violent authority embodied in it. We can at best, claims Derrida, have an oblique or indirect experience with justice (Derrida 1990, p 935). How might one have this indirect experience with justice? One might have an experience with justice through the deconstructive regard for the differential relation and tension between an incircumventible need for law and legal rules, on the one hand, and the impossibility of justice, on the other. Derrida articulates this differential tension further under the second aporia of justice elaborated in the essay: justice would demand that one simultaneously follow and not follow a rule (cf Derrida 1990, p 961). At issue here are two contradictory demands of justice that render the present materialisation or embodiment of justice impossible. A complete disregard for rules cannot be just. The just decision must follow the applicable rule. But the mere application of rules, however equitable, can also not do justice. It will presently become clear that these two irreconcilable demands of justice may well relate directly to two irreconcilable conceptions of justice in the history of Western or European legal thought.

How might this deconstructive articulation of the relation between justice and law be contextualised in the history of legal theoretical conceptions of the relation between law and justice? One must answer this question by considering the broader context of the late phase of Derrida's work to which the essay 'Force of Law' belongs. At issue here is the phase of Derrida's thinking in which the Levinasian concern with *hospitality* played a key role. According to Levinas and Derrida (leaving aside the differences between them for now), *hospitality* concerns the selfless submission to the demands of others upon us. It concerns, further, the absolute gift that expects or demands nothing in return. It concerns the selfless giving of that which one does not have to give. It concerns a completely asymmetrical relation in which the self gives itself to the demands of the other (Derrida 2000). This giving and this hospitality, just like justice, are impossible. There is no pure gift and no pure hospitality. Earthly relations, however generous or giving they may claim or aspire to be, always take place with the expectation of a return, an expectation of symmetry. There are key passages in the essay 'Force of Law' that clearly evince a direct connection or association of the impossibility of justice at stake in the essay, and the impossibility of the gift and of hospitality at stake in Derrida's engagement with Levinas in this phase of his thinking (Derrida 1990, pp 959, 965). Doing justice to others would require nothing less than absolutely selfless hospitality and giving. As we saw above, Derrida invoked 'nothing outside the text' to denote, obliquely, the limits of all language. This early concern with the limits of language takes an ethical turn in the works that would relate to his engagement with Levinas. The language that remains language in the wake of its poetic or mystic encounters with its own limits, the language that survives that encounter without giving way to incomprehensible delirium (Derrida often observed that deconstruction is an exploration of madness), is the precursor of the mad ethics of giving articulated in his later work. The ethics of giving articulated in this work evinces a deep fascination with the possibility of an insane disregard for mundane concerns of economic survival (Derrida 1990, p 965).

Evident in this ethics and in the deconstructive understanding of justice which Derrida articulates in 'Force of Law', is a clear departure from the Aristotelian understanding of justice in terms of just proportions that give to everyone that which is due to them (Aristotle 1981). This understanding of justice found its way into Roman law in the form of Ulpian's definition of justice as *jus suum cuique tribuere* – 'justice is to give to everyone his own' (*The Digest of Justinian* 1.1.10) – and can be argued to have remained, ever since, one of the pillars of Western legal thinking. The gigantic weight of the legal tradition that is challenged by the concept of asymmetrical justice articulated in 'Force of Law' should be clear. But 'Force of Law' is not the first articulation of this challenge. The Aristotelian concept of justice in terms of just reciprocities gave way for many centuries to the Christian ethics of asymmetrical giving and forgiving, the ethics of forgiving seventy times seven and of turning the other cheek. It was introduced to Western moral thinking by the works of St Augustine in the fourth to fifth century AD and it displaced the Aristotelian tradition of justice right up to the eleventh century. Aristotelianism experienced a revival in the twelfth century and from the twelfth to the fourteenth centuries these two pillars of Western legal thinking, Greek/Roman and Christian, competed fiercely with one another for the soul of Western or European morality and law. From the thirteenth to fourteenth centuries St Francis of Assisi and his followers articulated a remarkable example of the moral mysticism of selfless giving that haunts the Derridean concern with justice in 'Force of Law'. It gave rise to the famous poverty debate between the Dominican and Franciscan orders of the Catholic Church. Hotly contested was the question whether Jesus and his disciples owned property, whether they owned the clothes they wore and the food they ate, or just used and consumed these necessities without any claims to property. Like Benjamin, the Franciscans were aspiring to a life beyond property, beyond law (Villey 2003, pp 212–68).

Derrida's concern with the ethics and justice of selfless giving does not derive from this Christian background. He took it over from Levinas who, in turn, articulated it with reference to Jewish conceptions of ethics and justice. We cannot go into the difference between the Jewish and the Christian traditions here. Suffice it to say that both these traditions, together with the secular articulations they would find in the tradition of Marxism, embody a counterpoint to the Aristotelian (and Kantian) understandings of justice which today, perhaps in a fundamentally distorted way (one can presently basically forget about the ethics of selfless giving as modern legal systems can hardly claim in good faith to afford to each what is due to them), still inform dominant modes of legal thinking. One might say that these contrapunctual tensions in Western legal thinking evince the way legal language, like all language, incessantly resists itself and explores its own boundaries. Fundamental conceptions of law emerge from these and many other tensions. Only an anachronistic and recalcitrant metaphysics of law would endow them with stable and infinite presence.

Aspirations and claims to justice always emerge from the tensions of restless legal languages that explore and resist their own boundaries. The concern and experience with justice always comes from renewed instantiations of these tensions, explorations and resistances. Considered from this background, justice can never exist as a positive presence. It comes. It is always to come (Derrida 1990, p 969).

The contribution of deconstruction to legal theory is bound to remain controversial. But it is fair at least to credit Derrida with some of the most probing analyses of the precarious spectral dynamics and non-presence of law and legal language in recent philosophy and legal theory. The fact that a highly non-jurisprudential theoretical project such as deconstruction – something so far beyond the domain of rules of recognition, foundational norms, basic principles of morality, social and political legitimacy, and so on – has come to make such a forceful impression on legal theorists may well itself be explained in Derridean terms. Jurisprudence too is an unstable and restless discipline that continues to resist and explore its own outer limits and the outsides of its foundational texts. It is important to stress again in this regard the deconstructive regard for the fact that deconstruction is not something that some individuals or some legal theorists have done or are doing to law and legal theory. Deconstruction is what happens. It happens in law and legal theory because of the law's irreducible susceptibility to deconstruction. There is little point in dismissing these restless boundary explorations of jurisprudence as irrelevant or inappropriate as far as the 'proper domain of jurisprudence' is concerned, for there is little point in dismissing or being judgmental about that which happens, has happened and is likely to happen again. It is much more prudent and therefore also much more jurisprudent to endeavour to understand what really happens in law and legal theory. And it is for this reason that Derrida might be said to have made a huge contribution to jurisprudence, not only notwithstanding but perhaps also because of the obvious distances between his philosophical concerns and the more regular concerns of legal theory. If it is an aspiration of jurisprudence or legal theory to understand its own concerns more comprehensively, let alone fully, it cannot shy away from also exploring the outer limits of its fundamental textual organisations and constructions. And this may well require the traversal of considerable distances.

Reading

Students who wish to do more reading on deconstruction can consider the following books and articles:

Drucilla Cornell et al (eds), *Deconstruction and the Possibility of Justice* (1992) (Derrida's essay 'Force of Law' discussed above is also republished in the volume along with many other essays by other legal theorists who engage with Derrida's work).

Jonathan Culler, *On Deconstruction* (1985).

Christopher Norris, *The Deconstructive Turn* (2010).

Christopher Norris, *Deconstruction, Theory and Practice* (1982).

Christopher Norris, 'Law, Deconstruction and the Resistance to Theory', 1988 *Journal of Law and Society* 166–187.

Neil MacCormick, 'Reconstruction after Deconstruction. A Reply to CLS', 1990 (10) *Oxford Journal of Legal Studies* 539–558 (more broadly a response to the Critical Legal Studies movement than specifically a response to Derridean deconstruction).

References

Agamben, G, 2005, *State of Exception*, Chicago/London: University of Chicago Press.

Aristotle, 1981, *Nicomachean Ethics*, Harmondsworth: Penguin Books.

Ben-Dor, O, 2007, *Thinking about Law – In Silence with Heidegger*, Oxford/Portland: Hart Publishing.

Cornell, D [et al] (eds), 1992, *Deconstruction and the Possibility of Justice*, New York: Routledge.

Culler, J, 1985, *On Deconstruction*, New York: Cornell University Press.

Derrida, J, 1973, *Speech and Phenomena*, Evanston: Northwestern University Press.

Derrida, J, 1978, *Writing and Difference*, Chicago: University of Chicago Press.

Derrida, J, 1982, *Margins of Philosophy*, Chicago: University of Chicago Press.

Derrida, J, 1986a, 'Declarations of Independence', *New Political Science* 7–15.

Derrida, J, 1986b, *Schibboleth*, Paris: Galilée.

Derrida, J, 1990, 'Force of Law: The "Mystical Foundation of Authority"', 11 *Cardozo Law Review* 919–1726.

Derrida, J, 1994, *Specters of Marx*, New York/London: Routledge.

Derrida, J, 1995, *On the Name*, Stanford: Stanford University Press.

Derrida, J, 2000, *Of Hospitality*, Stanford: Stanford University Press.

Heidegger, M, 1971, *Erläuterungen zu Hölderlins Dichtung*, Frankfurt am Main: Vittorio Klostermann.

Heidegger, M, 1982, *Parmenides*, Frankfurt am Main: Vittorio Klostermann.

MacCormick, N, 1990, 'Reconstruction after Deconstruction. A Reply to CLS', 10 *Oxford Journal of Legal Studies* 539–558.

Norris, C, 2010, *The Deconstructive Turn*, London: Taylor & Francis.

Norris, C, 1982, *Deconstruction, Theory and Practice,* London and New York: Methuen.

Norris, C, 1988, 'Law Deconstruction and the Resistance to Theory', 15(2) *Journal of Law and Society* 166–187.

Van der Walt, J, 2011, 'The Murmur of Being and the Chatter of Law', 20(3) *Social & Legal Studies* 389–400.

Villey, M, 2003, *La formation de la pensée moderne*, Paris: Quadrige/PUF.

Wittgenstein, L, 1922, *Tractatus Logico-Philosophicus*, London: Kegan Paul.

❖ **TUTORIAL 1**

Read the Scottish case *MacLennan v MacLennan* 1958 SLT 12.

The aim of this tutorial is to help students to grasp the essence of *deductive formal reasoning*. *McLennan* was an early Scottish case on artificial insemination by the sperm of a donor without the consent of the husband. The case raised the question whether such an action constitutes adultery and, thus, whether it can provide the basis for an action for divorce. The judge, who appears to follow the model of deductive syllogism quite explicitly, reached the opposite conclusion.

Tasks and Questions

- Summarise the factual basis of the case and the opinion of Lord Wheatley.

- Focus on the precise structuring of the syllogism that sustains his decision and compare it to the 'model' of deductive argumentation provided by MacCormick's theory.

- Focus on the interpretation of the term 'adultery'. Is this a question of open texture, according to Hart's analysis? How does the judge deal with its meaning? Are you satisfied by his approach?

- Critically discuss the explicit contention of the judge that he is not to enter into the moral, philosophical and personal considerations that artificial insemination generates. Are you satisfied by this formalistic approach to the issue?

Corresponding Sections: Part II 1.1–1.2.

❖ **TUTORIAL 2**   Reading a text critically [1]: 'The case of the Speluncean Explorers'

Aim of this tutorial

The aim of this tutorial is to understand the complexity and contestability of legal argument over what is the right answer in hard cases. Look at how judges construct reasonable arguments about the *same* problem departing from radically *different* understandings of the presuppositions and meaning of the law and reaching radically different solutions too.

Reading

Lon Fuller, 'The Case of the Speluncean Explorers' (1949), 62 Harvard LR 616.

Tasks

Come prepared to discuss the following questions:

• How do we identify 'law'? What criteria do each of the judges use to identify law?

• What kinds of arguments do the judges in this fictitious case offer?

• Are they convincing?

• How would you decide the case and why?

Advanced

The limits of judicial discretion

Part I

In 1989, in Edinburgh, JD Stallard was charged with raping his wife in the matrimonial home while they were living together there. He took a plea to the relevancy of the charge, relying on Hume's statement (see below) that a husband cannot rape his wife because she has 'surrendered her person' to him. The plea was repelled at a preliminary diet, and the appellant appealed to the High Court.

Here are the facts:

> (2) [Y]ou being married to Evelyn Stewart or Stallard, care of Police Office, Bridge of Allan, and while residing with her at said house at . . . Stirling, did on 25th August 1988 at said house
>
> (a) assault said Evelyn Stewart or Stallard and did strike her on the face and punch her on the leg, to her injury;
>
> (b) order said Evelyn Stewart or Stallard to a bedroom within said house, there order her to remove her clothing and threaten to rip said clothing from her body if she refused, and she having removed her clothing you did assault her, place and lock a set of handcuffs on her wrists, order her to lie on a bed, lie on top of her, threaten her with violence if she screamed for help, have sexual intercourse with her against her will and thereafter kneel by her and emit semen on her face and did rape her; and
>
> (c) further assault said Evelyn Stewart or Stallard, tie her body and legs to said bed with ropes, force a sock or similar object into her mouth and place Sellotape over her mouth and face, and all this you did to her severe injury.

On 21st February 1989 the accused lodged a minute under s 76 of the **Criminal Procedure (Scotland) Act 1975** seeking a preliminary diet on the following ground:

> That the said Johnston David Stallard wishes to take objection to the relevancy of the indictment and more particularly objects that the charge (2)(b) is irrelevant insofar as it alleges that the accused committed the crime of rape upon his wife while they were residing together.

On 3rd March 1989 a preliminary diet was held in the High Court at Edinburgh before Lord Mayfield, when the plea to relevancy was repelled. The accused then appealed to the High Court.

Read the following extract from *HMA v Stallard* from the decision on appeal (emphases added):

LORD JUSTICE GENERAL (EMSLIE)

There is no doubt that if it was the law of Scotland that a husband is not amenable to a charge of raping his wife, the rule rests solely upon the sentence in Hume which was simply adopted and repeated in different language by the later commentators and writers on the criminal law. The statement in Hume that 'a man cannot himself commit a rape on his wife' appears in a passage in relation to a discourse on art and part of rape against a background of abduction. All who assist are involved in the same guilt as the actor.

'This is true without exception even of the husband of the woman; who, though he cannot himself commit a rape on his own wife, who has surrendered her person to him in that sort, may however be accessory to that crime . . . committed on her by another.' . . . The view expressed by Hume and echoed by, inter alios, Burnett, was taken from Hale's *Historia Placitorum Coronae* published in England in 1736 in which he said this [vol 1, p 629]:

'But the husband cannot be guilty of a rape committed by himself upon his lawful wife, for by their mutual matrimonial consent and contract the wife hath given up herself in this kind unto her husband, which she cannot retract.'

The first question accordingly comes to be whether, even in the eighteenth and early nineteenth centuries, the reason given for the husband's supposed immunity for the commission upon his wife of acts which would constitute the crime of rape was a sound one. That reason was, according to Hume, that the wife had 'surendered her person' to her husband 'in that sort'. This is the first oportunity which the court in Scotland has had to consider whether Hume's statement of the law was sound when it was written and whether it is sound today. It was not necessary in HM Advocate v Duffy or in HM Advocate v Paxton for the court to consider whether Hume's view was and is a sound one in any circumstances during the subsistence of a marriage, but we must do so now. In our opinion, the soundness of Hume's view, and its application in the late twentieth century, depends entirely upon the reason which is said to justify it. Our first observation is that if what Hume meant was that by marriage a wife expressly or impliedly consented to sexual intercourse with her husband as a normal incident of marriage, the reason given affords no justification for his statement of the law because rape has always been essentially a crime of violence and indeed no more than an aggravated assault. Even in Hume's time there was no immunity for a husband who assaulted his wife even if the assault contained elements of the grossest indecency. If, on the other hand, Hume meant that by marriage a wife consented to intercourse against her will and obtained by force, **we take leave to doubt whether this was ever contemplated by the common law** which was derived from the canon law, regulating the relationship of husband and wife. We say no more on this matter which was not the subject of debate before us, because we are satisfied that the Solicitor-General was well founded in his contention that whether or not the reason for the husband's immunity given by Hume was a good one in the eighteenth and early nineteenth centuries, it has since disappeared altogether. **What Hume meant to encompass in the concept of a wife's 'surrender of her person' to her husband 'in that sort', the concept is to be understood against the background of the status of women and the position of a married woman at the time when he wrote**. Then, no doubt, a married woman could be said to have subjected herself to her husband's dominion in all things. She was required to obey him in all things. Leaving out of account the absence of rights of property, a wife's freedoms were virtually non-existent, and she had in particular no right whatever to interfere in her husband's control over the lives and upbringing of any children of the marriage. By the second half of the twentieth century, however, the status of women, and the status of a married woman, in our law have changed quite dramatically. A husband and wife are now for all practical purposes equal partners in marriage and both husband and wife are tutors and curators of their children. A wife is not obliged to obey her husband in all things nor to suffer excessive sexual demands on the part of her husband. She may rely on such demands as evidence of unreasonable behaviour for the purposes of divorce. **A live system of law will always have regard to changing circumstances to test the justification for any exception to the application of a general rule.** Nowadays, it cannot seriously be maintained that by marriage a wife submits herself irrevocably to sexual intercourse in all circumstances. It cannot be affirmed nowadays, whatever the position may have been in earlier centuries, that it is an incident of modern marriage that a wife consents to intercourse in all circumstances, including sexual intercourse obtained only by force. There is no doubt that a wife does not consent to assault upon her person and there is no plausible justification for saying today that she nevertheless is to be taken to consent to intercourse by assault.

This development of the law since Hume's time immediately prompts the question: is revocation of a wife's implied consent to intercourse, which is revocable, only capable of being established by the act of separation? In our opinion the answer to that question must be no.

Revocation of a consent which is revocable must depend on the circumstances. Where there is no separation this may be harder to prove but the critical question in any case must simply be whether or not consent has been withheld. **The fiction of implied consent has no useful purpose to serve today in the law of rape in Scotland.** The reason given by Hume for the husband's immunity from prosecution upon a charge of rape of his wife, if it ever was a good reason, no longer applies today. There is now, accordingly, no justification for the supposed immunity of a husband. Logically the only question is whether or not as matter of fact the wife consented to the acts complained of, and we affirm the decision of the trial judge that charge (2)(b) is a relevant charge against the appellant to go to trial.

Questions

What **kind** of argument is the Lord Justice General relying on in the above quote? Is it an argument from principle? Is it an interpretation of existing law or does it involve a change of the law? How might the theories of Hart and/ or Dworkin help us to make sense of the legal reasoning in this case? Is the rule of law – or any aspect of it – sacrificed in the process?

Part 2

Read the Lord Advocate's Reference No 1 of 2001. It is reported at 2002 SLT 466 and 2002 SCCR 435.

The case was a Reference following the acquittal of an Aberdeen law student on a rape charge.

1 Summarise the arguments of EITHER the Lord Justice General OR Lady Cosgrove AND the dissenting opinion of Lord McLuskey.

2 Explain the point of disagreement and the legal arguments used to support the opposite opinions.

3 How do the judges view their role here? Do they view it as applying or as creating the law? What do you think is their proper role?

4 Compare with the reasoning in *Stallard*. What, if any, similar issues arise?

Part 3

Critically read L Farmer's 'The Genius of Our Law' (Farmer 1992). What does it say about the judges' 'practical legal approach' and does it help us understand the development of Scots Law as a 'living body of law'? In your opinion is it correct to sacrifice 'abstract legal rules' in the name of this more pragmatic approach?

Corresponding Sections: Part II 1.1–1.3.

❖ **TUTORIAL 4**   Rules and principles

Donoghue v Stevenson is one of the most famous common law cases. Read the following extracts of the opinions:

LORD BUCKMASTER

My Lords, the facts of this case are simple. On August 26, 1928, the appellant drank a bottle of ginger-beer, manufactured by the respondent, which a friend had bought from a retailer and given to her. The bottle contained the decomposed remains of a snail which were not, and could not be, detected until the greater part of the contents of the bottle had been consumed. As a result she alleged, and at this stage her allegations must be accepted as true, that she suffered from shock and severe gastro-enteritis. She accordingly instituted the proceedings against the manufacturer which have given rise to this appeal.

The law applicable is the common law, and, though its principles are capable of application to meet new conditions not contemplated when the law was laid down, these principles cannot be changed nor can additions be made to them because any particular meritorious case seems outside their ambit.

LORD ATKIN

. . . The liability for negligence, whether you style it such or treat it as in other systems as a species of 'culpa,' is no doubt based upon a general public sentiment of moral wrongdoing for which the offender must pay. But acts or omissions which any moral code would censure cannot in a practical world be treated so as to give a right to every person injured by them to demand relief. In this way rules of law arise which limit the range of complainants and the extent of their remedy. The rule that you are to love your neighbour becomes in law, you must not injure your neighbour; and the lawyer's question, Who is my neighbour? receives a restricted reply. You must take reasonable care to avoid acts or omissions which you can reasonably foresee would be likely to injure your neighbour. Who, then, in law is my neighbour? The answer seems to be – persons who are so closely and directly affected by my act that I ought reasonably to have them in contemplation as being so affected when I am directing my mind to the acts or omissions which are called in question.

It will be found, I think, on examination that there is no case in which the circumstances have been such as I have just suggested where the liability has been negatived. There are numerous cases, where the relations were much more remote, where the duty has been held not to exist. There are also dicta in such cases which go further than was necessary for the determination of the particular issues, which have caused the difficulty experienced by the Courts below. I venture to say that in the branch of the law which deals with civil wrongs, dependent in England at any rate entirely upon the application by judges of general principles also formulated by judges, it is of particular importance to guard against the danger of stating propositions of law in wider terms than is necessary, lest essential factors be omitted in the wider survey and the inherent adaptability of English law be unduly restricted. For this reason it is very necessary in considering reported cases in the law of torts that the actual decision alone should carry authority, proper weight, of course, being given to the dicta of the judges.

. . .

I have already pointed out that this distinction is unfounded in fact, for in Elliott v. Hall (4), as in Hawkins v. Smith (5) (the defective sack), the defendant exercised no control over the article and the accident did not occur on his premises. With all respect, I think that the judgments in the case err by seeking to confine the law to rigid and exclusive categories, and by not giving sufficient attention to the general principle which governs the whole law of negligence in the duty owed to those who will be immediately injured by lack of care.

LORD TOMLIN

My Lords, I have had an opportunity of considering the opinion (which I have already read) prepared by my noble and learned friend, Lord Buckmaster. As the reasoning of that opinion and the conclusions reached therein accord in every respect with my own views, I propose to say only a few words.

First, I think that if the appellant is to succeed it must be upon the proposition that every manufacturer or repairer of any article is under a duty to every one who may thereafter legitimately use the article to exercise due care in the manufacture or repair. It is logically impossible to stop short of this point. There can be no distinction between food and any other article. Moreover, the fact that an article of food is sent out in a sealed container can have no relevancy on the question of duty; it is only a factor which may render it easier to bring negligence home to the manufacturer.

The alarming consequences of accepting the validity of this proposition were pointed out by the defendant's counsel, who said: 'For example, every one of the sufferers by such an accident as that which recently happened on the Versailles Railway might have his action against the manufacturer of the defective axle.'

LORD MacMILLAN

What, then, are the circumstances which give rise to this duty to take care? In the daily contacts of social and business life human beings are thrown into, or place themselves in, an infinite variety of relations with their fellows; and the law can refer only to the standards of the reasonable man in order to determine whether any particular relation gives rise to a duty to take care as between those who stand in that relation to each other. The grounds of action may be as various and manifold as human errancy; and the conception of legal responsibility may develop in adaptation to altering social conditions and standards. The criterion of judgment must adjust and adapt itself to the changing circumstances of life. The categories of negligence are never closed. The cardinal principle of liability is that the party complained of should owe to the party complaining a duty to take care, and that the party complaining should be able to prove that he has suffered damage in consequence of a breach of that duty. Where there is room for diversity of view, it is in determining what circumstances will establish such a relationship between the parties as to give rise, on the one side, to a duty to take care, and on the other side to a right to have care taken.

I am happy to think that in their relation to the practical problem of everyday life which this appeal presents the legal systems of the two countries are in no way at variance, and that the principles of both alike are sufficiently consonant with justice and common sense to admit of the claim which appellant seeks to establish.

Discuss the following questions:

1 [General:]
    • Is the 'neighbour principle' a legal or a moral principle?
    • If, as Lord Atkin asserts, it is indeed 'found on examination that there is no case in which the circumstances have been such as I have just suggested where the liability has been negatived', then in what sense is *Donoghue* a hard case?

2 [In relation to MacCormick:]
    • Is it any of the business of the courts to decide cases on the basis of consequences they may have?
    • Discuss the role of coherence in law on the basis of the arguments made by the judges in this case.

3   [In relation to Dworkin:]
    • How would integrity's balance of 'fit' and 'justification' require
      Hercules to decide the case?

4   [In relation to the CLS:]
    • Discuss the contention that *Donoghue* exhibits nothing else but
      an early expression of a *politics* of legal reasoning in the judges'
      conviction that values of social solidarity should inform all social
      interaction.

Corresponding Sections: Part II 1.3.

❖ **TUTORIAL 5**   Discrimination and legal reasoning

Part 1

Read the paper by Ronald Dworkin: 'Bakke's Case: Are Quotas Unfair?' (Dworkin 1985, ch 14).

Questions

1   Summarise and explain the structure of Dworkin's argument.

2   In your opinion does Dworkin resolve the clash between the protection of individual rights and the pursuit of the common good in a satisfactory way?

Part 2

Consider the following scenario:

The medical school of Aberlour University in Scotland is concerned about the make-up of its student population. Measured against the overall population, too many of its students are female (75%), and they do not attract enough ethnic minority students or students from state schools. Recent research shows that state school students perform better at university than public school pupils with the same grades. As a result, the medical school introduces a quota in favour of state school pupils to address the imbalance. Since, statistically, most minority ethnic students are also state-school educated, the medical school hopes that as an indirect result, this policy will also increase the number of minority ethnic students.

John is a black African student, who studied at Fettes, an expensive private school in Edinburgh. His application to the university is rejected in favour of a lesser-qualified female student who studied at a Scottish state school.

Questions

1   Do you think that the introduction of the quota achieves a proper balance between the right to education and other social and political demands?

2   Do you think that John has been treated fairly?

3   In your view how might Dworkin answer this problem? How might Unger? Which approach do you find most persuasive?

Corresponding Sections: Part II 1.1–1.3. See also Part II 2.4.

❖ TUTORIAL 6   Legal reasoning, values and politics

Part 1
Essay questions

(1) All legal systems, argues Hart, 'compromise between two social needs: the need for *certain* rules, which can . . . safely be applied without weighing up social issues, and the need to *leave open for later settlement* issues which can only be properly appreciated and settled when they arise in a concrete case.' (Hart 1961, p 127)

(a) Do you agree?

(b) In your opinion can these two 'social needs' be reconciled?

(c) Is this a result of the 'open texture' of the law?

(d) Discuss this statement with reference to Dworkin.

(2) 'Clearly there is something wrong in regarding adversarial jurisprudence as an efficient tool for arriving at the truth. After all we know that others searching after facts – in history, geography, medicine, whatever – do not emulate our adversary system.'

Discuss.

(3) If law is a matter of rules, why does it matter that the great majority of judges are male, white, upper class and educated in private schools?

(4) 'Law's attitude is constructive: it aims, in the interpretive spirit, to lay principle over practice to show the best route to a better future, keeping the right faith with the past.' (Dworkin 1986)

(a) Do the terms 'best', 'better' and 'right' in the above quote introduce an irreducibly 'subjective' element to legal reasoning?.

(b) Discuss the contention that Dworkin's theory is a robust defence of the rule of law.

Corresponding Sections: (1) Part II 1.2; (2) Part II 1.2 and 2.3; (3) Part II 1.2–1.3 and 2.2; (4) Part II 1.2–1.3.

Part 2

(1) 'To regard the jury simply as a judicial institution would be taking too narrow a view of the matter for great though its influence on the outcome of lawsuits is, influence on the fate of society is much greater still. The jury above all is a political institution and it is from this point of view that it must always be judged.'

(De Tocqueville, *Democracy in America*)

In your opinion is a compromise possible between the role of the jury in deciding on the truth of the matter and its role as a 'political institution'?

(2) '[J]udges ought to strive to give the real reasons for their decision. It is my firm conviction that where courts of law have denied a remedy for the cost of bringing up an unwanted child the real reasons have been grounds of distributive justice. That is, of course, a moral theory. It may be objected that the House must act like a court of law and not like a court of morals. That would only be partly right. The court must apply positive law. But judges' sense of the moral answer to a question, or the justice of the case, has been one of the great shaping forces of the common law. What may count in a situation of difficulty and uncertainty is not the subjective view of the judge but what he reasonably believes that the ordinary citizen would regard as right.'

(McFarlane and Another v Tayside Health Board [1999]
4 All ER 961, per Lord Steyn at 977–78)

Discuss.

(3) 'A law of society prescribes what we may or may not do. It *can* be broken – indeed if we could not break it there would be no need to have it.'

Discuss.

(4) Discuss either of the following contentions:

(a) 'Legal reasoning is an inherently repressive form of interpretive thought which limits our comprehension of the social world and its possibilities.' (P Gabel)

(b) 'The intellectual core of the [formalist] ideology is the distinction between law and policy. Teachers convince students that legal reasoning exists, by bullying them into accepting as valid in particular cases arguments about legal correctness that are circular, question-begging, incoherent, or so vague as to be meaningless.' (Kelman)

Corresponding Sections: Part II, all sections.

References

Dworkin, R, 1985, *A Matter of Principle*, Oxford: Oxford University Press.
Dworkin, R, 1986, *Law's Empire*, London: Fontana.
Farmer, L, 1992, 'The Genius of our Law', 55(1) *Modern LR* 25–43.
Fuller, L, 1949, 'The Case of the Speluncean Explorers', 62 *Harvard LR* 616.
Hart, HLA, 1961, *The Concept of Law*, Oxford: Clarendon.

Part III

Law and modernity

1	General themes	203
2	Advanced topics	247

Chapter 1

General themes

Chapter Contents

1.1	The advent of modernity	204
1.2	Law and social solidarity	210
1.3	Law, power and exploitation	215
1.4	Formal legal rationality and legal modernity	224
1.5	Transformations of modern law	233

1.1 The advent of modernity

In this part of the book we change the focus of analysis to ask how some of the issues that have been addressed in the first two parts of the book might be understood as being specific to modern law. This requires that we ask whether there are legal issues or features of law that have developed only in the modern period, and what this can tell us about law as an institution. Further, if as many theorists have suggested, we are moving into a period of late- or post-modernity, this raises questions about how the functions of law might be changing and how we might need to revise our understanding of law. However, before we can begin to answer such questions, we must first consider what we mean when we talk about modernity, and more specifically, what we mean by the term legal modernity.

While the term 'modern' is often used in ordinary speech to describe something that is up to date or contemporary, the term modernity has a more specific meaning when used in social or political thought. In this context it is used to refer to a specific period of time (roughly the period from the European Enlightenment in the eighteenth century to the late twentieth century). This period saw the development of a specific set of beliefs or ideas that were manifested across the fields of knowledge and enquiry, characterised by a new freedom to contest what had previously been taken as given and removed from challenge. These in turn led to a radical change in the forms of political and social organisation.

The momentous changes that are ushered in with modernity include:

- In the field of ideas, scientific and philosophical enquiry:
  - The rise of science as no longer confined in doctrinal systems and hierarchies of authority
- In the field of material production and the economy:
  - The industrial revolution and the creation of markets in land, labour and money
- In the field of political organisation:
  - The separation of Church from State and the creation of the sovereign Nation-State in Europe and the entrenchment and deepening of colonialism.

Let us take each of these in turn.

We associate the Enlightenment with a shaking off of the shackles of tradition and with a belief in progress and in the capacity of rational thought to understand and organise the world. Enlightenment thinking challenged received wisdom as contained in doctrinal systems of thought with privileged interpreters of 'the truth', and instead sought to open these up to scientific and philosophical enquiry. In the field of science, for example, this led to the belief that the natural world operates according to natural laws (such as gravity, evolution and so on) as opposed to magical or mysterious forces, and that science can be applied to the understanding and eradication of particular social problems (such as disease or famine). This sets science and philosophy on a linear course of continuous progress, as mastery of nature and society.

Immanuel Kant's famous dictum *sapere aude* ('dare to know') captures something of the revolutionary moment in the field of knowledge and science. There was
a new optimism pervading the 'Age of Reason' that the world could be deciphered in
the sense of understanding the rules that underlie its function, tracking regularities,
submitting phenomena in the world to scientific analysis and experimentation. This
applied both to the natural and the social sciences. In the former, breakthroughs in
physics (Newton), astronomy, biology and so on drove the efforts to establish the
concepts, the rules and the measurements that would allow us to understand the
natural world. The latter was driven by efforts to understand the regularities of social
life, the underlying structures that determine how people interact in society. The
study of society, 'Sociology – both word and thing – was created by Auguste Comte'
wrote Levi-Strauss, and what is perhaps most remarkable about this invention is that
to understand society, Comte draws directly on the natural sciences. The discipline
of sociology was defined as 'social physics', deploying the logic of 'social statics' and
'social dynamics' directly from physics (the proper equilibrium of which determines
the proper functioning of society); the concept of 'social disease' was taken directly
from medicine; the understanding of 'social pathology' – as what transgresses the
'proper limits of variation' – from (evolutionary) biology. Moreover, the methodology of 'observation, experimentation and comparison', which was key to attaining
scientific knowledge about society, its 'laws of solidarity and sequence,' as he put it,
is of course the key method of the natural sciences. In philosophy, the shift was, with
Descartes, towards introducing the principle of doubt at the heart of epistemology
(the branch of philosophy that asks the question of what is knowledge) and, with Kant
in particular, to understand the frameworks of thought that conditioned people's
perception of reality, as well as the effort to delimit the concepts and categories in
terms of which we understand what is good (ethics) and what is beautiful (aesthetics).

These developments in thought and science were linked to dramatic changes in
the fields of production and the economy that have come to be known as the 'industrial revolution'. Driven in part by new scientific inventions, such as the steam engine
and the mechanisation of production, the industrial revolution was a transformation
of methods of production and a near-miraculous improvement in European societies' capacities to produce goods. However, at the same time, this also produced
arguably the most catastrophic dislocation ever of the lives of the common people of
Europe. It was in the period between the late 1790s and the 1840s in England that the
industrial revolution first made its impact and saw its greatest acceleration; the rest
of Europe followed later in the nineteenth century, and the impact was more gradual
and for the most part politically managed to protect society from the full impact of
rapid industrialisation.

Of course to understand the magnitude of both the massive increase in productive capacity and the scale of social dislocation one must go back in time to look at
how the conditions of such a transformation were set, in terms of the 'enclosures'
of the previous century in Britain. In the name of 'improvement', people's common
property in land was abolished, as Acts of Enclosure were passed depriving people of
access to the common land and its resources and thus depriving them of any means
of subsistence other than to sell their labour to the owners of the factories. During
this period which is sometimes referred to as the 'pre-history' of Capitalism, acts
of 'enclosing' were coupled, in England, with the draconian legal prohibition of

vagabondage, begging, wandering, and so on, and anything that might be perceived as an 'exit opportunity' from wage labour. This was not a process that was exclusively internal to the nation-state, as the industrial revolution in England was also driven by the ability to exploit the natural resources of the colonies. The extraction of wealth from the colonies allowed an extraordinary growth in the metropolis, and while this exploitation of the colonies often involved loot and plunder, it also took the more systematic form of enclosure of colonial lands and the exportation of the capitalist regime, or system of property relations to the periphery. The colonial adventure of the European States, each joining the 'race' (or 'scramble') at different stages and over different periods of time, and organising the exploitation in different forms, unfolded over a very long period and gradually encompassed the whole globe. Some of those forms became noted for their barbarity. Sven Lindqvist's *Exterminate all the Brutes* is one extraordinary account of this, while in *Red Rubber*, historian ED Moral famously exposed and denounced the excessive violence through which Leopold II of Belgium extracted wealth from the Congo. Both in its extreme forms and in the 'normality' of the everyday exercise of colonial rule, Marx reminds us in the first volume of *Capital*, that it (capital) came into the world 'dripping from head to toe, from every pore, with blood and dirt'.

But let us briefly return to the rise of industrial society and the capitalist economy at the beginning of the nineteenth century. Driving the developments of markets and industrial production and also enhanced by them is the emergence of new classes: on the one hand, those who owned the means of industrial production and, on the other, those who had no other means of subsistence than their ability to work. As those who could no longer sustain a livelihood in the old communities structured around attachments of 'blood and soil' fled to the industrial urban centres to find work, there was an unprecedented degree of geographical mobility, leading to the rapid growth of cities and significant changes in the forms of social life. We associate the industrial revolution, then, not only with the extraordinary advancement in technology and the use of machinery, but also the rise of factory towns, the emergence of slums, the long working hours of children, the increase in population and the concentration of industries. The fundamental change, however, is the emergence of the *market economy*. On the one hand, the market dynamic of bringing people together around new technologies of communication and exchange offered forms of freedom that directly countered the forms of traditional societies, with their limited possibilities of challenging hierarchies and received wisdom. On the other hand, this violent uprooting of life from local contexts could lead to a sense of meaninglessness or alienation. As people committed their work to what William Blake called the 'satanic mills' of industrial England, there developed a crippling dependency on the owners of the mills and the very real threat of destitution for those who could not find work or were laid off. A new freedom coupled with a new insecurity were constitutive of the new social experience.

Karl Polanyi describes it in this way in his book *The Great Transformation*, one of the most important analyses of the rise of capitalism:

> [A]n avalanche of social dislocation, surpassing by far that of the enclosure period, came down upon England . . . this catastrophe was the accompaniment of a vast movement of economic improvement; an entirely new institutional mechanism was

starting to act on western society; [and] its dangers, that cut to the quick when they
first appeared, were never nearly overcome.

(1957/1944, p 40)

Contrast this to an earlier pre-modern, pre-capitalist or traditional society. Where
pre-modern societies relied on agricultural forms of subsistence and were largely
rural, modern society is industrialised, organised around a capitalist economy, and is
largely urbanised. If traditional societies were based on face-to-face interaction with
family and acquaintances in small, self-contained, communities, modern society is
based on various forms of mediated communication and exchange with 'strangers',
that is those with whom no other bond or relationship *pre-exists* the exchange. And if
traditional societies were structured by beliefs in magic, and religious or mystical
symbols played an active role in the organisation of social life, modern society is
characterised by the declining importance of religion, and the belief that the social
and natural world can be demystified through the application of science. These transformations had a huge impact, not only on how people lived, but also on how they
began to think about themselves and their relation to the world. Indeed, it is not
surprising that sociology – the science of society – has its origins in the thought of
the eighteenth and nineteenth centuries as writers struggled to understand the nature
of the social changes that they were living through.

We have looked at the momentous changes in science and knowledge, and in
the economy with the creation of the market system. Let us close this introductory
section on the advent of modernity by looking at a final dimension of the great transformation, the dimension of the political.

If we look at Europe during the feudal period that preceded modernity, we see a
very different picture from that which we take for granted today, where the concept
of political authority lacked the sharp edges that the modern notion of sovereignty
furnishes it with today. For one thing political and religious authority remained
largely undifferentiated during the Middle Ages, fused in the encompassing notion
of the *respublica Christiana*. But the idea of this all-encompassing Christian empire
had neither the hierarchical structure nor the jurisdictional powers we associate
today with political authority. In fact authority was dispersed. To the extent that there
was rule as we understand it today, it was exercised in cross-cutting and undercutting
ways, by monarchs and ecclesiastical authorities, but also by commercial organisations, town councils or guilds. This was a radical form of what we would identify
today as legal pluralism. As Harold Berman puts it in his important book *Law and
Revolution: the Formation of the Western Legal Tradition*, it was not unusual for 'a
serf [to] run to the town court for protection against his master. A vassal might run
to the King's court for protection against his lord. A cleric might run to the ecclesiastical court for protection against the King' (p 10). This legal pluralism with its jurisdictional overlap of canon law, feudal law, royal law, merchant law (*lex mercatoria*),
was ill-suited to the project of the emergent bourgeois class and the need for stability
that a capitalist economy requires. Thus the reception of Roman law and the creation
of formal rational bodies of law in the form of constitutions and codes was crucially
linked with the emancipatory project of the new society.

Contrast this to the way in which sovereignty is understood today as central to
the understanding of how State power is exercised (internally) and as underpinning

the relationship between equal states (externally) [see Part I]. A unitary concept of sovereignty is central both to the internal – vertical – relationship between the State and its citizens, and in the external – horizontal – relationship between States that are formally equal, reciprocally recognised and with a corresponding right of non-intervention. To a large extent these developments that are captured by the key concept of sovereignty emerge with and around the Treaty of Westphalia of 1648.

It was in fact during the sixteenth and seventeenth centuries that the ecclesiastical-political order began to come apart under the pressures of the Reformation (initially in Germany) and the rise of the Italian city-states. With the Reformation there was both a challenge to the authority of the Catholic Church and its doctrine, and a shift from ecclesiastical to secular authority. As the latter developed as independent polit-ical entities emerged, a language and a logic of rule of statecraft and of 'reason of State' began to develop – that is the notion of rules as entailing the governing of states as self-contained and independent entities. Although these were processes that lasted a long time, it has become customary to refer to the Treaty of Westphalia, that ended the bloody Thirty Years War, as the significant watermark of this development toward the society of sovereign states.

If Westphalia is the important turning point, it was not necessarily perceived as such at the time (those who met in Westphalia still saw themselves as members of a Christian community, the agreement was expressed in Latin, and there was still no talk of 'sovereignty'). It is rather because, in retrospect, the Treaty ushered in a series of fundamental shifts in the institutions and language of politics. It by and large brought the church under state control; it abolished any supervisory authority (papal or other) over states and, most significantly, it established state jurisdiction over (contiguous) territory, and an exclusive one at that. States now, through their governing authorities, enacted the law that was binding on their citizens, and they had the monopoly of legitimate violence when it came to reckoning with breaches of the law or conflicts among its citizens.

Few works are as emblematic of the changing nature of sovereignty in this period as Thomas Hobbes's *Leviathan*. Written in France while Hobbes was in exile from the turmoil of the English civil wars it was published in 1651, two years after the execution of Charles I and the declaration of the Republic (which was to last only until 1660 when the monarchy was restored). Hobbes's work gave a rigorous philosophical justification for a strong unitary sovereign state, and its insights were influential far beyond its immediate historical context.

Two devices play a key role in the analysis: the 'state of nature' and the 'social contract'. Hobbes asks us to imagine what society would be like without a state, or where (as in civil war) state authority has completely broken down. According to Hobbes this 'state of nature' would be a place of profound insecurity and fear 'and the life of man, solitary, poor, nasty, brutish, and short'. Where everyone was roughly equal in capabilities and vulnerabilities – even strong men had to sleep! – the condition could be described as a war of all against all, and had this consequence: that 'nothing can be unjust. The notions of right and wrong, justice and injustice, have there no place.' There would be no property, only possession, no authority, only force. Hence the essential characteristic of a state of nature was that 'Where there is no common power, there is no law; where no law, no injustice' (Hobbes 1996/1651, pp 89–90). To remedy this condition required that individuals renounce their own strength and covenant with one another – the social contract – to establish a single source of authority, the sovereign. This sovereign – or Leviathan – had to be strong enough to secure peace and to establish, maintain and enforce law throughout the realm. But the social contract for Hobbes, is a contract of alienation (Loughlin 2000, p 129) since, once established, the multitude of subjects – though they are the authors of this instituted authority – have no ongoing contractual relationship with the sovereign; rather they owe it, in its now superior singular will, complete obedience. This unified, territorial authority therefore has, and must have, 'the use of so much power and strength conferred upon him, that by terror thereof, he is enabled to conform the wills of them all, to peace at home, and mutual aid against their enemies abroad' (Hobbes 1966/1651, pp 120–121).

Significantly, Hobbes describes this powerful Leviathan as 'a mortal god'. This apparently oxymoronic description – of a god-like power on earth, that is at the same time susceptible to death – captures the essence of modern sovereignty. Gone is the 'divine right' to rulership or claims to obedience by natural authority; gone is the plurality of competing jurisdictions, all to be replaced by one figure: 'this, our artificial man', the sovereign; a human, political, construct whose secular commands alone now count as law and to whom subjects, as individuals, owe allegiance and obedience for as long as the sovereign is able to protect them. Yet it is precisely as an artificial creation that this sovereign power is vulnerable, to sickness and ultimately death, either from internal discord (civil war) or from foreign invasion.

The core features of Hobbes's analysis are recognisably modern, even if their interpretation will be subject to modification: individualism, a role for consent in establishing secular authority, and complete obedience in law to a singular sovereign power. In terms of the development of political and legal theory, it is therefore 'Hobbes who makes the decisive break with the ancient world' (Loughlin 2000, p 134).

We have identified here the fundamental shifts in scientific understanding, the organisation of economic production and its impact on social life, and political forms that taken together can be characterised as modernity. We must now go on to explore how these had an impact on law and legal thought. We will do this by looking first at theories that have looked at the role that law has played in the production or maintenance of social order. We will then go on to look at theories of how the law has been used to sustain inequality or repress dissent, before looking at how the legal form itself has changed or rationalised in modernity.

Reading

For a classic statement of the 'Enlightenment project' in philosophy, see Kant (1991/1784). For an analysis of the limits of this approach see Foucault (1984). In terms of the changes brought about in the economy, Karl Polanyi's *The Great Transformation* (1957/1944) remains one of the most powerful accounts of the emergence of the market system and the extraordinary social changes it brought about.

Karl Marx's first volume of *Capital* remains the *locus classicus* of the account of 'original accumulation' or the early capitalist move to generate a class of labourers. In *Law and Revolution* (especially in volume 1) Harold Berman explains the changes in law during this period.

Thomas Hobbes's *Leviathan* (1996/1651) is the key text that tracks the changing understanding of sovereignty. A useful collection of papers on the concept and changing conceptions of sovereignty more generally is Walker (2003) and the historical essay by Robert Jackson (1999) is particularly useful on Westphalia and the new mapping of sovereignty in Europe.

The question of whether the state is still central or essential to the understanding of sovereignty and constitutionalism under conditions of globalisation has been in recent years the subject of much debate. On this issue see Bernard Yack (2001), David Held (2002) and Martin Loughlin (2000). This debate is more fully explored in 'Constitutionalism and citizenship' in Part I 2.2, above.

1.2 Law and social solidarity

In the last section we saw how the geographical mobility that industrial society required uprooted people from traditional communities so that identification with fixed locality was no longer possible. On the other hand, the 'release' from fixed social roles and the erosion of traditional forms of life based on status led to new opportunities to accumulate wealth or develop ways of life or new social identities in the fast-growing modern city. In practice though, the new industrial societies created vast asymmetries in the distribution of wealth, and a labour market to which, under the threat of starvation, the majority of the newly dispossessed were forced to commit their labour. The State and the Market become the two forces and organising principles of the new societies. In Polanyi's words, 'Hobbes's grotesque vision of the State – a human Leviathan whose vast body was made up of an infinite number of human bodies – was dwarfed by the Ricardian construct of the labour market: a flow of human lives the supply of which was regulated by the amount of food put at their disposal' (Polanyi 1957/1944, p 164).

A key problem that emerged in this period was thus the question of social order: what is it that holds society together in the face of the growing social divisions and tensions, the new risks and contingencies of social life ordered by the market, and the spectre of social dislocation where traditional forms of social ordering were being destroyed? How, therefore, in the face of these shifts and new uncertainties, and with the demise of traditional social structures, *was social order possible*? Such questions led in turn to an interest in the social functions of law as an instrument for the production of social order.

The three great social theorists of the period, the 'fathers of sociology', the new 'science' of society that emerged in the nineteenth century, all addressed and answered this question in different ways. The French sociologist Emile Durkheim (1858–1917), stressed the themes of social cohesion and collective belief, arguing that the changing forms of law could be seen as indices of different types of social solidarity. A second approach, exemplified by the work of Karl Marx (1818–1883), focuses, by contrast, on the theme of social conflict and dissensus. Marx argued that the main role played by institutions such as the law was to suppress class conflict and support the dominance of particular class interests, so that social order could be explained in terms of the domination of one class over the other. Finally Max Weber (1864–1920) studied law as a distinctive form of modern rationality. He placed a special emphasis on the idea of legitimation, and the connection between the form of law that emerges with capitalism and the specific type of legitimation it commands, and its role in securing social stability.

Durkheim and Marx raised important questions about the relationship between law and modern society, but they saw this relation as largely external and contingent – that is to say, that social changes were reflected in law, and that changes in the form or practice of law were best studied as a guide to understanding these broader shifts. Weber, while also being centrally concerned with the relations between law and modern Western capitalism, was mainly concerned with the development of an internal rationality of law and legal institutions, and how this process of rationalisation was linked to broader social and economic change.

For the remainder of this section we will focus on Durkheim and his notion of social solidarity. While the terms *Gemeinschaft* and *Gesellschaft* that will be introduced in this section are not his, and were in fact introduced later by Ferdinand Tönnies, they capture something of the correlation of social and legal orders, and the distinctiveness of the pre-modern as against modern types.

Durkheim's major work was *The Division of Labour in Society*, first published in 1893. This book analysed the transformation of the modern world in terms of the development of the division of labour – the extent to which work on particular tasks is subdivided between members of a community, and the subdivision of the labour involved in the production of particular objects – and its impact on the organisation of social life. He identified two forms of social solidarity, each of which was associated with a characteristic form of law. The first – *mechanical* solidarity – existed in small, undeveloped societies, where each clan or social group was a separate economic unit. In these societies labour was shared, and was geared primarily towards the subsistence and reproduction of that unit. Such groups were characterised by shared beliefs and values. Law in such societies was *repressive* – that is to say that it was primarily aimed at the reinforcement of social solidarity and the punishment or expulsion of those who threatened collective beliefs. The most prominent type of law to this form of social solidarity was criminal law as this was used both to protect the community against internal and external threats and as a means of expressing communal values. The second – *organic* solidarity – was typified by modern industrial societies. In these societies there are high levels of economic interdependence, as individuals typically work at the production of objects that must be sold to other economic producers, and are not producing their own means of subsistence. However, there are fewer shared beliefs, and Durkheim was concerned with the pressures that were created towards *anomie* (normlessness) or social disorder in such societies. The form of law corresponding to organic solidarity was *restitutive* law, which was aimed at the regulation and co-ordination of relations arising from the division of labour. The most prominent, but not exclusive, type of law was *contract law*, governing relations between producers and consumers in the marketplace. This clearly allowed the maintenance of the market and division of labour, but indicated a weaker form of social solidarity. For Durkheim, then, law played an important role in the maintenance of social solidarity, but the way that it did so was fundamentally different in different types of society.

One can explore the points that Durkheim makes here through the use of an important typology that was introduced by Ferdinand Tönnies. This is the distinction between *Gemeinschaft* and *Gesellschaft*, roughly translatable as 'community' and 'society' respectively (and thus corresponding in broad terms to mechanical and organic solidarity). With these terms Tönnies attempted to track the transition between societal change and the corresponding legal change. While these forms appear very much as ideal types in the Weberian sense (see section 1.4 below), they each have dominated (as paradigmatic) an epoch in the evolution of our legal tradition.

In the *Gemeinschaft* form of social regulation the emphasis is on law as expressing the will, the internalised norms and traditions of a community, to whom each individual member is part of the social family. In effect there is no clear distinction between what belongs to the private realm and what to the public, what is a legal as opposed to a moral issue, what is properly politics as opposed to justice, religion, morality. The normative order is all-encompassing and unyielding. This form of law is, in Weber's terminology as we will see, characteristically substantive. The arbiter of justice does not act under a legal capacity somehow detached from his own moral views, social position and politics. Rather s/he adjudicates on the basis of a justice that is the community's – the sense of which s/he embodies – and s/he does so (again in Weberian terms) irrationally, not by deducing from general premises but in a casuistic, ad hoc, manner, as the case at hand demands.

Gesellschaft law is in many ways the exact opposite of this. We move here from the cohesive community to liberal society and its need to co-ordinate differences in social and professional roles and contributions of labour. Where, in the former, society as a whole imposed the dictates of law, *Gesellschaft* law is geared to individualism. This requires that in the name of protecting the individual, the law must keep society at arm's length. The emphasis is now on the autonomous individual, motivated by self-interest, who enters the public arena to strike deals that will further his/her own interest. The law is there to set up and guarantee that process of exchange as well as the equality of all before it, and in a sense limits itself to the role of passive enforcer of individuals' agreements. To achieve its function this law of liberal society must assume the form of a system of rules that are clear, predictable, general (applying equally to everyone) and self-contained; recourse to outside moral, political or social considerations would undermine legal certainty and moral and political pluralism. The distinction between the two types of law brings into relief competing images of the person. In *Gemeinschaft* law the person is intimately linked with the community to which his/her own sense of identity is intimately tied. In *Gesellschaft* law the person is atomistic, self-determining and limited only by the rights of other individuals; s/he is first and foremost a bearer of rights, that is a cluster of entitlements through which public exchange and public life is possible.

But what is the lever of change between the forms of law? The answer to this question depends on the concept of *legitimation* (we will also be better positioned to understand this once we have explored what Weber says about types of legitimation). But to anticipate the point, the question that legitimation answers is this: given that the bottom line of law is that it is a coercive order, is it merely the threat of coercion that motivates people to accept it? Or is there something beyond threat that makes law appear, and makes people act, as if it were binding – which creates an obligation to obey? This matters because, although compliance with the legal order can be secured to a limited extent by coercion, compliance over time may be guaranteed only if the existing order commands the support or loyalty of the mass of the population.

In *Gemeinschaft* law, legitimation is based on shared values and shared under-standings. Legal rules (when law takes the form of explicit rules rather than custom) embody shared value commitments. Here society is held together through what Durkheim terms a *'conscience collective'* or shared set of beliefs and values, which is continually expressed and renewed through the operation of the law. (Weber will refer to the legitimation prevalent in *Gemeinschaft* law as being of the 'traditional' type.) The law is adhered to and respected because the opportunity to question it is absent: the social environment discourages dissent and rewards obedience. But the legitimation reaches deeper than mere external pressure. Allegiance to the rules derives from the fact that the rules give expression to the background common morality. With no dividing line between that morality and the legal expression of it no external measure of threat is needed to guarantee adherence to law. Since it is from this pool of common value that the community draws in order to make sense of the world in the first place, allegiance to law is guaranteed at the outset.

The changes, as analysed earlier, in economic and cultural conditions brought about a change in the legitimation process. The rise of the bourgeoisie in Europe, and the changed economic and social conditions, challenged the status society and subverted the *Gemeinschaft* form of law. As for legitimation, there arose due to the market as facilitator of exchange and of transaction among parties who did not share a world-view, a certain pluralism of values that undercut the sort of allegiance that was possible in *Gemeinschaft*. The logic of legitimation is reversed in *Gesellschaft* law: it no longer draws legitimation from shared substantive values, but instead from its very distance from those values. Religious or communal moral principles that grounded *Gemeinschaft* law are abandoned. *Gesellschaft* law frees itself from the sources from which a challenge to its legitimacy could originate, and appears as a rational system of self-justifying, neutral rules, which are independent of particular religious or moral beliefs. Law stays clear of promoting certain values against others, or certain ends against others, because that is the province of individual freedom of choice. Law merely fixes the formal framework within which individual wills will meet. It fixes common means to diverse ends, guaranteeing formal equivalence, the terms of exchange and the enforceability of the agreement. The legitimacy of law in the liberal era depends upon precisely its withdrawal to the formal side of the social inter-change. In a society where there is very little agreement on substantive issues across the board, it becomes important to agree the rules of disagreement. The law draws its legitimation from merely fixing the framework for settling conflict and abstaining from taking sides, as it were, in that conflict. It merely provides the technical means of compromising between conflicting interests. At the same time it provides institutional backing to a market economy where, in principle, everything is subject to agreement and exchange according to the free will of the parties. Law becomes legitimate in guaranteeing that kind of freedom, and in performing that function brings into play a different *kind* of solidarity, that which Durkheim calls 'organic'.

So liberal law, *Gesellschaft* law, is a type of law that relies on an image of the person that is not, to begin with, a creature of the community. The person is conceived of as pre-existing it, self-constituting, self-seeking and self-interested; s/he approaches the community in order to strike his/her bargains to realise his/her self-stipulated ends. That is why for Durkheim and Tönnies *contract* is the liberal law's *paradigmatic form*. And that is also why modern normative political philosophy draws so heavily on these kinds of assumptions. This image of the person as bearer of rights and of society as an association of individual persons is one developed by *social contract* political theorists like Locke and is one that still pervades liberal political theory. Contract, or agreement between individuals, in this view, dominates the constitution of society and the workings of society, and this crucial legal concept is coupled with those of property and rights. *Property* in liberal law becomes the inalienable entitlement to enjoy and dispose of objects to an unprecedented degree; unprecedented because any previous system of property circumscribed property more narrowly both as to the kind of things that could be owned (goods, capital, means of production, intellectual products, etc), and as to *the incidents* of ownership, that is the extent of power over the propertied: alienation, management, dividends, transmissibility. For a feudal lord, for example, ownership was hedged notably in terms of alienability. Liberal law thus extended (i) the number of incidents of ownership, that is, the range of entitlements to, dividends from, controls over and management of the propertied thing: in *Gesellschaft* law, ownership becomes absolute and property is freely disposable; (ii) the range of the kind of thing that may be owned: land and labour crucially, and later image/sound, ideas, or knowledge: there is a great increase of what may be propertied: in principle everything becomes exchangeable, alienable, saleable, including, notoriously, labour power; (iii) the priority and security given to the legal title of the owner against anyone with a different title. The development of a regime of individual property rights is tied to the development of a political economy based on the market and the principles that underlie it. These themes will be further developed in the following sections and in the Advanced Topics.

For Durkheim, then, the form and functions of modern law were to be studied as a means of understanding the nature of the underlying social solidarity. That is why he spoke of the *law as 'index' of social solidarity*. What makes social order possible under modern conditions of the division of labour, in the *Gesellschaft* type of society, is very different to that of the pre-modern type, but still intricately linked to law except that the law, for Durkheim, has shifted its internal emphasis towards the institutions of private law and the sanction of private agreements (rather than communal mores) in the form of contract, which becomes the characteristic of, and the lynchpin of, the emerging form of *organic* solidarity. In a move that 'frees' social relations from social stratification, from status and from the bonds that it entailed during the *ancien régime*, the law is severed from any substantive social and political content, and therefore body of values, and social order is possible in the new form of interdependence only because *pacta sund servanda* – that is, that obligations freely assumed, will be met – and the guarantee of the bond that makes society possible comes in the form of a law that underwrites this.

This generally, then, is a view of society that sees it as founded on forces that bring people together. The role of law, even in modern capitalist society, is to express this collective interest – albeit that this is a weaker form of social solidarity than traditional societies. We now turn to consider a view of law that starts from a radically different position, namely that society is characterised by conflict, and that rather than expressing collective interests the law defends or protects the interests of particular classes.

Reading

For a discussion of social solidarity and the division of labour see Durkheim, *The Division of Labour* (1963/1933), especially chapters 2 and 3. For one of the best analyses of Durkheim's thinking about law, see Cotterrell (1999), and more generally on his thinking about society see Giddens (1971) and Lukes (1973). Useful summaries and extracts of Durkheim's work are collected in Lukes and Scull (1983).

Durkheim has had a particular impact on criminal law, criminology and the social theory of punishment. Amongst the best analyses here are Garland (1990), chs 2 and 3 and Reiner (1984).

The transformation from *Gemeinschaft* to *Gessellschaft* (and then further to 'regulatory law') are analysed in the much discussed article by Kamenka and Tay (1975). For the classic account of the transition from 'status to contract' see Maine (1861), and for the changes in contract law during this transition Atiyah's magisterial account (1979).

1.3 Law, power and exploitation

As we discussed in section 1.1 above, the organisation of industrial production and the advent of capitalism was preceded, and was only made possible, by a systematic effort to secure the conditions under which the working population would commit their labour to factory production. Lands were 'enclosed', people were driven off the common lands (e.g. the clearances in Scotland), forms of nomadic living were outlawed, and opportunities to resist the new forms of economic activity were radically limited. For Karl Marx, the most acute and historically most influential critic of capitalism, these measures, secured primarily through the medium of law, were the conditions of driving the newly property-less class into wage slavery, and he called this moment that preceded capitalism 'original accumulation' – the moment when collective resources were defined as private property and taken into the ownership of a small social class. For Marx, once these conditions were in place, those deprived of any form of property had no option but to submit to the capitalist economy and the value of their work could now be misappropriated by those who owned the means of production, the bourgeois class, as a matter of 'free' agreement according to the logic of capitalist production.

To understand both the measure and nature of the injustice of the 'misappropriation' of the value of the work of the labouring masses, and the role of law in organising its conditions, we need to take a step back and to visit some fundamental premises of Marx's theory.

Marx's point of departure is the image of the productive man, who only realises the true nature of the being that he is ('species-being' Marx calls it) through creative labour. As history, for Marx, is conceived in terms of a continuing process of creation, satisfaction and reproduction of needs (as opposed to animals whose needs are fixed), man interacts with the material world in order to create the means to satisfy those needs. This interaction between man and society, *production*, becomes the very foundation of society. Labour underlies man's relation to the material world and his relations to others: since production requires co-operation and interdependence between people, at the basis of social life there is a co-ordination of individual labour, and thus there is no society that is not founded on a definitive set of relations of production. The social nature of the individual is a fundamental premise in Marxist theory, because one only realises one's own creative self through collective action and social interdependence. Marx goes on to examine and denounce the exploitative nature of that interdependence in societies which are organised in class terms. All human history, for Marx, was a history of a succession of forms of class societies, each with its distinctive form of 'relations of production': in slave societies the class structure took the form of ownership of the exploited; in feudal societies it was arranged through differential status (feudal lord and vassal). In capitalist societies classes polarise around the ownership of the means of production. There is the class of those who own the means of production – the factories, the land, the technology, the raw materials – and then there are those who own nothing except their ability to work, an ability that remains an empty abstraction if denied the means of its realisation. We saw how the stage that Marx called 'original accumulation' above secured the total dependency of the class of labourers exclusively on the class of owners of the factories. This compulsion to work for others in order to survive, however, finds 'expression' in the language of freedom, one of the many contradictions that Marx was incisive in identifying. The 'will' of those who own the means of production and of those who 'own' their labour power, employers and workers, 'meet' in the contract of employment, understood as a 'free agreement' entered into by both sides to exchange labour for a wage. Compulsion is thus expressed as freedom: to enter into or to abstain from the contract of employment. This, for Marx, is a key instance of what he describes as *ideology*.

The crux of what Marx denounces as the injustice of capitalism is that under capitalist conditions of production, a minority grouping (the bourgeois ruling class), by virtue of their ownership of the means of production, is able to appropriate the accumulated surplus production. 'Surplus value' is the difference between the value of what the product fetches in the market and the value that those who produce the goods (workers) are recompensed for, at subsistence level. The injustice of the system lies in the fact that those who produce the goods are recompensed (through their wages) for only a part of the value of the goods they produce; the capitalist class appropriates the rest. In fact, the more efficient workers are at producing goods, the greater the margin of value appropriated by the owners of production and in effect, paradoxically, the cheaper, therefore, the worker. Under capitalist conditions, surplus value is skimmed off, workers robbed of part of the value of their work, capital 'accumulates', and classes polarise as the capitalist class gets richer at the expense of the working class. Thus, under capitalist conditions, two fundamental classes emerge and gradually consolidate: a subordinate class that labours and a ruling class that appropriates surplus value. This creates a potentially explosive antagonism between an ever-shrinking minority of property holders (because powerful market players become increasingly powerful at the expense of weaker market players through economies of scale) and an increasingly pauperised working class, caught up in a vicious circle where the more dependent they become, the more expansive the 'reserve army' of the unemployed, the more able are their employers to suppress wages. Yet capitalism, argues Marx, contains the seeds of its destruction because it harbours this 'contradiction', between the different class interests, at its very core.

It is obvious in this analysis that Marx begins with production and treats the economic as fundamental. The economy is the base of every society, determining its shape and the nature of its institutions – at least 'in the final instance' – in the same way as the foundations determine and delimit the shape of what rests upon them. Marx famously used the metaphor of the 'base' and 'superstructure' to describe the social structure of class society. As the 'base' of society, the economy acts upon the (other) institutions of civil society in a way that can be described as causal (but in a loose sense; not in the sense that any change in the economy directly causes a change in society). He meant that the organisation of economic activity will determine the type of political, legal, religious, educational and cultural institutions. Law, located thus among the institutions of the superstructure is very much *in keeping with* the conditions of the mode of production. Its operation broadly reflects the necessities of the mode of production and its function is to sustain and regulate *capitalist* economic and social relations. For example, if the contract is the characteristic form of modern law, it is because the form of the contract governs economic relations – particularly the sale of labour. However, the form of law, which sees the contract as a fair exchange between two equal individuals, masks social inequalities and the fact that contract law systematically reproduces the economic interests of the bourgeoisie. For Marx, then, the form of law was a means of systematically reproducing the interests of a particular social class and masking or repressing the underlying economic inequalities, and in this way maintains and consolidates asymmetric economic relations.

If the economic base determines *in the last instance* the kind of institutions we have in the superstructure, the role of the superstructure is not confined simply to reflecting the economic relations of society. Of course, says Marx, the superstructural political institutions that we have will reflect, and facilitate rather than impede, economic interests (look, for example today at the relationship of the City of London and the UK government, the latter's meek attempts to control the former, or the bankrolling of the political parties by powerful economic interests); of course the educational institutions we have will reflect and reproduce relations of production (in an education system that discriminates between those who will receive expensive privately funded education and those who will receive education befitting their future role as workers); of course our cultural institutions will reflect and reproduce dominant values; and so on. But that, for Marx, tells only half the story. The other half is how the superstructure works to manage, alleviate and defuse the potentially destructive contradictions that arise as a result of the injustice of the economic system, and thus how the superstructure helps to alleviate class conflict. Its institutions are crucially implicated in providing legitimation of the capitalist mode of production, and the legitimation they provide is in turn linked to ideology. Ideology works to alleviate contradictions and render the society coherent and seamless. How to best understand this?

Take the example of religion. When Marxists called (the Christian) religion the 'opium of the people', their argument was that the religious teaching to 'turn the other cheek' to your aggressor, or the promise that it is the meek who will inherit the earth, served to disarm the dispossessed from a claim to justice in the here and now. Or when Marxists denounced the parliamentary system as a 'talking shop' of the bourgeoisie, their argument was that the populace is duped into thinking that they are represented in the processes of democratic will-formation in the legislature, while the real decisions that affect (and devastate) lives are taken behind the closed doors of the boardrooms of the bourgeoisie, or (to update Lenin's dictum) of the institutions of global capital, such as the World Bank, the IMF, the WTO and the G20. What we find in these examples is a clear legitimating function of the institutions of the super-structure: religion and politics in these examples function directly to mask, justify or redeem the injustice of capitalist social relations.

The function of law

Marx says little directly about the institution of law, at least in a systematic way, and much of his critique of modern law is scattered across his other writings. Like Durkheim, Marx also regarded the contract as the distinctive form of modern law, but on the basis of a fundamentally different analysis of social relations. The primary category of analysis for Marx, as we saw, was social class, and classes were defined and understood in terms of their position in relation to the means of production. But while the economic analysis that Marx offers focuses on how the bourgeoisie extracted profits from labour by forcing down the price of labour and maintaining the price of the objects produced through control of supply and demand in the market, there is a legal dimension to these processes that is highly significant. The economic *means* of production were accompanied by distinctive social *relations* of production, which aimed at the reproduction of the social position and power of the dominant class, significantly, though not exclusively, by means of law.

To explore this dimension we may usefully turn to the work of the Soviet jurist Evgeny Pashukanis whose tracking of the relationship of law to the economy through what he identified as the 'commodity form theory of law' has, belatedly, been hugely influential. Pashukanis argued that the form of law, especially the form that the law's basic categories of *legal subject, legal relation* and *legal norm* take, directly correlate to market relations of commodity exchange. The formation of capitalist production develops in tandem with bourgeois law, and the form of law coincides with that of commodity exchange. This is important. Pashukanis is in effect arguing that law is not merely an institution in the superstructure reflecting economic relations, but is instead crucially implicated in constituting them. If capitalist relations were struc-tured around ownership and the wage relation, it was the legal categories of prop-erty (ownership of means of production) and contract (the labour contract) that, so to speak, ran alongside the economic forms and allowed the economic system to func-tion as it did. Law was also centrally implicated in the commodification of social life, not merely by extending the category of property rights to cover one's very ability to work – for Marx the most *human* of activities, remember – but also by constituting the nodal points of social interaction in terms of contracts, rents, interests, and soon. In a capitalist society these were all legally sanctioned and policed. This is where the notion of *commodification* becomes important. For the market mechanism to operate, there needs to be an equation of goods in exchange, and thus a common denominator, which would allow comparisons, needs to be introduced. Equivalence is generalised across spheres of human activity, involving an abstraction from the use-value that made those activities meaningful to humans, individually and inter-personally. Now the logic of exchange takes over, and with it the hijacking of value by the profit motive. Money, Marx's 'cash nexus', allows the flow of all things in the marketplace as commensurable. It introduces a measure of all things in exchange. There is a loss in this, argued Marx: things are no longer of value for what they are (use value), but for what they are worth in exchange (exchange value). And where the cost is borne most heavily is in relation to that most fundamental of activities, labour. In the process of its double subjection to the logic of exchange value, and the material conditions of the organisation of factory production, the worker's creative labour becomes nothing but *expendable energy*, abstracted as merely time committed to the factory floor, that can be sold by the worker and bought by the capitalist. Throughout this it is the legal *form*, Pashukanis significantly adds, that is implicated in a way that is fundamental.

To summarise so far: the law enables the market to operate by establishing what it means to own a commodity and the conditions of its exchange. The legal concepts of property and contract are fundamental conditions for *giving form* to the economic relations of production. What is also of paramount importance is our identity in law as legal subjects. While for Marx our very sense of identity depends on our interaction with others, as legal subjects what ties us together is money and our ability to buy and sell. Law *abstracts* from social identity those features that are relevant to relations of commodity owners in the market. The legal subject is thus an abstraction from our social situation. We become in law merely bearers of rights and duties which, in liberal law, means that we are commodity owners, *free to* exchange commodities in the market and *free from* any interference (from the State primarily). (See, also, Habermas's account of the first epoch of juridification, Part III 2.2 below.) These form part of what Marx identifies as the processes of *alienation*, which take hold in capitalist societies. Co-operative productive activity is crucially undercut when exchange value stands in for what is of intrinsic value. The early Marx spoke passionately of the commodification of labour as 'reduc[ing] the worker into a fragment of a man, destroy[ing] the fruits of his labour . . .' (Marx 1844, pp 77–87). According to Marx, in the communist world that was to succeed the capitalist one this form of alienation would disappear alongside the withering away of the capitalist State and its law. Bourgeois law would be replaced by the technical norm, the regulation of things, not the class subjugation of people. We would then, for Marx, recover our true nature, currently *obscured* by the legal form, the legal description under which we understand ourselves as property owners and commodity exchangers.

Ideology

The notion of *legal ideology* as used by Marxists is relevant to this function of 'obscuring', used to explain how it works, how law operates to prevent visibility of the exploitative nature of social relations. We saw earlier that if Marx offers a theory of society in which the key determinant of its organisation is its mode of production, the superstructure does not simply passively reflect those economic relations. It also acts back on the base to manage, alleviate and defuse the potentially destructive contradictions that arise there, and to help alleviate class conflict. Its institutions are crucially implicated in providing legitimation of the capitalist mode of production, and the legitimation they provide is in turn linked to ideology.

While ideology in common parlance usually means a body of ideas and beliefs, in Marxist terminology it defines a *function*. This function is to sustain relations of domination by a move at the level of representation. Marx invites us to think about the following questions. Why, given the injustice of a system that is perpetrated by a minority grouping of society (the ruling class) on the majority (the working class), does the system continue its course of reproducing these unjust relations? Is this to do with how real relations are represented and lived? And how is man's relationship to the conditions of his own existence understood by him? Marx locates ideology as that system of representation that mediates man's relationship to the material conditions of his life, that is, in simpler terms, the grid or lens through which man perceives the lived reality of his situation in the social world. Ideology here accounts for a certain misrepresentation, a certain misreading of the conditions that allows the continuation of a system of domination that presents itself as free. As John Thompson has put it:

> the concept of ideology calls our attention to the ways in which meaning is mobilized in the service of dominant individuals and groups, that is, the ways in which the meaning constructed and conveyed by symbolic forms serves to establish and sustain structured social relations from which some individuals and groups benefit more than others.
>
> (1984, p 73)

How does 'misrepresentation' work exactly? At the most ordinary level, the superimposition of a framework of general, formal rules upon a sub-terrain of real inequality achieves both the 'mystification' – the cover-up – of the real disparities and also the accentuation of those underlying inequalities. According to the law of contract, as we know, parties to a bargain (whether this has to do with the buying or selling of goods or of labour) approach it on formally equal terms. Thus while a bargain is struck between parties of unequal bargaining power in real terms, legally it appears as an agreement between equals who are as free to reach agreement as they are to abstain. The realities of the vast disparities of bargaining power, or the threat of advancing unemployment are all screened off by the appearance of legal equality. The liberal legal order backs and sanctions individual freedom in the market, but this, as we saw Anatole France put it, is a freedom that works asymmetrically, in allowing 'both the rich and poor to sleep under the bridges of Paris'. Equality before the law hides material inequality, the uneven distribution of power and goods. Also, the market operates to give power to the most powerful market player (economies of scale, etc). And yet this privileging of the powerful party is hidden behind a guise of formal equivalence. This *concealment* is what in Marxist terms is understood as ideology. At the same time as it conceals and abstains from interference, formality boosts capitalist activity that further increases the disparity of wealth and power in society.

Marxists will not deny that coercion to support dominant economic interests often operates 'unmasked', especially when they are 'threatened' by subversive activity. However, such cynical instrumental accounts of law have a limited explanatory power and fail to take account of the vital dimension of legitimation, that is, the importance that power is presented not as brute power but as authority, as justified, fair and as creating obligation rather than obliging through force. No order, and in particular not one as unjust as the capitalist order, would be able to sustain itself over time if it did not appear as legitimate. Take an example that Hugh Collins uses in his study of *Marxism and Law* (1982, pp 41–2). Laws that criminalised 'combination' among workers were vital to an early capitalist system that felt the urgent need to protect itself from trade union activity. But such banning needed to present itself as legitimate and the ideological moment comes with its justification as upholding the equality of the parties to the labour contract; any combination that might allow workers to push for higher wages was thus made to appear unjust, a ganging up of sorts of one party against the other, irrespective of the fact that the bargaining positions were vastly uneven to begin with. It is in examples like this that we see clearly how a system seeks its justification in justice and equality, and is reluctant to rely on brute coercion alone to see through the reproduction of the relations of production.

There are multiple forms through which the ideological 'obscuring' works. Law, argue Marxists, operates ideologically to 'naturalise' concepts like private property and exchange through contract, as if they were essential to our constitution as human beings; to 'mystify' or cover up substantive inequality through formal equality, and powerlessness through equal rights; to 'depoliticise' social struggles, that is, remove their political dimension and make them appear as merely criminal; present them in a form that depletes them and renders them controllable. Here is Marx in his essay 'The German Ideology':

> The class which has the means of material production at its disposal, has the control at the same time over the means of intellectual production, so that thereby, generally speaking, the ideas of those who lack the means of intellectual production are subject to it.
>
> (1932, p 176)

There is a connection here between material production and the control of intellectual production, but that is not all. From the time of his earliest writings, Marx was keen to expose the subtle ways in which capitalism diffuses resistance and critique through subtle moves and strategies at the level of representation. One of his most famous denunciations is in 'On the Jewish Question' (1843), where he famously draws a distinction between political and human emancipation. He argues that the great political revolutions of the eighteenth century – the French and American – declared political emancipation while leaving the structures of 'private right' intact, notably the regime of property rights, including them as 'rights of man' in the name of which the revolutions were fought. But 'who is "man"?' asks Marx, and 'why are his rights called the rights of man?' He answers: 'No one but the member of civil society, i.e. egoistic man, man separated from other men and the community . . . who sees in other men not the realisation but the limitation of his own freedom' (1843, pp 52, 53). In proclaiming, and entrenching, the rights of 'egoistical' man as the rights of the citizen, the revolutions in fact served to install a system of bourgeois property relations in the name of freedom, and despite the universalism of their declarations and the extension of political rights, left citizens powerless before property owners (see Polanyi pp 225–226). For Marx this is 'revolutionary practice in flagrant contradistinction with its theory' (1843, p 54).

Legal ideology, then, functions by presenting contingent arrangements as natural, or by inscribing certain assumptions into the supposed nature of man. Is it really the case, for example, that, as Locke argued, the fact that no one owns me any longer (after the abolition of slavery) means that 'I own myself'? Or is it not rather that the category of property does not apply in this context? To secure its continuation capitalism must secure that relations of production are reproduced in their current form; that the disempowered remain in that state; and, thus, that class struggle is prevented from erupting in a way that might challenge the capitalist distribution of advantage through ownership of the means of production. To generate legitimation for the system, the law acts ideologically in a range of ways outlined here. In all these ways the 'critique of ideology' is far-reaching and has informed many critical stances today beyond strictly Marxist positions.

Marxists and the law

If these are the main elements of Marx's analysis of capitalist society, it should be noted that there are a number of different strands in the Marxist critique of bourgeois law, as different theorists have interpreted Marx's theory in diverse ways. These range from an extreme position that denounces law as merely reflecting exploitative economic relations of production, a mere instrument of oppression of the working class, to the acknowledgement of the 'relative autonomy' of law from the economic base. Rather schematically we can identify the following positions.

There is first a repressive–instrumental view of law that views the State and its law as instruments of class rule. This is the Marxist–Leninist line of 'class state – class law'. The rule of law and rights reflect and serve the interests of capitalists. Rights, with their emphasis on individualism, are incompatible with socialist ideals of justice and community; and the rule of law, with its emphasis on due process, merely inhibits the advancement of goals of substantive justice (Lenin 1917).

However, the argument that law is relatively autonomous of the economic base suggests that it does not merely reflect exploitation in a passive way, but might also develop according to its own logic or in response to other demands. On this view the law might provide opportunities to redress exploitation, and thus may have a strategic or substantive value for the proletariat. On this basis one might identify two further strands within the tradition.

On the one hand, Marxism as 'critical theory' emphasises and tries to expose the law's ideological effects. It is argued that the propounding of rights and the rule of law as the 'natural' expression of freedom sanctions a particular view of the 'natural' order of things in a competitive world of self-interested individuals.

The emphasis here is both on what law obscures (exploitation, class conflict), and on what it presents as necessary (individual rights, freedom of contract and property). This is no blanket rejection of the bourgeois law, but a thorough uncovering of the hidden disempowering assumptions that it embodies (Horkheimer 1972); and therefore the possibilities also that it might harbour, and of exploiting them strategically.

On the other hand there is a strand of Marxism that acknowledges value in the rule of law and the existence of rights. The celebrated historian Edward Thompson expresses this position (1977, pp 258–69). He suggests that the rule of law 'represents an unqualified human good' and that the existence of legal institutions independent of state manipulation or individual influence is a basic safeguard against arbitrary power and an effective inhibition upon class rule. He wrote: 'To deny or belittle this good is … a desperate error … which encourages us to give up the struggle against bad laws and class-bound procedures and to disarm ourselves against power. It is to throw away a whole inheritance of struggle about law' (1977, p 266). This line of argument, in one sense, builds on the critique of ideology for, 'if the law is evidently partial and unjust then it will mask nothing, legitimise nothing, contribute nothing to any class's hegemony' (1977, p 263). An important difference, however, is that it points to the way that the rule of law, or particular laws, can themselves become binding on the ruling classes, and might offer certain forms of protection against the abuses of political or economic power.

Reading

For an accessible analysis of some of the fundamentals of the theory see Marx's *The German Ideology*. His famous critique of rights and the French and American Declarations are contained in his early essay 'On the Jewish Question', and a discussion of equality in his *Critique of the Gotha Programme*. For his analysis of the labour contract see his 1849 essay 'Wage Labour and Capital'. His analysis of commodification, use- and exchange-value and 'original accumulation' are found in his major work of the later period *Capital*, especially vol 1.

For a concise introduction to Marx see Giddens (1971, chs 1–4). There is also a useful introduction in Collins (1982) and Cotterrell (1992, pp 106–18).

Marx wrote little directly on law; a useful collection of extracts is collected by Cain and Hunt (1979) (esp pp 52–3, 56–9, 116–17, 132–7, 164–5). For a discussion of Marxism and law the following are useful: Stone (1985), Collins (1982) and Giddens (1971). For other works on law in the Marxist tradition see especially Pashukanis's major work *Law and Marxism* and the very useful introduction by Arthur (1978). On commodification and reification with special reference to law, see Lukacs (1971). Louis Althusser (1971) provides one of the most famous, and controversial, accounts of the function of ideology as tied to the material practices of what he identifies as 'Ideological State Apparatuses'.

For a work discussing the conception of ideology in relation to international law see Marks (2000, ch 1) and more generally to law Hirst (1979). In his edited volume, Zizek (1994, especially chs 1, 6, 9, 12 and 13) has compiled one of the best collections of writings in the Marxist tradition of ideology.

1.4 Formal legal rationality and legal modernity

While the two analyses that we have looked at up to this point have focused on the changes in social and economic relations and their impact on law, the German sociologist Max Weber was more concerned with questions of how particular forms of rationality developed in different areas of social life, including the law, and the extent to which there were common themes or affinities in this process of rationalisation. Weber's central project was thus a historical sociology of the distinctive forms of modern Western rationality. Central achievements of occidental rationality were seen as the capitalist economy, organised religion, the Nation-State and modern forms of bureaucracy or political administration, and the rule of law. This did not mean that he ignored the relation between economy and society, but rather that he did not see a clear causal relation between developments in the one and the other. His sociology of law, then, was an attempt to analyse the distinctive features of modern Western law by focusing on the conditions that he saw as central to its unique development, and to trace the relationship between the law and the other forms of rational organisation of social life.

Weber saw modern Western law as having certain distinct features. It was a system of general norms of universal application, organised and backed by the power of the State, applied and interpreted by a specially qualified staff of lawyers. In addition, modern law was relatively independent from politics, although the modern bureaucratic State was itself dependent on a particular legal form. These were not viewed as necessary features of all law, but were understood as the outcome of a particular process of historical development. The study of the form of modern law (as with the study of all other forms of rationality) thus required the development of a particular methodology, focusing on the forms of legal rationality and political authority and the relationships between them. We shall look at these, before going on to see how Weber used them in his historical sociology of the development of modern law.

Forms of legal rationality

Legal rationality was analysed in terms of four forms; formal and substantive (informal); rational and irrational. These were 'ideal-typical' forms, not intended to refer to any actually existing legal system, but to allow the analysis of the principal characteristics of specific legal systems on the basis of variations in legal technique and forms of political organisation. There are two major dimensions of comparison: the degree of *rationality* and the degree of *formality*. The former measures the generality of the rules employed by the system and the systematic character of the legal order, the latter the extent to which criteria of decision intrinsic to the legal system are used. Thus the degree of rationality is aimed at the analysis of the internal consistency of a legal system, while the criteria of formality are concerned additionally both with the extent to which legal norms are formally articulated and with the autonomy of the legal system from political institutions and pressures. It must, therefore, be noted that these forms refer not only to the internal characteristics of legal systems, but also to the relation between legal systems and other forms of social and political organisation.

If we look at each of the different types of rationality, we can distinguish the following principal types of legal systems:

informal irrational	formal irrational
informal rational	formal rational

● Informal irrational

In these types of systems there may be no formally established body of laws, and no established criteria on which decisions are to be made in individual cases. There may or may not be recognised judges, and each case will be judged on its own merits. Decisions will commonly have no binding force beyond the particular case to be adjudicated. Weber sometimes referred to this as 'khadi-justice' after the practice in certain Muslim courts (Weber 1968, pp 845, 976–8).

● Formal irrational

This refers to those types of systems where there is some form of established law, but the law derives its authority from the lawgiver, as in the case of sacred law, or from a formalised set of customary practices. This was regarded as irrational in the sense that the authority of the law was not related to an internal quality of the rules themselves or their efficacy in organising social life, but was derived wholly from the oracular quality of their source (for example, forms of sacred or religious law). Thus in the sphere of law-finding, there might be recognised judges who follow certain established procedures for the settling of disputes, but the criteria of decision-making are unknowable. A good example of this type of practice would be the trial by ordeal or battle, which was a highly formalised system, but which appealed to divine intervention for the determination of guilt.

● Informal rational

This refers to those systems where there is a rational process for the making and enactment of law, but this is directed towards set extrinsic or external aims, such as ethical imperatives, utilitarian ends or political purposes. Law is used instrumentally, and its authority depends on the extent to which it is able to fulfil these ends. The application of law must meet similar criteria. It would therefore be conceivable that in cases where the facts were similar, different decisions might be reached depending on, for example, the status or social class of the litigants as a matter of the policy or values to which the law was oriented.

● Formal rational

This refers to systems with a formal process for the enactment of laws, but where the laws would be regarded as relatively autonomous from particular social policies or ethical ideals. There would be specialised institutions for the application of the law, and the discretion of judges would be limited. There would be a strong expectation that cases that were alike in their relevant legal characteristics would be treated alike. This requires the development of techniques for determining the relevant legal characteristics of a case and for the identification and application of general rules. Alternatively, it may simply demand the adherence to certain external characteristics of the facts, such as a signature on a deed or the utterance of certain words. This is to distinguish two different variants of formal rationality, which can be referred to as logical formality and the formal recognition of extrinsic characteristics. The former is in many respects the key to Weber's analysis of modern law, and we shall be examining it at some length below. It is first necessary, however, to look at his analysis of the forms of political authority.

Forms of political authority

Weber defined a State as 'a human community that (successfully) claims the monopoly of the legitimate use of physical force within a given territory' (1948a, p 78), arguing that political organisation could not typically rely on coercion alone, but would have also to establish some legitimate grounds for political authority. The forms of political authority or domination were, therefore, analysed in terms of the types of legitimacy that were typically claimed by, or which actors ascribed to, political orders. Political authority or domination was also seen as taking certain characteristic or ideal-typical forms. Weber identified three pure types of legitimate domination:

- *Traditional* domination, which rested on the 'established belief in the sanctity of immemorial traditions and the legitimacy of those exercising authority under them' (Weber 1968, p 215).
- *Charismatic* domination, which rested upon the extraordinary heroism or exemplary character of an individual leader and the order created or revealed by him or her.
- *Legal* domination, which rested on the belief in the legality of a consciously created order and the right to give commands vested in certain persons designated by that order. This is seen as the specifically modern type of administration.

The last is an impersonal form of order where obedience is demanded and given out of respect for the order itself, while the other two depend on the status of an office or the characteristics of certain individuals. In legal domination legitimation is thus intrinsic to the order, rather than being dependent on external factors. However, Weber goes on to argue that, to the extent that legal domination is a rational form of domination, it will tend to have certain further characteristics relating to its administrative staff: official business is bound by rules; it is carried out within certain demarcated spheres or jurisdictions; it takes place within an official hierarchy of rule and supervision; and it requires some degree of professional training of officials. In addition, in a rational system there is a strict separation between the ownership and the means of administration, with no office being owned by its incumbent: that is to say that there is a separation between the office and the individual, which guarantees the impartiality and technical efficiency of the bureaucracy. Thus 'the purest type of exercise of legal authority is that which employs a bureaucratic administrative staff' (Weber 1968, p 220), for this leads to an increase in the technical knowledge and competency of the administration, which is essential to economic organisation and organisation of social life under the conditions of the division of labour. In this sense, then, Weber contends that rational bureaucratic organisation is essential to modernity, since it alone is capable of dealing with the problems of distribution of goods and management of the economy, as well as ensuring the continuous regulation of social life.

Through these ideal types Weber traces an affinity between formal rational law and legal domination – legal domination as the rule of law, but also seeing bureaucracies as rule-bound institutions of government – a relationship that would be confirmed by his historical sociology of Western law. However, it is important to note that there are ambiguities here that reflect tensions between law and politics in the modern State.

The key point here concerns the distinction between forms of legal and political organisation and the way that the different forms of law could interact with the types of legitimate political domination. Thus while certain forms of law require some sort of extrinsic guarantee for the legal order, as informal rational law relies on religious (charismatic) or political ends and authority, formal rational law claims an intrinsic authority or validity based on the legal form itself. In this way it makes a claim to autonomy from political or economic or ethical ends or rationality (although as we have suggested in Part II 1.2 the commitment to formalism is in itself a commitment to a particular set of political values). The question of legitimacy, however, is primarily a political question, and legal domination is a form of political legitimacy. This is a claim to a form of intrinsic authority (while the other two types rely on extrinsic factors) that depends on, for example, the legal codification of political relationships in the form of a constitution and the legal definition of the scope of political offices or powers. It thus overlaps conceptually and historically with formal rational law. The ambiguity lies in the fact that while legal domination appears to rest on an internal claim to validity (government by laws not men, the rule of law), it in fact depends on the organisation of the legal system and the sustainability of the distinction between law and politics. There is a necessary tension in the juxtaposition of formal rational law and legal legitimacy, for though the latter would seem to require the former, the reverse of this is not the case. This captures an important feature of the relationship between law and politics in the modern State. This relationship is slanted towards the question of how law can guarantee political order, rather than vice versa. This means that the question of the legitimacy of the legal system itself can appear as a problem under certain conditions, such as, for example, when legal questions become politicised or where law is required to adjudicate in political disputes, because while the political system might draw on the formal rational law for legitimacy, this can come at a cost for law. Historically, Weber suggests, the difficulty is bridged through the conjunction between formal legal rationality and the development of bureaucracy as the highest forms of rational and autonomous administration in the modern State. However, as we shall see, the distinction between law and politics has become increasingly unstable.

The development of legal modernity

The relationship between forms of law and political organisation becomes clearer if we consider it in the context of Weber's basic outline of a historical sociology of Western law, the central feature of which was the increasing rationalisation of legal thought and the triumph of formal rational law. In this we can illustrate how Weber uses the ideal types as a means of analysing a specific pattern of development, as well as seeing how the development of legal modernity relates to the forms of political organisation.

The broad outline of development of legal modernity is laid out in the following passage:

> From a theoretical point of view, the general development of law and procedure may be viewed as passing through the following stages: first, charismatic legal revelation through 'law prophets'; second, empirical creation and finding of law by legal *honoriatores*, i.e. law creation through cautelary [reasoning on a case-by-case basis] jurisprudence and adherence to precedent; third, imposition of law by secular or theocratic powers; fourth and finally, the systematic elaboration of law and professionalised administration of justice by persons who have received their legal training in a learned and formally logical manner. From this perspective, the formal qualities of the law emerge as follows: arising in primitive legal procedure from a combination of magically conditioned formalism and irrationality conditioned by revelation, they proceed to increasingly specialised juridical and logical rationality and systematisation, sometimes passing through the detour of theocratically or patrimonially conditioned substantive and informal expediency. Finally, they assume, at least from an external viewpoint, an increasingly logical sublimation and deductive rigour and develop an increasingly rational technique in procedure.
>
> (Weber 1968, p 882)

This describes a double movement combining the increasing rationalisation of law, in the sense of generalisation in its elaboration and enactment, and the increasing formalisation of the law and its autonomy from systems of religious and political power. At the same time, however, this describes the subjection of political power to the forms of legal rationality, one of the more significant achievements of formal rational law and a characteristic of legal modernity.

These achievements can be broken down into four broad categories. First, the development of rational law frees the individual from traditional forms of power based in superstition, religion or arbitrary sovereign action, through the development of universalisable norms and the rational administration of justice. The development of modernity thus establishes a particular kind of relationship between formal legal rationality and political power, which is constituted in legal form. This form of legitimacy enables those holding political power to do certain things, in particular when associated with the development of the capacities of rational bureaucratic administration, but (in its formal rational expression) the law now sets limits on arbitrary power. It is thus (paradoxically) both a means of achieving individual and political freedom and the means through which the rational administration of the modern State is constructed.

The second achievement is the creation of a law of general validity and universal application. As the State has a monopoly over the means of violence within certain territorial boundaries – the classic definition of the modern Nation-State – this leads to the creation of law that is universal within the territory, superseding all local laws and privileges based on status and special jurisdictions. Formal rational law achieves its ideal expression in the form of a code. Laws must be published in advance in a form that can be understood by all subjects, and are merely applied by judges and other legal officials who are formally independent of the sovereign. The actions of the State and its officers are subjected to legal controls, and so become more predictable. Equally, in the area of private law, the protection of private property and the enforcement of contracts become more secure and predictable, allowing the more certain regulation and future planning of economic affairs. By this means the rule of law creates and sustains security in economic, governmental and social life.

Third, there is the development of a sophisticated and specialised type of reasoning that requires that those interpreting and applying the law receive professional training. The idea that the law is both gapless and internally consistent with itself is derived from the reception of Roman law, which took rules that were developed by an inductive process and were context-dependent and generalised them to the level of abstract principles that could be applied deductively since they were believed to be the highest achievements of reason. Legal problems are thus seen as individuated cases that can be solved in a systematic manner by identifying the legally relevant facts and subsuming them within abstract legal norms. Cases are to be solved only by looking at the combination of law and facts, and by excluding consideration of factors such as moral values or social status.

Finally, as part of a wider process of secularisation, the law is separated from the sphere of ethics. Although this was initially understood in terms of the separation of law and religion, both at the level of the disestablishment of State religion and in terms of the content of individual laws, this has a number of important consequences for our understanding of modernity. Weber traced the reception of Roman law through its transformation into modern or revolutionary natural law, in which the legitimacy of the norms was derived from the immanent or teleological qualities of the law – the working out of the principles of 'reason and justice' – which allowed it to transcend its origins in princely or priestly power. This, he argued, was the 'only consistent type of legitimacy of a legal order which can remain once religious revelation and the authoritarian sacredness of a tradition and its bearers have lost their force' (Weber 1968, p 867). However, he also pointed out that this form of legitimacy was undermined by the development of a formal rational law whose authority was grounded only in the formal question of the internal validity of the norm. The development of legal modernity thus broke the connection between law and reason or justice. Formal positive law need have no particular content, and is limited by no other ethical or moral principles. It is non-interventionist – not pursuing particular social or policy ends – and it is clearly differentiated from other sources of normative ordering. It is therefore implicit in both the idea and the historical development of formal rational law that there be some form of specialisation and autonomy from other spheres of values and social life.

From this brief account we can see how Weber's conception of formal rational law describes important features of legal modernity. It is tempting to see these achievements as the inevitable result of the unfolding of an immanent process of rationalisation – a march of progress towards better, more rational, law – a temptation that is exacerbated by the language of ideal types and Weber's description of formal rational law as the highest form of rationality. However, it is necessary to ask why this form of law should have developed uniquely in the West, for this was not an inevitable process, even when considered in conjunction with the development of the capitalist economy.

To begin with, it is important to note that Weber did not see this question as one simply of the relation between law and economy, or between forms of legal and economic thought, although he clearly regarded this relation as being of central importance. Indeed, unlike Marx, he was at pains to deny the existence of a strict correlation or causal relation between the two: changes in external conditions, such as changes in the form of the economy might have some impact on individual or collective conduct, but could not in any sense be regarded as determinants of such conduct. Equally, the law might protect certain economic interests, but it was clear both that these interests might be protected in other ways, and that the law also served other interests that could not be reduced to purely economic factors. It is thus important to note that while Weber wished to place the forms of economic organisation at the centre of his sociology, he was also distancing himself in two important respects from Marx's analysis of the development of law and the capitalist economy. First, he was concerned to establish the full range of relations between the economy and other relevant social spheres, without seeing these relationships as being uni-causally determined in any way. Second, in contrast to Marx's class analysis, Weber was concerned with individual activity and orientations towards forms of conduct or ideas as a means of understanding social and economic activities: 'the ability and disposition of men to adopt certain types of practical rational conduct' (Weber 1930, p 26; Ewing 1987). However, unlike many forms of methodological individualism that begin from the assumption of certain natural or intrinsic characteristics, such as self-interest or the ability to reason, for Weber there is no intrinsic quality attaching to human actions or persons, and thus there can be no organising principles beyond the orientation towards certain rationally structured activities. This problematises the idea of rationality, for it is implicit in this view that the world is fundamentally non-rational. This gives his analysis of the rise of formal rational law further distinctive characteristics, notably an emphasis on the contingency of social relations and a scepticism about the capacity of rationality to organise human affairs. The explanation for the rise of formal rational law was sought, then, in the coincidence of, or affinity between, certain interests, combined with an analysis of the intrinsic or internal demands of a developing legal profession.

This can be seen in his treatment of the rise of the national economic system and its impact on traditional forms of economic and political organisation. Weber argued that an economic system of the modern type could not exist without a legal order backed by the State that could guarantee the predictability and stability of economic relations:

> [M]odern economic life by its very nature has destroyed those other associations which used to be the bearers of law and thus of legal guaranties. This has been the result of the development of the market. The universal predominance of the market

consociation requires on the one hand a legal system the functioning of which is calculable in accordance with rational rules. On the other hand, the constant expansion of the market consociation has favoured the monopolisation and regulation of all 'legitimate' coercive power by one universal coercive institution through the disintegration of all particular status-determined and other coercive structures which have been resting mainly on economic monopolies.

(Weber 1968, p 337)

In this passage, then, Weber is pointing to the central importance of legal order in counteracting the social effects of economic development, as well as the way in which economic development created the conditions in which a rational legal system could supersede other forms of social and political organisation. Law functioned to promote the security of the interests of commerce and business and the protection of property. It did so by structuring economic relations in ways that made them more efficient, predictable and enforceable, specifically through the contractual form, but also through the development of devices such as agency and negotiable instruments, which facilitated economic transactions. However, Weber was also at pains to point out that this was not a function of legal rationality as such, for 'the consequences of the purely logical construction often bear very irrational or even unforeseen relations to the expectations of the commercial interests' (Weber 1968, p 855). The formal abstract character of law was also of decisive merit to those with economic power in securing freedom from arbitrary government interference, as it was to those 'who on ideological grounds attempt to break down authoritarian control or to restrain irrational mass emotions for the purpose of opening up individual opportunities and liberating capacities' (Weber 1968, p 813). Once again, however, this was accompanied with a caveat, pointing out that there was no necessary connection between economic freedom of contract and political freedom.

Weber identified two other principal factors in the rise of formal rational law: the influence of political authority, and autonomous developments in the study and professional organisation of the law. With respect to the former, he argued that the more rational the administrative machinery of princes or religious leaders became (in the sense of the use of paid, qualified, officials and the development of a permanent bureaucracy), then the more rational would become the law. This, however, was not a matter of articulated policy, but was generally driven by the immanent needs of their own organisation, whether fiscal or administrative. In general, Weber identified princely or patrimonial forms of law with either arbitrary command or the creation of privileges in the 'estates', but he argued that this limited the effectiveness of princely rule, since the administration was limited by the fragmentation of the realm and the discontinuity of laws across special jurisdictions. The elimination of these privileges served the interests of officials in the expansion of the extent of the law and the creation of order and unity, also coinciding with the interests of the bourgeoisie in a more objective and rational law. In fiscal terms, as the size of the administration grew beyond the household of the prince, the costs of maintenance increased, and these needs were met by increasingly rational (regular and general) rather than arbitrary forms of taxation as the princes sought to tie themselves to certain economic interest groups. Perhaps most importantly of all, however, Weber stressed the importance of technical factors associated with learning and professionalisation that drove the autonomous development of the law. The crucial factor here was the reception of Roman law, initially in the canon law and later as a more abstract system of legal learning, which offered the basis for a universalisation of law that transcended traditional forms and particularistic norms. This had important consequences for the education of lawyers in the early universities. The study of law based on the formal qualities of Roman law became a specialised form of knowledge and encouraged the formation of the legal profession (though these did not necessarily serve economic interests). It also had important consequences for the administration of justice as trained lawyers, whether acting as officials or judges, demanded the rationalisation of law and procedure. This underlines, once again, the close connections that Weber drew between formal rational law – the development of rational administration in the form of bureaucracy – and legal domination.

In summary, then, legal modernity for Weber was characterised by the development of formal rational law, a development that coincided with, and contributed to the development of the capitalist economy. The notable achievements of this form of law were to provide a legal form that enabled both the stable and continuous regulation of the economy and social life and the constitutionalisation of political power, through the creation of an autonomous, specialised form of legal reasoning. However, as we shall see in the following section, both internal and external pressures on the law have threatened these achievements.

Reading

Weber's major work was carried out between the years of 1904 and 1905 – when he first published the essays that subsequently made up the book *The Protestant Ethic and the Spirit of Capitalism* (Weber 1930) – and his death in 1920. The bulk of his great synthetic work – *Economy and Society* (Weber 1968) – was published posthumously in 1921, though it was not fully published in English until 1968.

Weber provides an excellent short introduction to the questions that animate his sociology in the introduction to *The Protestant Ethic and the Spirit of Capitalism* (1930, pp 13–31).

The classic analysis of Weber's sociology of law based on the ideal types can be found in Rheinstein (1954, pp xlvii–lxiii). A similar account can be found in Kronman (1983, ch 4). See also Part II 1.1 and II 1.2 for a discussion of legal formalism.

The types of legitimate domination are set out in Weber 1968 ch III (you should read pages 217–26 for an analysis of legal authority).

Weber's theory generally is discussed in Cotterrell (1995), Turner (1996) and Murphy (1997).

1.5 Transformations of modern law

If there were disagreements between Durkheim, Marx and Weber in the analysis of the function of law in modern society and its relation to economic development, there are also certain shared elements. All three recognised that the form of law was changing in response to the social changes that came with the development of the capitalist economy, and the significance of formalism in legal reasoning as being necessary to the securing of a particular kind of stability in legal, social and economic relations. And all recognised the importance of the role of law in reshaping and legitimating the modern state. Yet even as they wrote, the law was changing in response to social and political pressures – in response to what is often described as the 'social question'. In this section we outline some of these changes and the transformations that they brought about to the legal form and the function of law in modern society, notably with the emergence of the welfare state. We will then conclude the section by discussing how modern law is being exposed to a fresh set of pressures with the development of what has come to be known as globalisation.

The materialisation of modern law

Weber's argument, as we saw in the last section, was that modern law was an autonomous and technical discipline which, with the rise of the modern nation-state, had to fulfil the end of legitimising the political system. However, he recognised that there was an inherent tension between law and political power since the political demand for the implementation of particular policies tended to undermine the formal rationality of the legal system. 'Juridical formalism', in Weber's formulation, 'enables the legal system to operate like a technically rational machine' (1968, p 811) – implementing policy through legislation – but this had the consequence of undermining its capacity to stand opposed to political power. Legal modernity had created a formal rationality without ideals, where the legal profession acted as technicians serving established power, and where law was used to promote instrumental ends. Thus:

> [i]nevitably the notion must expand that the law is a rational technical apparatus which is continually transformable in the light of expediential considerations and devoid of all sacredness of content. This fate may be obscured by the tendency of acquiescence in the existing law, which is growing in many ways for several reasons, but it cannot really be stayed.
>
> (Weber 1968, p 895)

He identified three developments, which were bringing specific pressure to bear on the formal rationality of modern law – what he called the 'materialisation' of formal law. In the first place, he noted the revival and growth of 'particularism' in the law specifically, though not exclusively, in the areas of commercial and labour law. While, as we have seen, the development of modernity had been characterised by the removal of status privileges and jurisdictions and their replacement by norms of general application, writing in the early part of the twentieth century, Weber noted a trend towards the weakening of legal formalism by considerations of substantive expediency specific to certain areas of law. Thus he noted that in the area of commercial transactions the application of the law was coming to be determined by the substantive qualities of a transaction, that is to say the economic purpose of the transaction, rather than the formal properties of the contract. This was accompanied by the development of special tribunals, such as commercial courts, which explicitly sought to develop principles of adjudication that were adapted to the activity that they sought to regulate. The continuation of this trend has been noted by later theorists who have observed, for example, that the outcomes of commercial contractual disputes are more likely to be determined by the relationship between the contracting parties than the letter of the contract, and that the law is used only as final resort (Macaulay 1963; *Social & Legal Studies* 2000). We can also note the continued development of specialised informal dispute settlement institutions, such as tribunals or courts of arbitration, which have their own specialised jurisdiction and rules.

Second, Weber noted the operation of the status demands of lawyers. Legal formalism seeks to minimise the contribution of the lawyer by bowing to the political demand that the law be accessible and intelligible and attempting to reduce judicial discretion in the interpretation and application of the law. Weber, however, argued that this conflicted with the professional ideology of lawyers, which is based on the claim that the law is a complex science, the understanding of which requires specialised training and knowledge. Indeed he suggests that lawyers have an interest in maintaining the complexity of the law, and react to political movements for legal codification, or the simplification of the sources and mode of expression of the law, by seeking to defend their interests and preserve their social status. There is thus a fundamental conflict between professional demands for complexity and political demands for intelligibility, the outcome of which in practice has been the development of increasingly technical and internally differentiated bodies of law.

Third, he noted the impact of social conflict and inequality on the law, as the law was increasingly used as a tool for the management of class conflict. This, he argued, affected the ability of the law to be an abstract and impartial system of adjudication in one of two ways. On the one hand, the existence of social conflict called into question the abstract claims of the law to treat all individuals as equals, which led to political demands for a more social law that would be responsive to certain inequalities. There was thus also a politicising of law – that is to say the use of law as a means of achieving certain policy ends – in order to preserve the legitimacy of political authority. On the other hand, in the process of legal interpretation and application there was an assertion of the need for judicial creativity to supplement the abstract formulation of the law with evidence relating to the meaning and context of certain disputes. Thus lawyers would claim to discover the 'real' intentions of the parties to a contract, rather than looking at its purely formal qualities, and demand the recognition of categories such as 'good faith' or 'fair usage', which would require the judge to be more evaluative rather than merely enforcing the formal terms of an agreement. This reflects an inherent incompatibility between the 'utilitarian' meaning of a proposition and its formal legal meaning as this was governed by the demands of logical consistency. These could only be brought together at the cost of the renunciation of the formal qualities of law, and in particular the idea that the law was complete and 'gapless', in favour of more amorphous and ethical standards of substantive justice.

Although his analysis concentrates mainly on the external pressures that were being placed on the law, it is worth noting that it reflects a general and underlying internal tension in the legal form. This can be seen in the two different aspects of the positivisation of the law – a development that (as we have already noted) Weber regarded as a central achievement of legal modernity. On the one hand, positivisation reflects a fundamental conflict between legal and social fact, which can be traced to the relation between formal and substantive legitimacy in modern natural law. Modern natural law sought to establish the normative legitimacy of the law by codifying the natural qualities of social relations. It thus claimed a direct relation between legal and social fact. However, this form of law is vulnerable to disruption by the evidence of actual social facts or substantive demands made in the name of an ethical claim about legal justice. There is thus a necessary gap between legal and social fact that follows from the failures of social life to correspond to the model of law. Thus while the model of formal law is apparently founded on the premise that legal and social justice are commensurate, the experience of modernity suggests that this is not the case, and the law in practice swings between retreating into formalism and its dissolution in the pursuit of particular substantive ends. That is to say that there is a privileging of either the normative quality of the legal or that of the social, as a result of the unbridgeable gap that has been created between law and society. At the same time, the positivisation of the law results in the specialisation of the legal sphere. This accentuates a fundamental tension between the universalism of the ideology of the legal form and the limited social capacity of the law to resolve social conflicts.

Law in the welfare state

The diverse social developments that Weber identified came together with the emergence of the welfare state in developed Western nations in the middle decades of the twentieth century. It developed initially as a response to the devastating effects of the Great Depression and the Roosevelt administration's 'New Deal' in the United States, and later with the post-Second World War concern with justice and equality. This was the case for the victorious Allied Nations, where in Britain, for example, the Labour government of 1945 committed itself to an unprecedented programme of building up the education and health systems according to a vision of social democracy whereby the inability or denial to meet people's basic needs in terms of subsistence, health, education, employment and housing were seen as a violation of their dignity. But it was also the case for the defeated Germany where – perhaps paradoxically for those who today declare their unwillingness to fund it in times of recession – the commitment to the welfare state was tied to the very attempt to rebuild a strong economy. Subsequently, in what proved to be the final step of expansion of welfarism, the 1960s and early 1970s saw popular mobilisations and student/worker upheavals in Europe and America and the demand for the further expansion of social rights and protections. With the market's pretence to be free of power exposed, and with class inequalities and social hierarchies increasingly pronounced, there ensued a legitimation crisis that tried the 'staying power' of liberal capitalism which conceded what came to be known as the 'Welfare State compromise'. But by the end of the 1970s, as we will see, the seeds of the 'undoing' of this compromise and the breakdown of the post-war settlement were already visible.

We will say something more about this history, but it is important first to identify the features of the new role for the State that emerged with the development away from the classic model of economic liberalism. The State becomes an interventionist one, it undertakes the macro-management of the economy, is increasingly involved in redressing social inequalities, improving the living and working conditions of workers and extending social rights. In performing the tasks of redistribution of income and resources, regulation and planning ('social engineering'), it changes from the liberal state, the impartial guarantor, to the welfare state.

The hallmark of the welfare state, then, is that it dissolves the strict separation between state and society. In liberal society there were rigid boundaries between various social spheres – the economic, the familial and more generally the private – and the State and its law. The emergent welfare state moves into these spheres in the name of governing and regulating them. In the economic sphere, it supplements the market model with that of a state-regulated capitalism, for example through state demand for unproductive commodities, monopoly regulation and regulation of various forms of economic concentration. In the sphere of labour, the state provides protections for workers in the workplace and against dismissal. In the social sphere, the state provides education and health care through forms of national insurance. The state also replaces the market on occasions when it redirects capital investment into neglected sectors, or relieves capital of the need to amend certain social costs of production (by providing unemployment compensation, or assuming the costs of ecological damage).

But the interventionist role of the state is felt also in the transformations of modern law itself. Take contract law for example. The law of contract reflects this transformation from liberal to post-liberal law as it earlier reflected the shift from *Gemeinschaft* to *Gesellschaft* societies. Contract law was liberal law's paradigmatic form because it expressed the meeting of the wills of individuals, free to enter and shape the agreements. Contract law is now no longer the same. Think of the employment contract and the role of the state as a 'third' party to it: the fixing of the minimum wage, regulating for compulsory maternity and other leave, compensation thresholds and other interferences of all kinds from allocating rights of employment to regulating union membership, to policing the 'fairness' of contracts. In his analysis of contract law Thomas Wilhelmsson (1995) offers a conception of 'social contract law' as one which takes as its central notion not the freely reached agreement to satisfy individual *desires*, but the notion of (objectively) fair bargaining which satisfies (objective) *needs*. Drawing his examples from Swedish private law, he describes a system where judges have the power to rewrite the contract for the parties, and change unfair terms (rather than to declare them simply void), and where state agencies will intervene in negotiations with big companies to set standard terms which are in the public interest and which protect consumers. Unlike 'classical' liberal contract law which is content-neutral, welfarist contract law is content-oriented, with judges looking to interpret the contract in the light of legal policy and social interest. Where classical contract law is conceptualised as the expression of antagonistic tendencies in societies, the contract law of the welfare state may interpret contracts in the light of co-operation. Long-term contracts, especially employment contracts, become the role model of contract law and replace sales of goods. Another typical modern expression of this development is the idea of granting pressure groups, such as consumer organisations, legal standing to challenge companies in the name of 'the public'.

One might extend a similar analysis to property law. Classic *Gesellschaft* notions of ownership comprised the right to possess, to use, to manage, to destroy, the right to the capital, the right to the income of the thing, and an immunity from expropriation. By contrast, a welfarist understanding of property might limit these rights in the name of a common interest, for example in the environment, public access or communal water rights, in such a way that the owner is virtually unable to use the land in a profitable way. Societies where the liberal ideas of free ownership still predominate, such as the United States, will typically use forms of restrictions very reluctantly, and in the case of expropriation, grant the full market value as compensation. Societies in which the welfarist argument is predominant will use public law regulations intensively to guarantee that the use of private property is beneficial, or at least not detrimental, to the public.

We have taken these examples from private law as key 'indices' of the paradigmatic change that the regulatory welfare state ushers in. If in the *Gesellschaft* model, as we have seen, individuals could only be held liable for actions that could be attributed to them (criminal law and tort/delict) or transactions they freely entered into (contract), this principle becomes variably displaced or 'supplemented' by another, that of strict liability. Take the example of accidents in the workplace. Factory work carries risks and the question of who pays for the cost of injuries is crucial to our industries and economies. If the principles of welfarist legal systems commit to strict liability, and therefore the duty of employers to shoulder the costs of industrial accidents even when no negligence can be proven on their part, it is because it is assumed that those costs should not be borne by those less able to afford them, the workers, and because the social costs of production need to burden also those who most benefit from its organisation.

The more general question of our analysis here can now perhaps be posed in this way: how has the different function that law assumes as an instrument of regulation affected its form, and (in effect) the rule of law? Putting it in very general terms, we could say that the welfare state has changed law from formalistic to policy-oriented, and has shifted its concern from one with formal justice to one with substantive justice.

We might identify the following features as characteristics (and tensions) in the regulatory-welfarist form of law.

● **Bureaucracy, justice and instrumentalism**

Most writers identify welfare state law with the growth of large state bureaucracies, which are viewed as increasingly expensive and inefficient – more likely to preserve themselves or apply rules in formal and mechanical ways than be sensitive to the needs of individuals. There is an interesting contrast here with Weber's view, which, in describing late-nineteenth-century state bureaucracies, saw not a conflict but a fruitful convergence between bureaucratic structure, the spread of formal rationality and the rule of law. Bureaucracies provided a social and administrative guarantee of formal justice and control of the judiciary. The hierarchy of supervision and division of labour was the most efficient way to handle cases and the uniform and regular application of rules was an effect of the institutional structure. Conversely, however, this guarantee may turn into a threat to the rule of law, for the connection between efficiency and due process is not straightforward. Many contemporary analyses of legal administration have thus focused on the general trend towards mechanical regulation and bureaucratic goal displacement.

● **The uses of discretion**

This second trend associated with the growth of the modern welfare state converges with the first in involving an alleged increase in discretionary powers and a shift away from rights-based law to social management. State bureaucracies have increasingly involved themselves in substantive ethical and policy issues associated with welfare interventionism. The expansion of judicial discretion is thus associated with: (i) the increasing abstractness or open-endedness of statutory provisions and standards; inherently discretionary concepts such as 'the best interests of the child' replace fault-based legal actions; (ii) an increase in short-term government-of-the-day policy uses of law; (iii) a blurring of boundaries between broad policy-administrative and narrowly legal aspects of legal administration – such as in the use of law to effect social justice (e.g. equal opportunities legislation). Judges are increasingly expected to adjudicate in fields of expertise – social and economic policy – that are outside their competence. Also, an extended use is made of tribunals and regulatory agencies such as the Equal Opportunities Commission that rely on informal procedures, as do reconciliation procedures in family law.

Weber suggested that the features of law that dominated its liberal era – formality and neutrality – would pervade future development. Neutral rules, Weber thought, were particularly conducive to the workings of bureaucracies and they would persist and expand to new ground without challenge, due to their apparent indispensability to the logic of bureaucratic organisation. While regulatory law has shifted significantly from legislatures to administration, its form remains what Weber predicted it to remain, formal rational. But that, of course, is only part of the story. Let us say that between bureaucratisation and welfarism in law there is both a tension and a convergence. Tension because bureaucratic law is rational law, its form is that of general abstract rules, while welfarist regulation is substantive, particular and casuistic. Convergence because often welfarist concerns key in with bureaucratic ones, for example the welfarist shift away from fault (as socially inappropriate) meets with the efficiency demand of bureaucracy, the speedy processing of cases thus far inhibited by the requirement to explore *mens rea*.

● **Particularised legislation**

The materialisation of law marks the tendency toward particularised legislation: the movement towards breaking up the general categories into sub-categories towards which law applies differentially. The grand category of the legal person gives way to a specification of categories, and the formal equivalence of the legal subject gives way to a proliferation of different legal statuses: consumer (consumer law), worker/trade union member, employee, welfare recipient, business franchisee. In each case the law addresses the legal subject under that more specific description and there is a move from the formal to the material in this. But further: natural and artificial persons, grouped together under liberal law, become differentiated for specific legal purposes, so that, for example, the privacy of the natural person is protected where that of the company is not (access to data, freedom of information).

● Erosion of the separation of powers

The separation of powers, that other lynchpin of liberal law, is eroded, for example, once courts are called upon to determine whether a government has acted in the public interest. Equally this happens when the legislature delegates responsibility for fixing the terms of what appear as general directives, as the executive state machinery has the resources to do the job better.

● The undermining of formal equality

Formal equality is undermined once 'reverse discrimination' or 'affirmative action', that is a reverse preference to a disadvantaged group, become institutionalised in law in order to redress existing inequalities.

The welfare state and globalisation

Transformations in law are unlikely to be total revisions. In the transformation from *Gemeinschaft* to *Gesellschaft* law, elements of the former survived in the latter. The transformation of *Gesellschaft* law to the regulatory-welfarist type meets with a similar inertia. The core of liberal law cannot be easily side-stepped in the name of expediency, of getting things done. Liberal values still inform the way we speak about law and the legitimacy we see in it. On the other hand we expect a responsiveness from law. That is, we expect law to meet social needs and aspirations. And in this, legal action comes to serve as a vehicle by which groups and organisations may participate in the determination of public policy.

This important tension, while still with us in some respect, has also receded to a significant degree. The welfare state and its ideological foundation in social democracy has been on the retreat, at different rates and to different degrees certainly, but retreat nonetheless. And with it, the law of the welfare state entered its own period of crisis. With the rise of the New Right in Europe and the US in the late 1970s and 1980s, the adoption of deregulatory strategies and monetary policies by the Thatcher and Reagan governments initially, and with the gradual prevalence of the Washington consensus globally, there began the 'undoing' of this compromise and the breakdown of the post-war settlement. As Maurice Glasman puts it:

> The New Right combined an economic theory which limited welfare, marginalized unions and forbade direct productive interference by the state in the economy with a moral theory that identified the state with oppression and the market with freedom in the sphere of material distribution.
>
> (1996, p xiii)

Politically speaking, the welfare state compromise appeared to have let both sides down. The Left were (too) quick to protest about the dependency that it created, a tendency encouraged by the practices of the administration of social security law that 'foster the idea of requesting assistance rather than asserting social-welfare rights' as Cotterrell put it. Or more polemically, as Habermas denounced it in his more radical days, the welfarist state had become a 'technocratic administered capitalism' (Habermas 1976). The Right on the other hand discovered that redistribution worked against incentives, that unemployment benefits undercut management power by offering the workers 'exit' opportunities from employment, that regulation placed burdens on competitiveness, and that economic growth could only be achieved through priorities that ran counter to welfarism. In effect business became increasingly unwilling to fund the welfare state, an unwillingness that we continue to observe today.

These developments combined with (and combined to precipitate) an extraordinary degree of withdrawal (or rolling back) of the State, and a newfound freedom for capitalist activity on the global level. 'Globalisation' is the term used to describe the process of capitalist integration beyond the level of the State, facilitated by new international organisations, international investment treaties and other international instruments. These shifts require that we also adjust our conceptual tools and legal theories to address and understand these changes. The phenomenon of globalisation indeed challenges many of the core assumptions that underpin this account of legal modernity. Thus, for example, where Weber saw legal modernity in the consolidation and singularity of state law, globalisation sees the fragmentation of sovereignty; and where our understanding of legal modernity is based on the generality and universality of state law, globalisation sees the pluralisation and diversity of legal orders. To what extent then does this require us to revise or replace our understanding of legal modernity?

The literature on globalisation is vast, covering a wide range of subjects often unfamiliar to the legal curriculum. The question of where to start elaborating the relevance of globalisation studies for legal theory can appear quite daunting. It is therefore important to be clear what our purpose is in referring to debates about globalisation. Here, we focus on the key issue of whether the pressures on the Nation-State discussed under the rubric of globalisation represent the demise of the paradigm of modernity. This has important implications for legal theory, given the close relationship outlined above between modernity and contemporary understandings of law: if modernity is in crisis, this may require us to revisit some core assumptions of current legal thought. We set the context for this discussion by outlining the main contours of the debates on globalisation, before considering in more detail why this has led to claims of epochal change. We then contrast the response that these challenges can be accommodated by adapting existing legal concepts with the argument that we need to transform the basis of existing legal knowledge and conclude by considering what law, after modernity, might look like.

Debates about globalisation often divide between those who argue that the Nation-State is no longer the main organising principle of society, and sceptics, for whom globalisation means very little. One key issue is whether the link between national territory and politics is being undermined, with the state being supplanted at the supra-, sub- and non-state levels as the primary locus of political authority. Claims that technological innovations that compress business time and space have led to the organisation of economic activity on a global scale are met with the response that the global economy is a myth designed to suggest there is no alternative to prevailing neoliberal policies. Some argue that a global culture is being created, evocatively referred to as 'McWorld', while others highlight the still powerful connection between national identity and cultural institutions. These two perspectives on political, economic and cultural globalisation provide helpful tools for engaging with the debates, but they are only a starting point. Moreover, they are far from distinct positions, being connected with varying degrees of complexity. For example, does the development of institutions for regulating the global economy limit the scope for national policy innovation? Are cultural changes driving other forms of globalisation or are they secondary phenomena?

The question that runs through these debates is whether globalisation represents a period of paradigmatic transition. In other words, do the changes discussed above signal the intensification (but continuation) of existing processes, or do they represent a more fundamental rupture with the past? Are forms of knowledge that take the Nation-State as the privileged unit of analysis still adequate for understanding ongoing changes? This also engages with claims of modernity's political failure: some see the crises attending globalisation as evidence of the Nation-State's inability to deliver its promise of greater emancipation, while others emphasise the resilience of existing institutions. These debates are necessarily linked, and give us a flavour of the politics of globalisation. A paradigmatic reading, which advocates a new framework of enquiry, is generally linked to a transformative political strategy that imagines forms of social organisation beyond neoliberalism. A subparadigmatic reading tends to assume capitalism's continuation, but seeks to adapt the resources of modernity to manage its excesses.

We can identify three important ways in which globalisation undermines some deep-rooted assumptions of modern legal thought. First, it makes it increasingly difficult for legal study to be contained within the territorial boundaries of national legal systems. To understand the operation of formal State law, we have to take into account the proliferation of supranational sources of law, such as those emanating from the European Union (EU) or the World Trade Organization (WTO). The obverse of this is that at the international level, sovereignty is undermined by greater acceptance of interference in the internal affairs of states, for example, through the doctrine of humanitarian intervention. Second, while traditional jurisprudence focused exclusively on municipal and public international law, globalisation requires notice of other forms of legal ordering, such as the *sui generis* legal order of the EU. But not all have a formal pedigree. One prominent example is transnational *lex mercatoria*, which regulates interactions between global commercial firms outside official law through practices such as international arbitration. Other types not readily slotted into standard categorisations include Islamic law, which operates across national boundaries, sometimes in opposition to State law. A third challenge addresses how globalisation may be undermining the cultural specificity of law, and asks whether in response, we can construct a theory of law that reaches across legal cultures. In other words, can we develop a conceptual language that can make sense of the relations between, for example, national and supranational, formal and informal, sub-State and non-State contexts?

'Unthinking' modern law

An important and influential analysis of these questions can be found in the work of the Portuguese theorist Boaventura de Sousa Santos, who contends that the problems engendered by modernity cannot be solved within the latter's intellectual and political resources. His primary motivation is to develop an emancipatory conception of law in response to the political crisis of modernity, ushered in by globalisation. While overtly socio-political, Santos's response to globalisation also addresses our categories of legal knowledge. For him, the two are deeply connected, as it is only by 'unthinking' the current basis of legal knowledge that law's emancipatory potential can be realised.

Santos's theory of law and globalisation is situated within his broader account of the demise of modernity. Modernity, for Santos, established a dynamic tension between regulation (or order) and emancipation (or good order). Its success was predicated on the promise that a sufficient weight of expectations (of emancipation) could be translated into experiences (emancipatory struggles translated into new forms of regulation), so that incompatible values, such as equality and freedom, could be held in balance. This was to be delivered through the Nation-State, applying scientific knowledge through legal instruments. However, he argues that what marks our time is the wholesale collapse of emancipation into regulation, as, for example, the welfare state comes under pressure from the global economy in neoliberal mode.

Santos defines globalisation as 'the process by which a given local condition or entity succeeds in extending its reach over the globe and, by doing so, develops the capacity to designate a rival social condition or entity as local' (2002, p 178). He distinguishes first between two hegemonic forms of globalisation: 'globalized localism', which is 'the process by which a given local phenomenon is successfully globalized' – for example, the spread of US popular culture – and 'localized globalism', which connotes 'the specific impact of transnational practices and imperatives on local conditions that are thereby destructured and restructured in order to respond to transnational imperatives' (2002, p 179) – such as the emergence of free trade areas. The core industrialised countries specialise in exporting to the former, whereas developing peripheral countries are the prime importers of localised globalisms. Each operates in subparadigmatic mode as they assume the continued existence of global capitalism. Alongside these, he outlines two forms of counter-hegemonic globalisation: subaltern cosmopolitanism, referring to transnational resistance to hegemonic globalisation, for example, the new forms of political activism under the umbrella of the World Social Forum; and the common heritage of humankind, which motivates political struggle around issues such as the depletion of the ozone layer and the proliferation of nuclear weapons. These represent paradigmatic approaches to globalisation as they are addressed to audiences that seek to imagine different forms of social organisation beyond capitalism. Santos is critical of those approaches to law and globalisation that concentrate solely on hegemonic processes, as this neglects the significance of new forms of law, which are emerging from daily struggles in diverse settings.

Santos sees the 'globalisation of the legal field' as a constitutive element in these processes. An important example is the spread of liberal democratic constitutional reforms to newly established democracies in Central and Eastern Europe, and Latin America. While often sponsored by international agencies as the epitome of good governance, Santos sees these reforms as globalised localisms, elevating Western-style democracy as the single global model. However, these processes are not just hegemonic in substance, reinforcing North–South power asymmetries, but also in form through their partial understanding of legal phenomena. Accompanying these reforms is a series of measures designed to shore up the rule of law, for example, by providing for the protection of property rights. Not only is law understood here solely in terms of formal State law, but also this conception is seen as vital to providing the infrastructure for global capitalist activity.

This brings us to the key point of Santos's critique, namely that the reduction of law to State law is a deeply contingent political product of modernity, and which helps explain the latter's emancipatory limits. For Santos, this reduction rests on an artificial distinction between the State and civil society, which obscures the existence of political authority beyond official processes, for example, in the workplace. Moreover, the identification of law solely with the State played a key role in sustaining capitalism. First, autonomous and scientific State law was held up as the instrument for securing societal progress by managing capitalism's worst excesses. But this was also a strategy of depoliticisation, which legitimated the confinement of democratic politics to the State, while excluding them from other sites of social power. So although modernity has, for example, promoted formal democracy in the State, by legislating for equal voting rights among citizens, it has left in place unequal power relations in the workplace.

Santos argues that globalisation makes this limited conception of law implausible when it attempts to describe law as it is and is unacceptable as a vision of what law should be. For him, one feature of the paradigmatic transition is the increasing visibility of forms of law beyond the State. This requires us to widen our knowledge to include, *inter alia*, the laws generated by transnational corporations, resurgent forms of indigenous law such as the assertion of historic rights by aboriginal peoples, and the broad international human rights regime, which covers the activities of both international agencies and NGOs. The objective is not simply to catalogue different types of law, but also to account for the uneven ways in which they interact with and influence each other – what Santos calls interlegality. In this picture, State law is one of a number of legal orders and not necessarily the most influential – often, for example, operating in the shadow of the (legal) norms of the neoliberal global economy.

Santos thus links this reconceptualisation of law to the political dimension of globalisation. For Santos, the recoupling of law with social power lies at the heart of the counter-hegemonic agenda. This is not just aspirational rhetoric, as his later work discusses the various struggles, whether campaigns against water privatisation in Latin America or the fight for affordable antiretroviral drugs in Africa, which he sees as providing the basis for new international legal regimes. Thus Santos emphasises the need to consider both hegemonic globalisation from above, but also counter-hegemonic globalisation from below. This necessarily changes how we think about State law, as now only one route among many open to legal activists; but to the extent it can be successfully deployed in a broader campaign of resistance it may retain an emancipatory character. For example, he discusses the transnational coalition for the elimination of sweatshops as an attempt to politicise the law of the workplace in a counter-hegemonic way.

Santos's work provides an ambitious framework for making sense of law and globalisation as part of a broader account of paradigmatic change. His project aims at returning law to its emancipatory potential. This requires us to shift our focus away from traditional State legal forms to the practices of oppressed groups. These new forms of law, found in the interstices of the State and in non-Western settings, may appear alien subjects for legal study to students educated in the Western tradition.

But that is precisely his point: that the paradigmatic transition highlights the ways in which old certainties are being undermined, and which require us to 'unthink' many core assumptions of the modernist conception of law.

Reading

On the shift from the liberal to the regulatory paradigm, see Santos (2002), pp 39–60. In the sphere of contract law see Atiyah (1979) and, for a normative analysis of the two paradigms, contrast Wilhelmsson (1995) and Collins (1982) on the one hand with Fried (1981) on the other. In Fried's *Contract as Promise* (1981) contract law and the promise principle are contrasted to the socially imposed obligations of compensation, restitution and sharing. Deploying 'economic analysis of law', a school of thought deeply rooted in the liberal paradigm, Fried argues that the idea of obligations created by promises is the fundamental and operative principle of contract. See also generally the symposium on contract law and legal theory in *Social and Legal Studies* (2000).

On the question of crisis that underlies the transformations, see Habermas (1976), Santos (2002) and Glasman (1996). Nelken (1982) looks at the question of 'crisis' in the law. There is also a good discussion of the transformation of formal law in Unger (1976), chs 2 and 3, Cotterrell (1992), ch 5 and in Kamenka and Tay (1975). For a discussion of diverse impacts of welfarism on law see the essays by Criller and Morris and McClintock in Adler and Asquith (1981).

For an introduction to debates on globalisation, see Held and McGrew (2003) and Scholte (2008). For an introduction to globalisation and law see Twining (2000), especially chs 1, 4 and 7, and (2009), especially chs 1, 2 and 9. For an account of paradigmatic and subparadigmatic readings of globalisation, see Santos (2002, pp 172–7). Other aspects of Santos's analysis covered here can be found in more detail in Santos (2002, pp 1–11, 89–98, 177–93 and 465–70). For an account of alternative ways of conceptualising globalisation, drawing on work in the global South, see Santos and Rodríguez-Garavito (2005), ch 1. For a discussion of Santos's theory by Twining, see (2000), ch 8.

References

Adler, M and Asquith, S (eds), 1981, *Discretion and Welfare*, London: Heinemann.
Althusser, L, 1971, 'Ideology and Ideological State Apparatuses', in L Althusser (ed), *Lenin and Philosophy, and Other Essays*, London: New Left Books.
Atiyah P, 1979, *The Rise and Fall of the Freedom of Contract*, Oxford: Oxford University Press.
Berman, H, 1983, *Law and Revolution: the Formation of the Western Legal Tradition*, Cambridge, MA: Harvard University Press.
Cain, M and Hunt, A, 1979, *Marx and Engels on Law*, London: Academic Press.
Collins, H, 1982, *Marxism and Law*, Oxford: Oxford University Press.
Cotterrell, R, 1992, *The Sociology of Law. An Introduction*, 2nd edn, London: Butterworths.
Cotterrell, R, 1995, 'Legality and Legitimacy: The Sociology of Max Weber', in Cotterrell, *Law's Community*, Oxford: Clarendon.

Cotterrell, R, 1999, *Emile Durkheim: Law in a Moral Domain*, Edinburgh: Edinburgh University Press.

Durkheim, E, 1963/1933, *The Division of Labour in Society*, New York: Free Press.

Ewing, S, 1987, 'Formal Justice and the Spirit of Capitalism: Max Weber's Sociology of Law', 21 *Law and Soc Rev* 487–512.

Foucault, M, 1984, 'What is Enlightenment?', in P Rabinow (ed), *The Foucault Reader*, Harmondsworth: Penguin.

Fried, C, 1981, *Contract as Promise*, Cambridge, MA: Harvard University Press.

Garland, D, 1990, *Punishment and Modern Society*, Oxford: Oxford University Press.

Giddens, A, 1971, *Capitalism and Modern Social Theory: An Analysis of the Writings of Marx, Durkheim and Weber*, Cambridge: Cambridge University Press.

Glasman, M, 1996, *Unnecessary Suffering: Managing Market Utopia*, London: Verso.

Habermas, J, 1976, *Legitimation Crisis*, London: Heinemann.

Held, D, 2002, 'Law of States, Law of Peoples: Three Models of Sovereignty', 8 *Legal theory* 1–44.

Held, D and McGrew, A, 2003, 'The Great Globalization Debate: An Introduction', in D Held and A McGrew (eds), *The Global Transformations Reader*, 2nd edn, Cambridge: Polity Press.

Hirst, PQ, 1979, *On Law and Ideology*, London: Macmillan.

Hobbes, T, 1996/1651, *Leviathan*, Cambridge: Cambridge University Press.

Horkheimer, M, 1972, *Critical Theory*, New York: Herder & Herder.

Jackson R, 1999, 'Sovereignty in World Politics: A Glance at the Conceptual and Historical Landscape', 67 *Political Studies*, 431–56.

Kamenka, E and Tay, A, 1975: 'Beyond Bourgeois Individualism: The Contemporary Crisis in Law and Legal Ideology', in E Kamenka and R S Neale (eds), *Feudalism, Capitalism and Beyond*, London: Edward Arnold.

Kant, I, 1991/1784, 'What is Enlightenment?', in H Reiss (ed), *Political Writings*, Cambridge: Cambridge University Press.

Kelman, M, 1987, *A Guide to Critical Legal Studies*, Cambridge, MA: Harvard University Press.

Kronman, A, 1983, *Max Weber*, London: Edward Arnold.

Lenin, VI, 1917, *The State and Revolution*, various editions.

Loughlin, M, 2000, *Sword and Scales*, Oxford: Hart Publishing.

Loughlin, M, 2003, 'Ten Tenets of Sovereignty', in N Walker (ed) *Sovereignty in Transition*, Oxford: Hart.

Lukacs, G, 1971, 'The Phenomenon of Reification', in *History and Class Consciousness*, London: Merlin Press.

Lukes, S, 1973, *Emile Durkheim. His Life and Work: A Historical and Critical Study*, Harmondsworth: Penguin.

Lukes, S and Scull, A, 1983, *Durkheim and the Law*, Oxford: Robertson.

Macaulay, S, 1963, 'Non-contractual Relations in Business: A Preliminary Study', 28 *Am Soc Rev* 55–67.

Maine, HS, 1917/1861, *Ancient Law*, London: Dent.

Marks, S, 2000, *The Riddle of All Constitutions*, Oxford: Oxford University Press.

Marx, K, 1865, *Capital*, vol. 1, many editions.

Marx, K, 1843, 'On the Jewish Question', in D McLellan (ed), *Karl Marx. Selected Writings*, 1977, Oxford: Oxford University Press.

Marx, K, 1844, 'Economic and Philosophical Manuscripts' in D McLellan (ed), *Karl Marx. Selected Writings*, 1977, Oxford: Oxford University Press.

Marx, K, 1849, 'Wage labour and Capital' in D McLellan (ed), *Karl Marx. Selected Writings*, 1977, Oxford: Oxford University Press.

Marx, K, 1851, 'The Eighteenth Brumaire of Louis Bonaparte', in D McLellan (ed), *Karl Marx. Selected Writings*, 1977, Oxford: Oxford University Press.

Marx, K, 1932, 'The German Ideology', in D McLellan (ed), *Karl Marx. Selected Writings*, Oxford: Oxford University Press.

Murphy, WT, 1997, *The Oldest Social Science? Configurations of Law and Modernity*, Oxford: Oxford University Press.

Nelken, D, 1982, 'Is there a Crisis in Law and Legal Ideology?', *Journal of Law and Society*.

Pashukanis, EB, 1978, *Law and Marxism. A General Theory*, London: Pluto Press.

Polanyi, K, 1957/1944, *The Great Transformation*, New York: Beacon Press.

Reiner, R, 1984, 'Crime, Law and Deviance: The Durkheim Legacy', in S Fenton (ed), *Durkheim and Modern Sociology*, Cambridge: Cambridge University Press.

Rheinstein, M, 1954, 'Introduction', in M Rheinstein (ed), *Max Weber on Law in Economy and Society*, Cambridge, MA: Harvard University Press.

Santos, B de Sousa, 2002, *Toward a New Legal Common Sense*, 2nd edn, London: Butterworths.

Santos, B de Sousa and Rodríguez-Garavito, CA (eds), 2005, *Law and Globalization from Below: Towards a Cosmopolitan Legality*, Cambridge: Cambridge University Press.

Scholte, Jan-Arte, 2008, 'Reconstructing Contemporary Democracy', 15 *Indiana Journal of Global Legal Studies* 305.

Social & Legal Studies, 2000, Symposium on Contract Law and Legal Theory, 397–447.

Stone, A, 1985, 'The Place of Law in the Marxian Structure-Superstructure Archetype', *Law and Society Review*, vol 19, pp 39–67.

Teubner, G (ed), 1997, *Global law without a State*, Aldershot: Ashgate.

Thompson, EP, 1977, *Whigs and Hunters*, Harmondsworth: Penguin.

Thompson, J, 1984, *Studies in the Theory of Ideology*, Cambridge: Polity Press.

Turner, B, 1996, *For Weber. Essays on the Sociology of Fate*, London: Sage.

Twining, W, 2000, *Globalisation & Legal Theory*, London: Butterworths.

Twining, W, 2009, *General Jurisprudence: Understanding Law from a Global Perspective*, Cambridge: Cambridge University Press.

Unger, RM, 1976, *Law in Modern Society*, New York: The Free Press.

Walker, N (ed), 2003, *Sovereignty in Transition*, Oxford: Hart.

Weber, M, 1930, *The Protestant Ethic and the Spirit of Capitalism*, London: Allen & Unwin.

Weber, M, 1948a, 'Politics as a Vocation', in HH Gerth and CW Mills (eds), *For Max Weber*, London: Routledge & Kegan Paul.

Weber, M, 1948b, 'Science as a Vocation', in HH Gerth and CW Mills (eds), *For Max Weber*, London: Routledge & Kegan Paul.

Weber, M, 1968, *Economy and Society, An Outline of Interpretive Sociology*, 2 vols, Berkeley: University of California Press.

Wilhelmsson, T (ed), 1995, *Social Contract Law and European Integration*, Aldershot: Dartmouth.

Yack, B, 2001, 'Popular Sovereignty and Nationalism', 29 *Political Theory* 517–36.

Zizek, S, 1994, *Mapping Ideology*, London: Verso.

Chapter 2

Advanced topics

Chapter Contents

2.1	Legal pluralism	248
2.2	Juridification	255
2.3	Displacing the juridical: Foucault on power and discipline	264
2.4	Law in the risk society	271
2.5	Law and autopoiesis	278

2.1 Legal pluralism

The question at the heart of legal pluralism is that of what separates law from non-law. For many students, teachers and practitioners of law, the instinctive answer to this is that law is the formal product of the State, consisting primarily of statutes made by legislatures, or the decisions of courts. According to this view, special training is required to become 'learned in the law', and so be able to administer and use it. Legal pluralism contends that this view of law – sometimes referred to as 'lawyers' law' – gives us only a partial account of the nature and scope of law. Instead it is argued that there are many other non-official, often unwritten, normative orders operating in society – whether setting standards for conduct in workplaces, within clubs and associations or among neighbours – which should also be regarded as sources and forms of law.

Legal pluralism presents an alternative paradigm of law to that of legal modernity. As discussed above, the dominant legal understanding that emerged from the eighteenth century onwards saw law as one of the principal achievements of Enlightenment rationality. This view emphasised law's singularity, its universality and its effectiveness. Law was regarded as a coherent body of norms, emanating from a single source – the State; rational law was the culmination of human progress, and the aspiration and mark of all 'civilised' societies; and law was one of the primary instruments of social engineering available to the State, shaping society through various inducements and sanctions. Legal pluralism challenges not only the State-centredness of legal modernity, but also its main attributes. In place of singularity and unity, legal pluralism sees multiplicity and relative disorder; in place of universality, legal pluralism sees legal modernity as but one, deeply contingent, way of imagining law, tied to a particular (European) time and place; in place of effectiveness, legal pluralism highlights the ways in which State law is often stymied by non-State law, and so fails to live up to its own standards of instrumental rationality.

Renewed interest in ideas of legal pluralism is generally attributed to anthropological research, conducted in colonial societies in the mid-twentieth century. The nature of this work – often focused on the customary habits of tribal communities – led to legal pluralism being depicted as 'exotic,' and so kept on the margins of legal study. However, in the 1970s, interest in non-State forms of law extended to the mainstream law and society movement, and more recently ideas of legal pluralism have become a central feature of debates about globalisation. While much of this scholarship was conducted over the past 50 or so years, it is important to note that exponents of legal pluralism claim that they are recovering an older tradition, which was temporarily displaced by legal modernity. We now consider some of the key claims from each of these periods to illustrate the more specific arguments advanced by legal pluralists.

Classical and contemporary legal pluralism

The issue of the basis of legal authority in colonial societies crystallises some of the principal themes of legal pluralism. The paradigm of legal modernity played an important role in justifying European colonialism. According to the Europeans, if land was unoccupied – *terra nullius* – it was open to settlement and governed according to the law of the coloniser. But the territories that the settlers encountered were still occupied by their original inhabitants, and in many cases had been for thousands of years. This problem was overcome by contrasting the stage of development of European societies, with their formal, rational laws, with indigenous forms of social organisation that were deemed 'so low in the scale of social organisation' that they could not be 'reconciled with the institutions or legal ideas of civilized society'.[1] Without law, there could be no rights of ownership on the part of aboriginal peoples and so, as John Locke put it, there could be no injury to them by the assertion of European sovereignty.

Various legal–anthropological studies over the past century have disputed the idea that law arrived in modern-day North America, sub-Saharan Africa or Australasia with the European settlers. These studies – often referred to as 'classical legal pluralism' – emphasised two points. First, that indigenous peoples formed relatively complex societies with their own normative structures and forms of political organisation. Legal anthropologists identified many developed systems for regulating social life, whether for exchanging goods, raising children, exploiting the land or settling disputes. These rules were often expressed through (to Western eyes) unfamiliar forms, such as woven belts, and operated within different cultural assumptions – private ownership of land is simply incomprehensible to many indigenous peoples. The settlers did not recognise this as law because it failed to meet their own cultural predispositions (as would be the case with Western law for the aboriginals). The second argument running through classical legal pluralism is that indigenous forms of law did not disappear in the colonial state. Indeed, the coexistence of both formal and indigenous law is said to be the more accurate account of the colonial era (Asch 1997). For example, the early settlers often entered into treaties with aboriginal groups, adopting the latter's rites of solemnification, such as exchange of wampum belts (although, when inconvenient, these treaties were dispensed with by asserting the ultimate authority of the colonial state). Moreover, colonial officials often found it more pragmatic to license the use of customary norms, which in many cases continued to be followed by the local population, to govern areas of social life such as the family (Chanock 1985). Thus legal pluralists argue that claims that official State law provides the sole criterion for legal order simply do not accord with reality.

The key development that marked a move from classical to 'new' or 'postcolonial' legal pluralism was the growth in empirical socio-legal studies. This research adopted a different approach to traditional legal scholarship, concerned less with doctrinal analysis – 'law in the books' – and more with how it operated in practice – 'law in action'. This led many to conclude that an exclusive focus upon State law only gave a limited picture of legal relations in developed countries. An important impetus here was research on forms of alternative dispute resolution (ADR). This demonstrated that citizens who lacked the wherewithal to have access to the formal machinery of justice often cultivated their own informal means of settling disputes (Abel 1982). The idea that informal law was not only to be found in colonial societies was taken forward by other studies, for example in the field of

1   *Re Southern Rhodesia* (1919) AC (PC) 210 at 233.

industrial relations. Legal pluralists here contrasted State labour law with the 'indigenous law of the workplace', such as codes of conduct, informal agreements and customary patterns of behaviour, and argued that the latter were often more important in shaping workers' day-to-day activities (Arthurs 1985b).

The advent of globalisation has further refocused attention on plural forms of legal ordering. This is unsurprising, given that the principal argument across the globalisation literature is that the Nation-State should no longer be the privileged object of study. Some commentators highlight the profusion of sites of formal political authority in the global era, and suggest that citizenship is now necessarily multiple, and that we negotiate our rights and obligations within overlapping legal orders at the subnational, national and supranational levels (see Part III, 1.5, The welfare state and globalisation). Others argue that the new legal forms, which have helped lubricate the operation of the global economy, can only be explained by a pluralist perspective. For example, an important feature of contemporary economic activity is global *lex mercatoria*, which includes various business practices, codes of conduct, standard form contracts and arbitration awards, all of which can be described without reference to State law. Economic globalisation may also recast what we regard as sources of law, and see multinational corporations as exercising significant normative authority, for example, in setting standards in the fields of agricultural production or medical research (Hertz 2001).

Strong and weak legal pluralism, and the position of the State

It should already be clear that legal pluralism itself takes many forms. One way in which we might characterise different approaches adopted in the various phases is the distinction between 'strong' and 'weak' legal pluralism. According to John Griffiths, 'weak' legal pluralism entails the 'formal acquiescence by the state' in accepting 'different bodies of law for different groups in the population' (1986, pp 7, 5). The archetypal, but not only, example of this is the coexistence within the colonial state of Western and indigenous legal rules, with the State's courts authorising reliance on customary law to resolve disputes before it. Griffiths argues that this situation should not count as proper legal pluralism, as it accepts the State as the ultimate sovereign authority: in our example, customary norms apply because the State legal system 'recognises' them. He contrasts this with 'strong' legal pluralism, which he defines as 'that state of affairs, for any social field, in which behaviour pursuant to more than one legal order occurs' (1986, p 2). Accordingly, State law is but one legal order, whose authorisation is unnecessary for the empirical operation of other forms of law.

A leading account of 'strong' legal pluralism is found in the work of Boaventura de Sousa Santos, in particular his complex 'structure-agency map' of modern capitalist society. Santos posits six structural places – the householdplace, the workplace, the marketplace, the communityplace, the citizenplace and the worldplace. Each generates its own distinct form of law: for example, the domestic law of the householdplace refers to the unwritten codes that govern social relations within the family, while the exchange law of the marketplace denotes the trade customs and normative standards operating among producers, merchants and consumers. For Santos, the actual legal rules that apply at any one time are not dependent on one type of law, but will necessarily be a combination of the different forms. For example, the legal regulation of the family includes a mixture of formal State law and informal domestic law.

The distinction between strong and weak legal pluralism is a controversial one, and not everyone accepts Griffiths's dismissive stance towards the latter. It highlights though, that attitudes towards the State remain an important fault line within legal pluralist scholarship. This raises important methodological and normative issues. Regarding the former, legal pluralists have sought to provide a definition of law that captures the full range of legal phenomena.[2] However, Brian Tamanaha (1993) claims that many of these attempts underscore the difficulty of conceiving of law without reference to the State. He argues that legal pluralists tend to posit their criteria for law by focusing on what appears essential to State law – whether the enforcement of norms or the resolution of disputes – but then subtracting the indicia of the State from this equation. For him, this shows that the State remains the starting point even for some leading pluralist accounts of law.

A related question is whether, even if legal pluralism could escape the analytical framework of State law, it is desirable that it should. This addresses the connection between description and prescription in legal pluralism. While Griffiths argues that legal pluralism is simply a fact, it is part of his mission to debunk the 'ideology' of centralising approaches that hold that law ought to be the law of the State. It would seem to follow that legal pluralists think that law ought to be regarded other than in State-centred terms, and some writers appear to valorise non-State forms of law for their own sake. Others, though, are concerned by the normative implications of this position. First, they suggest there is no special reason to believe that plural forms of law will be necessarily progressive: for example, some socio-legal scholars saw the rise of ADR as problematic as it potentially restored the advantages of the financially and socially powerful, which the formal law had sought to equalise. Moreover, to confer the term 'law', with its connotations that what is lawful is right or moral, on some aspects of social life, is to confer upon them a legitimacy that they do not deserve (for example, the often oppressive regimes generated within prisons) (Tamanaha 2000).

These are important questions, but to some extent, they are unanswerable in their own terms: how, for example, do we 'prove' what law is? Rather, they direct us to an enquiry into the usefulness of plural understandings of law, and the objectives that they serve, to which we now turn.

Empirical, conceptual and political approaches to legal pluralism

The points just discussed highlight the importance of the qualifying adjective. In traditional terms, State law is simply 'law,' while plural forms of law, such as indigenous or informal law, require qualification or demotion, so that they are customs, or habits, or social norms, but not law. There are various strategies that legal pluralists employ to cast off the burden of the qualifying adjective, and so affirm that they are

---

2   Santos (2002, p 86) defines law as 'a body of regularized procedures and normative standards, considered justiciable – i.e. susceptible of being enforced by a judicial authority – in any given group, which contributes to the creation and prevention of disputes, and to their settlement through an argumentative discourse, coupled with the threat of force'.

indeed talking about law. We might categorise these strategies on the basis of their empirical, conceptual and political emphases (although these categories are far from watertight, and overlap in practice).

Empirical approaches to legal pluralism seek to provide a more comprehensive account of the actual norms that influence everyday life, and argue that this requires a broader research field than an exclusive focus on State law. This engages with the influential command theory of law, that is, that through people's subservience to law, the State can direct the future shape of society. Legal pluralists argue that if this is what distinguishes State law as law, then it frequently fails to live up to this ideal. Moreover, other forms of normative order often seem better to approximate the special characteristics claimed for State law. In place of the model of (State) law acting upon a passive society, legal pluralists see it as constantly interacting with other legal orders. For example, to return to the example of relations in the family, the limitations of State law in addressing problems such as domestic violence can be attributed to the fact that it does not wholly displace the (often patriarchal) norms of domestic law. The objective here is to understand better how the interaction between these different forms of law may facilitate or impede different policy objectives.

While empirical approaches may lead to a more nuanced account of State law, with more feasible expectations, it could still be objected that we lose conceptual clarity if the category of law becomes overbroad. Conceptual approaches to legal pluralism respond by arguing that the singularity associated with State-centred views provides a distorted basis for legal study, and necessarily gives way, once we accept that law reflects the society within which it is embedded. This approach is grounded in a pluralistic social theory, which views social life in terms of a disorganised struggle between different groups. Seeing law as one part of a larger web of varied and complex social relations, it is argued that legal relations must also be asymmetrical (Sampford 1991). This goes further than some empirical approaches: not only is law decoupled from the State, but also all forms of law tend towards disorder and incoherence. From this perspective, even if our focus is on State law, this has to be recast as inherently plural, with full account taken of its crosscurrents and contradictions (and so the difference between strong and weak legal pluralism may not be as pronounced as has been suggested).

One might accept that the empirical and conceptual approaches present important challenges to traditional legal thought, but still insist there is value in maintaining the distinction between law and other social norms. This brings us to the political dimension of legal pluralism, which reverses the enquiry so far conducted, and asks what purposes are served by presenting State law as the sole category for legal study. For Santos, this reflects less an analytical imperative, and more the operation of a politics of definition designed to portray the State as the only form of political authority in society. He argues that the main consequence of this politics of definition is to mask other sites of social power, and their attendant forms of law, such as the market.[3] Thus the political purpose of pluralising law is not to suggest a moral equivalence, say, between norms produced by states and multinational corporations;

3　For discussion of the operation of the politics of definition in the context of globalisation, see Part III, 1.5 above.

rather, it seeks to expand questions about the legitimate use of power across all those institutions (State and non-State) which exercise coercive power.

Future directions in legal pluralism

Ideas of legal pluralism now occupy a more prominent place in legal scholarship than has historically been the case, and have recently been employed to address main-stream subjects such as constitutional law (Anderson 2005) and transnational law (Buchanan 2006). With this expanded interest, debates within and about legal pluralism have continued to adapt, and we conclude by briefly discussing three key innovations in the literature. The first, variously termed 'governmentality' or 'governance', can be considered less an elaboration of legal pluralism than a cognate development within a different intellectual tradition. This school of thought emerged from Michel Foucault's social theory, and focuses on the various agencies, tech-niques and forms of knowledge that seek to govern human behaviour (see Part III, 2.3 below; see, also, Dean 1999). There are strong affinities with legal pluralism to the extent that it is concerned with normative regimes beyond the State: for example, a major strand of research considers the extent to which the governance of security is now located beyond the State (Shearing and Wood 2003, pp 402–3). There are, though, important differences of emphasis, with governance more interested in how social problems are created in the first place, than necessarily with the interaction between different normative systems (Rose and Valverde 1998).

A second approach follows the 'linguistic turn' in political philosophy, and seeks to develop a form of legal pluralism that is both sensitive to the limitations of the State-centred conception, and retains a distinction between law and social norms. The solution, it suggests, lies in a conventionalist approach under which law is what people generally designate as law. Gunther Teubner, one of the leading exponents of this view, argues, for example, that global commercial practices (*lex mercatoria* discussed above) should be seen as a form of law as the binary coding 'legal/illegal' is used by key actors such as international arbitrators (Teubner 1997, p 4). While this approach may provide a relatively straightforward threshold test for the existence of law, it has been criticised on the grounds that it retains the view that certain functions are essential to law – on Teubner's terms, the controlling and co-ordinating behav-iour – which are ultimately derived from the State-based understanding (Tamanaha 2000, pp 308, 312–21).

An approach that seeks to avoid any preconceived notion of how law should be defined comes under the rubric of critical legal pluralism (Kleinhans and Macdonald 1997). This departs from empirically based scholarship, arguing that techniques of mapping tend to see law in positivist terms as something that can be measured 'out there', apart from the human agents who created it. Critical legal pluralists reject this view of law as external knowledge, and instead highlight the role of knowledge in creating our perception of reality. This results in a different test for legal order. The focus is no longer simply on which external legal order exercises normative authority over individuals: we also have to ask within which legal order do individuals regard themselves as acting. This places more emphasis on the legal subject, who is not just a passive recipient of law, but has an active role in producing and shaping legal knowledge. As we perceive ourselves to be working within different legal orders at different times, the legal knowledge produced, and as perhaps the various views canvassed in this section affirm, will be necessarily and irretrievably plural.

Reading

A helpful overview of the principal differences between legal pluralism and State-centred accounts of law is found in Arthurs (1985, ch 1). For a discussion of the shift from 'classical' to 'new' legal pluralism, see Merry (1988, pp 872–4), and for the application of ideas of legal pluralism in the context of globalisation, see Santos (2002, pp 194–200) and Twining (2009, ch 12). For a review of the debate concerning the utility of the distinction between strong and weak legal pluralism, see Woodman (1998). Davies (2005) highlights the various empirical and conceptual strands within legal pluralist scholarship, and for an elaboration of the 'politics of definition' see Santos (2002, pp 89–91). For a discussion of critical legal pluralism, and its responses to some of Tamanaha's criticisms, see Kleinhans and Macdonald (1997, pp 30–43). A recent revisitation of the major themes of these debates can be found at Melissaris (2009).

References

Abel, R (ed), 1982, *The Politics of Informal Justice*, vols 1 and 2, New York: Academic Press.

Anderson, GW, 2005, *Constitutional Rights after Globalization*, Oxford and Portland, OR: Hart.

Arthurs, HW, 1985a, *Without the Law*, Toronto and Buffalo: University of Toronto Press.

Arthurs, HW, 1985b, 'Understanding Labour Law: The Debate over "Industrial Pluralism"', 38 *Current Legal Problems* 83.

Asch, M (ed), 1997, *Aboriginal and Treaty Rights in Canada: Essays on Law, Equality and Respect for Difference*, Vancouver: University of British Columbia Press.

Buchanan, R, 2006, 'Legitimating Global Trade Governance: Constitutional and Legal Pluralist Approaches', 57 *Northern Ireland Legal Quarterly* 1.

Chanock, M, 1985, *Law, Custom and Social Order: The Colonial Experience in Malawi and Zambia*, Cambridge: Cambridge University Press.

Davies, M, 2005, 'The Ethos of Pluralism', 27 *Sydney Law Rev* 87.

Dean, M, 1999, *Governmentality: Power and Rule in Modern Society*, London: Sage.

Griffiths, J, 1986, 'What is Legal Pluralism?', 24 *J Leg Pluralism* 1.

Hertz, N, 2001, *The Silent Takeover: Global Capitalism and the Death of Democracy*, London: Heinemann.

Kleinhans, M-M and Macdonald RA, 1997, 'What is a Critical Legal Pluralism?', 12 *Canadian Journal of Law and Society* 25.

Melissaris, E, 2009, *Ubiquitous Law: Legal Theory and the Space for Legal Pluralism*, Aldershot: Ashgate.

Merry, SE, 1988, 'Legal Pluralism', 22 *Law & Soc Rev* 869.

Rose, N and Valverde, M, 1998, 'Governed by Law?', 7 *Soc & Leg Stud* 541.

Sampford, C, 1991, *The Disorder of Law*, Oxford: Blackwell.

Santos, B, 2002, *Toward a New Legal Common Sense*, 2nd edn, London: Butterworth.

Shearing, C and Wood, J, 2003, 'Nodal Governance, Democracy, and the New "Denizens"', 30 *Jnl of Law & Soc* 400.

Tamanaha, BZ, 1993, 'The Folly of the "Social Scientific" Concept of Legal Pluralism', 20 *Jnl of Law & Soc* 192.

Tamanaha, BZ, 2000, 'A Non-Essentialist Version of Legal Pluralism', 27 *Jnl of Law & Soc* 296.

Teubner, G (ed), 1997, *Global Law Without a State*, Gateshead: Athenaeum Press.

Twining, W, 2009, *General Jurisprudence: Understanding Law from a Global Perspective*, Cambridge: Cambridge University Press.

Woodman, GR, 1998, 'Ideological Combat and Social Observation', 42 *Jnl of Leg Pluralism* 21.

Case

Re Southern Rhodesia (1919) AC (PC) 210.

2.2 Juridification

Introductory remarks

A development that has preoccupied many recent theorists of legal modernity has been the growth in the scale and scope of legal regulation in the modern State, a phenomenon that can be described as the juridification of social relations. This, indeed, has become a central theme in contemporary political debates over the role of the State, with (broadly speaking) politicians of the right decrying the over-regulation of the economy and society, and arguing for a reduction in the amount of legal regulation, and politicians of the left defending the necessity of such regulation as a means of remedying social inequalities produced by the operation of the market. This is a debate that has taken on added significance in the context of globalisation. On the one hand, the emergence of supranational bodies such as the European Union (EU), which seek to regulate the conditions of labour and production at a supra-State level, has led to political clashes over questions of national sovereignty and the 'democratic deficit' in European institutions. On the other, the globalisation of the economy has greatly facilitated the capacity of economic producers, such as multi-national corporations, to evade or shape particular regulatory regimes, leading to concerns about the impact of certain practices on the environment, and on the health and working conditions of workers in particular industries. It is not our intention to take sides in this particular debate, though it is important to understand the way that these debates are connected to jurisprudential themes. Our purpose is rather to open a different perspective on these debates by situating them in the context of our understanding of legal modernity.

The central issues here are, first, how to explain the growth of legal regulation, and second, what this can tell us about the place of law in the modern State. Underlying these issues, there is the broader question – a theme that runs through the whole of this part of the book – that of whether the development can be understood and explained within the paradigm of modernity, or whether we need to develop new theoretical resources in order to understand these processes. Before we go on, however, we must set out a basic description of the phenomenon of juridification.

We can imagine juridification as having both horizontal and vertical dimensions. Horizontally, we can observe that in modern society law increasingly spreads its regulatory reach across an increasingly diverse range of social activities – a feature that corresponds to Weber's observations about the instrumentalisation of modern law. It has spread, for example, into areas that were formerly considered private and beyond the proper reach of the law, such as aspects of domestic and family relations; it has spread into the area of what were once considered as matters purely of nature, such as the environment, genetics and life and death (as one English Court of Appeal judge put it, 'Deciding disputed matters of life and death is surely and pre-eminently a matter for a court of law to judge');[4] and it has spread increasingly – though incompletely and unevenly – into the political realm. This has led public law theorist, Martin Loughlin, to comment that one of the most important features of this, our 'age of rights', is that the 'politicization of law' goes hand in hand with the 'legalization of politics' (2000, ch 13). In each realm legal norms gain prominence as a means of organising factual and normative aspects of social relations, which were previously under- or unregulated by law. The vast increase in legislation in recent years (at subnational, national, and supranational levels, for example), as well as more popular perceptions of ours being an increasingly litigious society are both symptomatic of this trend.

In tandem with this, the vertical aspect concerns the ways in which legal norms not only tighten their hold on already or newly regulated areas through increased legislation or judicial activity, but do so by way of increasingly detailed normative standards. That is, rather than legal standards being general principles of reasonably broad coverage, there is an observable tendency for these standards to become more detailed in their specification of the factual circumstances that are being legally regulated. Again, this is observable across a broad range of areas of legal practice, such as administrative, corporate and criminal law: the United Kingdom, for example, has seen the creation of more than 3,000 new criminal offences in the last 15 years – offences that tend to be concerned with detailing more and more precisely the operative facts, rather than in responding to whole swathes of new forms of criminality.

Juridification, then, in the words of Jürgen Habermas, one of the leading analysts of this phenomenon:

> refers quite generally to the tendency toward an increase in formal (or positive, written) law that can be observed in modern society. We can distinguish here between the expansion of law, that is the legal regulation of new, hitherto informally regulated social matters, from the increasing density of law, that is the specialized breakdown of global statements of the legally relevant facts into more detailed statements.
>
> (1987, p 357)

---

4   *Re A* [2000] 4 All ER 961 per Ward, LJ at 987.

Habermas on juridification

Habermas argues that the process of juridification can generally be understood as part of a series of processes by which the modern State and economy developed as distinctive bodies or systems that operate subject to their own distinctive rationalities. While the spheres of politics and the economy are increasingly subject to the instrumental demands to reproduce systems of power and money, the rest of society – which he designates by the term the lifeworld – operates according to a non-instrumental, communicative rationality. Juridification, then, is a process by which system and lifeworld, and the relationships between them, are legally structured and regulated. This process facilitates the growth of the capitalist economy but also, and crucially, establishes and guarantees political and social liberty as the State seeks to legitimise its actions through the concession of political rights and freedoms.

He designates four distinctive epochs or thrusts of juridification. These begin in the seventeenth century with the emergence of the bourgeois State and the capitalist market economy. Here law is primarily concerned with regulating relations between individual commodity or property owners, and the authorisation of a 'sovereign state power with a monopoly on coercive force as the sole source of legal authority' (1987, p 358). That is to say that the legal order formally guarantees both the capacity of private individuals to own and alienate commodities in the market, through the laws of contract and property, and the political liberty and security of the individual, to the extent that it does not conflict with the security of the State. What is crucial here is the drawing of the distinction between public (the State) and civil society or the private, which is left unregulated. The succeeding epochs see the expansion of the scope of civil society vis-à-vis the State, as the lifeworld makes demands on the State for greater political freedoms, but these come at the cost of the increasing legal regulation (juridification) of social relations.

The second and third epochs, then, are the development of the constitutional State and the democratic constitutional State. In both these stages 'the idea of freedom already incipient in the concept of law as developed in the natural law tradition was given constitutional force' (1987, pp 360–1). In general terms, State power was first constitutionalised, giving citizens rights against the State (for example, not to be detained or punished except by due process of law), then democratised, as citizens were given rights to political participation (with, for example, the extension of suffrage and the freedom to organise political associations and parties). Political power is thus made subject to law and then, with the juridification of the legitimation process, its legitimacy is anchored in the democratic process.

While the first three stages mirror Weber's account of the achievements of legal modernity, as in Weber's account we see a more complex and ambivalent picture emerging in the fourth epoch. Here Habermas suggests that while the welfare state continues the line of freedom-guaranteeing juridification of the earlier epochs by 'the institutionalizing in legal form of a social power relation anchored in class structure' (1987, p 361), it does so in ways that, in fact, restrict freedom. Where the capitalist economy, supported by the laws of contract and property, had permitted the unlimited pursuit of self-interest and tolerated the resultant inequality and social deprivation, the welfare state sought to regulate the economy and intervene in the social sphere (or lifeworld) to mitigate the worst effects of the capitalist system. Classic examples of the juridification of economic relations would be measures to improve working conditions, the right to unionise and collective bargaining, and so on – all of which seek to protect or enhance the freedom of labour. Other social welfare measures can be described as the 'juridification of life-risks', including measures such as State provision of pensions and benefits, socialised health care, public education and so on – measures which seek to secure individuals against economic risks and to improve equality of opportunity. While these measures aim to guarantee freedom, Habermas contends that bureaucratic interventions in the lifeworld may also limit freedom by creating new forms of dependency. This occurs because bureaucracies must, of necessity, intervene in ways that require individuals to conform to general legal conditions in return for monetary compensation. This abstracts individuals from their life-situations, obscures the more general social conditions that might have given rise to particular problems, and damages pre-existing networks of social support or communication. Juridical intervention demands a restructuring – or 'colonisation' – of the lifeworlds of those entitled to social security. As he puts it generally:

> The negative effects of this wave of juridification do not appear as side effects; they result from the very form of juridification itself. It is now the very means of guaranteeing freedom that endangers the freedom of the beneficiaries.
>
> (1987, p 362)

He thus concludes by pointing to the dilemmatic structure of this type of juridification:

> [W]hile the welfare-state guarantees are intended to serve the goal of social integration, they nevertheless promote the disintegration of life-relations when these are separated, through legalized social intervention, from the consensual mechanisms that coordinate action and are transferred over to media such as power and money.
>
> (1987, p 364)

Juridification and the 'regulatory trilemma'

Where Habermas sees the problem of juridification in the dilemma of under- or over-regulation, Gunther Teubner's analysis of juridification suggests that it should rather be understood in terms of a 'trilemma'.

Teubner begins by asking why it is that many regulatory initiatives, such as attempts to limit polluting emissions, fail. He suggests that among the many reasons why such a measure might fail – expensive and inaccurate means to detect marginal violations, corruption, excessive budgetary costs on industry due to enforced slow-downs, and so on – is a response that we might even deem expected. Industry's typical response will be to deal with the penalties of breaching the law as an added cost. And, more often than not, such costs enter the balance sheets and are returned to consumers in terms of higher prices for the products without any effect on environmental damage. Or, to take another perhaps more complex problem, a government committed to fair housing policies may introduce measures to prevent landlords from raising rents. As a direct economic result of such a policy, capital is redirected away from the housing industry towards more lucrative ventures. As a result, tenants find themselves in a housing market where the rents may be affordable, but there is very little supply of rented accommodation.

Note that in these scenarios we have crossings of boundaries between the political, legal and economic systems. A political demand (for cleaner environment, for cheaper housing) is translated into a legal measure, operating a distinction between what is legal and illegal (penalties, fair rents), which is then retranslated by the economy into a language of prices and costs. Teubner identifies the problem of regulatory failure as the mistranslations that have occurred from each system using a different register to translate the 'stimulus' they receive: in the political system in which the demand is generated it is about the use of power; the legal system 'picks up' that demand as one that has to do with acting legally or illegally; the economic system picks it up in terms of what makes good economic sense. In this process the systems (political, legal, economic) do not operate causally on each other, but through what Teubner, following Niklas Luhmann, calls 'structural coupling'. It is a moment of reciprocal interference that sends each of the 'interacting' systems in the direction that the limited range of its own possible responses pre-ordains. Regulatory failures are a direct result of this inevitable mismanagement, inevitable because of the change of register that any 'structural coupling' between systems involves.

Teubner thus invites us to think about 'juridification' in the context of the increased instrumentalisation of law in the regulatory State. This use of law stumbles, he argues, on a 'regulatory trilemma', which confronts it with three possibilities – all three detrimental: 'either [to be] irrelevant, or produce disintegrating effects on the social area of life or else disintegrating effects on regulatory law itself' (1987, p 21). What do these three options mean? The first – indifference – denotes an absence of impact: the law has failed to make its demands felt at all and has had no regulatory effect. In the second case, regulation has a disintegrating effect on the field it attempts to regulate: under the bombardment of regulation the field loses its distinctive character, and becomes in a sense 'colonised' by the legal medium. Examples of this kind of failure abound: think of the family and the way the legalisation of reciprocity within it in terms of rights and duties erodes what we value most about it; or systems of childcare, where bureaucratic–legal criteria come to colonise and substitute for what are hugely nuanced and difficult judgements over what is in the best interests of the child in any concrete case. In the final horn of the trilemma it is law itself, the regulatory mechanism, that in a sense becomes 'colonised' by its object. If the law, in order to avoid riding roughshod through the societal field it is called to regulate, attempts instead to introduce too much complexity in order to respond more sensitively to its object, it runs the risk of undermining itself as a system. That is because the law draws its identity from introducing general standards and subsuming individual cases under them. If it is responding on an ad hoc, case-by-case, basis, readjusting itself as it goes, then it no longer provides that certainty and stability of expectations that it must produce and guarantee, leading to the disintegration of what was distinctive about law.

In locating the problem in the specific context of regulatory law, Teubner (unlike Habermas) invites us to understand juridification as a pathology associated with this type of law. Juridification becomes an umbrella term to cover questions of the function, legitimacy, structure and success of this 'managerial' type of law. Teubner pursues the explanation as a question of 'structural coupling' between the political system, where regulatory strategies are hammered out, the legal system, which is the former's means of implementing that policy, and the social field to be regulated, each with its own autonomous logic that defies direct manipulation. Problems of juridification then appear as failures to respect the boundaries and logics of the systems involved. It is all too easy to overstep boundaries on all sides in this delicate process; the result of such overstepping is experienced as juridification.

From within this theoretical framework, only two options remain open in respect of our ability to act through law to fashion our own future. The first is a conservative, laissez-faire option, espoused by Hayek and renewed by Luhmann, which calls us to respect differentiation and the autonomy and integrity of different systems. A functionally differentiated society is one that has no 'centre' remaining from which social demands can be articulated and directed to other systems. If we do not, however, want to give up on the possibilities of intervention, Teubner's social democratic alternative attempts to base such possibilities in the concept of 'reflexive' law – a procedural alternative to substantive intervention. This circumvents the regulatory trilemma by avoiding direct intervention and instead seeking to guarantee the conditions for autonomy and self-reproduction in the system under regulation.

Juridification as depoliticisation

These two approaches to juridification identify it as a crisis of the legal system, a problem that emerges with the growth of regulatory law in the welfare state. The instrumentalisation of law damages social relations (Habermas) or undermines the function of the legal system (Teubner); the response to this must be to limit the function of law by respecting the autonomy of the legal system. An alternative approach, however, sees juridification as a political problem – that is to say a problem that arises as a result of the legal system appropriating, or juridifying, conflicts that should more properly be dealt with politically. On this view, political disputes or problems are distorted by being made to fit legal categories; legal reasoning (which is oriented towards fitting particular cases within pre-existing general rules) excludes the possibility of a consensual or future-oriented resolution. This view does not start from an assumption of the autonomy of the legal system, but sees law as a tool (or strategy) that might be used by the State for the control or management of social relations. The crisis, then, is not one of law, but one that legal regulation brings about in the social field to be regulated (Santos 2002, pp 55–61).

Perhaps the most revealing historical examples of this kind of expropriation are in the area of labour law and industrial relations. It is in fact in this context that the term itself originates, in the polemical writings of early labour lawyers in Germany for whom 'juridification' was explicitly a moment of depoliticisation of industrial conflict, which could only properly be conceived and played out in political, class-conflictual terms. To use legal categories instead of political ones in the workplace not only alienates workers from a conflict that is vital to their sense of identity and their plight, but also hands it over to legal experts and disempowers them further.

The idea that juridification involves 'depoliticisation' is not of course confined to the sphere of industrial relations and labour law. It is in fact possible to establish that the increasing density of law can be witnessed in the regulatory modes employed generally by governments, national and supranational. These modes may themselves be more or less public, may themselves exist in regulatory competition, and overall will tend to an increasing specialisation of knowledge and norms in comparison with traditional legal principles. Of greatest importance here is the observation that while a range of legal mechanisms is used to discipline actors and practices, there is no necessary correspondence – in ideal or practice – to furthering goals of political freedom, in particular since the trajectory of freedom-enhancing measures in the pursuit of social or public goods is no longer paramount. Instead, the density of regulation, and the importance of private law mechanisms in this juridical matrix, is geared largely or almost exclusively to economic or efficiency ends.

What are we to take from all this? One response is to see these developments as symptomatic of a general decline in politics, what Isaiah Berlin (1969) saw as the demise of genuine political disagreement and its replacement with debate over means only. Evidence of this is normally of the kind that draws attention to voter apathy, the decline of differences between political parties, and the almost total demise of genuinely influential public political deliberation. However, what is significant is the way that the adherence to particular regulatory regimes or frameworks is used to 'depoliticise' certain issues. So, for example, the augmented and privileged role of private law as an institutional mechanism in public and economic life (in private finance initiatives (PFIs) or the contracting out of government services) acts to signal a decline in political participation in favour of corporate influence and demands.

These changes are not only taking place at a national level, but are replicated at the transnational and global level. The 'constitution of global capital', as Stephen Gill calls it, is made up of institutional mechanisms that discipline markets and states, forcing states, for example, to restructure market and regulatory institutions internally in return for loans or investment. This is done, says Gill, to accord with the 'Three Cs': confidence of investors, consistency of policies and credibility of governments (2000). In this sense, national, but also EU institutions and policies, have to adapt to transnational networks and deregulated markets, such as agreements on competition in services and intellectual property in formerly locally protected markets. Significantly, these forces are locked in through more or less formal legal agreements and conventions, and are implemented by a range of legal institutions – EU, WTO, IMF, central banks – operating at different levels of locality. For these reasons it is appropriate to talk about a 'constitution' of global capitalism.

It is arguable, however, that rather than representing a depoliticisation, these trends could also, or perhaps better, be understood as an immense repoliticisation in favour of a certain style of politics. This politics is geared to the naturalisation of unequal distribution of resources and opportunities, to its enforcement through disciplinary mechanisms (including law and the sanctity of contracts and private governance regimes) and in which democratic participation, where it exists at all, tends to be merely formal. Pierre Bourdieu talked insightfully of this 'new' politicisation as:

> a conservative revolution ... a strange revolution that restores the past but presents itself as progressive, transforming regression itself into a form of progress. It does this so well that those who oppose it are made to appear regressive themselves.
>
> (Bourdieu and Grass 2002, p 65)

A fifth epoch?

The analysis so far has analysed juridification from the perspective of regulatory law in the welfare state, but it could be contended that recent developments, such as those referred to in the last section, require us to develop a new theoretical framework for the analysis of juridification. Should we, in other words, be asking whether we have entered a fifth epoch?

The starting point for this would be the observation that the welfare state is variously seen in many Westernised countries as being in decline, under pressure, or, more actively, being dismantled. The post-war ideals and institutions that saw its establishment and development, and around which there existed a broad political consensus, have decayed to a point where the very existence of the welfare state might be in doubt. Such developments, it is important to note, do not signify the triumph of the free market over the State. Rather the State has realigned itself in relation to capital (and in particular corporate capital) in such a way as to demonstrate that the State and the market are not in competition. We can thus identify an increased 'marketisation' of social life in areas formerly considered public. This takes many forms, but is most commonly carried through by the privatisation of the delivery of public goods and services (and in some cases the privatisation of these as public goods themselves). The UK in particular has successfully pioneered and exported models of 'private finance initiative' (rechristened 'public private partnerships (PPP)' by New Labour) where companies pursue profit through the provision of public services, such as schools and hospitals, both in terms of investment capital and ongoing management and delivery. The processes of individualisation and monetarisation established in the fourth epoch continue, but no longer simply in the guise of public-welfare entitlements, but rather as part of a complex web of private or 'public–private' economic relations.

Central to this process is the re-embedding of private law mechanisms – contract and property law in particular – within formerly public, State-owned areas. These carry with them techniques (such as commercial confidentiality clauses, etc) that exclude more conventional public supervision. In addition, these mechanisms themselves are structured within competition law frameworks, which draw on supranational legal sources, and which at the academic level have seen demands for the convergence of private law at a conceptual level: the development of European private law codes, harmonisation of trade and contract laws, UNIDROIT, and so on. Together, these signal a decentralisation of power in contrast to the welfare state model, but also a reconfiguration of power at the supranational level. As MacNeil has put it:

> These 'private' institutions [such as corporations] are delocalized, being almost totally mobile. Many dwarf half the 'sovereign' countries of the world. By their power over money, information and communication they can and do manipulate and control even the largest of 'sovereigns'.
>
> (MacNeil 2000, p 431)

One could say more about these processes, but together they might suggest that a new epoch of juridification is upon us. If we map these changes onto Habermas's definitions we may note the following. First, there can be little doubt about the increased volume of formal law within particular states and in the EU more generally. This might best be seen as part of a longer trajectory, that in itself does not amount to a new epoch. However, when we consider that aspect, which identifies the expansion of law, we find that regulatory activity has in fact expanded into new areas. To take only one, emblematic example: the regulation of biomedical sciences and, in particular, those relating to genetics – human, animal and plant – exemplifies a rethinking of the very means and modes of the reproduction of basic social and material life.

Crucially, however, regulation in this and other areas is driven by private enterprise and the desire for commodification, and only secondarily as a public welfare concern. It is for this reason that we can speculate whether the fourth epoch of juridification identified by Habermas is giving way to a fifth.

Reading

For a general account of the epochs of juridification and the problems encountered by law in the fourth epoch, see Habermas (1987, pp 357–73). Teubner (1987) presents a challenge to this interpretation of the problems of juridification. There is some useful background discussion in Cotterrell (1992, pp 65–70 and ch 9), and the debate between Rottleuthner (1989) and Smith (1991), and the further response in Teubner (1992) provides further illustration of the issues here.

For historical accounts linking juridification to the development of the welfare state see Kamenka and Tay (1975) and Unger (1976, pp 58–66, 192–223), and for a critical dismissal of the whole debate, see Santos (2002, pp 55–61).

The question of whether we have entered a fifth epoch of juridification is addressed in Veitch (2012).

References

Berlin, I, 1969, 'Political Ideas in the Twentieth Century', in Berlin, *Four Essays on Liberty*, Oxford: Oxford University Press.

Bourdieu, P and Grass, G, 2002, 'The "Progressive" Restoration: A Franco-German Dialogue', *New Left Review* (Mar/Apr) 62–77.

Cotterrell, R, 1992, *The Sociology of Law. An Introduction*, 2nd edn, London: Butterworths.

Gill, S, 2000, 'The Constitution of Global Capitalism' at www.theglobalsite.ac.uk/press/010gill.pdf.

Habermas, J, 1987, *The Theory of Communicative Action. Vol. 2 Lifeworld and System*, Cambridge: Polity.

Kamenka, E and Tay, AE, 1975, 'Beyond Bourgeois Individualism: The Contemporary Crisis in Law and Legal Ideology', in E Kamenka and RS Neale (eds), *Feudalism, Capitalism and Beyond*, London: Edward Arnold, pp 127–44.

Loughlin, M, 2000, *Sword and Scales*, Oxford: Hart.

MacNeil, I, 2000, 'Contracting Worlds and Essential Contract Theory', *Social & Legal Studies* 431–8.

Rottleuthner, H, 1989, 'The Limits of the Law: The Myth of a Regulatory Crisis', 17 *Intnl Jnl of Soc of Law* 273–85.

Santos, B de Sousa, 2002, *Toward a New Legal Common Sense*, 2nd edn, London: Butterworths.

Smith, SC, 1991, 'Beyond "Mega-Theory" and "Multiple Sociology": A Reply to Rottleuthner', 19 *Intnl Jnl of Soc of Law* 321–40.

Teubner, G, 1987, 'Juridification: Concepts, Aspects, Limits, Solutions', in G Teubner (ed), *Juridification of Social Spheres*, Berlin: de Gruyter.

Teubner, G, 1992, 'Regulatory Law: Chronicle of a Death Foretold', 1 *Soc & Leg Stud* 451–75.

Unger, RM, 1976, *Law in Modern Society*, New York: The Free Press.

Veitch, S, 2012, 'Juridification, Integration and Depoliticisation', in D Augenstein (ed), *'Integration through law' Revisited*, Aldershot: Ashgate.

Case

Re A [2000] 4 All ER 961.

2.3 Displacing the juridical: Foucault on power and discipline

Introductory remarks

Our discussions of legal modernity up to this point have accorded a central role to the law. In analyses such as Weber's, for example, the development of modernity is linked to the law playing an ever more central role in the constitution of political power, in the regulation of economic transactions and in the government of social life. These replicate the arguments in, say, liberal political theory that emphasise the role of the law in developing human rights and democracy and protecting the autonomy of the individual. This is challenged by theoretical approaches which seek to displace the centrality of the law in the development or analysis of modernity. These approaches go beyond merely attempting to displace the centrality of State law, such as we see in Santos's discussion of globalisation and legal pluralism, to the argument that in the development of modernity law is transformed in such a way as to reduce the significance of juridical categories. It is argued that law is no longer a category through which we can understand or analyse the operation of power in modernity. We shall examine these types of claims through an examination of the work of the French philosopher and social theorist Michel Foucault (1926–1984).

Foucault famously, and controversially, contended that the period of modernity is a 'phase of juridical regression', and that a focus on the constitutions and legislation that had been passed since the eighteenth century would prevent us from understanding fundamentally important shifts in the nature of the operation of power in modernity (1979, p 144). He argues that new techniques of government that developed in the modern period were distinct from the traditional juridical forms of sovereignty. The juridical, he suggests, has been displaced as a principle of power, and modern society should be analysed in terms of the development of a 'governmentality', which constitutes both 'society' and the individual as effects of the operation of power.

Foucault's work has been important and influential, and though it rarely focuses on the law directly, it raises radical questions about the social role and function of law in modern society. In this section we will first of all examine the key terms of discipline and biopower, and their place in the complex of techniques that Foucault called 'governmentality'. We will then look at the concept of power in Foucault's work before addressing the question of how his work can contribute to our understanding of law in modern society.

Discipline and biopower

Some of Foucault's most intriguing and important remarks on power and the law are contained in the short section entitled, 'The Right of Death and the Power over Life', which concludes volume I of the *History of Sexuality* (1979, pp 135–59). Here Foucault sets out two models of political power: the pre-modern, or classical, model of juridical power, and the modern normalising power. In the juridical model, the sovereign had the right to take the life of those who threatened the internal or external order of the State, or to demand that his subjects give up their lives in the defence of the State. This power could be characterised as a right of seizure (of things, time, bodies, even life itself): a power of life and death exercised by a sovereign over his subjects. The normalising model, by contrast, is characterised by its power over life: to administer, sustain, develop and multiply the life of the population of a particular territory. This did not necessarily exclude the right to take life, but to the extent that it remained, it was part of a complex of forces that were aimed primarily at the fostering or production of life – the administration of bodies – rather than its seizure or negation. Thus if juridical power was characterised by negativity (the prohibition), exemplified in the use of the death penalty, this new form of power was productive or positive in its effects, and subtle and diverse in the techniques and strategies that it employed. Where juridical power relied on the single intervention, these new powers were continuous and regulatory in their effect. Most important of all, he claims that these new apparatuses of power increasingly incorporated and transformed the judicial institution, leading to the decline, or regression, of the juridical.

The normalising power:

> evolved in two basic forms . . . two poles of development linked together by a whole intermediary cluster of relations. One of these poles . . . centered on the body as a machine: its disciplining, the optimization of its capabilities, the extortion of its forces, the parallel increase of its usefulness and its docility . . . [A]ll this was ensured by the procedures of power that characterised the disciplines: an anatomo-politics of the human body. The second, formed somewhat later, focused on the species body . . . [S]upervision was effected through an entire series of interventions and regulatory controls: a bio-politics of the population.
>
> (1979, p 139)

These two forms, then, are discipline and biopower. While the former operates on individuals located in institutions such as prisons, factories, schools and hospitals by surveillance and control with the constant aim of the more efficient distribution and use of power, the latter is concerned with the management of populations through the science of statistics and techniques of political economy.

Discipline

Foucault's analysis of discipline is developed in what is probably his most famous book, *Discipline and Punish*, first published in France in 1975 (Foucault 1977).[5] Although the primary subject of the book is the birth of the prison, that is to say an analysis of the dramatic shift that took place in the early nineteenth century towards the systematic and large-scale use of incarceration as a form of punishment in its own right, Foucault's main concern is with how institutions such as the prison were based on (and in turn fostered) new techniques for the disciplining or control of the body. He is concerned here with the question of how power operates in institutions such as the prison, for he observed that the modern prison did not seek simply to segregate the prisoner from society. The prison, he argued, developed techniques that sought to operate on the mind or soul of the prisoner, placing them in a network of power relations aimed at creating a new kind of individual. It was, in short, a form of discipline. This, he argued comprised three techniques or modalities of power: hierarchical observation, normalising judgment and the examination (1977, pp 170–94).

Hierarchical observation enabled coercion through the means of surveillance or monitoring. While observation, of course, was not new, what was distinctive about the modern period was the way that it became embedded in the architecture and design of certain institutions. Prisons were designed in such a way as to make the prisoner physically visible to other inmates or to prison officers, who were themselves being watched and supervised. At the same time, the network or hierarchy of management was an apparatus that placed individuals in a field of relations in which all were continuously supervised by their superiors and inferiors. These institutions and networks made possible the exercise of a continuous control over conduct. *Normalising judgment*, by contrast, refers to the breaking down of actions and behaviours into evermore distinct elements, the normal (or average) way of behaving or performing an action, the departure from which is corrected by discipline aimed at training or instilling in the individual the proper way of acting. Corresponding to the deviations from the norm, there was a new microeconomy of penality, of rewards and punishments, according to which individuals could be compared, differentiated, hierarchised, homogenised and excluded (1977, p 183). Last, Foucault suggests that these first two techniques are combined in the *examination*. The importance of the examination (the physical examination of the patient or prisoner, the assessment of the student and so on) lies in the fact that it constitutes the object of the examination as a field of knowledge, something that is to be known. The examination, then, made possible the gathering of a certain kind of knowledge (of individuals, of cases), that could be systematised, made more scientific, and which would in turn enable more effective future examination and control. The examination thus 'linked to a certain type of the formation of knowledge a certain form of the exercise of power'

---

5   The French title is *Surveillir et Punir*, but see the translator's note to the English edition.

(1977, p 187). The aim of all these techniques was the production of more efficient distributions of power or mechanisms of control, but central to them was the constitution of the individual as both the object of power and the instrument of its exercise.

The importance of these 'modest' techniques goes well beyond the analysis of the prison, for Foucault argues that these represent a new political technology of the body, that is to say, a set of techniques and forces that aimed at maximising the productivity and obedience of the individual. Indeed, he took Jeremy Bentham's model of the panopticon – the prison in which the prisoners are continually visible to their jailer, and must believe themselves to be observed even when they are not – as a model for the operation of this form of power throughout the social body (1977, pp 200–9; Bentham 1995). The mechanism could be used for the surveillance of prisoners and patients, but also of workers in a factory to increase their productivity. This form of constant observation was more effective, inducing people to act as though they were always being observed, and thus to internalise the operation of discipline. It was a form of police power, systematic, far-reaching and intense that allowed the government of society as a whole without the need of recourse to repression or the outward display of force. The panopticon internalised the operation of disciplinary power, while maximising the numbers of people on whom it could be exercised. Most important of all, it was capable of being transferred between different contexts or institutions, making possible a generalised surveillance. It was, in this sense, 'the diagram of a mechanism of power reduced to its ideal form' (1977, p 205).

Biopower

Where discipline works on the individual, 'biopower' is aimed at the administration and production of life. This, Foucault proclaims rather grandly, was 'nothing less than the entry of life into history' (1979, p 141), by which he meant that the conditions of biological existence became the concern of politics.

Foucault remarks here that the modern period sees the development of a new kind of concern with public health. States and sovereigns had had to contend throughout history with disease and epidemics, and their damaging consequences. Famine and natural disaster had caused economic slumps. However, he noted that the eighteenth century saw the beginning of attempts to regulate or manage public health, and to adjust the life and well-being of the population to the needs of economic production. This was made possible by the development of three techniques. First, the collection of social statistics allowed the monitoring of the size and well-being of the population, the recording of birth and death rates, and the measuring of the incidence of disease. It was observed that there are regularities or patterns in these figures at the level of the population – in birth or mortality rates, or the incidence of certain illnesses – and that the social body has a life that can be studied and regulated. Second, interventions in public health could improve collective welfare or security at the level of the population. Thus, for example, improvements in drinking water and sewage disposal eradicated certain diseases; mass vaccination programmes led to dramatic improvements in health and mortality rates; the provision of public housing led to improvement of the collective health of the working classes; and the regulation of sex and the family, through programmes of contraception and sex education, could alter birth rates and infant mortality. Third, population dynamics have economic effects – the size, health, level of education and wealth of the population are all, more or less, directly linked to the economic capacity of the State. The new science of political economy arose out of the perception of these links between population, territory and wealth, and was accompanied by new forms of intervention: managing economic production through the provision of social infrastructure such as roads or housing; establishing systems of public education for an educated workforce; the provision of benefits to workers to sustain the workforce even during economic slumps, and so on.

We can thus see how this biopower was central to the development of capitalism: inserting bodies into the machinery of production and adjusting the phenomena of population to economic processes. However, Foucault wants to contend that this was neither the outcome of the process of economic development nor a process that was directed by the State. It was, he argued, a new rationality of government, or governmentality, based around techniques for the management of individuals and populations, but which was not reducible to changes in the form of State institutions.

Governmentality

Governmentality, he argued, is a specific and complex form of power (institutions, procedures, analyses, tactics), which 'has as its target population, as its principal form of knowledge political economy, and as its essential technical means apparatuses of security' (2000, p 220). There were thus certain techniques of individualisation and totalisation that characterise the operation of power in modern society: the production of knowledge through statistics as a means of establishing the social as a field of intervention; the production of collective welfare, health, wealth; the production of the citizen through discipline as a certain way of relating inner being and outer behaviour; and the production of new apparatuses of security and surveillance (the prison, the hospital, the asylum, police) that created and regulated social space.

The importance of these forms of power is that they do not necessarily emanate from the State, nor are they employed exclusively in State institutions. Indeed, he is at pains to contrast governmentality with traditional juridical forms of sovereignty centred on the State. There are three important differences between the two forms of power. First, while juridical power is repressive and negative, Foucault argues that normalising power is productive. It is an action upon an action, not upon a thing, and through action it produces or constructs knowledge about its object and the processes of its application. It thus constructs society and the individual as the targets of power. Second, it is not a property, but a strategy. Power is not located at a particular point in the social body (the sovereign, the constitution), and it cannot be possessed, either in itself (as a right) or as a consequence of the ownership of something else (such as the means of production). Power is a relation and it operates through clusters of individual relations or nodal points in the social body. And third, then, its operation is always localised rather than centralised. Power is not handed down from the great institutions of State, but operates through diverse and multiple networks. Thus in his radical formulation, the State and the rights-bearing individual appear as an effect of power rather than as its source.

However, while this analysis does not take the State and State institutions as its starting point, it is also important to note that Foucault sees the State as having been 'governmentalised' in the sense that problems of sovereignty, such as the competences of the State, come to be thought of within the matrix of powers and knowledge that have been produced by governmentality (2000, p 221). In a more specific sense, governmentality goes hand in hand with the modern liberal State and capitalist economy as the means by which population and individuals are managed so that individuals can become the self-governing subjects of the liberal legal order. However, where traditional political theory has interpreted sovereignty in juridical terms – founded on a contract, and structured by rights – the analysis of governmentality argues that political and social relations cannot be reduced to the legal relation, and that we should additionally focus on the governmental practices that shape the subject as the self-governing, rational actor presumed by political theory (Dean 1999, ch 6).

A theory of legal modernity?

Let us now return to the question with which we started: to what extent can Foucault's theory contribute to our understanding of the place of law and modernity? We can now see that Foucault is making two claims about the law. First, that with the development of governmentality the law is transformed by normalising power. Second, that the basis of sovereignty, which before the modern period was constituted in juridical terms, requires to be rethought.[6] Let us look at each of these in a little more detail.

The characteristic form of modern law, Foucault argues, is not the absolute rule or prohibition, but the norm as 'the judicial institution is increasingly incorporated into a continuum of apparatuses (medical, administrative and so on), whose functions are for the most part regulatory' (1979, p 144). Consider, for example, the end of life. Death no longer merely marks the limit of sovereign authority, but is surrounded by detailed legislation regulating the point of legal death, how a person may die (euthanasia, medical intervention), the responsibility for the well-being of the terminally ill patient, and even the disposal of the body so as to protect public health. The norm is not an absolute rule, referable to an external source of authority, but is produced through the logics of discipline and government; a norm of behaviour is established through observation and then applied to the same objects that it seeks to govern. The norm as a standard of behaviour is thus strictly self-referential, not emanating from a sovereign power. The strengths of the norm, however, are that it is a common, even objective, standard of measurement, and that it can measure and adjust the behaviour of different individuals. Modern law thus operates as a series of continuous regulatory and corrective mechanisms, rather than on the basis of the sovereign prohibition. It is constituted with reference to the object of regulation rather than according to a set of universal principles. And the sources, objects, institutions and practices of law are necessarily plural. Law in this sense must be understood as a medium rather than a principle of power.

We can now see that claim about modernity as a phase of juridical regression is not necessarily a claim about the declining importance of law so much as a claim about the declining significance of a particular form of sovereignty. The juridical should thus be taken as a way of describing a particular historical form of monarchical sovereignty. However, this is important because this conception of sovereignty has been of importance in shaping our theoretical understanding of the concept. On this view, law is increasingly sidelined, as it is no longer the principle of power: real power is neither

---

6   See Ewald (1991, p 139) for a slightly different formulation.

constituted nor defined in legal terms, but operates through non-legal strategies and mechanisms. The importance of law may be merely that of legitimising certain actions of the State; indeed, Foucault suggests at various points that formal legal liberties are founded on the corporeal disciplines, and that these were the forms that made normalising power acceptable (1977, p 222; 1979, p 144). We believe power is constituted in legal terms (rights, constitutions, etc) and so are distracted from the real operation of power in society.

The claim of juridical regression is, however, significant in two further and closely linked senses. On the one hand it is a claim about the declining capacity of the categories of the law to capture or define the nature of society (Murphy 1991). On this view law is neither a measure of rationality nor an index of social solidarity; the study of law can reveal nothing essential or fundamental about the nature of society. On the other hand it raises a question about how sovereignty is to be constituted in the absence of an external source of power such as the monarchical sovereign, for we cannot start from any assumptions about the nature or proper function of law as distinct from its actual operations. How, that is to say, can we theorise a sovereignty that is referable only to its own practices? How do we theorise law if it possesses no fundamental characteristics? And how, as a question of politics, can law limit the operation of power in the knowledge that there is no space 'outside' in which law can stand against power? These questions are not easily answered, but the importance of Foucault's theory is that he raises them in particularly acute form.

Reading

The starting point for any understanding of Foucault must be the original texts, because of his distinctive style. The most accessible are probably *Discipline and Punish* (1977) and Volume I of the *History of Sexuality* (1979). It is also worth bearing in mind that Foucault published a number of interviews, which also provide short, accessible introductions to his work. Many of these have now been reproduced in the three-volume *Essential Works*. You will also find a selection in Foucault (1980). Gordon (1987) offers a useful comparison with the work of Max Weber. There is little secondary literature directly on Foucault and law, but Ewald (1991), Murphy (1991) and Golder and Fitzpatrick (2009) are most useful.

On governmentality, you should begin with Foucault (2000), while Dean (1999) provides a very useful summary and discussion of the ideas and of the literature spawned by the lecture. The lecture is also published in Burchell *et al* (1991), together with a number of other essays discussing and applying the ideas.

Finally, it is worth reading some of the more recent attempts to extend and apply Foucault's thought. The themes of governmentality and police are explored in the essays in Dubber and Valverde (2006), and the legal construction of categories of gender in medicine and law in Sheldon (1997). Hardt and Negri (2000), and Agamben (1998) are stunning and important attempts to address the questions of sovereignty and biopower in a globalised world.

References

Agamben, G, 1998, *Homo Sacer. Sovereign Power and Bare Life*, Stanford: Stanford University Press.

Bentham, J, 1995, *The Panopticon Writings*, M Bozovic (ed), London: Verso.

Burchell, G, Gordon, C and Miller, P (eds), 1991, *The Foucault Effect: Studies in Governmentality*, London: Harvester Wheatsheaf.

Dean, M, 1999, *Governmentality: Power and Rule in Modern Society*, London: Sage.

Dubber, MD and Valverde, M (eds), 2006, *The New Police Power*, Stanford: Stanford University Press.

Ewald, F, 1991, 'Norms, Discipline and the Law', in R Post (ed), *Law and the Order of Culture*, Berkeley: University of California Press.

Foucault, M, 1977, *Discipline and Punish. The Birth of the Prison*, Harmondsworth: Penguin.

Foucault, M, 1979, *The History of Sexuality. Vol I. The Will to Knowledge*, Harmondsworth: Penguin.

Foucault, M, 1980, *Power/Knowledge. Selected Interviews and Other Writings 1972–77*, C Gordon (ed), Brighton: Harvester.

Foucault, M, 2000, 'Governmentality', in *Essential Works of Foucault 1954–1984. Vol III Power*, New York: New Press.

Golder, B and Fitzpatrick, P, 2009, *Foucault's Law*, London: Routledge.

Gordon, C, 1987, 'The Soul of the Citizen: Max Weber and Michel Foucault on Rationality and Government', in S Whimster and S Lash (eds), *Max Weber, Rationality and Modernity*, London: Allen & Unwin.

Hardt, M and Negri, A, 2000, *Empire*, Cambridge, MA: Harvard University Press.

Murphy, WT, 1991, 'The Oldest Social Science? The Epistemic Properties of the Common Law Tradition', 54 *Mod LR* 182–215.

Sheldon, S, 1997, *Beyond Control: Medical Power, Women and Abortion Law*, London: Pluto Press.

2.4 Law in the risk society

Introduction

We might think, plausibly enough, that law and legal institutions are centrally concerned with the organisation of risk. This might be in the private law of delict (or tort), where legal rules and principles are employed to govern the allocation of benefits and burdens consequent on negligently or intentionally caused harms; or in contract law, which organises the formation and consequences of consensually reached bargains in the market; or in public or international law, where rights and responsibilities are set out in legal norms as a means of addressing and trying to plan around the uncertainties of events and the practices of power associated with particular spheres of action. In all these areas, risks and the way they are dealt with are an indispensable element of the legal world. We might believe that this observation merely acknowledges the fact that the world is an inherently 'risky' place, and that legal mechanisms, particularly of the type associated earlier with the formal rationality of Weber's analysis, provide ways of organising these risks in a relatively predictable way in order to secure some kind of human control over an inevitably unpredictable future. While we might be tempted to see risk in that sense as a negative feature of social life, we should also acknowledge that it is absolutely fundamental to social life, including of course the fact that risks are crucial to the capitalist form of economic organisation.

But our concern with risk in this section has a different emphasis. Here we will concentrate on what the German sociologist, Ulrich Beck, has labelled 'risk society', and by which he means something much more specific. In what follows we will outline its main features and some of the challenges it poses to legal order. It is important to analyse these for a number of reasons. First, the social and environmental conditions that mark the emergence of risk society in Beck's terms are of great and potentially enduring significance to human communities on a global scale. Second, these conditions arguably work to undermine the effectiveness of the rationalities associated with modernity, but – and this is the key point – such undermining is a consequence of these very rationalities themselves. Finally, as a crucial component of this, the legal rationality associated with modernity is itself threatened in ways that put in question its ability to deal with the kinds of risks that have emerged. All together then, the question of risk society is a question of the very future viability of law in, indeed of law and, modern society.

Features of the 'risk society'

Risk society, according to Beck, is a catastrophic society. It is one in which the technological developments of modernity produce risks of such magnitude and such potentially vast environmental devastation that they threaten human, animal and plant life on the planet. Progress in terms of chemical, nuclear and biological science may have led, in the West at any rate, away from a society of scarcity, but it is now precisely in terms of wealth and overproduction that risks appear most prevalently. Environmental pollution, nuclear radiation, toxins in food and genetic engineering, for example, stem directly from the practices of modern society, but all arise from or produce hazards that put in jeopardy the successes of modernity. As Beck puts it, 'at the turn of the twenty-first century the unleashed process of modernisation is overrunning and overcoming its own coordinate system' (Beck 1992, p 87), and it is this, he argues, which signals that we have now entered a period of 'reflexive modernity' in which modernity itself 'is becoming its own theme' (1992, p 19).

In comparison with earlier phases, what is so specifically dangerous and novel about the nature of the hazards associated with reflexive modernity is that they are irreversible and incalculable. Such risks are often difficult to detect, both spatially and temporally, until they result in harms and hence they affect the future in ways that are highly unpredictable. They tend to render traditional calculations about cause and effect problematic, as hazards become not only potentially uncontrollable, but perpetrators (where they can be singled out at all) are identifiable only once irremediable damage has occurred. Moreover, risks such as those associated with environmental devastation or global warming respect no national boundaries and, while they are not dissociable from existing structures of wealth, they no longer conform to these in traditional ways – as Beck puts it succinctly, 'poverty is hierarchic, smog is democratic' (1992, p 36). Finally, given the global nature of the dangers these processes produce, action in response to them can no longer be plausibly understood in modernity's traditional terms; for example, actions undertaken by states acting alone to defend their own populations will not be able to combat the effects of global warming, no matter how 'environmentally friendly' their own political programmes. As such, the State's sovereign powers are diminished under threats that they can no longer directly or unilaterally control, and risk society thus renders the effectiveness of the Nation-State system highly problematic. In these respects, and others, the hazards of risk society come to undermine many of the basic elements we have seen associated with modernity. Beck describes the effects of these developments in stark terms:

> The dangers of highly developed nuclear and chemical productive forces abolish the foundations and categories according to which we have thought and acted to this point, such as space and time, work and leisure time, factory and nation state, indeed even the borders between continents.
>
> (Beck 1992, p 22)

As part of this process, Beck identifies what he terms the 'boomerang effect' of risks under conditions of globalisation. According to this, even those who might think themselves safe from the disastrous effects of socially harmful activities – the rich and the powerful – cannot escape these risks. At its most extreme, for example, the physical effects of a nuclear war perpetrated by a powerful nuclear State, would be such that the damage caused could not be confined to the 'enemy' State (and would affect third-party countries not part of the conflict); the perpetrator itself would not be able to immunise its own population from the effects of radiation carried back on the winds or in the food chain. Such modernisation risks, says Beck, mean that 'perpetrator and victim sooner or later become identical' (1992, p 38).

This boomerang effect, moreover, does not apply only to human life, but also to central elements of the dominant world order, such as 'money, property, and legitimation. It does not just strike back directly at the individual source; in a wholesale, egalitarian way it impairs everyone' (1992, p 38). Environmental devastation, for example, will return at some point to have an impact on those who might be thought to have been most culpable in permitting or committing the original wrong, such as powerful states or economic actors. Unable to escape from the effects of the interdependency of global financial, productive and consumer activity, the very successes of these actors – in political or economic terms – will themselves be put in danger by the hazards they have been involved in creating. This is a process amply demonstrated by the ongoing financial crisis in the world financial system, triggered by the collapse of the US 'sub-prime' market, but which spread rapidly to all areas of the global banking system and economy. Thus the 'boomerang effect' impacts on all levels of social interaction, including the security and stability of property relations subject to its impact.

Beck sums up this point in the following terms:

> Everything which threatens life on Earth also threatens the property and commercial interests of those who live from the commodification of life and its requisites. In this way a . . . contradiction arises between the profit and property of interests that advance the industrialization process and its frequently threatening consequences, which endanger and expropriate possessions and profits (not to mention the possession and profit of life).
>
> (1992, p 39)

States and economic actors have acknowledged these features only slowly, and many are still in denial about them (as the refusal of the US government to sign up to the Kyoto agreement confirms; see also the UK's Stern Review of 2006). Ironically, of course, as Beck points out, it is often the case that where proposed solutions to these problems are sought within the terms of capitalist development itself, one effect is to commodify these risks themselves, turning them into business. (Carbon emissions trading, for example, involves making a market out of pollution.) As such, the 'diffusion and commercialisation of risks do not break with the logic of capitalist development completely, but instead they raise the latter to a new stage' (1992, p 23). But for how long, it might be asked, will such development remain development, when the very conditions of the reproduction of life may be put at risk by such activities? This is precisely the problem Beck identifies for reflexive modernity.

Law in the risk society

The issue of property returns us to questions about the impact of the risk society on law and legal regulation. There are two aspects to this that we should consider. First, in line with the earlier observations, it would seem that traditional legal categories are threatened by the consequences associated with the large-scale hazards produced under conditions of reflexive modernisation. Thus, as we have already seen, the legal powers of states to have a monopoly on determining internally the conditions of their citizens' life and opportunities may be threatened by global risks that cannot adequately be dealt with by national legislation. Even regional regulation (such as within the EU) may be insufficient to stem the production of hazards on a global scale. Moreover, where the environmental costs of production might be thought to be locatable elsewhere (in terms of industrial production being displaced from one region to another for the sake of increasing profit) these costs will not remain in the place they are generated where the boomerang effect cannot be avoided.

At a more theoretical level, however, given the extensive nature of the hazards that have emerged, it is also the case that traditional legal concepts and categories may themselves become redundant in the face of global ecological threats. Thus conventional legal categories of causation, individual liability and foreseeability of harm are no longer adequate conceptual means of redressing the harms of risk society. In the face of incalculable threats and in situations where the identities of victims and perpetrators merge, modernity's legal mechanisms for dealing with risk allocation might be thought to provide inadequate resources. We will return to this point again in a moment.

Finally, the relation between law, politics and science is reconfigured in the risk society in ways that challenge the very ability of legal and democratic accountability to organise regarding the dangers faced and ways of dealing with them. Because risks tend to be 'knowledge based', they are 'open to social definition and construction'; consequently they can, says Beck, 'be changed, magnified, dramatized or minimized within knowledge' (1992, p 23). What this means is that they are open to conflictual understandings in such a way that the politics of the definition of risks becomes a crucial feature of attempts to acknowledge or alleviate them. One of the central problems here is the emergence of an asymmetry between, on the one hand, the production of, and knowledge about, risks, and on the other, the responsibility for them.

This plays out directly in the context of the relationship between law, politics, science and business. As Beck maintains, 'The structuring of the future is taking place indirectly and unrecognisably in research laboratories and executive suites, not in the parliament or in political parties', adding that the potential is that 'politics is becoming a publicly financed advertising agency for the sunny sides of a development it does not know, and one that is removed from its active influence' (1992, pp 223–4). This asymmetry is compounded by the fact that, at the level of social expectations, governments and states are still seen as the key players in legitimating the practices and consequences of scientific 'progress', even when in fact they are ill-equipped to do so. Government is still perceived as the main port of call in terms of trying to alleviate or compensate for harms caused by business. However, business sees these harms as side effects, which are not their responsibility. The consequence is that 'business is not responsible for something it causes, and politics is responsible for something over which it has no control' (1992, p 227).

This leads us to our second observation about the role of law in the risk society. This is to suggest that law and legal institutions may themselves be complicit in the ongoing production and normalisation of global risks. If this is so, then we are confronted by the possibility, not only of law's inability to confront global hazards, but by the fact that it actually promotes them. This is a far more devastating critique of law's role than merely pointing to its inadequacy. Let us see how Beck argues this point.

If the modern industrial society was centrally concerned with the distribution of goods, says Beck, then the risk society is concerned with the distribution of 'bads'. But such distribution takes place according to certain dynamics, including importantly that of legal regulation. But here, law, instead of operating to regulate responsible behaviour and impose consequences for irresponsible behaviour – that is, to set standards and impose sanctions consequent on their breach – actually operates as a way of organising irresponsible behaviour. In other words, dangerous actors – be they states or corporations – carry out activities that contribute to global risk, but these harmful activities are legalised through a regime that claims still to be there to protect people and the environment from such harms. The reason this happens is because the principles law has for organising responsibility – in particular those regarding causation, individual liability, and proof – are rooted in an earlier form of modernity and have not caught up with the nature and extent of the dangers now being faced. Thus their operation is not only inadequate, but contributes to the problem. This, says Beck, is the 'concealed gap of the century' and, in the context of ecological harms, in fact legalises universal pollution:

> [D]angers worldwide make it harder to prove that a single substance is the cause; the international production of harmful substances works against proving the culpability of a single company or perpetrator; the individual character of criminal law contradicts the collective danger; and the global character of the danger has abolished 'causes' as our industrial forefathers understood them.
>
> (Beck 1995, pp 131–2)

By assigning responsibilities only under certain well-established legal categories, what modern law and legal institutions do is to organise a system of non-liability, a regime of unaccountability: environmental harms continue at an alarming rate, and yet either no one at all can be or is held responsible for them (or everyone and thus no one is responsible for causing them), or responsibility is massively asymmetrical to the harms caused (small fines, say, for massive damage caused). Here, then, is how Beck sums up the overall effect:

> If one wanted to think up a system for turning guilt into innocence, one could take this collaboration between justice, universal culpability, acquittal and pollution as one's model. Nothing criminal is happening here, nothing demonstrably criminal anyway. Its undemonstrability is guaranteed precisely by compliance with, and strict application of, the fundamental rule of justice – the principle of individual culpability, whereby both pollution and non-pollution, justice and (coughing) injustice, are guaranteed.
>
> (1995, p 135)

In this way modern law is not simply inadequate to the task of combating the dangers of the risk society, but is rather directly involved in perpetuating their ongoing development. This, says Beck, shows how law in the risk society engineers a global system of organised irresponsibility.

Individualisation

There is one further aspect to Beck's analysis that is worth paying attention to here, since it returns us to certain themes covered earlier. In his work, Beck includes an important discussion of the notion of 'individualisation', which he sees as central to an understanding of the risk society. Under conditions of reflexive modernisation, even though patterns of inequality remain, traditional categories of family, work, class and gender tend to break down. For Beck, in contemporary Western capitalist societies, it is instead, increasingly, the case that the individual becomes the reproduction unit for the social in the lifeworld. But the 'individual' is not to be understood in a natural or pre-social way. In ways reminiscent of Foucault's work (see Part III, 2.3 above), the individual should be thought of as something produced, not something pre-existing, the result or gathering point of the effects of external social forces. As such, the 'individual' is something whose characteristics, expectations and sensibilities change over time. Of course there is a paradoxical aspect to this: if individuals are products, then they are not truly individual precisely to the extent that they are produced, and, more decisively, produced as similar individuals. But this is what in fact is happening: the process of individualisation is also one of standardisation, through which the characteristics of the individual are formed with reference to a range of social and bureaucratic institutions and demands, be they financial, educational, or legal systems. This paradoxical situation is described by Beck as:

> [T]he contradictory double face of institutionally dependent individual situations. The apparent outside of the institutions becomes the inside of individual biography. The design of life situations spanning institutional boundaries results from their institutional dependency (in the broadest sense). The liberated individuals become dependent on the labour market and *because of that*, dependent on education,

consumption, welfare state regulations and support, traffic planning, consumer supplies, and on possibilities and fashions in medical, psychological and pedagogical counselling and care. This all points to the *institution-dependent control structure* of individual situations. Individualization becomes the *most advanced* form of socialization dependent on the market, law, education and so on.

(1992, pp 130–1, emphasis in original)

But if this is so, then it follows that the individual becomes 'emphatically dependent on situations and conditions that completely escape its reach' (1992, pp 130–1). That is, to the extent that individuals are the deposit of social institutions, and that individuals as individuals do not themselves control these institutions or the logics according to which they operate, then they are therefore condemned to live out their lives according to demands and risks that these institutions generate. As Beck therefore points out, 'under these conditions, how one lives becomes the biographical solution to systemic contradictions' (1992, p 137).

This point signals one further aspect to this situation that compounds the problem. For it is of the utmost importance that these are processes of individualisation; that what is produced are individuals who are thereby deemed themselves to be responsible for their own destinies and treated as if they were in fact able to manage these external forces. The individual is thus valorised as a key achievement of modern society – a key focal point of work responsibilities, leisure and consumption activities, financial and legal decisions, and so on – and yet they are in fact at the mercy of external forces over which they have little control for the very reason that these systems are what produce the sense of individuality in the first place. Hence the full force of the paradox: 'At the same moment as he or she sinks into insignificance, he or she is elevated to the apparent throne of world-shaper' (1992, p 137).

In some ways, the liberal mind-set – the liberal personality of capitalist society – is the most problematic of all versions of individuality, since it fulfils this paradoxical condition expertly, by internalising choices given from outside but making them their own. And where this is so, individuals are subject to the power and risks of social systems in ways that are not at all persuasively captured by the stereotypical claims of modern society being 'individualist'. In many respects this was also the insight that Foucault's technologies of the self provided in such a nuanced but cogent manner, for it exemplifies his apparently counterintuitive claim that we are 'governed through our freedoms'. To the extent that Beck's analysis is accurate then, it is precisely these processes of individualisation that unsettle an optimistic account of modernity as releasing the individual from the bonds of conventional forms of power. To the extent that individuals were released from, for example, religious or mystical forms of domination, they are reinserted far more thoroughly – because far more invisibly – within other forms of systemic control, whether economic, bureaucratic or governmental. For as we are increasingly aware, through techniques such as biometric testing, DNA profiling and identity surveillance, under legal authority, governments (as well as some corporate actors) are able to set in motion powers that are not properly understandable or made accountable through conventional forms of legal regulation. It is this that leads one commentator on Foucault to observe that, 'the modern Western state has integrated techniques of subjective individualisation with procedures of objective totalization to an unprecedented degree' (Agamben 1998, p 5).

Reading

Beck's most famous work (Beck 1992) remains the best starting point for research on the risk society. The question of 'organised irresponsibility' is identified in Beck (1995), and its implications for law explored most fully in Veitch (2007). For a more recent treatment of ways to think about addressing the problems of the risk society, and which also connects directly with themes of globalisation, see Beck 2005.

There is a burgeoning secondary literature on the risk society; see, indicatively, Adam *et al* (2000). For a concise treatment of risk and law, though one that tends to focus on the traditional ways in which law has managed risk, see Steele (2004).

References

Adam, B *et al* (eds), 2000, *The Risk Society and Beyond*, London: Sage.
Agamben, G, 1998, *Homo Sacer: Sovereign Power and Bare Life*, Stanford: Stanford University Press.
Beck, U, 1992, *Risk Society: Towards a New Modernity*, (trans) M Ritter, London: Sage.
Beck, U, 1995, *Ecological Politics in an Age of Risk*, (trans) A Weisz, Cambridge: Polity Press.
Beck, U, 2005, *Power in the Global Age*, Cambridge: Polity Press.
Power, M, 1997, 'From Risk Society to Audit Society', 3 *Soziale Systeme* 3–21.
Steele, J, 2004, *Risks and Legal Theory*, Oxford: Hart.
Veitch, S, 2007, *Law and Irresponsibility. On the Legitimation of Human Suffering*, London: Routledge-Cavendish.

2.5 Law and autopoiesis

The concept of autopoiesis

The term 'autopoiesis' was borrowed by German social theorist Niklas Luhmann from biology and introduced to help understand social (rather than biological) systems. The concept, which was coined by biologists Maturana and Varela, in order to describe the self-reproduction of organic life – the production of living cells from living cells – was transported by Luhmann to the study of society, significantly not as a metaphor. Luhmann insists that social systems are autopoietic in as real a sense as living systems are: they too produce their own elements from their own elements, the difference being that their elements are not cells but communications.

The distinction of system and environment (common to, and constitutive of, living and social systems) is fundamental to this approach to society. The system identifies itself in an environment and maintains itself in constant relationship to that environment. The system organises its own processes and reproduces its own elements (hence autopoiesis: self-production), and its environment is that against which it defines itself and in constant 'coupling' with which it reproduces itself. This maintaining itself alongside an environment is a key to understanding one of the most important insights systems-theory has to offer, over the idea of closure (from the environment), openness (to it) and the relationship between closure and openness in the operations of a system. This dialectic of closure and openness is crucial across the typology of systems Luhmann distinguishes: living systems, psychic systems and social systems. The autopoiesis of living systems has to do with the self-reproduction of life, of psychic systems with that of consciousness, and of social systems with that of communication. We will limit ourselves to the discussion of the latter only, and out of the range of social systems primarily with the social system of law.

The theory of autopoietic social systems is admittedly difficult and pitched at a challengingly abstract level; it demands 'high entry costs' as Luhmann himself put it once, and we cannot hope but simply to introduce some of its main tenets here. And yet the theory, despite its complexity, has generated an extraordinary level of interest, in particular in Continental Europe, and a considerable amount of controversy, not least in Anglo-American legal theory. We will try and say something here both about what makes it so useful to the study of law as well as to what makes it controversial. To do so we will need initially to set up an inventory of key notions: the key analytical distinction between operations and observations, and that between communication and action, the notions of complexity and contingency, and of coding and programming. After that we will look at what systems theory takes to be the function of law, and then explore more concretely 'how the law thinks', to use Gunther Teubner's famous formulation (Teubner 1989).

An inventory of concepts
● Operations and observations, communication and action

Autopoiesis means self-reproduction and is consequently defined at the level of *operations*: operations whereby elements reproduce elements of the system. It is because the system exists as the linking up of operations that Luhmann sees as the most important question relating to the concept of society: 'which is the operation that produces the system of society and, we must add, produces it from its products, that is, reproduces it?' He says:

> My proposal is that we make the concept of communication the basis and thereby switch sociological theory from the concept of action to the concept of system. This enables us to present the social system as an operatively closed system consisting only of its own operations, reproduced by communications from communications.
>
> (Luhmann 1992, p 71)

Thus Luhmann identifies communication as the operation that reproduces the social system and designates society, the most comprehensive social system of all, as *the totality of communications*. By positing communication as the element, Luhmann proposes something much more precise than the social category 'relations' and side-steps the problems associated with employing individuals, conflict/co-operation and most significantly action, as the basic units or categories of sociological inquiry.

The *shift* of sociological inquiry *from action to communication* is treated by Luhmann himself as a 'conceptual revolution'. Society is for Luhmann the totality of communications, not of individuals or groups, nor of their relations, nor of their actions. Unlike Habermas for whom communication is a way of acting, Luhmann conceives of acting as a way of communicating. This reversal brings far richer possibilities into sociological inquiry, he argues, and circumvents some fundamental problems of action theory. Importantly it circumvents the problem that action is not necessarily social, which has made it necessary for sociologists (e.g. Weber) to impose criteria upon actions as to what counts as their *social* meaning. Secondly because it addresses the problem of treating in the framework of action the active decision to *abstain from action*; maintaining one's silence in the courtroom, to use an important example, can be fruitfully thematised in the context of communication rather than action. Finally it redresses the problem that the focus on action screens off an essential social aspect of action, that is the *impact* of the action, that is something – what else? – *outside* the action (someone is talked *to*) but not outside the communication that always involves communicators (in the plural). These are not mere problems that are avoided in the shift from action to communication, but are in fact *brought back into sociology as questions that enrich sociological inquiry.*

Because the communication is always unfinished, it is in anticipation of a response. The system exists not as an aggregate of communicative acts, but as a linkage of new communicative acts to those past. Between the two there is a sense in which meaning is pending, because without memory or anticipation there can be no meaning. It is through this '*capacity for linkage*' (*Anschlussfähigkeit*) that the system exists and its autopoiesis consists of this generation of new elements from existing ones.

To summarise: the operations of the social system are communications. A social system is autopoietic in that it produces and reproduces its own elements, new communications from a network of existing communications. The system does not exist as the aggregate of its elements but as their succession: it exists as dynamic, in the continuing linkage of new communications to ones already communicated. Systemic meaning is thus based on the instability of elements, their connectability, the opportunities they raise, the potentiality that is actualised in linkage.

Observation is defined by Luhmann as the unity of an operation that makes a distinction in order to indicate one or the other side of this distinction. A system's operation is tied to a system's observation. Operations are communications about system and environment, internal and external reference, therefore observation. Observation, on the other hand, equips communication with a reference in terms of which it can continue, link up, and thus allows the system to effect its operations, produce new elements from existing ones and continue its autopoiesis. The system 'observes' (the law 'thinks') with the help of distinctions, and we will return to this below.

● **Complexity and contingency**

The world is infinitely complex, it admits of a variety of ways it can be talked about, it possesses many aspects and possibilities of its description. New perspectives displace older ones, the false necessities of 'natural' descriptions are shaken as they do; every such new description reminds us of the world's complexity but also increases that complexity by adding to the possibilities of describing it. So every time that a new system draws a boundary and establishes a specific difference of system and environment it of course adds to the overall complexity but also, importantly, reduces it to that specific difference of system and environment. This *reduction of complexity* is a reduction of the possible states and events to ones that can be envisaged by the system as determined through its specific means of making selections and establishing relevance. Not every societal communication, not every state of affairs that can be talked about, may become the subject of each system's communication. More importantly competing categorisations, interpretations of events will not all find expression in the system's terms; each system will restrict the modes in which the world can be talked about by perceiving it in a categorically pre-formed way. That is how the reduction of complexity occurs and is managed by each system. Much of what happens in its environment the system remains indifferent to. Some of it it picks up as relevant to what it is 'attuned' to. The system creates 'order from noise' by drawing selectively on the surplus of possibilities – the domain of high complexity – potentially available in the environment. 'Noise' is what is not yet reduced. In the process of this selective depiction the system constructs the external world that it could not conceive in its complexity. A system knows by simplifying, and then by choosing among, manipulating and combining these self-produced simplifications that stand in for that which is too complex for the system to conceive. Systems are agents of reduction only in terms of which the unbearable complexity of the world becomes meaningful. This reduction, as Gianfranco Poggi puts it well, allows the system 'a simple hold upon possibly highly complex stretches of reality' (Poggi 1979, p x). As complexity in the environment increases, the system adapts its own capacities for resonance by building up its own complexity; but it will never match that of its environment (or it would merge with it).

To summarise: meaning is always system-specific according to Luhmann. It depends on a reduction of complexity, a reduction in the scope of possibilities of all that may be communicated. A system comes about as a specific, reductive, selective way of observing a complex world, with a surplus of possibilities, is established. When a system observes its environment, it observes it through a form of selection that has to do with the distinction that guides it. Put another way, the world is a horizon; it is not yet meaningful except as a background against which certain possibilities are actualised. This is what Luhmann is saying too, except in the more precise terms of infinite complexity (horizon, the World) and reduced complexity (the system). Systems are thus islands of reduced complexity in a world of infinite complexity. Significantly, complexity is not eliminated in the process but reduced. It needs to be preserved, like the horizon, not only to furnish further selections but more importantly to make present ones meaningful. The dimension of time is also of the essence here: every actualisation as selection transforms the system and forms the basis for future selections. It is the specific form of *selectivity-in-progress* that constitutes the identity of the system.

The coding of social systems

Systems observe by introducing a guiding difference and by making the world relevant to this guiding difference. The guiding difference organises, permeates and 'over-determines' the network of differences, the set of further distinctions and demarcations that meaning requires. Semantic codes specify the differences which form the basis for something to be received as information. The world is, in the case of each system, submitted to the difference that, for that system, makes a difference. A pattern of difference lies at the basis of the system's observation of the environment. The idea of the 'code' of the system is pivotal to this.

At the very root of the matter, then, the possibility of cognition for the system, springs from difference-controlled observation. According to Luhmann, 'the formulation of the concept of difference makes it possible for events to appear as information and to leave traces behind within the system'. In view of this, the interesting question is: 'with the aid of what distinctions can a [social] system observe internal and external objects?' (Luhmann 1985b, p 393)

Binary codes are simply a difference between a yes and a no, the difference between a positive and a negative value. The value and counter-value of the code, unlike 'thick' values, have formal equivalence for the system: designating something as legal or true is not a more likely or favoured choice for the legal and scientific system respectively, than deeming it illegal or false. The power of the code lies in the notion that the very constitution of the identity of a system involves the play between positive value and negative value: the designation of every position is always identified in relation to (in the mirror of) its counter-position. 'Communication x is legal, y is true', claim the lawyer and the scientist. How could things be different? They could be different in being illegal or false. The identity of x as legal involves situating it in the difference between legal/illegal. Only by reflecting it in the mirror of its negation does the identity of x as legal come about.

This is how the identity of the system comes about: identity as tautology (legal is what is legal) is replaced by identity as difference (the law is the difference between legal and illegal). It may be true that this 'identity as difference' means very little before it can be shown how through the latter the system can relate to the world. But it is crucial to note that in whatever context the legal/illegal dichotomy may be used in communication, it will underpin, cause, raise and furnish the identity of any information. This is what the theory's critics do not see when they criticise the theory's exaggerated reliance on the code.

The point is that the code gives a communication in law its very identity as legal, allowing in the first place any further state of information about concepts, conditions, incentives, strategies, etc, to appear, and all this in an immediate way. However legal information is to be processed, and the variety here is immense, it first comes about as such through coding. Experience, action, facts are grasped through difference, by virtue of their being submitted to the guiding distinction; information is possible only in this situating, this channelling into a pattern of difference. It is in the situating of a stimulus (noise) in the pattern of 'this rather than that' that codes can be understood as duplication rules. They duplicate the reality they observe. Reality acquires a dimension other than that of being normal. When exposed to the code difference, say the legal code, the 'facticity' of the world becomes information. Actions become legal or illegal, events become legally relevant. How they are allocated to either value is itself not a matter for coding. What duplication means is that the very identity of x as legal involves its negation, that is its reflection in the counter-value (x is not not-legal). A statement about x can be made meaningfully, the system activates a perspective by duplicating reality and making 'x is legal' meaningful because it could be the case that 'x is not legal'. It is this duplication that determines in what sense things could be different. Reflecting in the counter-value enables observation, by setting an assertion against the background of another possibility (this rather than that). Pure fact now acquires the possibility to register, to be observed.

At the same time the duplication through the negative value opens up a contingency space: x could be legal or illegal. The negative value allows us to see how things could be different. In view of this everything is neither necessary nor impossible, therefore contingent. This is a contingency that is bound by the bivalency of the code; it is, in other words, a 'first-order contingency'. There are other levels too at which we encounter contingency and we must be careful to keep these distinct.

We will look at an example of how this works in the final section below.

Society, sub-systems and the law

Society, as we said earlier, is the sum total of communications. In Luhmann's words, 'society is the closed system of connectable communications'. But a paradoxical situation arises. Whatever unity the formula 'all communication' makes apparent is in fact dispersed; for within society's ambit there develop a multitude of sub-systems, each developing a selective and exclusive mapping of the world. Where society cannot communicate with its environment, since it already consists of all that is communicable, between sub-systems there does develop a communication of sorts. Each system of the 'social' type is a sub-system of society and each makes sense of the world in different, mutually overlapping, mutually undercutting ways. Sub-systems are not strung together in any pattern of co-ordination. Society's sub-systems are not patterned in a whole/part schema, but instead each system repeats a system/environment distinction within society, distinguishing itself from society through that distinction. For Luhmann, 'the unity of the world is not the unity of an assemblage . . ., but rather the unavoidable, indestructible possibility of moving from one thing to another – not an aggregation, but rather a correlation of meaningful experience and action' (Luhmann, 1975b, 411). Every formation of a sub-system is nothing less than a new exposition of the unity of the whole social system from its perspective. And yet, every formation of a sub-system breaks that unity of the whole system into a specific difference of system and environment.

How does this differentiating out of a sub-system occur? As far as functional sub-systems are concerned, these are differentiated-out of society on the basis of performing a unique function in society. Luhmann writes:

> I propose to characterize modern society as a functionally differentiated social system. The evolution of this highly improbable social order required replacing stratification with functional differentiation as the main principle of forming subsystems within the overall system of society. In stratified societies the human individual was placed in only one subsystem. . . . This is no longer possible in a society differentiated with respect to functions such as politics, economy, intimate relations, religion, sciences and education. Nobody can live in only one of these systems.
>
> (Luhmann 1986b, p 318)

Functionally differentiated systems are not 'manned' or 'lived in'. They consist of sets of differentiated and specialised resources and activities each articulating with others and each contributing through its own operation to the functioning of the whole. Each develops its own partial rationality, options and demands, goals and means. Partial rationalities do not combine in a comprehensive social rationality as such, however, and in one sense at least, the sum of the parts is more than the whole. No system is of primary importance to the functioning of the whole, none provides a 'summit' (as was the case in stratified societies) or a 'centre' for society. Finally, according to the principle of functional differentiation each sub-system performs a function that is unique: were that exclusivity to be compromised the principle of differentiation itself would give way. Sub-systems do not simply perceive the world in different and competing ways but also perceive their differences in different ways. As Teubner (1993, ch 7) describes it, society is a *unitas multiplex*: a society that is at once unity (all communication as distinct from life and consciousness) and multiplicity. And at the same time, in the current evolutionary phase of functional differentiation, it is also a 'heterarchy'; the multiplicity of descriptions of society cannot be co-ordinated hierarchically. This is how Luhmann summarises this:

> Each system is universally competent and at the same time a system within the world, able to distinguish and observe and control itself. It is a self-referential system and thereby a totalizing system. It cannot avoid operating within a world of its own. Societies [social systems] constitute worlds. Observing themselves, that is communicating about themselves, societies cannot avoid using distinctions which differentiate the observing system from something else. Their communication observes itself within its world and describes the limitation of its own competence. Communication never becomes self-transcending. It can never operate outside its own boundaries. The boundaries themselves, however, are components of the system and cannot be taken as given by a pre-constituted world.
>
> (Luhmann 1986c, pp 178–9)

How does 'the law think'?

Let us now try and apply all that we have seen so far to the legal system, to understand in what sense it might constitute a 'reduction achievement', what constitutes its specific operations, what furnishes its observations, and how to understand its function. It is in this sense, in particular, that we might begin to untangle, then answer, Teubner's challenge:

> What is the precise meaning of the somewhat ambiguous statement that law constitutes an autonomous reality? Similarly, what is meant by saying that the individual is a mere construct of society and law? And, above all, how does the law 'think'?
>
> (Teubner 1989, p 730)

Like every other social system, the legal system's operations are communications. They are communications that are 'coded', that is aligned to the code of the legal system legal/illegal. Any communication that concerns the allocation of one of those values qualifies as legal, whether it be someone asserting their right ('I have a right to speak'), assuming a duty ('I will deliver the merchandise tomorrow') or interpreting a legal provision ('surely the law cannot be interpreted to authorise the killing of innocent civilians'). Of course certain communications will be pivotal and others less so. Decisions of courts, officials and parliaments, interpretations of the law offered by courts or legal academics, promises, offers and verbal transactions, and so on, fall into the first category; lay communication invoking the law, falls into the latter. But all communication thematised along the legal/illegal coding is 'part' of the legal system, the world of legal communication.

In what sense does this system, thus broadly understood, constitute a *reduction* achievement and what accounts for its '*closure*' as a system?

If the world, as we discussed earlier, admits of a variety of ways it can be talked about, every system restricts on its own terms the ambit of what is meaningful by filtering communication through system-relevance established by the code. Competing categorisations and interpretations of events will not all find expression in the system's terms; out of the infinite possibilities of describing a person's action, for example, the legal system addresses what is relevant to deeming it legal or illegal. Only on that basis can a person's will further be thematised as intention or motive on the basis that it is conducive to a legal characterisation of his/her action. The economic system may recast that expression of the will as economic-rational preference, the political system will assess it in terms of support or disaffection to Government or Opposition, and so on. Each system will restrict the modes in which the world can be talked about by perceiving it in a categorically pre-formed way. Further distinctions (programming) build on the code: intended/not-intended, fault/strict liability, incitement/free expression, occupational/political demand, speech/action. All the distinctions on the one hand draw on the system's reduction of the world to a single difference (legal/illegal), while at the same time building up the system's internal complexity, that allows it to 'see' more things, and cope more adequately with external reality.

In this sense the code enables the system to 'construct' its environment, to set itself in context; it enables it to observe environmental stimuli on the basis of the distinction and deal with them by each time indicating one side of the binary schema. The structural technique that makes this possible is a 'difference technique'.

The system introduces its own distinction and on that basis grasps states and events as information. The 'difference technique' is the device that the system employs to decipher complexity by enacting a system-specific reduction which results in a system-centric representation of reality. It is thus that the distinction 'establishes a universe, sets up systemic boundaries, structures a discourse'. Together coding and programming provide the cluster of differences through which the world is localised within the system. Primacy of course lies with the code that underlies the identity of the system and ultimately generates information; it does not determine, however, 'which pieces of information are called for and which selection they trigger'. Programming provides criteria for fixing the conditions for the suitability of selections. In science, for example, the requirement of suitability belongs to theory and method, on the basis of which the truth or falsity of scientific statements can be assessed. Structures themselves can be changed at the level of programming, as is ultimately the case with a paradigm shift in science, without the system thereby losing its identity, which depends on the coding. To move this to law: norms (programmes) provide the correctness of the allocation of legality and illegality (code), method (programme again) here consisting of rules of interpretation of norms; structural variations, in law, occur when norms are varied through new legislation or new constitutional interpretations.

To recapitulate: the identity of the system comes about at the level of the code. The system's identity as tautology (legal is what is legal) is replaced here by identity as difference (the law is the difference between legal and illegal). But the symmetry has to be broken because it is otherwise unproductive for the system. On the basis of programming (the deployment of other schemes of differences aligned to coding) the system is allowed to steer its operations by allocating events to either side of the contrast-schema. Together coding and programming allow the system to see the world in a certain way (it can be legal or illegal), and to operationalise its mode of seeing. We do not need any more background information in order to make sense of those cryptic and controversial descriptions of systems as 'closed and open at the same time'; of the legal system, for example, as 'cognitively open because normatively closed'. It is the difference of coding and programming that makes possible the combination of closure and openness in the same system. These are flip-sides of the same coin, internally linked, mutually supportive, reciprocally enabling: it is the very structural constraints that enable the system to relate to the environment. The system's capacity for reaction to the environment, 'resonance', which is steered through programming, rests on the closed polarity of the code. The possibility that the environment registers at all is due to the code, and in that sense closure is a precondition for cognitive openness.

The function of law, for Luhmann, is the very rule-of-law-like imperative to provide for the 'stabilisation' of normative expectations. Let us explain this. Contexts can be fixed at a number of levels. Simple interactions between, say friends, lovers, colleagues, develop as contexts that allow reciprocal perspective-taking and thus expectations to articulate. Interactions in wider settings also develop elementary contexts that allow meaningful interchange. But the greatest constancy of the context of reciprocity is achieved at the level of functional systems like science, the economy, and of course law. Law has a special, enhanced role here. Law secures this constancy by narrowing the *expectability* of expectations, by abstracting from various 'irrelevant' contingencies of the pragmatic situation, by providing norms that involve sanctions should the other not conform, but, most importantly for present purposes, by abstracting from the concrete parties involved and the reciprocal perspective-taking that in turn would involve knowledge of the other party and the contingencies that entails. It renders this context independent of the indeterminacy that comes from concrete interactions: it allows people to encounter each other as role-players, here, as legal actors.

Motive, identity, implied reciprocities that stem from role, are always-already aligned to systems. For Luhmann role-indeterminacy as context-indeterminacy becomes settled by the system but only for the system. Legal expectations allow uncertainty in specific, controlled ways and immunise the system towards other uncertainties it cannot control. The legal system reduces the complexity of possible contingencies: it allows for some, and reproduces itself by responding to them. By the same token it immunises itself against others, that are precluded because expectations are not attuned to them. A system modulates its reaction to its environment by changing expectations and controlling this change at the level of expectations of expectations.

The legal system's *openness* to the world consists, therefore, in its reading disappointment or fulfilment of the expectations it itself projects. Of course the system is neither static nor insensitive to change; to remain responsive to a changing world the system must also vary the expectations it projects. New legal possibilities need to be projected to respond to new situations. New expectations test new patterns of conflict around new issues, and their fulfilment or disappointment, is fed back into the law as valid new premises for future decisions. The legal system thus varies its structures, reconstructs and alters them, and in the process 'learns' and evolves. It does this by providing legal answers to the conflictual expectations that face it requiring litigation. Conflict is necessary for law because it provides input into the reproductive process without which the system of law would stagnate. But in dealing with conflict, law only achieves a new return to order. It pushes back the threat of disorganisation by conceiving and resettling disturbed practice on the basis of uncontroverted practice. Law conceives of conflicts as disturbances that must be overcome. The conflictual pattern is transitory; a destabilisation that allows legal evolution through successive steps of return to order. The uncertainty of expectations that face law in a situation of social conflict is fruitful ground for internal innovation and simultaneously for the regeneration of legal order. The system overcomes the turbulence that it sees conflict as presenting it with, by resettling disturbed practice and sanctioning the resettlement with permanence for the time being. For the legal system the conflictual pattern is a pathology in the healing of which law evolves.

Note that the only way in which a claim for change may register is if it manages to surprise projections of expectations. Following the principle that we can only see what we know how to look for, perception must be based upon an already existing preconception of what is to be seen or understood. For a challenge to register, that is, the system's memory has to be tapped. The degree to which the system is open to learning is, of course as always, an internal matter. In Luhmann's terms this would be expressed in the following way: the system itself controls the balance of redundancy and variety. It is a distinction that bears on the system's readiness to vary its structures in the face of an evolving environment. Variety is about increasing responsiveness, redundancy about suppressing it.

It is *because* the system needs to react to, and keep up with, a changing environment that 'variety' comes into play. Significantly the practice of distinguishing and overruling 'occasionally invents new [grounds] to achieve a position where the system can, on the basis of a little new information, fairly quickly work out what state it is in and what state it is moving towards' (Luhmann 1993, p 291). The reason why it requires 'a special effort' to shake the redundancy of the system and stretch its imagination is because the system tends to 'reduce its own surprise to a tolerable amount and allow information only as differences added in small numbers to the stream of reassurances' (Luhmann 1993, p 291). In an extract that could easily have been written by critical legal scholars had it not preceded them by a decade, Luhmann says:

> Suitable information . . . must be specially produced, brought to light by uncovering some latent aspect of existing order, or retrieved from the existing decision-making process by incongruent questions.
>
> (Luhmann 1990, pp 33–4)

'How the law thinks', then, has to do with the opportunities and limitations that pertain to what is specifically institutional about it: the imposition and entrenchment of certain reductions in the possibilities of describing and talking about the world. Law as such an institution gives us a language to conceive of identity, interdependence, conflict, benefit and harm, concepts of risk and time, what is owned and what is due. These are precisely the kinds of reductions in the possibilities of communicating about the world that give rights their specific legal nature as an institutional achievement. The selection of what is legally relevant occurs over and against the background of other possibilities that remain legally underdetermined. The system actualises something over and against other possibilities – that is the crux of institutionalisation, of the drawing of the legal system's boundary.

How the legal system controls that boundary, to what extent it stands to 'learn' from the changing environment or to remain indifferent to it by reproducing the same set of expectations and immunising itself from 'noise' from it, is a matter for the law and the law alone. There is, as has often been discussed, something profoundly self-referential about this, tautological even: 'the law is what the law is' or, put differently, 'the law is what it says it is'. Positivism taken to an extreme, perhaps. But Luhmann insists that we should not shy away from the self-reference that one encounters at the foundation of things but instead focus on the way it is 'breached', unfolded and made productive. And Teubner will add this:

> The theory of autopoiesis deals with these paradoxes of self-reference in a different way: Do not avoid paradoxes, but make productive use of them! If social discourses are autopoietic systems, that is, systems that recursively produce their own elements from the network of their elements, then they are founded on that very self-referentiality. As autopoietic systems, discourses cannot but find justification in their own circularity and cannot but produce regularities that regulate themselves and that govern the transformation of their own regularities. The paradox of self-reference then, is not a flaw in our intellectual reconstruction of discourse that we have to avoid at all costs, but is its very reality that we cannot avoid at all.
>
> (Teubner 1989, p 736)

Reading

Luhmann's *opus magnum*, where he introduces the term 'autopoiesis' is his *Social Systems* of 1984, which appeared in English in 1993. His major work on the legal system, *Das Recht der Gesellschaft*, was translated into English ('Law as a social system') in 2006. For a concise account of how coding works and how it links to programming', see Luhmann (1986).

The application of systems theory in law is connected primarily with the work of Gunther Teubner. See in particular (1989) and (1993).

Among the growing secondary literature on systems-theory in English, King and Thornhill (2006) provide a very good introduction to Luhmann's theory of law and politics. For an early, highly creative, introduction to autopoiesis, see

Smith (1991) and on the concept of 'redundancy' in legal reasoning, Smith (1995). For an application of systems theory to the relation between law and politics, see Christodoulidis (1998). See also the recent monograph on Luhmann's legal theory by Andreas Philippopoulos-Mihalopoulos (2009).

References

Christodoulidis, E, 1998, *Law and Reflexive Politics*, Dordrecht: Kluwer.

King, M and Thornhill, C, 2006, *Niklas Luhmann's Theory of Politics and Law*, Basingstoke: Palgrave Macmillan.

Luhmann, N, 1985, 'Some Problems with Reflexive Law', in G Teubner and A Febbrajo (eds), *State, Law, Economy as Autopoietic Systems*, Milano: Giuffré.

Luhmann, N, 1986a, *Ecological Communication* (trans J Bednarz), Cambridge: Polity.

Luhmann, N, 1986b, 'The Individuality of the Individual: Historical Meaning and Contemporary Problems', in T Heller *et al* (eds), *Reconstructing Individualism*, Stanford: Stanford University Press.

Luhmann, N, 1986c, 'The Autopoiesis of Social Systems', in F Geyer and J van der Zouwen (eds), *Sociocybernetic Paradoxes; Observation, Control and Evolution of Self-Steering Systems*, Beverly Hills: Sage.

Luhmann, N, 1990, 'Meaning as Sociology's Basic Concept', in *Essays on Self-Reference*, New York: Columbia University Press.

Luhmann, N, 1992, 'The Concept of Society', 31 *Thesis Eleven* 67.

Luhmann N, 1995a, *Social Systems*, Stanford: Stanford University Press.

Luhmann, N, 1995b, 'Legal Argumentation: An Analysis of Its Form', 58 *Modern Law Review* 285.

Luhmann, N, 2006, *Law as a Social System*, Oxford: Oxford University Press.

Philippopoulos-Mihalopoulos, A, 2009, *Niklas Luhmann: Law, Justice, Society*, London: Routledge.

Poggi, G, 1979, 'Introduction', in N Luhmann, *Trust and Power*, Chichester: Wiley.

Smith, SC, 1991, 'Beyond "Mega-Theory" and "Multiple Sociology": A Reply to Rottleutner', 19 *International Journal of the Sociology of Law* 321.

Smith, SC, 1995, 'The Redundancy of Reasoning', in Z Bankowski, I White and U Hahn (eds), *Informatics and the Foundations of Legal Reasoning*, Dordrecht: Kluwer.

Teubner, G, 1989, 'How the Law Thinks: Toward a Constructivist Epistemology of Law' 23/5 *Law & Society Review* 727–58.

Teubner, G, 1993, *Law as an Autopoietic System*, Oxford: Blackwell.

Responding to pressure from the trade union movement and left-wing political parties, the Ukanian Parliament passed legislation in 1930 to require employers to continue to pay workers who were sick when they were unable to work, for a period of up to two months. The legislation came into force on 1st January 1931.

In February 1931 a dispute arose at the factory of United Washers Ltd, a company that produced components that were essential to the manufacture of domestic appliances. Six workers were sacked after failing to turn up to work for three consecutive days, a situation which the company argued had led to a significant reduction in output. The men argued that they had been sick and unable to work and that they should have received sick pay during their absence. The company responded that the men had been paid for days that they were absent before they were sacked. The case was taken up by the men's trade union who brought a legal action against the company, requiring that the men be reinstated. The court of first instance held that the men should not be reinstated: there was nothing in the legislation that prevented a company from sacking those who were too sick to work, and that they had been paid by the company for the period that they were sick, in accordance with the legislation.

The union appealed the case to the Supreme Court of Ukania, where the five judges delivered the following opinions.

JUDGE ANTONY:

The central issue in this case is the wording of the legislation which alone expresses the intention of Parliament. The courts cannot and must not go beyond that wording in the determination of a case, for to do so would undermine the very legitimacy of the legal system. In this case the legislation provides for the protection of employees who are sick, but there is nothing in the legislation to prevent a company from terminating the contract of employment at any point, irrespective of the health of the worker.

JUDGE BELINDA:

I am not persuaded by the argument of my brother Judge Antony. The intention of Parliament is expressed in the legislation as a whole and it is very clear that the spirit or intention of this legislation was to protect workers against just these types of actions by their employers. The rights given by the statute become meaningless if they can be avoided so easily, and so the legislation must be interpreted in the light of the intention of Parliament to protect the security and quality of employment. The legitimacy of the law will not survive unless it is interpreted in such a way.

JUDGE CHARLES:

There is much that is of merit in the argument Judge Belinda. She is right to focus on the question of the legitimacy of the law, but unfortunately her argument is purely speculative. The present case cannot be decided simply on the basis of the narrow interpretation of the legislation. If the courts are to deal with such issues properly they must be provided with more information about the profitability of washer manufacture; about time lost through sickness and injury in this sector of the economy; about the income and employability of workers, skilled and unskilled in this sector; about the attitudes to the law of all workers and so on. As we know, such information is central to the management of modern society and the economy, and is the basis for decision-making by all other organs of government. If the courts continue to confine themselves to the interpretation of the wording of statutes alone, then they run the risk of becoming increasingly irrelevant.

JUDGE DIANA:

I am not persuaded that this is a question for the courts at all. It is clear to me that the legislation has been poorly drafted, in that it allows employers to act in a way which is clearly contrary to the spirit of the law. Parliament should, as a matter of urgency, revisit and amend this statute to close this loophole. This, however, is a political question, and the courts should not be drawn into such political disputes. The law must stand apart from politics.

JUDGE ERIC:

The issue in this case can best be dealt with by placing it in the context of our existing law concerning the relations between master and servant. This is an important body of law, which has developed over centuries, which both expresses and regulates the nature of the employment relation. New legislation must not be understood as replacing this traditional law but as merely developing and extending it to new situations. According to this traditional law trust is the fundamental basis of the master–servant relation, and the courts should move to prevent any action, by either party, which seeks to undermine this trust. The actions of the employers here do precisely this and so the men should be reinstated.

Questions

1   How might we categorise these arguments in the light of Weber's typology of legal rationality?

2 Do these different arguments express differing attitudes towards and understandings of legal modernity?

3 The different judgements express different attitudes towards the legitimacy of the legal system. Which of these do you think most accurately expresses the proper basis of legal legitimacy and why?

Corresponding Sections: Part III 1.2–1.4.

❖ TUTORIAL 2   Law and modernity

1 Discuss the significance of formal legal rationality to Max Weber's account of the development of modern law.

2 Does law always serve the interests of the ruling class, or has it developed in a way which is independent of particular interests?

3 Why has it been argued that globalisation requires that we reassess our understanding of the nature of modern law?

Corresponding Sections: Part III 1.3–1.5.

❖ **TUTORIAL 3** Legal rights as ideology

1 Read *On the Jewish Question* (Marx 1843), pp 44–7 and 51–7.

Answer the following questions:

- What does Marx mean when he argues (p 44) that through the right to freedom of religious worship 'man liberates himself from an impediment through the medium of the state'? Why should this liberation be only 'limited, abstract and partial'?

- He goes on to argue (p 45) that the political annulment of private property actually presupposes it. Why?

- What is the basis of the distinction he draws (pp 45–6) between 'material' life and 'species' life? How does this correspond to the distinction between public, political, life and private life?

- Consider Marx's analysis of the rights to freedom of conscience, liberty, property and security (pp 52–3). What is the basis for his criticism of these rights?

- What is the basis of the character of the political revolution he discusses at pp 55–6?

- In his conclusion he argues that the 'actual individual man must take the abstract citizen back into himself' (p 57), and that emancipation requires the ending of the separation between political and social forces: what does this mean?

2 Can a Marxist believe in human rights?

Corresponding Sections: Part II 1.1 and Part III 1.3.

Advanced

❖ TUTORIAL 4   Law and discipline

1   Read M Foucault, *Discipline and Punish* (Foucault 1977), pp 264–85.

Answer the following questions:

- Why does Foucault argue that the prison is denounced as a failure, even from the very moment of its adoption as a common and generalised mode of punishment? To what extent do these criticisms correspond to contemporary arguments against imprisonment?

- What does Foucault argue is the invariable response to such criticisms (pp 268–70)?

- Why does he argue (p 271) that the supposed failure is part of the functioning of the prison?

- What does he mean by the terms 'discipline' and 'surveillance'?

- 'It is not so much that they render docile those who are liable to transgress the law, but that they tend to assimilate the transgression of the laws in a general tactics of subjection' (p 272). What does this mean? How does this differ from our normal understanding of the function of the criminal law?

- What does Foucault mean when he argues (p 277) that the prison *produces* delinquency? What, does he suggest, are the 'uses' of delinquency? Think of some contemporary examples of delinquency that are used in this way. What does this tell us about the relationship between power and knowledge?

2   What conclusions, if any, can we draw from this passage about the function of law in modern society?

Corresponding Sections: Part III 2.3.

❖ TUTORIAL 5   Globalisation and juridification

Washers Unlimited International PLC (WUI) is a multinational corporation based in Ukania. In 1999 they closed all their manufacturing plants in Ukania and opened factories in Ruritania, an ex-Soviet-bloc country that offered cheap labour and low levels of regulation of health and safety. Ruritania is, however, a member of the Council of Europe and a signatory to the European Convention on Human Rights.

In 2003, the nationalist neo-liberal party that had been in power in Ruritania lost the general election and was replaced by the Social Democratic Party, which had campaigned on the basis of improving working conditions and limiting the power of foreign corporations in Ruritania. Their first acts on taking power were to introduce a new tax on the profits of foreign corporations and to introduce a new system of health and safety regulation which they promised would be actively enforced. WUI immediately declared that this was unduly restrictive and that they would be investigating ways of closing their factories in Ruritania. As an interim measure they immediately sacked 100 employees who had engaged in a public protest against the employment practices of the company, citing the increased costs of conforming with regulation as the reason for this measure.

Consider the following issues arising from this scenario:

1   The Ruritanian government approaches you for advice on how best to modify the proposed regulatory schema. They understand that regulation might be expensive for business, but they are keen to fulfil their democratic mandate. How might theories of juridification help us to analyse this situation?

2   The sacked workers take legal advice. In the absence of any employment rights under Ruritanian law they decide that they want to bring a legal action against WUI for breaching their right to peaceful protest under the ECHR. WUI argue that the ECHR cannot apply against private corporations, and that Ruritanian law is sovereign. The Ruritanian government supports the sacked workers' legal action, arguing that their independence has been undermined by the actions of corporations like WUI.
    (i)   What are the different types of legal order that are involved in this dispute?
    (ii)   How might a theory of globalisation help us to understand the complexities of this dispute?
    (iii) Discuss the theoretical basis for the non-application of human rights to private bodies. Why might this exemption be challenged by the process of globalisation of law?

3 Does this scenario confirm or contradict the assertion that we are entering a fifth epoch of juridification (Part III 2.2.5)?

Corresponding Sections: Part III General Themes 1.5, Advanced Topics 2.1 and 2.2.

❖ **TUTORIAL 6**   The public/private distinction

1   Evaluate the significance of the public/private distinction in thinking about the role of law in contemporary society.

Discuss with reference to either:

(a)   theories of legal pluralism, or

(b)   the development of the 'risk society', or

(c)   theories of juridification.

2   Is juridification a legal or a political problem?

Corresponding Sections: Part III 2.1–2.4.

References

Foucault, M, 1977, *Discipline and Punish: The Birth of the Prison*, Harmondsworth: Penguin.

Marx, K, 1843, 'On the Jewish Question', in D McLellan (ed), *Karl Marx: Selected Writings*, Oxford: Oxford University Press, pp 39–62.

Index

Page numbers in *italics* refer to tutorials.

A

accountability in political transitions 89–90
Ackerman, B. 68–70
acts, subjective and objective meaning of 38–9
adjudication, rules of 36
administration *see* bureaucracy
Agamben, G. 174–5, 277
Alexy, R. 45–6
American legal realism 123–31
    critique 130–3
    fact-scepticism 128–9
    faith in science 129–31
    'Path of the Law' 125–6, 129–30
    prophecy/prediction principle 126
    rule-scepticism 126–8
analogy
    argument by 136–7
    hospitality and justice 183–4
Anti-Terrorist Act 2001 83, 114–15
Arendt, H. 67, 72, 90
Arthurs, H.W. 250
Austin, J. 16, 33–4, 35
Australian Aborigines (*Mabo* case) 168–73
authority
    mystical foundations of 180, 181, 182
    political 226–7, 231–2
    and violence 182–3
autopoiesis 278–89
    coding of social and legal systems 281–3, 284–6
    concept of 278–9
    related concepts 279–81
    society and sub-systems 283–4

B

Bartlett, R. 171
basic goods 151–2
Baxi, U. 31, 32
Beck, U. 272–7
Benjamin, W. 182–3
Bennett, W. and Feldman, M. 164
Bennion, F. 117
Bentham, J. 16, 28, 33–4, 52, 118, 267
Berman, H. 207
Bernstein, B. 164
Bingham, Lord 83, 114–15
biopower 265–6, 267–8
'boomerang effect' of risks 273
Bourdieu, P. 261
Brennan, Chief Justice 169–70
Browne-Wilkinson, Lord 150, 152
bureaucracy 237–8
    and justice, conflict between 165–7
    and political authority 226–7, 231–2

C

capitalism
    critique of 60–3
        function of law 218–19
        legal ideology 219–22, *294*
        theoretical positions 222–3
    historic development of 205–7
    and welfare state 236, 257–8
    see also globalisation
change, rules of 36

citizen–government reciprocity 24–5
citizenship 13, 28
    liberal and republican 70–3
civil rights 28–9
class conflict 234
    see also capitalism, critique of
classification, relevancy and
        interpretation 134, 157–9
coding of social and legal systems
        281–3, 284–6
Cohen, L.J. 56, 60
coherence – and legal reasoning 136–7,
        141
Collins, H. 144, 221
colonialism 206
    Australian Aborigines (*Mabo* case)
        168–73
    legal pluralism 248–50
commodification 218–19
common good(s) 151, 152
communication
    codes 281–3, 284–6
    operations, observations and action
        279–80
community
    and capitalism 63
    and society (*Gemeinschaft* and
        Gesellschaft) 211, 212–15, 236–7,
        239
complexity and contingency 280–1
consistency and legal reasoning 136
constitutional legitimacy 16–17
constitutional 'moments' 68–70
constitutional state, elements of 11–13
constitutionalism
    beyond the state 78–80
    liberal and republican citizenship 70–3
    paradox of 65–7, 68
    representation and foundation 67–8
contract law 143–4, 150–1
    historical perspective 211–12, 214,
        219, 236
courts 13–14, 41–2
    fact-scepticism 128–9
    language and narrative of 162–5
critical legal pluralism 253–4
critical legal studies (CLS) 142–5

D
Davis, M. 62
deconstruction 174–86
deduction *187*
    and legal formalism 120–2
democracy 41, 61, 66–7
depoliticisation, juridification as 260–1
derogation of rights 81–4, 114–15
Derrida, J. 174–6, 177–81, 182–4, 185
Detmold, M. 152–3
dignity 53–4, 63
discipline *see under* power
discretionary powers 166, 238
distributive justice 51–63, 92
Durkheim, E. 210, 211–12, 213, 214
Dworkin, R. 137–42

E
economy
    and advent of modernity 204, 205–7
    and rational legal system 230–1
    see also capitalism; globalisation
Ely, J. 66
emancipatory concept of law 241–4
emergency powers *see* state of
        emergency
'entitlement' theory of justice 54–5
environmental issues 272–4, 275–6
equality/fairness issues 62–3
    discrimination and legal reasoning
        197
    gender 62
    and liberty 22–3, 56–9
    racial 62, 168–73
    and social conflict 234
    and welfare state 239
    see also capitalism, critique of;
        feminist critique of legal reasoning
European Union (EU) 14–15, 18–19,
        37–8, 76, 77, 78
Ewing, K. 82–3, 84
'extended' formalism 133–7

F
fact-scepticism 128–9
    legacy of 159–62
facts and rules in legal reasoning 116–17

fairness *see* equality/fairness issues
feminist critique of legal reasoning 154–9
    challenges 154–5
    form 155–7
    relevancy, interpretation and
        classification 157–9
Finley, L. 156
Finnis, J. 25, *34*, 46–7, 150–3
Fletcher, G. 163
formalism *see* legal formalism
Foucault, M. 253, 264–71, 277
Frank, J. 128–9, 159–60, 161
Fraser, N. 61–2, 157
Fuller, L. 23–5

G

Gaita, R. 171
Gemeinschaft and *Gesellschaft* 211,
    212–15, 236–7, 239
gender inequality 62
    see also feminist critique of legal
        reasoning
'general public norms' 42
Gill, S. 79, 261
Gilligan, C. 155
Glasman, M. 239
globalisation
    'boomerang effect' of risks 273
    and constitutionalism 78–80
    and emancipatory concept of law
        241–4
    and injustice 62–3
    and juridification 255, 261, *296–7*
    and legal pluralism 250
    and reconfigured state 74–5
    and rights 31–2
    sovereignty after 75–8
    and welfare state 239–41
government–citizen reciprocity 24–5
governmentality 268–9
Grass, G. 261
Griffiths, J. 250, 251

H

Habermas, J. 72, 73, 239, 256, 257–8
'hard' cases 137–40, *188*
    moral reasoning and 149–50

Hart, H.L.A. 25, 33–4, 35–8, 131–3
Hayek, F.A. 123, 260
Heidegger, M. 175, 180–1
Hobbes, T. 16, 208–9, 210
Hoffmann, Lord 83
Holmes, O.W. 125–6, 127, 129–30, 150
hospitality and justice analogy 183–4
human rights *see* rights
Human Rights Act 1998 21, 82, 83,
    114–15
Hume, D. 34, 51

I

ideology, legal 219–22, *294*
individualisation paradox 276–7
industrial revolution 205–7
inequality *see* equality/fairness issues
injustice and invalidity of law 44–7
inner morality of law 22–6
instrumental and justice reasons for rule
    of law 22–3
integrity of law 140–1

J

Jackson, B. 162–3, 165
judicial discretion, expansion of 166, 238
juridical regression 264–5, 269–70
juridification 255–6
    as depoliticisation 260–1
    epochs 257–8, 262–3
    and globalisation 255, 261, *296–7*
    horizontal and vertical 256
    and 'regulatory trilemma' 258–60
jurisdiction, state and legal system
    13–15
justice *105–7, 110*
    and bureaucracy, conflict between
        165–7
    deconstructionist perspective 183–5
    distributive 51–2, 92
    fairness and liberty 56–9
    and instrumental reasons for rule of
        law 22–3
    socialist perspective 59–63
    types 51–2
        in political transitions 90–3
    utilitarianism *vs* libertarianism 52–6

K

Kant, I. 53–4, 63, 66, 205
Kelsen, H. 14, 33–4, 38–40, 118–20

L

Lacey, N. 157–8
language
   deconstructionist perspective 176–83,
      184, 185
   elaborate and restricted codes 164
   and narrative of courtroom 162–5
   'open texture' of legal language
      131–3
legal formalism 117–23
   critiques 130–7, 155–6
   and deduction 120–2
   definition 117–18
   'extended' 133–7
   promise of 122–3
   see also American legal realism; pure
      theory of law
legal ideology 219–22, *294*
legal norms 38–40
legal pluralism 248–55
   classical and contemporary 248–50
   concept of 248
   empirical, conceptual and political
      approaches 251–3
   future directions 253–4
   strong and weak: position of state
      250–1
legal positivism 16, 18, 33–40
   critiques 40–7
legal profession 233–4
legal rationality
   forms 224–6
   and modernity 224–32
legal realism *see* American legal realism
legal reasoning 111–86, *187–99*, 229
   colonial context 168–73
   relevancy, interpretation and
      classification 134, 157–9
   see also feminist critique; moral
      reasoning
legality
   characteristics of 23–4
   and validity of law 40–4

legitimacy
   constitutional 16–17
   modern natural law 235
legitimation concept of 212–13
Levinas, E. 183–4, 185
lex mercatoria 241, 250, 253
liberal and republican citizenship 70–3
libertarianism, utilitarianism *vs* 52–6
liberty 22–3, 56–9
Llewellyn, K. 124–5
Locke, J. 27, 55, 249
Loughlin, M. 18, 27–8, 77–8, 209, 256
Luhmann, N. 259, 260, 278, 279–80,
     282, 283–4, 286, 287, 288

M

MacCormick, N. 22, 37, 39, 66–7, 76,
     120, 121–2, 133–7, 157
MacIntyre, A. 63
MacKinnon, C. 155–6, 158
MacNeil, I. 262
Marshall, T.H. 28
Marx, K. 28, 60, 210–11, 215–22, 230
   and Engels, F. 60
materialisation of law 233–5, 238
Michelman, F. 72
Mill, J.S. 52
modernity/legal modernity *290–3*
   advent of 204–10
   globalisation and emancipatory
      concept of law 241–4
   and legal rationality 224–32
   materialisation 233–5, 238
   power as medium of 269–70
   reflexive 272, 274, 276
   and social solidarity 210–15
   see also capitalism; juridification;
     power; risk society; welfare state
moral reasoning 150–3
   'hard' cases 149–50
morality of law, inner 22–6
mystical foundations of authority 180,
     181, 182

N

narrative of courtroom 162–5
natural law 46, 152–3

formal and substantive legitimacy 235
and legal positivism 34–5, 47
natural rights 27, 28
new constitutionalism 79, 80
Nozick, R. 54–6

O
'open texture' of legal language 131–3

P
Pashukanis, E. 218
'Path of the Law' 125–6, 129–30
Poggi, G. 281
political authority 226–7, 231–2
political and legal power 10–11, 227
political rights 28–9
political transitions 88–95
    accountability and responsibility issues 89–90
    dilemmas 88–9
    forms of justice 90–3
politics
    and law, relationship between 10–15, 98–104
    of legal pluralism 252–3
    science and business in risk society 274–5
Polanyi, K. 206–7, 210
Positivism see legal positivism
'positivity of law' 42
post-sovereignty 18, 76, 77
Pound, R. 124–5
power
    biopower 265–6, 267–8
    and discipline 265–6, 295
        techniques 266–7
    and exploitation see capitalism
    governmentality 268–9
    juridical regression 264–5, 269–70
    political and legal 10–11, 227
    theory of legal modernity 269–70
prediction/prophecy principle 126
prisons 266, 267
privatisation 262–3
property
    historical perspective 214, 219, 237

rights 54, 55–6, 237
    and risk society 274
psychology of fact–finding 128–9, 160–1
public–private relationship 262–3, 298
'publicness' of law 42–3
pure theory of law 38–40
    and self-containment notion 118–20

R
racial inequality 62, 168–73
Radbruch, G. 44–5, 46–7
rationality see legal rationality
Rawls, J. 56–9, 61, 63
realism see American legal realism
reciprocity between government and citizens 24–5
recognition, rule of 36–7
reflexive modernity 272, 274, 276
'regulatory trilemma' of juridification 258–60
relevancy, interpretation and classification 134, 157–9
republican and liberal citizenship 70–3
responsibility in political transitions 89–90
restorative justice 91–2
retributive justice 90–1
'right answer' 140–1
rights 26–8, 108–9
    civil, political and social 28–9
    derogation in state of emergency 81–4, 114–15
    as evolutionary process 27–8
    Human Rights Act 1998 21, 82, 83, 114–15
    indivisibility of 30–1
    international and global context 31–2
    legalisation and politicisation 29–30
    Marxist perspective 221–2
    origins of 27
    positive and negative 29–30
    utilitarianism vs libertarianism 52–6
risk society 271–2
    features 272–4
    individualisation paradox 276–7
    law in 274–6

Roman Law 229, 232
rule of law 12–13, *96–7*
   challenges to 20–2
   formalism 123
   and inner morality of law 22–6
   justice and instrumental reasons for 22–3
   meaning and value 20
   validity 40–4
rule-scepticism 126–8
rules
   and facts in legal reasoning 116–17
   and 'open texture' of legal language 131–3
   primary and secondary 35–7
   and principles *193–9*
Rumble, W. 127

S

Sale of Goods Act 1979 122
Sandel, M. 71
Santos, B. de Sousa 241–4, 250–1, 252, 260
Sassen, S. 77
Saussure, F. de 178
Schmitt, C. 84–6
science
   American legal realism 129–31
   and modernity 204, 205
   politics and business in risk society 274–5
self-containment notion 118–20
separation of powers 11–13, 17, 21, 23, 29
   erosion of 116, 239
simplification and diversion techniques 165–6
Singer, J. 130–1
Smith, A. 1, 59
'social contract' 208–9
'social contract law' 236
social rights 28–9
social solidarity 210–15
social systems and sub-systems 281–4
socialism 59–63
society and community (*Gesellschaft* and *Gemeinschaft*) 211, 212–15, 236–7, 239

sociology 205, 210–11
sources of law 115–16
sovereignty 15–20
   after globalisation 75–8
   attribution of 16–18
   contested concept of 15
   and the exception 84–6
   historical perspective 207–9
   and identity of 'the people' 68, 69
   modernity and juridical regression 269–70
   post-sovereignty 18, 76, 77
   see also colonialism
state
   constitutional, elements of 11–13
   constitutionalism beyond 78–80
   jurisdiction and legal system 13–15
   position in legal pluralism 250–1
   'Westphalian state' 12, 17–18
state of emergency 81–8
   derogation of rights 81–4, 114–15
   sovereignty and the exception 84–6
Steyn, Lord 149
supra-national constitutionalism 78–9
supra-national law
   EU 14–15, 18–19, 37–8, 76, 77, 78
   and international law 241
surveillance 266, 267
'systematicity' of law 43

T

Tamanaha, B. 251, 253
'temporal' dimension to justice 92–3
territorial validity of law 14–15, 229
terrorism and derogation of rights 81–4, 114–15
Teubner, G. 253, 258–60, 284, 288
Thompson, E. 223
Thompson, J. 220
Tönnies, F. 211, 212, 214
torture 21, 52–3, 81–2, 161–2
trials *see* courts
Truth and Reconciliation Commission (TRC), South Africa 91–2

U

Unger, R. 118, 142–5
utilitarianism *vs* libertarianism 52–6

V

validity of law 40–4
  injustice and invalidity 44–7
  legal positivist perspective 33–40
  territorial 14–15, 229
violence, authority and 182–3

W

Waldron, J. 40–4, 53
Walker, N. 65, 76, 78, 79
Ward, Lord Justice 137
Weber, M. 161, 165, 166, 226–7,
  228–35, 238, 257

welfare state 235–9
  bureaucracy, justice and
    instrumentalism 237–8
  and capitalism 236, 257–8
  discretionary powers 238
  erosion of separation of powers 239
  and globalisation 239–41
  and juridification 262
  particularised legislation 238
Westphalia, Peace/Treaty of 12, 208
'Westphalian state' 12, 17–18
will and reason 65–6, 68
witness testimony 160, 163
Wittgenstein, L. 176, 179–80

Y

Yntema, H. 130
Young, I.M. 63